Hilda Gamlin

Emma, Lady Hamilton

An old Story retold

Hilda Gamlin

Emma, Lady Hamilton
An old Story retold

ISBN/EAN: 9783337106591

Printed in Europe, USA, Canada, Australia, Japan

Cover: Foto ©ninafisch / pixelio.de

More available books at **www.hansebooks.com**

EMMA
LADY HAMILTON

AN OLD STORY RE-TOLD

BY

HILDA GAMLIN

WITH PORTRAITS, FACSIMILES, AND OTHER
ILLUSTRATIONS

LIVERPOOL
EDWARD HOWELL, 28 CHURCH STREET
LONDON
SIMPKIN, MARSHALL, HAMILTON, KENT & CO. LIMITED
MDCCCXCI

PREFACE.

Once upon a time it was customary for an author to solicit a man of genius to write the introductory matter to his work, but the powerful phrasing of a master mind has a tendency to depreciate the weaker composition, which suffers by comparison. I had the intention of asking some literary scholar to preface my own effort, but lest his superior style should overshadow my more homely essay, an afterthought suggested the wisdom of endeavouring to find my own way into the good graces of my readers. I will therefore be brief, and explain that this new Life of LADY HAMILTON has been undertaken in the hope that a better insight into her character, gleaned from the correspondence of herself and her associates, may tend to elevate the memory of one whose failings have been unnecessarily magnified.

Great care has been exercised in endeavouring to arrive at the actual relations between LORD NELSON and LADY HAMILTON, and, though the line taken in these pages differs from that of other works on the same subject, an attentive reader will see that there are ample grounds for questioning the truth of much that has been written to LADY HAMILTON'S detriment, every statement that *appears having been culled from authentic sources. Lovers of romantic fiction will find in the narrative incidents equally astonishing with those of any of their favourite stories: the humble birth of the heroine, the charmed life carrying all before it, the flight of worldly wealth, and the friendless death-bed. An unparalleled career! Her own letters teem with amusing quaintness.*

I beg most gratefully to thank the many influential persons who have readily afforded me access to their valuable possessions, and courteously given me their aid, thereby contributing points of invaluable interest. I wish particularly to specify His Grace the DUKE OF ABERCORN, *the* MARQUESS OF HERTFORD, *the Right Hon.* W. E. GLADSTONE, M.P., *etc.*, ALFRED MORRISON, ESQ., *of Fonthill, Wilts, the* MISSES RIGBY, *of Hawarden*, MISS HOLTBY, *York*, Mrs. RAGLAN SOMERSET, THE ARMY AND NAVY CLUB, ROBERT GRIFFIN, ESQ., F. H. GOLDNEY, ESQ., *Camberley*, W. S. WINTLE, Esq, *The Foundling Hospital, and* E. F. J. DEPREZ, ESQ., *London.*

HILDA GAMLIN.

CAMDEN LAWN,
    BIRKENHEAD.

LIST OF ILLUSTRATIONS.

	PAGE
FRONTISPIECE.—EMMA, LADY HAMILTON, *from a Miniature found in the Cabin of* LORD NELSON, *after his death.*	
THE ATTITUDES, *Plate I*	4
FOUR OF ROMNEY'S PICTURES OF LADY HAMILTON *as* THE BACCHANTE, NATURE, THE SPINSTRESS, *and* SENSIBILITY	12
PORTRAIT OF GEORGE ROMNEY, ESQ., *from an Old Print*	18
DR. THOMAS'S HOUSE AT HAWARDEN	20
LADY HAMILTON *as* CASSANDRA, *from a Painting by Romney*	24
THE HON. CHARLES GREVILLE, *from a Drawing in Sepia, in possession of the* AUTHORESS	34
THE ATTITUDES, *Plate II*	44
ELIZABETH GUNNING, DUCHESS OF HAMILTON, *from an Oil Painting in possession of the* AUTHORESS	56
SIR WILLIAM HAMILTON, K.B., *from a Picture by Grignion*	59
LADY HAMILTON, *from a Sketch by Lawrence, in* 1791	62
THE ATTITUDES, *Plate III*	70
BURNHAM THORPE RECTORY, THE BIRTHPLACE OF LORD NELSON	88
LADY HAMILTON, *from a Miniature by Cosway, lent by* F. H. GOLDNEY, ESQ.	98
THE ATTITUDES, *Plate IV*	104
SIR WILLIAM HAMILTON, K.B., *from an old Drawing*	111
MARIA CAROLINE, QUEEN OF NAPLES, *from a Picture given by herself to Lady Hamilton*	114
LORD NELSON, *from a Portrait by Abbott*	124
AUTOGRAPH LETTER OF LADY NELSON TO HER HUSBAND	128
EXTRACT FROM AUTOGRAPH LETTER FROM LORD NELSON TO MAJOR-GEN. VILUTUS	128
THE FONTHILL REVELS IN HONOUR OF LORD NELSON	132
THE ATTITUDES, *Plate V*	134

FACSIMILE OF SPURIOUS VERSES SAID TO HAVE BEEN WRITTEN BY LORD NELSON	146
AN AUTOGRAPH LETTER FROM LORD NELSON TO LADY HAMILTON	146
THE ATTITUDES, Plate VI	152
SEAL OF LORD NELSON, A PROFILE OF LADY HAMILTON	154
LADY HAMILTON, from a Miniature in the possession of MISS HOLTBY, York	165
THE ATTITUDES, Plate VII	168
MERTON PLACE, SURREY, THE RESIDENCE OF LORD NELSON	170
LADY HAMILTON, from a Portrait in a Locket, lent by the RIGHT HON. W. E. GLADSTONE, M.P.	178
SIR W. HAMILTON, K.B., from an old Print	180
THE ATTITUDES, Plate VIII	186
AUTOGRAPH LETTER OF LADY HAMILTON TO LORD NELSON	205
LORD NELSON, from a Miniature by Jackson	208
EMMA HAMILTON, from a Drawing by Lawrence, 1791	216
THE ATTITUDES, Plate IX	222
LADY HAMILTON as a "MAGDALEN," from a Painting by Romney, a commission from the Prince Regent	233
PORTRAIT OF LADY HAMILTON, from a Sketch in possession of one of her relatives	236
THE ATTITUDES, Plate X	238
LADY HAMILTON, from a Miniature by Dun, given by herself to her former mistress, Mrs. Thomas, of Hawarden	244
THE ATTITUDES, Plate XI	256
LADY HAMILTON—the last Portrait of her painted by Romney, in 1791	266
MRS. HORATIA NELSON WARD, from a Photograph in possession of her granddaughter, MRS. RAGLAN SOMERSET	273
FOUR PICTURES OF LADY HAMILTON:—A BACCHANTE and ARIADNE, from Paintings by Sir Joshua Reynolds; A PORTRAIT and EMMA, from Paintings by Romney	282
THE ATTITUDES, Plate XII	288
FACSIMILE OF A LETTER WRITTEN BY HORATIA (NELSON'S ADOPTED DAUGHTER) TO LADY HAMILTON, written across one from her Governess to Miss Charlotte Nelson	292

CONTENTS.

CHAPTER I.
PARENTAGE—EARLY LIFE—DR. GRAHAM 1

CHAPTER II.
GEORGE ROMNEY AND THE PORTRAITS ... 13

CHAPTER III.
EMMA VISITS PARKGATE; LETTERS TO GREVILLE. SIR WILLIAM HAMILTON MAKES HER ACQUAINTANCE 21

CHAPTER IV.
GREVILLE'S FINANCIAL DIFFICULTIES; HE SEEKS SIR WILLIAM HAMILTON'S ADVICE CONCERNING EMMA, AND WRITES ABOUT HIS OWN MATRIMONIAL PROSPECTS; HE SUGGESTS THAT HIS UNCLE SHALL INVITE EMMA TO NAPLES 29

CHAPTER V.
EMMA PREPARES TO VISIT ITALY; HER ARRIVAL AT NAPLES. SIR WILLIAM'S ATTENTIONS; HER BEAUTY ATTRACTS CROWDS 41

CHAPTER VI.
GREVILLE'S CONCERN ON HEARING EMMA'S RESOLVE TO RETURN TO ENGLAND. HER GRAPHIC DESCRIPTION OF VESUVIUS IN ERUPTION. THE DUTCH COMMODORE GIVES AN ENTERTAINMENT IN HER HONOUR 50

CHAPTER VII.
MME. LE BRUN PAINTS EMMA'S PORTRAIT. SHE SITS FOR HER PORTRAIT TO SIR THOMAS LAWRENCE. HER LETTER TO ROMNEY, AND HIS REPLY. THE MARRIAGE OF SIR WILLIAM AND EMMA 59

CHAPTER VIII.

QUEEN CHARLOTTE REFUSES TO RECEIVE LADY HAMILTON AT COURT. HORACE WALPOLE'S SARCASM ON HER MAJESTY'S ACT. MARIE ANTOINETTE SHOWS HER MUCH CIVILITY AT THE COURT OF FRANCE 67

CHAPTER IX.

GREVILLE CONSIDERS SIR WILLIAM THE RIGHT PARTY TO PROVIDE FOR "LADY HAMILTON'S *PROTEGÉE*." SIR WILLIAM'S ILLNESS. EMMA ASSISTS HER GRANDMOTHER 72

CHAPTER X.

THE QUEEN OF NAPLES ADMITS LADY HAMILTON TO CLOSE FRIENDSHIP. SHE FINDS HER PIN MONEY TOO LIMITED FOR HER REQUIREMENTS. HER RECEPTIONS AT THE EMBASSY 78

CHAPTER XI.

NELSON—HIS BOYHOOD; HE TAKES TO THE SEA; HIS YOUTHFUL LOVE AFFAIRS; HIS MARRIAGE 88

CHAPTER XII.

NELSON'S INTRODUCTION TO LADY HAMILTON. SHE USES HER INFLUENCE WITH THE QUEEN OF NAPLES IN THE INTEREST OF THE BRITISH FLEET. THE BATTLE OF THE NILE ... 96

CHAPTER XIII.

LADY HAMILTON ASSISTS THE FLIGHT OF THE ROYAL FAMILY OF NAPLES; THE EXECUTION OF CARACCIOLO 105

CHAPTER XIV.

REJOICINGS IN HONOUR OF NELSON. SIR WILLIAM BEECHEY'S PORTRAIT OF OLD MR. NELSON. JOSIAH NISBET IN TROUBLE. NELSON AND THE HAMILTONS RETURN TO ENGLAND ... 114

CHAPTER XV.

LADY NELSON'S RESENTMENT. THE FONTHILL REVELS: LADY HAMILTON'S IMPORTANT REPRESENTATION OF THE ATTITUDES. MR. BECKFORD'S ECCENTRICITY 127

CONTENTS. xi

CHAPTER XVI.

PAGE

THE THOMSON LETTERS. IMPORTANT EVIDENCE FAVOURING THE ASSERTION THAT LADY HAMILTON WAS NOT THE MOTHER OF HORATIA 140

CHAPTER XVII.

NELSON'S REGARD FOR HORATIA. "EMMA HAMILTON" OF THE FOUNDLING HOSPITAL 155

CHAPTER XVIII.

MERTON PLACE. GILLRAY'S CARICATURES. NELSON OBJECTS TO PAY FEES FOR HONOURS CONFERRED. NELSON'S FATHER ACKNOWLEDGES LADY HAMILTON'S KINDNESS. THE HOUSEKEEPING ACCOUNTS OF THE COMBINED HOUSEHOLD 164

CHAPTER XIX.

DEATH OF SIR WILLIAM HAMILTON. HIS LEGACY TO LORD NELSON. GREVILLE REALISES HIS EXPECTATIONS. LADY HAMILTON APPLIES FOR A PENSION FROM THE GOVERNMENT 179

CHAPTER XX.

NELSON'S UNPROFITABLE ESTATE OF BRONTË. HIS PLANS FOR HORATIA. HIS GREAT CHARITY. FAREWELL TO MERTON 190

CHAPTER XXI.

THE BATTLE OF TRAFALGAR. NELSON'S MESSAGE TO THE FLEET. DEATH IN THE HOUR OF GLORIOUS VICTORY 202

CHAPTER XXII.

THE FUNERAL AT ST. PAUL'S. NELSON'S MEMORY AFFECTIONATELY HONOURED. THE REV. EARL SHOWS HIS HAND. *PUNCH* SPEAKS HIS MIND 211

CHAPTER XXIII.

ENGLAND IGNORES THE LEGACY. DR. SCOTT SYMPATHISES. HIS GRIEVANCE AGAINST EARL WILLIAM. WAS HORATIA OF FOREIGN EXTRACTION? ... 224

CHAPTER XXIV.

POOR RELATIONS. LADY HAMILTON MAKES HER WILL. THE DUKE OF QUEENSBURY RELIEVES HER. THE DEATH OF MRS. CADOGAN. YOUTHFUL MEMORIES BETRAY A SECRET 234

CHAPTER XXV.

LADY HAMILTON ENDEAVOURS TO OBTAIN A PENSION. HER PETITION TO THE PRINCE REGENT 243

CHAPTER XXVI.

LADY HAMILTON TRUE TO NELSON'S TRUST. THE FLIGHT TO CALAIS. HER POVERTY, DEATH, AND BURIAL. DR. BEATTIE'S BEAUTIFUL VERSES ON HER NEGLECTED GRAVE 259

CHAPTER XXVII.

HORATIA'S TROUBLES. THE PRINCE CONSORT ENDEAVOURS TO BEFRIEND HER. SHE APPEALS FOR A PENSION. PLEASING RECOLLECTIONS OF LADY HAMILTON'S ASSOCIATES. INTERESTING RELICS AND FINALE ... 274

LADY HAMILTON.

AN OLD STORY RE-TOLD.

CHAPTER I.

PARENTAGE—EARLY LIFE—DR. GRAHAM.

OLD stories re-told have ever a charm to interest the people of a later day. As the world rolls on, each generation leaves some few whose lives have shone out with a clearer light, marking a record for themselves, while the memories of those who ran the race of life alongside them fade into oblivion. No story so attractive, both to tale-teller and auditor, as the relation of incidents in the life of a beautiful woman; and, standing supremely above the people of her day, was one who, with smile and wile, ruled the destinies of great nations, a one-time cottage beauty, known to fame as Emma, Lady Hamilton. So many articles have been written to the prejudice of this wonderful woman, that the present undertaking is attempted in the endeavour to produce her character in a more pleasing light; the facts introduced having foundation in correspondence gathered from one source and another, which, it will be admitted, is a good groundwork for a display of truth.

Amy Lyon, afterwards known as Emily Lyon, Emma Hart, and ultimately the world-renowned Lady Hamilton, was born at Denhall, in Nesse, in the county of Cheshire, presumably in the year of grace 1765. No actual record of her birth is traceable, but in the register of baptisms in the church of Great Neston is to be seen the certificate of her admission to Christianity. She always celebrated the anniversary of her birthday on the 26th of April. The certificate is entered as follows:—"Emy, D^r of Henry Lyon, smith, of Nesse, by Mary his wife. Bap. 12 May, 1765." This document settles the important point as to the position in life occupied by the father of the rising beauty. As she signed her marriage certificate "Amy," it may reasonably be assumed that the spelling "Emy" was the result of the country dialect, with which a non-native minister would not be thoroughly conversant. She received the name of Amy out of compliment to an aunt, Amy Moore, of Liverpool, wife of John Moore, whose daughters were mentioned in one of the wills she made as Lady Hamilton, in 1811, when she recorded their residence as Moore Street, Liverpool, at which time they were keeping a small beerhouse. Her mother was the daughter of a peasant woman at Hawarden, Flintshire, named Kidd, and her father, Henry Lyon, a blacksmith of Denhall, a village on the outskirts of Great Neston, in Cheshire. In Mortimer's *History of the Hundred of Wirral*, Neston is recorded as one of the most miserable villages in the locality, consisting of a mass of hovels inhabited by colliers. Emma's father survived her birth a very short time; his burial is registered within six weeks of his little daughter's christening, in these lines—" Henry Lyon, of Denhall, smith, Bur. 21 June, 1765." The young widow, finding her support gone, and unable to contend alone amid comparative strangers in the effort to make a living for herself and infant, returned to Hawarden to share the kindly shelter of her mother's roof. In the quiet country village the early days of her child were spent, and one writer asserts that, as a young girl, Emma was frequently to be seen walking alongside a donkey, offering coals for sale, which is by no means improbable, the district including collieries, and insomuch as the occupation of grandmother Kidd was the conveyance of coal between Hawarden and Chester, which pursuit is still followed by an eccentric old lady who is known to her neighbours as "Lady Margaret." Mrs. Kidd also acted in the capacity of carrier between the great people at the Hall and Chester. Broad Lane Hall it was called in those days—Hawarden Castle it is now.

On one occasion, as Mrs. Kidd was wending her homeward way, in charge of her horse and cart, she was overtaken by the shades of night, under cover of which an attack was made upon her by two men. Her screams for help reached the ears of some farm labourers, who were proceeding home after their day's work. Exclaiming "There's old Mrs. Kidd in trouble," they ran to the rescue. The assailants made quick retreat on their approach, but not before they had cut away the old woman's loose pocket, containing the money received in Chester on behalf of the occupant of the Hall, which it was the nightly duty of Mr. Kidd, her husband, to walk up to the Hall and deliver. The old man gained his living by minding sheep on Saltney Marshes. The River Dee flowed up much farther than at present.

Great loss and annoyance was caused by dogs worrying the flocks; at that time there was no dog tax, and, therefore, they abounded in numbers. In order to rid himself of these troublesome pests, Mr. Kidd dug a hole in the ground, in which he stood breast high, and lay in wait with his gun, which he discharged at the depredators whenever they came within range, until he effectually cleared them away.

An old lane used to run down under the park wall, on the opposite side of the road to the "Glynne Arms," which led to a mill; at the end of this lane stood the cottage and outbuildings of Grandmother Kidd. The humble dwelling was of the usual thatched and whitewashed type, and went by the name of "The Steps," from the entrance being gained by the ascent of a flight of steps. The actual house was pulled down a few years ago, and modern structures occupy the spot.

A good opening presented itself to Mrs. Lyon as needlewoman in the establishment of Lord Halifax, of Stanstead Park, who, noticing her bright pretty child, undertook the expenses of a little education, and put her to a day-school, where she made rapid progress. The Earl marrying again, the mother's services were dispensed with, and Emma (as she was called in Hawarden) was placed as nursemaid to the children of Mr. Honoratus Leigh Thomas, surgeon, of Hawarden. This gentleman had settled in that village about the year 1759, and soon attained a respectable and lucrative practice. This was probably due to his marriage on January 28th, 1760, with Maria Margaretta, younger sister of the celebrated Alderman John Boydell, engraver and printseller, and Lord Mayor of London in 1791; whose father, Josiah Boydell, at the instigation of his friend and patron, Sir John Glynne, had settled at Hawarden. In 1768, Mr. Thomas, in conjunction with a brother surgeon named Sutton, made inoculation for smallpox a speciality, their joint advertisement in the *Chester Courant* of June 27th, 1768, stating that the success that had attended their method of inoculation rendered it unnecessary to expatiate on the utility of a practice so universally approved. Old Mr. Thomas is spoken of as having possessed an exceedingly kind disposition; charitable to the poor, but unwishful that his many acts of mercy should be known; no sufferer in the little village need refrain from seeking advice from want of means, for the services of the worthy man were ever at the command of the destitute, and were often supplemented by gifts both in money and kind. His wife, Mrs. Thomas, was in every way a desirable mistress for young Emma; though she exercised great control over the giddy girl, and held her exuberant spirits in check, she retained her love and respect to the last hour of her life. When her little serving maid had attained an elevated position on the rung of the social ladder, she frequently sent her former mistress evidences of affection which are still in the possession of the descendants and relatives of Mr. and Mrs. Thomas, and are highly regarded as heirlooms by their owners.

When Mrs. Thomas first undertook to train Emma for domestic service, she had much to contend with from the thoughtlessness and untidiness of her little dependant, and it was no unusual thing to find Emma running about with the holes in her stockings pinned together, for she totally dispensed with the use of a darning-needle; but much allowance can be made, for she was merely a child of twelve years old, and had everything to learn, and as her mistress found her very amenable to correction, she became greatly attached to her little nursemaid. It was, therefore, with feelings of deep regret that a summons arrived from Mrs. Lyon, who had found her way up to the great metropolis; this summons contained the announcement that there was an opening for her little girl in the family of Linley, the great composer, who at that time was part owner of Drury Lane Theatre, and Emma must proceed at once to London. Young as she was, she had become a general favourite among the villagers, with a bright word here, and a quick retort there, as she ran her errands. One and all felt her loss greatly when the girl had departed in company with one of her male cousins to join the stage coach at Chester *en route* for London. At Chester they were met by Mrs. Burt, wife of an artist, who took charge of them on the journey. Some of the old residents of Hawarden remember hearing their grandparents speak of Emma Lyon as a very well disposed girl, generous to a fault. To console the weeping girl at parting, Mrs. Thomas promised that she should return and pay them a visit, which pleasure was carried into effect eventually; but London scenes and life had done their worst for the country maid, and her giddiness caused much annoyance and anxiety to Mrs. Thomas, who was a religious and good-living woman. A climax was put to the visit by Emma's attending Wepre Fair, held in the neighbourhood, which was the resort of light characters, whom Mrs. Thomas rightly judged to be unfitted for the companionship of young people, and as the entertainments proved so attractive that Emma did not return home until a very late hour, her old mis-

PLATE I.— ATTITUDE OF LADY HAMILTON, FROM A DRAWING BY REHBURG.

tress resolved to have no further responsibility, and sent her back to London. It was in the year 1777 that Emma entered the service of Mrs. Linley, who at that time was mistress of Drury Lane Theatre. Emma had to accompany her to the playhouse, and it was her province to convey messages from the actresses behind the scenes to Mrs. Linley seated in her private box. It was no uncommon thing to find Mrs. Linley in ill-humour, and her little maid had not unfrequently to be the bearer of an unpleasant retort to those who considered themselves of equal importance to the lady. It was in this capacity that she imbibed her love of attitudinising, the natural result of being a frequent witness of theatrical rehearsals and representations; and it was during her period of service in the family of the composer Linley that she first displayed her extraordinary inborn talent for music. Her conduct was in every respect satisfactory, and the cause of her leaving her situation was perhaps the first romance of her life. She had formed a girlish attachment to one of her young masters, Samuel Linley, a midshipman on the *Thunderer*; his father received the intimation that he was seriously ill of a fever, and hurried to the vessel to convey his son to his home. Emma assiduously nursed and tended him during his illness, which, despite all that love and care could do, had a fatal termination. So heartbroken was the affectionate girl that she quitted the house immediately after the funeral. Mrs. Linley told a lady that Emma was so attached to her son, and her affliction made such an impression on her mind, that she was unable any longer to dwell in the scene of her trouble, and no entreaties could prevail upon her to remain even a day.

Her next situation was in the family of Dr. Budd, who then resided in Chatham Place, Blackfriars. This gentleman was one of the physicians at St. Bartholomew's Hospital. Her fellow-servant was a lively, clever girl, who, in later years, became known as a popular and celebrated actress at Drury Lane Theatre, by name Mrs. Jane Powell. One day the two giddy girls conceived the idea of perpetrating the following escapade, which they successfully carried out. Full of life, and bent on fun, they started for Cocksheath Camp* as ballad singers, thereby emulating "*la belle* Jennings," afterwards Duchess of Tyrconnel, who donned the garb of an orange girl, and vended her wares among the audience of the old playhouse. Two gentlemen like-

* Mrs. Montague, a last century lady, writes: "It is much the fashion here to go and see the Camp at Cocksheath."

wise in search of pleasure, one Mr. Perry, afterwards proprietor of the *Morning Chronicle*, the other, Mr. Bish, who became director of a well known lottery office, were struck with the wit and deportment of the two girls, and though they really took them to be ballad singers, they considered them to be of a superior degree, and endeavoured to make their acquaintance. This the young women resented, and they obstinately refused refreshment at a tavern, which civility the young men pertinaciously proffered to them. Regarding these attentions as persecution, they determined to return home, and contrived to elude their admirers for a time. However, the young fellows followed them until they reached London Bridge, where they suddenly missed them. Perry happened to look over the bridge, and saw the girls in a wherry crossing over to the other side of the river. As Emma caught sight of his face above the parapet, she stood up, and waved her arms at him in derision! Many years afterwards, Lady Hamilton, then in the zenith of her power and beauty, visited Drury Lane Theatre, attended by her husband, and the audience at the old playhouse divided their admiration between the accomplished and entertaining actress, Mrs. Powell, on the stage, and the baronet's fascinating wife in her own box, the fellow servants of Chatham Place, a coincidence in the annals of domestic service which it is safe to assert is without parallel.

Bestowing too much time on the productions of the printing press to the neglect of the linen press, Emma received her discharge from Mrs. Budd, and she next entered into the establishment of a fruiterer in St. James's market. In after years, when Madame Le Brun was painting the portrait of the Prince Regent, he told her that he had seen Emma standing at the door of this fruiterer's, and though she was poorly dressed and wore clogs, her lovely face had attracted his attention. It would most probably be "Betty's" noted fruit shop, where men of fashion assembled and talked the gossip of the day.

In this situation she was noticed by a lady who possessed more goods than good, and who, by holding out tempting promises of a life of pleasure, induced her to take up her residence in her house in Arlington Street; this lady, by name Mrs. Kelly, was known by the soubriquet of "the Abbess." Many and many a time was Emma heard in later years to regret the manner in which she passed her days under the roof of this devotee of pleasure.

Meanwhile, news reached her that the cousin, who had been her escort on her first journey to London, had been impressed and conveyed on board a vessel lying in the Thames. The intelligence caused her much distress, and induced her to seek an interview with Captain, afterwards Admiral, John Willet Payne, for the purpose of soliciting her cousin's release. Incapable of resisting her earnest entreaties, the Captain granted her request, but it was given conditionally, at great cost to herself, for the audience closed with her promise to accept the overtures he made, and led to her first mistake in life. In a few months orders arrived for the Captain's vessel to proceed to sea, and the poor girl found herself abandoned in a condition deplorable to relate. In these straits she sent for her mother, who remained with her, attending her through her great trouble, and when she parted from her daughter, to revisit the little Welsh village, she carried with her a little child to be reared and tended by old Mrs. Kidd, to whom they always reverted in their hours of need, and the heart of the hard-working old countrywoman was easily moved to aid and help then. The infant, a girl, was named Emily, or Emma, after her mother.

Captain Payne, on becoming Admiral, was appointed Comptroller of the Household of George, Prince of Wales. He commanded the squadron in 1795 which brought to England Caroline of Brunswick, the Prince's young bride.

The next step taken by the foolish beauty was equally reprehensible with the last. Making the acquaintance of a fast-living baronet, Sir Harry Featherstonehaugh, she was soon found presiding over his splendid establishment at Up Park, Surrey, where she received great applause on account of her equestrian prowess, sitting her horse with uncommon elegance, and rivalling the boldest huntsman in speed and daring; while she was the life and soul of the party, amusing all Sir Harry's friends with her quaint and lively sallies and prattle. This was without exception the worst period of her life. New to social splendour, a giddy girl, who owned to doing many acts from pure bravado and wildness; with no checking hand to stay her in her headlong course, what wonder that the flattered young beauty went astray? This fatal beauty, and a kind of natural grace which she possessed in a striking degree, made her presence distinguished. She should not be judged by our ordinary standard. Her early surroundings, and the entire want of education in her day among the class in which she lived in childhood, would, to a nature like Emma's, mean more than deprivation, and doubtless led the way to a life in which she seemed to be a prey to every undisciplined impulse. Her reign at Up Park was brilliant and brief; Sir Harry breaking up his household on the plea of her extravagance, and, though she may not have been entirely responsible for the catastrophe, we may infer that he had some grounds for his complaint by reading the following extract from a letter of Mr. Charles Greville, who was destined to play a prominent part in the history of her life, and whose acquaintance she made about this time :—

January 10*th*, 1782.

MY DEAR EMILY,

I do not make apologies for S' H.'s behaviour to you, and altho' I advised you to deserve his esteem by your good conduct, I own I never expected better from him. It was your duty to deserve good treatment, and it gave me great concern to see you imprudent the first time you came to L. (London) from the country; and as the same conduct was repeated when you was last in town I began to despair of your happiness. To prove to you that I do not accuse you falsely, I only mention 5 guineas and a half a guinea for coach. But, my Emily, as you seem quite miserable now, I do not mean to give you uneasiness but comfort, and tell you that I will forget your faults and bad conduct to Sir H. and to myself, and will not repent my good humour if I find that you have learnt by experience to value yourself and endeavour to preserve your friends by good conduct and affection. *

Finding herself cast adrift by the baronet, she had made her way to her grandmother's cottage at Hawarden, where she remained in a state of great depression—her coming trouble weighed heavily on her mind; Sir Harry had acted most shabbily, and barely supplied her with enough money to convey her home, as she herself had written to Mr. Greville : " I have not a farthing to bless myself with, and I think my friends looks coolly on me, I think so I do, o G—— what shall I Dow ? what shall I dow ? o how your letter affected me wen you wished me happiness." She writes of herself as a girl in distress, for she says : " What else am I but a girl ? " And she closed her letter with the piteous appeal : " Don't tell my mother what distress I am in, and dow aford me some comfort." Mr. Greville was a man much older than herself, and he had frequently exerted himself to control her

* The Morrison MSS.

PARENTAGE—EARLY LIFE—DR. GRAHAM.

during her late wild career; his response was in a firm and kindly tone. He advised her to return to town, as her friends looked coolly on her it was time to leave them. He told her to part with her maid, take a new name, and live retired until she could re-appear, when no one would have it in their power to betray her if she kept her own secret, and as he would gradually get her a new set of acquaintances, he hoped to see her respected and admired. He enclosed her a sum of money, telling her not to throw it away, but to reserve it for her journey in case she might feel fatigued and wish to take her time, but that when she arrived in town she might send some presents to her relatives. He furthermore advised her that her conduct be staid and quiet, and that so long as she acted with strict adherence to his desires, he would provide her with a home, but with this condition, that she must renounce all her relations, as he would not be troubled with any of them except her mother.

It was during this visit to Hawarden that, in accordance with Mr. Greville's bidding, she obtained a copy of her baptismal register, and received from the hand of the curate of Great Neston Church the document which decides her original name. The copy was supplied to her on December 19th, 1781, and was forwarded by her to Mr. Greville. Inside the envelope she scrawled the following specimen of her defective orthography: " My age was got out of the Reggester, and I have sent it to my dear Charles, once more adue, once more adue, O you dear Grevil."* At the period of her second trouble she had only just completed her seventeenth birthday, and pitiable though it is to assert, there seems to be no reason to surmise that she was any older, or that she was other than an unusually precocious girl. A few years later, Greville wrote of her: " She is but twenty," and she herself mentioned her birthday in the year following as being her twenty-first, which dates would place her birth as 1765. The certificate was evidently obtained so as to decide her age, as she clearly writes: "*My age* was got out of the Reggester." Of the occurrence which happened in town there is no further mention, therefore the probability is that death intervened and removed a living reproach.

At this point it will not be inopportune to introduce the connection ascribed between Emma and Dr. James Graham, a famous charlatan, who deluded the fashionable world more than a century ago. Investigation has

* In the Morrison MSS.

disproved the fable of Emma's association with the noted exhibition, which was the outcome of a scurrilous and anonymous attack, published within a few months of her death. On enquiry her time has been found fully occupied during the period when her services were said to have been at the command of Dr. Graham, so that it would have been an impossibility for her to have represented the character in question, that of the Goddess of Health in his far-famed temple. Nothing on modern record can equal the mysteries introduced by this first-rate impostor. His house on the Adelphi Terrace was splendidly lighted up, and the rooms set apart for the show were gorgeously furnished, comparable only to a scene from the *Arabian Nights*, and his lectures upon no very decorous subjects were attended by ladies as well as gentlemen of the highest rank. A thousand strange stories were whispered of the scenes that occurred beneath his roof. At the door stood two gigantic porters, near seven feet high, each supplied with a long staff having ornamental silver heads, like those borne by parish beadles, and wearing superb liveries, with large gold-laced cocked hats; they were retained at the entrance to keep back the crowds; when not engaged at the door of the exhibition, they were employed in distributing handbills round the town. A writer of the period has left the following lines, which vindicate Emma Lyon so far as posing at the doctor's show is concerned. "It has been asserted," he says, "that it was the late Lady Hamilton who prefigured the Goddess of Health, but it certainly was not she; I remember the carriages drawing up to the door of this modern Paphos, with crowds of gaping sparks on each side to discover who were the visitors, but the ladies' faces were all covered, all going *incog*."

One means which the quack advocated for ensuring health and longevity was the frequent use of the "mud bath," and that there might be no error as to his practising what he preached, he was to be seen in his garden buried up to the chin in mud,* accompanied by a lady to whom he gave the title, "Vestina, Goddess of Health." While sitting in the mud bath her head was most elaborately dressed in the prevailing fashion with powder, pearls, feathers, and flowers; while her "Companion of the Bath," the doctor, appeared in a full-bottomed-wig. His goddess, Vestina, instead of drawing

* The house of the father of one of the actors of the period was situated back to back with this exhibition; the lads annoyed the doctor and his patients by propelling paper pellets in their faces with unerring aim.

new life from her semi-burial, nearly succumbed during its exhibition on the northern tour, which he made when his show was played out in the capital, and in consequence the lady withdrew her services. He worded his advertisements: "The rosy, the gigantic, the stupendous Goddess of Health." and anon, "Vestina, the Gigantic," which produce the rational inference that the character was undertaken by a fully-developed, massive woman, whereas Emma, at this time, was only a tall, lithe girl of fourteen or fifteen years. Again, he announced that "before and after the lecture one of Vestina's fairy train will warble forth sweet celestial sounds." He would not have deputed a subordinate to sing had Emma with her magnificent voice been the exponent of Vestina.

A younger sister of Mrs. Siddons, by name Mrs. Curtis, who was the cause of much trouble and annoyance to her family, gave lectures on health in connection with the Doctor's celebrated imposition, but she only appeared very shortly before the expiration of his metropolitan lease. To annoy her relatives, she appended to the announcement that she took in plain sewing, that she was " Mrs. Curtis, sister to Mrs. Siddons."

Progressing gradually northwards with his show, the Doctor arrived at Edinburgh, where he was condignly committed to the Tolbooth on the score of impropriety. Records of the well-merited sentence passed on the infamous impostor are to be found in *The Gentleman's Magazine* for 1783 as follows:—"On the 19th of July came on to be tried, before the Lords of Session, a bill of suspension and liberation, at the instance of the noted Dr. James Graham, against the Lord Provost and Magistrates of Edinburgh for false imprisonment and exacting exorbitant bail, when their Lordships were pleased to approve the imprisonment, but to discountenance their proceedings as exacting exorbitant bail, as they no doubt had in view the assumed character and apparent opulence of the Doctor; whereas, the Doctor was in reality an inferior person, and therefore their Lordships were pleased to restrict the bail from £1,000 Scots to 50 marks (about three guineas), on payment of which the Doctor was liberated from prison, but was bound to take his trial for the several offences with which he was charged."

This announcement was succeeded in the next month's issue by the result of his appearance at court, August 15, 1783. A letter received from Edinburgh, dated August 9, says—" This day Dr. James Graham was committed prisoner to the Tolbooth by a warrant of the Magistrates, on the application of the Procurator Fiscal, in order to take his trial for his late injurious publications in the City. Nothing," continues the *Magazine*, "can be a stronger satire on the police of this country for suffering this man's pernicious exhibitions to have their full effect than this commitment." A well-earned rebuke, for during his metropolitan career he had kept his equipage, maintained a splendid retinue, and, for a short time at least, was invited to many of the first tables, and in return, contrived to give his claret and champagne. He dispensed one quackery, which he averred was infallible—an Elixir of Life; and one would have thought that, being in possession of so valuable a receipt for prolonging life for ever and ever, he would have made use of it in his own interest. If he did, it failed to act, for he died at Glasgow, in indigent circumstances, aged fifty-two.

Fond as Emma was of attitudinising, there is no record of too much freedom of display. Her unrivalled poses were chiefly from the antique, portraying the most refined perception and graceful delineation. No artist of her day has left one line to record that she was other than proper in her personifications. It having been said that she had sat in the "life" school at the Royal Academy, numerous Academicians contradicted the assertion, and Wilkie—who was specially questioned as to her having posed in that capacity—replied that he "had no recollection of her as a model when he was a student."

THE SPINSTRESS—ROMNEY SENSIBILITY—ROMNEY

CHAPTER II.

GEORGE ROMNEY AND THE PORTRAITS.

UNDER the guiding influence of a man well disposed to goodness, and owning more straightforward ideas than could be placed to the credit of many men of his period, the tractable Emma became most pliable in the hands of Greville. Possessing a quick, warm nature, more easily led to good than evil, she put forth her best endeavours to make a seasonable return to one who had placed her in comfort and happiness, and whom she sincerely loved and respected. Now commenced the training and development of her naturally well-inclined heart, and if Mr. Greville's monetary position had not necessitated his mating with a well-dowered wife, and had he been able to marry Emma at this stage, she would in all probability have left behind a name as highly honoured for goodness as she became notorious by the power of her beauty. His companionship and judicious kindness had the most beneficial effect on her in every respect. The men who assembled at his table were only those of great refinement and artistic worth; one of his intimate friends being George Romney, and to his facile brush are we indebted for the loveliest portrayals of her winning face. It was during her residence with Mr. Greville that she first sat to the painters Romney and Henry Tresham, in accordance with his wish; and at most sittings she was accompanied by himself or her mother, Mrs. Lyon, who from henceforth will be known as Mrs. Cadogan. Left a young widow, there is every likelihood of her having re-married with some one bearing the name of Dogan or Cadogan. In deference to the desire of Mr. Greville, she had become an inmate of his establishment. He entertained a high feeling of respect for her, and considered that her companionship would act as a restraint on his young *protégé*. Writers have looked askance at her taking up her residence under her daughter's roof; but it must be borne in mind that those times were not these times, nor must we judge the people of that day as we would the people of this day. We cannot but regret the nature of the household in Edgeware Road; and, though we sincerely deprecate it, we must take into consideration the tone of society in general at the period of which we write, and not expect to find people of humble origin acting with the propriety which their superiors ignored. Mrs. Cadogan's position was merely that of a considerate housekeeper, who busied herself in seeing to the comfort of each one, and all who knew her at any time of her life liked her. The assistance she gave added materially to the well-being of the household, for she personally superintended the culinary department, and the various little dinners served to the coterie of talented men who frequented the house reflected the greatest credit on the hard-working woman's knowledge of tasty dishes produced at little cost. Life ran smoothly and most enjoyably, the limited circle living in happy accord among themselves, seldom appearing at any of the public places of entertainment. Some hours daily were devoted to self-improvement. Emma's vocal gifts were of an extraordinary quality, of great power and brilliancy, though slightly incorrect in intonation. She performed bravuras with the utmost facility, her dramatic ability enabling her to give superior force and finish to all her performances. Music had ever a charm which carried her out of herself. One evening, by way of a treat, Mr. Greville took her to a fashionable resort of the past, Ranelagh Gardens, where her feelings so overcame her on hearing the singing of the principal lady, and the applause that followed it, that she was carried away by her excitement, and so far forgot herself as to burst forth into one of her most brilliant scenas, trilling and shaking in emulation of the rival vocalist. At first her interruption caused annoyance and astonishment to the visitors, who showed unmistakable signs of disapprobation at so unusual a proceeding, but, as they listened, entranced by her vocalisation, they broke into a volley of applause as she concluded. Mr. Greville was too much ashamed of her exhibition to own or check her, and as soon as order was restored he quietly withdrew and took her home, speaking his mind in no measured terms, telling her she had shown manifest inclination to please fools rather than respect his sentiments, which avowal gave her great discomfort and distress. On their return to their house she retired to her own room and cast aside her holiday finery, crying as if her heart would break; then she clothed herself in one of her plain, homely gowns, sought her companion and asked him to dismiss her; for, having caused him so much shame, she was unfit to remain with him. He was touched by her evident repentance, and it was the *only* occasion on which he had to be severe with her, so amenable was she to correction.

In the beginning of the year 1782, Emma, who then went under the name of Mrs. Hart, first sat to Romney for her portrait, and to his delineations of the beautiful girl he owes his immortality. We can do no better than quote the words of the artist's son, the Rev. John Romney, who, in the year 1830, published a memoir of his talented father. He says, "She was brought by the Hon. Charles Greville to sit for a three-quarters portrait. It was a beautiful one, so full of *naïveté*, in which she is represented with a little spaniel lap-dog under her arm. This picture was afterwards bought by Mr. Lister Parker, at Sir William Hamilton's sale. Another portrait of her, full-length, in the character of 'Circe,' was begun about the same time. It had the same expression of countenance, and was very fascinating; but suffered the fate of many others in never having been finished. The brutes which the enchantress had metamorphosed, could not be painted at that time without much personal inconvenience to Mr. Romney, so the picture was set aside. Gilpin was to have painted them afterwards, but from some cause never did. Had any person, however, offered a hundred guineas for it, I have no doubt but it would have been completed." Besides the two above-named pictures, the following is a list of the principal portraits of Emma, painted by George Romney:—"Iphigenia," whole-length, not finished; "St. Cecilia," half-length, bought by Mr. Montague Burgoyne for seventy guineas; "Sensibility," bought by Mr. Hayley for one hundred guineas; "A Bacchante," half-length, sent to Sir William Hamilton at Naples—the most enchanting of all her portraits, lost at sea on its return to this country. "Alope exposed with her Child," bought by Admiral Vernon for sixty guineas; "The Spinstress," bought by Mr. Curwen for one hundred and fifty guineas; "Cassandra," bought for the Shakespeare Gallery, for one hundred and eighty guineas; a three-quarters, in a straw hat, called "Emma," for Mr. Crawfurd; "A Bacchante," three-quarters, bought by Sir John Leicester; a half-length, in a black gown and pink petticoat, sent to Naples; a half-length, painted after she was Lady Hamilton, given, at her request, to her mother; a "Calypso" and a "Magdalen," painted from her when Lady Hamilton for the Prince of Wales, two hundred pounds; whole-length of "Joan of Arc," unfinished; "The Pythian Priestess," half-length, unfinished; "Cassandra," whole-length, unfinished; a half-length, in which she is represented reading a paper, having the light reflected on her face, given to Mr. Hayley; a three-quarters, sent to Mr. Deutens in 1792; a three-quarters portrait, side face, shoulders bare; and two heads.

The picture of "Joan of Arc" was purchased by Mr. Stewardson, the artist, at the sale of Romney's pictures. The picture of "Cassandra," for the Shakespeare Gallery, influenced the public taste, and was instrumental in the discarding of the long and shapeless waists then in vogue, by the introduction of a more simple and graceful mode of dress approaching the Grecian. Succeeding painters copied Romney in this reform, and thereby gave their portraits more elegance. Many of the finest portraits of Sir Joshua and Romney are disfigured by the preposterous fashions of their time.

In Romney's picture of Emma as "Nature," we see the girl as she might have been in the rural lanes of her country home, hatless and laughing, running with the little pet dog in her arms as playfellow. Not in any picture of Romney's does she stand represented with the faintest suggestion of boldness of expression—all shadow forth a loveable, frank, sweet face. What picture could be lovelier than the "Emma" of Romney's master brush?—a modest, rarely-beautiful face in a large straw hat, tied round the head and under the chin with a handkerchief; from beneath the broad brim she peeps with shy, half-bent head; her dress of muslin, simple and high-fitting, with a long scarf thrown round her neck, and her sleeves quite plain to the wrist: what an unassuming girlish form and sweet coy face!

The picture known as "Sensibility"* had its origin in a curious way, from a suggestion of Hayley, the poet, life-long friend and biographer of Romney. He thus describes it himself:—"During my visit to Romney, in 1786, I happened to find him one morning contemplating a recently-coloured head on a small canvas. I expressed my admiration of his unfinished work in the following terms: 'This is a most happy beginning; you never painted a female head with such exquisite expression: you have only to enlarge your canvas, introduce the shrub mimosa growing in a vase, with a hand of this figure approaching its leaves, and you may call your picture a personification of "Sensibility."' 'I like your suggestion,' replied the painter, 'and will enlarge my canvas immediately.' 'Do so,' I answered with exultation, 'and I will hasten to an eminent nurseryman at Hammersmith and bring you the

---

* This picture was sold at Messrs. Christie's auction rooms, on March 29, 1890, and was purchased by Mr. Henson for the sum of £3,045.

most beautiful plant I can find.'" The poet coveted the possession of the picture which he had thus helped to create. He obtained it by a stroke of business. A gentleman whose estate lay contiguous to some property of Hayley's took a fancy to one of his farms, and desired to buy it. "If you pay a fair and full market price for the land, according to the valuation of an uninterested person," said this most prudent of all the sons of song, "and purchase and present to me the 'Sensibility' of Romney besides, the land shall be yours." The terms pleased, and, presently, both money and picture were in the hands of Hayley.*

The picture called "The Spinstress" was painted to the order of Mr. Greville, but his limited finances prohibited his completing the purchase. Romney received an offer from a Mr. Curwen to take the picture; but as it had been painted originally for Mr. Greville, with whom the artist had long been on very intimate terms, he did not feel himself at liberty to sell it until he had ascertained Greville's views. He accordingly wrote to the latter gentleman, and informed him of the offer made, saying that if he still continued in the intention of purchasing it, he (Romney) would reserve it for him, and postpone the payment till it might suit Greville's convenience, to which Romney received, in reply, a letter dated Feb. 25, 1788:—

> The separation from the original of the "The Spinstress" has not been indifferent to me, and I am but just reconciled to it, from knowing that the beneficial consequences of acquirements will be obtained, and that the aberration from the plan I intended will be for her benefit. I, therefore, can have no reason to value "The Spinstress" less than I have done; on the contrary, the just estimation of its merits is ascertained by the offer from a person who does not know the original. Yet I find myself daily so much poorer that I do not foresee when I can pay for it; and I am already too much obliged to you to avail myself in any degree of your kindness to me. Perhaps Mr. Christian might accept my resignation of it, and pay for it, and give me the option of re-purchasing, if the improbable event of my increase of means shall enable me to recover what I now lose with regret; but I can make no condition, and I leave the full and entire disposal of it to you.†

* Allan Cunningham's *Lives of the British Painters*.
† Mr. Christian was a gentleman from the Isle of Man, who, marrying an heiress named Curwen, adopted her name, and became Mr. Christian Curwen.

Mr. Christian Curwen was agreeable to possess the picture in conformity with Mr. Greville's desire to purchase it from him, should he ever be able to do so; but Mr. Curwen enjoined this condition, that Romney would undertake, at a convenient opportunity, to paint another picture to replace "The Spinstress," if he should be required to give it up; and after this interchange of courtesies, the picture was handed over to him. Romney first conceived the idea of the attitude from observing a cobbler's wife sitting in a stall.

"The Spinstress" was engraved by both Bartolozzi and Cheeseman. Nor was Romney the only artist who rejoiced in portraying that face beyond compare. Lawrence drew a chalk head of "the artist's queen," signed "Emma, 1791," and subsequently a full-length figure. The "Emma" is a profile, with head turbaned in gauze. It can be seen in the British Museum among the prints of Lady Hamilton.

Sir Joshua Reynolds painted her as a Bacchante, but he certainly did not develop so pleasing a result as his despised rival Romney, whose name he feigned to forget, and whom he always designated as "the man in Cavendish Square." The spirit of jealousy invades every phase of society, asserting itself whenever an equally clever rival appears on a similar trade ground. Reynolds' Bacchante conveys more the idea of an untidy, half tipsy woman, and for this portrait at least he must stand below Romney. Hoppner painted her as a "Magdalen" and "the Comic Muse"; they were formerly at Ragley Hall, the seat of the Marquess of Hertford, but they have strayed away into strange hands. Romney always treated Emma with a fatherly consideration, checking her temper and endeavouring to improve all her weak points. Later on letters will be inserted, showing in themselves the relative positions of painter and model. In the hands of such able men as the poet Hayley, and the artist Romney, both highly intellectual, her mind put forth its latent energies, and she successfully aimed at refinement and cultivation. Little as it was merited, George Romney fell under the lash of the slanderous tongues which respected neither man nor woman in that disreputable era of our annals. Let us hear what his son says in vindication of the injured memory of his father, which is to be found in his *Life of George Romney* in these words: "Far be it from me to become her apologist, but as I know that her conduct in the former part of her life has been misrepresented,* and that many extravagant stories have been told of her, implicating Mr.

* Regarding her connection with Dr. Graham's show.

GEORGE ROMNEY, ESQ.

Romney, which have not the shadow of foundation, it is no more than common charity and justice to state such circumstances as will place her character in its true light. In all Mr. Romney's intercourse with her she was treated with the utmost respect, and her demeanour fully entitled her to it. In the characters in which she has been represented, she only sat for the face, and a slight sketch of the attitude; and the drapery was painted either from other models or from the layman. The only figure that displayed any licentiousness of dress was the Bacchante, and it was as modest as the nature of the character would admit of, but in this she only sat for the face. There is no doubt but the talent of representing characters by action, and by the expression of countenance, which she afterwards displayed with so much success when Lady Hamilton, was acquired when she sat to Mr. Romney, she being requested to imitate those powerful emotions of the mind which he wished to paint. It was a great gratification to her to sit as a model; it amused her, and flattered her vanity. From the peculiarity of her situation, she was excluded from society—justly excluded ; and the only resources she had for amusement in her loneliness, were reading and music at home, and coming once or twice a week to sit for her picture. She always had a hackney coach to bring and take her away, and she never appeared in the streets without her mother. She told Mr. Romney that soon after she became acquainted with Mr. Greville, he took her to Ranelagh, where she attracted so much notice, that she perceived it gave him pain ; she therefore of her own accord put off her gay attire, and assumed the garb of a lady's maid in which she ever after appeared, and never again went to any public place."

Hayley, too, has recorded his tribute to the graces of her person, and the excellence of her accomplishments. We find the following lines in the life of his friend Romney, which he compiled mostly at the suggestion of Emma, then Lady Hamilton. He writes: "The talents which nature bestowed on the fair Emma led her to delight in the two kindred arts of music and painting. In the first she acquired great practical ability, for the second she had an exquisite taste, and such expressive powers as could furnish to an historical painter an inspiring model for the various characters, either delicate or sublime, that he might have occasion to represent. One of his earliest fancy pictures from this animated model, was a whole length of Circe, with her magic wand. It could not be painted later than 1782, as I recollect a letter from a friend in that year, describing the very powerful impression made by this picture on a party who had surveyed it." Anon he says: "Her features, like the language of Shakespeare, could exhibit all the feelings of nature, and all the gradations of every passion, with the most fascinating truth and felicity of expression."

Romney was exceedingly rapid in the execution of his work. As an instance, it may be mentioned that he painted the drapery in the picture of Emma Hart, as Alope (Cercyon's daughter), in one hour, from a living model.

Before passing from the subject of Romney for the present, it may be of interest to some to insert the fact that he never put his name to any of his pictures; his confidence in the quality of his compositions taught him to feel that his signature would not be necessary to the people of coming ages to enable them to recognise his works.

DR. THOMAS'S HOUSE, AT HAWARDEN.

CHAPTER III.

EMMA VISITS PARKGATE ; LETTERS TO GREVILLE. SIR WILLIAM HAMILTON MAKES HER ACQUAINTANCE.

In the midsummer of the year 1784 Emma was much troubled with a skin affection, for the cure of which her medical attendant recommended sea air and bathing. Mr. Greville proposed Abergele, and suggested that she should first call at Hawarden and spend a few days with her grandmother and her little girl, and when she fixed on her marine residence she should let the child have the benefit of a change; he also offered that her mother should make one of the party, of which kindness she gladly availed herself. After spending a few days at her early home, she proceeded to Parkgate, a quiet seaside place on the river Dee, distant about one mile from her birthplace, and which at this period was a station for the Irish packets that sailed four times a week. Passing through Chester in her course to Parkgate, she wrote from there to Mr. Greville, saying how very unhappy she was at the non-receipt of any letter from him; at the same time asking him not to be angry with her, but "I gave my granmother 5 guines For she had Laid some out on me, and I would not take her a whay shabbily "—the " her " referring to her little Emma. The description she gives of the small village and surroundings as they were one hundred years ago must interest their many inhabitants of to-day, who will scarcely be able to realise that the popular resort of Hoylake was rejected by her on the grounds which she set before Mr. Greville. It was thus that she wrote of that now highly sought after and charming district :—

PARKGATE, *June* 15, 1784.

MY DEAREST GREVILLE,

You see by the date where I am gott and likely to be, and yett it is not through my neglect of seeking after other places for I have. and as to Abbergely it is 40 miles, and so dear that I could not, with my mother and me and the child, have been there under 2 guines and a half a week, it is grown such a fashionable place ; and high lake (Hoylake) as 3 houses in it, and not one of them as is fit for a Christian. The Best is a Publick house for the sailers of such ships as is oblidged to put in there, so you see there is no possibility of going to either of those places. Has to where I am, I find it very comfortable, considering from you. I am in the house of a laidy whoes husband is at sea; she and her granmother live together, and we board with her at present till I hear from you. The price is high, but they won't lodge anybody without boarding, and as it is comfortable, decent, and quiet, I thought it wou'd not ruin ous till I cou'd have your oppinion, which I hope to have freily and without Restraint, as, believe me, you will give it to one who will allways be happy to follow it let it be what it will, as I am sure you would not lead me wrong; and though my little tempers may have been sometimes high, believe me I have allways thought you right in the end when I have come to reason. I bathe and find the water very soult; there is a great many laidys batheing, but I have no society with them, as it is best not so. Pray, my Dearest Greville, write soon and tell me what to do and I will do just what you think proper, and tell me what I am to do with the child, for she is a great romp and I can hardly master her. I don't think she is ugly, but I think she is greatly improved, she is tall, good eyes and Brows, and all together she will be passible, but she has overgrown all her cloaths. I am makeing and mending all as I can for her. Pray, my dear Greville, do let me come home as soon as you can, for I am all most broken hearted being from you, indead I have no pleasure nor happiness. I wish I could not think on you, but if I was the greatest laidy in the world I should not be happy from you, so don't let me stay long . . . Indead, my dear Greville, you don't know how much I love you, and your behaviour to me even when we parted was so kind. Greville, I don't know what to do, but I will make you a mends by my kind behaviour to you, for I have Grattitude, and will show it you all as I can, so don't think of my faults, Greville, think of all my good, and Blot out all my Bad, for it is all gone and berried never to come again. So good by, my dear Greville, think of nobody but me, for I have not a thought but of you; and praying for you and for ous to meet again, God bless you, and believe me yours truly and affectionately,

EMMA H——T.*

From such a letter only one inference can be drawn—that the girl of nineteen possessed innate goodness of heart: though retrenching her own

* The Morrison MSS.

personal expenses, and seeking a secluded second-rate watering-place in preference to a fashionable one where her outlay must necessarily be larger, yet she honourably endeavoured to recoup her old grandmother for the expenses she had incurred for her child. We cannot but feel leniently towards a fellow being who, though little more than a child, could word so well-intentioned a letter, and who spent her holiday in making and mending for her little girl.

The next letter is almost sublime for so young a woman, and its careful perusal can only leave on the reader's mind keen sympathy with a creature who, possessing real wish to be good, and straining earnestly after right, was nevertheless led into evil ways.

PARKGATE, *June the* 22, 1784.

MY EVER DEAR GREVILLE,

How teadious does the time pass a whay till I hear from you; I think it ages since I saw you, and years since I heard from you; indead I should be miserable if I did not recollect on what happy terms we parted, parted but to meet again with tenfold happiness. Oh, Greville, when I think of your goodness, your tender kindness, my heart is full of grattutude that I want words to express it. But I have one happiness in view which I am determined to practise, and that is evenness of temper and steadiness of mind, for indead I have thought so much of your aimable goodness, when you have been tried to the utmost, that I will, indead I will, manige myself, and try to be like Greville. Endead I can never be like him, but I will do all I can towards it, and I am sure you will not desire more. I think if the time would come over again I would be different. But it does not matter, there is nothing like Bying expearance; I may be happyer for it hereafter, and I will think of the time coming, and not of the time past, except to make comprapasons to show you what alteration there is for the best, so, my dearest Greville, don't think on my past follies, think of my good, little as it has been, and I will make you amends by my kind behaviour; you shall never repent your partiality, and if you had not behaved with such angel-like goodness to me at parting it would not have had such an effect upon me, but I have done nothing but think of you since; and O, Greville, did you but know when I do think, what thoughts, what tender thoughts, you would say, "Good God! can Emma have such feeling sensibility? No, I never could think it, but now I may hope to bring her to conviction, and she may now prove a valluable and aimable whoman." True, Greville, and you shall not be disapointed, I will be everything you can wish. But mind your great, your two great, goodness has brought this to bear, for you don't know what I am. Would you think it, Greville—Emma, the wild unthinking Emma, is a grave and thoughtful phylosopher? It is true, Greville, and I will convince you I am when I see you. But how I am runing on! I say nothing abbout this guidy wild girl of mine. What shall we do with her? She is as wild and thoughtless as somebody when she was a little girl; there is no telling, but there is one comfort, she is a little afraid on me. Would you belive, on Satturday she had a little quarel—I mean Emma and me—and I did slap her on her hands; and when she came to kiss me and make it up, I took her on my lap and cried. Now do you blame me or not, pray tell me? Oh! Greville, you don't know how I love her. Endead I do! When she comes and looks in my face and calls me mother, endead I then truly am a mother, for all the mother's feelings rise at once and tell me I am or ought to be a mother, for she has a wright to my protection, and she shall have it as long as I can; and I will do all in my power to prevent her falling into the error her poor miserable mother fell into. . . . I must not forget to tell you my knees is well as there is hardly a mark, and my Elbows is much better, and I eat my vittuels very well, and I am quite strong, and feel hearty and well, and I am in hopes I shall be very well. You can't think how soult the water is, and there is a many Laidys bathing here. But, Greville, I am oblidged to give a shilling a day for the bathing horse, and twopence a day for the dress, it is a great expense, and it fretts me wen I think of it. But now I think how well I am, and my Elbows likely to get well, it makes me quite happy, for at any rate it is better than paying the doctor. But wright your oppinion truly, and tell me what to do.*

Poor Emma! two guineas a week covered the whole of her outlay! Who could accuse her of extravagance on that seaside trip?

In all her correspondence she ignored punctuation, but in order to render it more intelligible, stops are inserted. A month later she wrote again, commenting on the quiet and peaceful life she was leading, having no associates save her landlady and her sister, the latter a good-natured genteel young lady whom the grateful visitor declared to be always trying to please her. For the

* The Morrison MSS.

LADY HAMILTON AS "CASSANDRA"

EMMA VISITS PARKGATE; LETTERS TO GREVILLE.

relief of her troublesome ailment she had tang or seaweed applied to her knees and elbows each night on retiring to rest, which had a beneficial effect on the eruption, and soon restored the affected parts to their original smoothness. The people with whom she stayed were most attentive, and carried up the salt water for her use four or five times each day. The name of the lady who contributed in so effectual a manner to the comfort of the future ambassadress was Mrs. Darnwood, of Parkgate.

On the return of Emma to London, she was seized with an alarming attack of sickness which proved to be measles, but with care and her mother's good nursing she soon regained her usual strength and spirits; her little daughter had returned to town with her by the desire of Mr. Greville, who placed the child in the charge of a Mr. and Mrs. Blackburn, to be reared and educated in return for the stipulated sum of £65 per annum.

While Emma had been enjoying the retirement in Cheshire, Greville and his uncle, Sir William Hamilton, whose heir presumptive he was, were making a tour together in South Wales, overlooking the Welsh property that would some day pass from the one to the other.

Sir William Hamilton was born in the year 1730. He used to say he began life with an ancient name and £1000. His father, Lord Archibald Hamilton, was Governor of Greenwich Hospital, and Governor of Jamaica. His mother, Lady Jane Hamilton, was daughter of the sixth Earl of Abercorn. She enjoyed the post of Governess to the children of Frederick Prince of Wales, and gossip said, "companion to the Prince," which caused her son to be named the foster brother of George the Third from his constant companionship with the royal children; to this he was indebted for the lucrative appointment he received of Envoy Extraordinary and Minister Plenipotentiary at the Court of Naples, which comfortable post he held at this phase in the narrative.

As Sir William plays a most important part in subsequent events, a few words in reference to him will not be out of place. He was at this time a widower; his first wife had been a Miss Barlow of Clarges Street, a Welsh heiress, with whom he lived twenty four years, and though he was no ways backward in conveying to his friends that he married the lady in consideration of her possession of the comfortable income of £5000 per annum, rather than for any violent attachment to her person, yet he managed to live decently with her, bury her decently, and regret her decently (for a very limited period). The only issue of this *mariage de convenance* was a daughter, who died in 1775.

Michael Kelly, manager of the King's Theatre and Drury Lane, visiting Naples for voice training in his youth, called upon Sir William, and presented letters of introduction. On reading them, Sir William received him very kindly, assuring the young student that he would be happy to give him all the advice in his power, and asserting his willingness to be of service to him. To use Mr. Kelly's own words--" Sir William invited me to dinner that day. I returned, and was introduced to the first Lady Hamilton. The taste and partiality for music of this highly-gifted lady are too well known to need a remark from me. At that period she frequently gave concerts to which all the best performers were invited. She was herself considered the finest pianoforte player in Italy." At parting, his host desired him to call upon him next morning at eight o'clock. He did not, however, arrive until a quarter to nine, when he found Sir William with Mr. Drummond, his physician, and a couple of antiquaries. The table was covered with cameos, intaglios, and lava. As soon as he entered the apartment, Sir William said, " My good boy, you were to have been here at eight, and it is now three quarters of an hour past "—then, looking severely at the abashed youth, he added, " You will never be a good musician if you do not learn to keep time."

Sir William Hamilton was the king of antiquaries; his knowledge was so true that he keenly enjoyed the absurdities committed by self-estimated connoisseurs, appreciating their pretensions at their just worth. In 1780 he trained an Indian monkey to examine his antiques with the aid of a magnifying glass, as he told his nephew, Charles Greville, " in imitation of the art critic, and to skit the antiquaries." The air of deep investigation assumed by the clever little animal was ludicrous in the extreme.

Sir William was a man of great muscular power, which remained with him to his later days. In the *Reminiscences of Sir Nathaniel Wraxall* mention is made of Sir William, with whom he was personally acquainted at this epoch—" One of the most interesting portions of my life," he says, " was the time I passed at Naples in the summer of 1779. Sir William Hamilton, His Majesty's Minister, constituted in himself the greatest source of entertainment, no less than of instruction, which the capital then afforded to strangers. He honoured me with his friendship, which he continued to the end of his life. In his person, though tall and meagre, with a dark complexion, a very aquiline nose, and a figure which always reminds me of 'Rolando,' in *Gil Blas*, he had, nevertheless, such an air of distinction in his countenance, as powerfully attracted and conciliated the beholder. His mother, Lady Archibald Hamilton, enjoyed, as is well known, a very distinguished place in the favour of Frederick, late Prince of Wales, and Sir William himself was brought up from early life with his present Majesty,* to whom (after his accession to the Crown) he became an equerry. The versatility of his character constituted one of the most interesting features of his composition." Sir Nathaniel's memory of the first Lady Hamilton was that of a most superior and accomplished woman. Another diarist, Mrs. St. George—or, as she is better known, Mrs. Trench—writing of an escapade of Sir William's as he passed through Dresden in the year 1800, says—"He greatly astonished her and a host of courtly people by hopping about the room on his back bone, his arms, legs, star and ribbon all flying about. This at seventy years of age."

As Mr. Hamilton, he was sent to dispense British hospitality at the Court of Naples in 1764, which enabled him to pursue his studies on volcanic geology. His collection of volcanic matter was given to the British Museum in 1767, and his splendid and valuable ancient Greek and Etruscan vases† were purchased by the nation in 1772, for the sum of £8,400; and the same year he was made a Knight of the Bath.

There are two portraits of Sir William Hamilton in our National Portrait Gallery. One, painted by David Allan in 1775, represents him as a full-length figure, attired in the robes of the Bath, standing towards the left, on a marble pavement. His plumed hat is placed on a chair to the right; above which, in a cabinet, appears a large Magna Græcia vase, the whole surmounted by a standing figure of Jupiter with an eagle. To the left, above a richly-gilt table, seen through a verandah, is a distant view of Mount Vesuvius. The artist's name and date are inscribed on a paper lying on the ground in the left hand corner, "Painted by D. Allan, and by him humbly presented to the British Museum, Anno Dom¹ 1775." This "humble" gift

* George the Third.
† Sir William supplied D'Hancarville with materials for his celebrated work on Greek and Etruscan vases.

measures 7 feet 5 inches by 5 feet 4 inches, and was transferred from the British Museum in June, 1879.

Mrs. Hannah More, breakfasting with Miss Hamilton in 1783, met Lord Stormont, Sir William Hamilton and Monsieur de Luc. The lady found the society of the learned geologists oppressive, and has left us the following comment on their dissertations:—"As we had Mr. de Luc and Sir W. Hamilton, we had a little too much virtu, and Calabria, and Vesuvius, all of which were more interesting to them than to his lordship and me."

Horace Walpole, too, had his word to say on the coming to town of him whom, in his own peculiar fashion, he quaintly dubbed "The Professor of Earthquakes," and who, he said, would not be quite out of his element, as they had had pigmy earthquakes, much havoc by lightning, and some very respectable meteors. Sir William received great assistance in the composition of his works from one of the monks of Mount Etna.

It was during the visit to England, in 1783, that Sir William saw for the first time the woman who, at a future date, was destined to be his second wife, and who, in the position to which he raised her, became for the time being the most notorious, sought after, and popular beauty of the age. As a matter of course he visited the house of his nephew and heir expectant in Edgeware Row, and there received his introduction to its elegant mistress, Emma. Like one and all who came in contact with the vivacious girl, he was full of admiration of her wondrous beauty, amused by her outspoken sallies and prattle, and fascinated by the display of her dramatic ability in her exquisite rendering of her famous attitudes, or what we would call *tableaux vivants*.

CHAPTER IV.

GREVILLE'S FINANCIAL DIFFICULTIES; HE SEEKS SIR WILLIAM HAMILTON'S ADVICE CONCERNING EMMA, AND WRITES ABOUT HIS OWN MATRIMONIAL PROSPECTS; HE SUGGESTS THAT HIS UNCLE SHALL INVITE EMMA TO NAPLES.

We have now arrived at a very important epoch in the progress of the memoir—the transfer of Emma from the care of Greville, in London, to that of his uncle, in Naples. Many reckless assertions have appeared, wherein it has been stated that the nephew resigned in favour of his relative on the condition that his debts were paid, a statement which collapses on the attentive perusal of the many letters which passed between the two men before Emma was informed of their plans for her future.

Finding himself in monetary straits, Greville had no alternative but to reduce his establishment. His allowance, as a younger son of the Earl of Warwick, only reached £500 per annum, a small sum for a man who possessed artistic tastes and was burdened with financial embarrassments. He wrote to Sir William (who, according to Horace Walpole, "had returned to his kingdom of cinders") that he was offering to sell his pictures, in order to rid himself of "the Humberstone engagements;" that he had a thousand pounds ready, but had another thousand to provide, and, if the pictures failed, he would ask Sir William to join him in security to free himself of Humberstone's affairs: and as it was indifferent to him whether what he valued was in the keeping of himself or his uncle, he would deposit with Sir William gems over and above the amount for which he would stand security, in case he (Greville) should " dye," and that it was only on that condition he would involve him, as " favour I take as a favour, and business as business."

Conscientiously feeling that Emma was too good to be recklessly cast adrift, and aware that his uncle felt a real regard for the girl whom he had jocularly called "the tea-maker of Edgeware Road," Greville wrote to Naples, laying open his financial dilemma and enforced retrenchment, and as he was wishful to place Emma in comfort, he suggested that Sir William should provide her with a home—a curious arrangement; but Greville was undoubtedly actuated by self-considering motives, fully aware that his faithful little friend would watch his interests, and perhaps stand in the way of Sir William's taking a second wife, which step might possibly deprive him of his prospective fortune. The young girl was ignorant of their designs, and the plotters agreed to coax her into yielding to the change by holding out the promise of foreign masters for the perfecting of her accomplishments, and, if she proceeded in advance, Greville would follow when he had settled his affairs. The innocent dupe was elated at such a prospect, and easily induced to prepare for a visit to lovely Italian cities.

Extracts from Greville's letters to Sir William will convey a more definite idea of the position of parties, and demonstrate the propriety with which the household was conducted, and the pliability with which the girl's character was moulded to goodness. In the first of the series he says :—

> Emma is very grateful for your remembrance. The picture shall be sent by the first ship. I wish Romney yet to mend the dog. She certainly is much improved since she has been with me. She has none of the bad habits which giddiness and inexperience encouraged, and which bad choice of company introduced. She has much pride, and submits to solitude rather than admit of one improper acquaintance. She is naturally elegant, and fits herself easily to any situation, having quickness and sensibility. I am sure she is attached to me, or she would not have refused the offers which I know have been great, and such is her spirit that, on the least slight, or expression of my being tired or burthened by her, I am sure she would not only give up the connexion, but would not even accept a farthing for future assistance. This is the awkward part of my situation. If I was independent I should think so little of any other connexion that I would never marry. I have not an idea of it at present, but if any proper opportunity offered, I should be much hampered, and not know how to manage or how to fix Emma to her satisfaction. . . . Give me your opinion honestly how you would act in my situation. If I followed only my own inclination advice would be unnecessary.
>
> Believe me ever y^{rs} affec^{ately}
>
> C. F. GREVILLE.*

In reply, Sir William disclosed his intention of making him his heir, a

* The Morrison MSS.

confidence reposed in his nephew to support him in any matrimonial scheme he might determine upon, and he furthermore offered to provide for Emma in Naples. These avowals drew from his naturally grateful relative this effusive response :—

> My dear Hamilton,
> Whatever degree of sincerity accompanied my professions of attachment to you, I trusted much to your disposition and a congeniality which, with pleasure, I had observed in our opinions and pursuits, which I believed would make up for the deficiency of expressions which, if attempted by words, become fulsome. I will not tell you what I think of your letter, but shall, if possible, respect and love you more than I have hitherto done. I must endeavour to cultivate that kindness which you feel for me, and which was more strongly exerted towards me when you wrote your last letter than when you made the original plan of what you communicated to me by that letter, and I should be ungrateful indeed if I did not feel your goodness to me. I am doubly so that you did not withdraw it when I risqued appearing, as I might have done to a less partial friend, mean and interested.*

He proceeds to inform his uncle that his next-door neighbour in Portman Square (Lord Middleton, of Nottingham,) has a son and two daughters, that he has had the good fortune to please them, and has cultivated their friendship. He says, in continuation :

> The eldest married last year, the youngest presented only this winter. You know me sufficiently to know that beauty and disposition are both requisites, and the youngest in both respects is beyond the reasonable mark for a younger brother. I understood their fortunes to be 30, but since find the eldest had only £20,000. Such, however, to sensible people might be sufficient for the present; but it must be an impudent person who could propose it, being only possessed of £500 a year and some incumbrances. I have always avoided the least particularity, and considered it as impracticable, but also convinced that if I could secure any jointure, and show any prospect in future, that a certain moderate provision for her, joined to the preference the old people have for me, might obtain their consent to become a suitor. Distant and imperfect as the prospect is, I wished to state it to you, and had it not been a subject so nearly connected

* The Morrison MSS.

with yourself, I should still have consulted you, and, believe me, no person living knows my thoughts or intentions. The awkward situation of public affairs do not open to me a favourable plan, and I could not continue my present establishments. To leave Emma unprovided for I could not, and take her to Naples might do for a time, and to what would it lead? To go there without her would be debarring her from her last chance of happiness —your protection. I therefore determined to write to you, and to trust, as I would have done on every occasion, to your good sense and to your good heart, and I have not been disappointed. I have already wrote to Ld Middleton, and communicated to him the letter you wrote. . . . . "

After thus dilating on his own interests, he turns to those of Emma, enlarging to his uncle on the marked improvement in her character and disposition. He says:—

She never has wished for one improper acquaintance. She has dropt everyone she thought I could except against, and those of her own choice have been in a line of prudence and plainness which, though I might have wished for, I could not have proposed to confine her. If you can find only one or two acquaintances, and let her learn music and drawing, or anything to keep in order, she will be as happy as if you gave her every change of dissipation. She is no fool; but there is a degree of nature in her that she has the same pleasure in a retired and confined line as in a more extensive one, and she has no difficulty in confining herself, and yet she has natural gentility and quickness to suit herself to anything, and take any hint that is given with good humour. I have often heard people say, you may do anything by good humour, but never saw anyone so completely led by good nature, and I believe she would die before she yielded to ill-treatment. If you could form a plan by which you could have a trial, and could invite her, and tell her that I ought not to leave England, and that I cannot afford to go on, and state it as a kindness to me if she would accept your invitation, she would go with pleasure. She is to be 6 weeks at some bathing place, and when you could write an answer to this, and enclose a letter to her, I could manage it, and either by land by the coach to Geneva, and thence by Vetturino, forward her, or else by sea. I must add that I could not manage it so well later. After a month's absence, and absent from me, she would consider the whole more calmly.

' The Morrison MSS.

... I would, in case nothing happens from my letter,* pass the principal part of the winter in Edinburgh, and my pretence should be chemistry with Dr. Black. I shall live cheap and retired, and break all expenses by being out of the way of temptation, and if called to town by call of the House, I should be less confined in my plan of settling, if possible, to advantage, or, at least, put myself more in the way of fortune. I must now say a few words about Wales. I am glad what I have done and am doing was previous to your kind letter to me, lest you should think my zeal increased by personal interest. I have already got a post established 3 times a week to Hubberston. I want only the name of a person to be postmaster, and I cannot, till prompted, give in a name. I am now treating with the Custom House about removing the Custom House from Pembroke to Hubberston, and a memorial about pacquets from Waterford to Hubberston is before the Treasury, and I have been acting with Mr. Knox and Mr. Beresford, the Irish Negociator, who takes it up warmly. If it was not building on your Intentions further than you propose, and should my letter lead to my present settling, I should incline to settle about Pembroke in preference to other parts, unless I could find some part in Devonshire or Cornwall where I could bring to profit some manufacture of china. If I went to Wales, I would bring it there, and promote any plan for increasing the Industry of the Natives, and their exports might arise from the increased Intercourse with Ireland without any charge to you; and in Dec. last, when the Irish proposed to build an Inn, I told them if they came in the summer I would meet them and consult with Meyrick. But unless I hear from them I shall proceed on my tour with Robert† through N. Wales, and thence through S. W. to Cornwall, a party which has been for some months settled. Except to Lord Middleton, you may depend on my not mentioning to any person whatever the contents of your letter.

Believe me
ever gratefully and affectionately yours
C. F. GREVILLE.‡

It will be noticed that in this lengthy letter Greville refers to the keeping of two separate establishments. That in Portman Square, and the less pretentious one where Emma was the presiding genius, the upholding of which

---

* To Lord Middleton, advising him of his prospects.
† His brother, the Hon. Robert Fulke Greville.   ‡ The Morrison MSS.

would certainly strain the limited £500 to its fullest extent. In a letter from King's Mews, dated March 10, 1785, he tells his uncle that he hears he is in love, and "I know you love variety and are a general Flirt, & of the 60 English, what with widows and young married ladies, an amateur may be caught. Some have said you have had the gout. I say I neither know whether your heart or feet are lightest, but that I believed them both sound, & altho Harry Harpur says he was witness to the deluge of blood of Boars which flowed around you, I know that your heart is neither callous to friendship nor to beauty. I hope I shall ever have the usual share of the one, and I shall as readily give up as much as you chuse to bestow on beauty. I do not consider them as incompatible guests in a good heart, & it must be a very interested friend indeed who does not sincerely wish every thing that can give comfort or happiness to a friend. I sincerely wish that happiness to you."*
The wily man was far from feeling so easy as he would fain appear; but it was his policy to seem satisfied that his uncle should please himself, even though it should act to his own detriment. At the same time he wisely conjectured that if he sent Emma to Naples she might serve as a foil in deterring Sir William from any matrimonial alliance. While apparently considering his relative's pleasure, he had mainly one object at heart—his own interest! He proposed, in a communication that he made to his uncle, to settle on Emma £100 a year, which he could ensure by parting with a portion of his articles of *virtû;* he was desirous of closing the little house before he was so far involved as to be unable to extricate himself, and while yet there was a chance of providing for her, as he had no wish to be unjust to her. He said he thought she was too young and handsome to retire into a convent, and as she was honest, honourable, and could be trusted, he volunteered to hand her over to the custody of his uncle.

Responsive to the suggestion thrown out that Sir William should write and invite Emma to Naples, that gentleman forwarded the missive agreeably to his nephew's dictation, but the time of its arrival was inopportune, as the devoted girl was suffering much distress from the alarming illness of her mother, Mrs. Cadogan, who was threatened with paralysis, and the matter had to remain in abeyance until a more suitable period should arrive for broaching the important design, and accordingly he acquainted Sir William of the postponement of their plans in the following letter:—

* The Morrison MSS.

GREVILLE'S FINANCIAL DIFFICULTIES.   35

May 5, 1785.

MY DEAR HAMILTON,

On my return to town I found the message just as I expected. Emma had been much alarmed & distressed at her mother's illness. It was not so severe an attack as I understood it to be when I informed you of it from Cornwall, but anything which the faculty style Paralysis is alarming, & I left her by no means recovered. You may suppose that I did not increase Emma's uneasiness by any hint of the subject of our last correspondence; at any rate it cannot take place before the spring, & she goes on so well, and is so much more considerate & amiable than when you saw her, & also improved in looks, that I own it is less agreeable to part, yet I have no alternative but to marry or remain a pauper. I shall persist in my resolution not to lose an opportunity if I can find it, and do not think that my idea of sending her to Naples on such an event arises from my consulting my own convenience only. I can assure you she would not have a scarcity of offers. She has refused great ones.
. . . I know that confidence & good usage will never be abused by her, and nothing can make her giddy. . . . How true it is that the interior of few families exhibits coincidence of opinion or Harmony. Sr H. Harpur is already tired of his son, and they will I fear soon be at open War, it has already been within an ace of his quitting the house; what will be the consequence I know not, but I came here to try & do good, & I shall take my nephew to Lord Middleton's, as I mentioned in a former letter. If he is lucky enough to settle in a good family, he will be happy in a creditable society, if not, he will sink into nothing, & be lost to the world.

During my short stay in town, I saw Hamilton* twice; once I called on him, & the next I brought him to dine with Emma. He says he has not seen anything like her in G. B.,† and that she reminds him of a person in Rome whom he admired much, though she was deficient in the beauties of the mouth, & that Emma is both beautiful & uncommon. He has been meditating for a subject; he says he shall not rest till he has prevailed on her to sit; you may suppose she is flattered, and she told him at once she had put him on her list of favourites because you had spoke of him as a person you regarded, and also because he bore your name. I am told he has lately settled with his brother to take an annuity of £500 a year, & give up the Estate for ever. I think he will do wisely. He finds the

_{* Gavin Hamilton, the artist.   † Great Britain.}

expense of London very high. He was obliged to give 4 guineas a week for a painting room for two months, & 2½ guineas for lodging, which made six guineas & a half per week, without Fire or victuals. His health is not the worse; on the contrary, his journey to England and from thence to Scotland has improved his looks. I hope you have had pleasure in unpacking your pictures, and that they arrived safe. While I was in town I saw Bartolozzi and the plates; one of them is almost finished, and will be very fine; the others were so far advanced that in about a month they will be quite finished. He wanted money, and I called on Ogilvy and directed him to pay him £100, and to take his receipt for it as part payment. I also told him that I should send Romney for payment of the picture he sent. When the plates are finished I will take them, and you will give orders for the payment of the remainder. (I am sure you will be satisfied with them.) And you will give me directions in what manner you would have me proceed to distribute the prints that you may be repaid, and also what inscription, and what letter-press. If you will give the outline you will find me punctual. The publication may be made more bulky by an etching from Piranese or F. Bartolozzi of the sepulchre, and also of the sarcophagus in which they were found, and most people love bulk.

I should have wrote to you during my stay in town if I had not been very much hurried, & wished to delay until I could inform you, as I now can, that all the plan relative to the Irish & London Mail to Hubberston is actually established. I shall attack the Custom House at Pembroke on my return to town, and I have on foot a plan to settle a colony of American Fishermen at Hubberston to carry on the whale fishery from thence to the South of Falkland Islands. You know how difficult it is to get assistance from Gov^t, and how impossible it is to do much without money. You know that my establishment will render the Farms contiguous more valuable, and that you are advised not to grant leases at Hubberston, that some good plan may be established. If I cannot get the aid of Gov^t nothing can be done. But if my plan is adopted, I shall bring a colony & fix them on your Estate, and build them habitations, and enable them to establish the manufactures necessary for the fishery without any expense to you. You must, therefore, give me *carte blanche* on this scheme, which you cannot think bad if it can be brought about. It will only occasion a capital of £100,000 to be embarked on your land. The Banks of the Pill which bring you in nothing will about do what I want, and you will have the improvement of your neighbouring land certain without embarking any money at all. It is too good a scheme to be certain of succeeding; but I do think it possible, & I bring it forward without delay, and if assistance is wanted from Parliament I must follow it up there also. I propose to lay it before Mr. Hamilton,* whose friendship to you may be mellow if not ripened yet, and I shall, through him, lay it before Mr. Pitt. When I have finished my plan, I will send you a copy of my letter; you must not think me mad till my letter arrives, nor mention it in your letter to others, for it is a negociation of delicacy to move a colony from the American States to G. B.,† and is better not talked of till executed. ‡

Sir William suggested that Emma should proceed to Naples, to preside over and do the honours of his household, which proposition Greville earnestly deprecated, rightly considering the prominence of such a situation would cause questionable comment which it was better to avoid. Accordingly he sent a remonstrance to his uncle, contained in a letter bearing date November 11, 1785:—

MY DEAR HAMILTON,
I received your letter. I have no doubt of your kind wishes towards me, therefore the interest you take in my situation is by me very sensibly felt. If I could have thought that no line could be taken but that of making E. do the honours of your house, I confess I never should have dreamt of it. This is a line so different from what I have practised, that I should be among the first to lament that you adopted an unwise plan. I tell you fairly that your expressions of kindness to E., & the comfort you promised to her in case anything happened to me, made such impression on her that she regards you as her protector & friend, and in moments of her thinking over your goodness she related to me your last conversation, & I concluded that your regard to me had been the only reason for not making present offers. You know that from giddiness & dissipation she is prudent & quiet, and that, surrounded with temptations, I have not any the least reason to complain of her; & my attentions do not lead me to make a parade of her, or a sacrifice of my amusements or business. The secret is simple—she has pride and vanity. I have for some years past directed them for her happiness. . . . She

* Gavin Hamilton. † Great Britain. ‡ The Morrison MSS.

does not wish for much society, but to retain 2 or 3 quiet, creditable acquaintances in the neighbourhood. She has avoided every appearance of giddiness, and prides herself on the neatness of her person and the good order of her house. These are habits both comfortable and convenient to me. She has vanity, and likes admiration; but she connects it so much with her desire of appearing prudent, that she is more pleased with accidental admiration than that of crowds, which now distress her. In short, this habit of 3 or 4 years' acquiring is not a caprice, but is easily to be continued. . . . She is not led by interest, but by kindness, and she appreciates favours from the intentions. . . . She is but 20. An early experience makes a strong impression, & if giddiness, or avarice or vanity could have run away with her, she would not have improved & resisted great offers. . . . If things remain as they are, I shall be sure to be much straitened in finances. I shall be so whether she remains or not, and literally her expences are trifling; but when income is very small a trifling expence is felt.

He proceeds to inform his uncle that he had seen his (Sir William's) brother, and with what must look like utter absence of delicacy on the part of the expecting nephew, he notifies that that gentleman had expressed that—

He was perfectly satisfied with the Fortune he had. He had enough for his family, & that he should be very glad to hear you declare openly your successor, & particularly so if you named me. I write without affectation or disguise. If you find me either reserved or artful, you may despise me; but in opening my heart & thoughts, do not impute concealed designs. I wish you every happiness in this World, & long life to enjoy it. I protest I do not think the odds in our lives are proportioned to the difference in our years.

In continuation, he reverts to the prospects of a matrimonial union, and as the intention of Sir William to make him his heir was so far a secret between the two men, the wily nephew felt it would be more to his advantage if the rumour were allowed circulation, to which end he suggests—

I fairly own that the only case in which I should ever wish to have the kind intentions you have made known to several of our friends made any ways certain would be, that it could be the means of my being married to a lady of at least £30,000. I could not have your decision for a less ample fortune, because a less fortune would not at present enable me to live comfortably, & I never could permit your goodness to be exhausted which might be the case if you adopted me a beggar.

No modest store did this selfish man set upon himself, when he placed his valuation of himself and limited income of £500 (pretty well condemned by his debts) as an equivalent to a lady, pretty and good, with a fortune of £30,000. He next alluded to the plan of introducing the American colony on to the Pembrokeshire property, and certainly he does not show himself wanting in business enterprise, on which he propounds sensible arguments. He says:—

> The great object to bring to bear is a project such as mine, which brings capital, introduces industry and improvements of Agriculture, & raises at once the rents of Lands where it is established. What renders property on the Banks of the Thames, of the Avon at Bristol, valuable, but a spirit of enterprise and the employment of great capital, which returns itself manifold, and generally in proportion to the amount?*

In the forepart of this somewhat lengthy letter Greville, in writing of Emma, says " She is but 20." These words, written in 1785, would fix the year of her birth as 1765. Greville had known her intimately for some four years at least, and was a man of sufficient discernment not to mistake a girl of sixteen for one of eighteen, which first number would be the reckoning of her years when she came under the notice of the intelligent man of the world. We must, therefore, consider her as a precocious young girl who had fallen into very bad hands.

The valuable extracts we have quoted must surely bear testimony in favour of the girl's native worth, and to the improvement which had taken place since the days when the pin did the work of the darning needle. There appears to have been no hand to direct her to a better course; and as it was at this period that the insinuations were levelled against her concerning her intercourse with Romney, the artist, the careful reading of Greville's correspondence will eminently determine that his strict line of conduct, and its unqualified adherence on the part of his *protégé*, destroy the probability of

* The Morrison MSS.

truth in such accusations. Romney had never seen Emma until she was introduced to him by Greville, in the year 1782. George Romney was the artistic friend of Charles Greville, and in good fellowship the latter was desirous that the pretty face of his *protégé* should be at the service of the artist; but any foolishness on her part would immediately have caused Greville to put a veto on the visits to the studio, for he was most rigid in his demands for decorous conduct, and he repeatedly asserts that her inclinations all tended towards propriety.

CHAPTER V.

EMMA PREPARES TO VISIT ITALY; HER ARRIVAL AT NAPLES. SIR WILLIAM'S ATTENTIONS; HER BEAUTY ATTRACTS CROWDS.

UPON the recovery of Mrs. Cadogan, her daughter was informed of the advancing crisis to Greville's affairs, which would necessitate the disbanding of his little household, and that while he remained in England to wind up his estate, she and her mother would proceed to Naples, at the invitation of Sir William, whither he would follow when everything was settled.

Emma was elated at the prospect of visiting Italy, and, backed by a very kind letter from Sir William, Greville easily induced her to prepare for the coming change. His uncle had entrusted fifty pounds to him to cover the expenses of travelling. All arrangements completed, the day of departure was announced to Sir William, in a letter dated March 11, 1786 :—

MY DEAR HAMILTON,

You will by this time have received the trunk which went by sea, & on Thursday Emma is to set out. I write to assure you that nothing but the comfort which Mrs. Hamilton's company will be to her, would have made me consent to the delay of a few days, which, from the absence of letters, may be material to you. The letter which you wrote was received, as it should be, by a grateful heart. Emma felt much your kindness to her and to myself. I shall pay 30 g^s to Mr. H. for her journey to Geneva, the remainder of the £50 she shall carry in her pocket. By the sale of some pictures and one of my statues, I have cleared Emma and myself of everything connected with our establishment. My mind and inclination have been at war with prudence; but necessity has turned the scale, and that necessity has become less severe from your kindness and friendship to me, and from your attachment to her. In short, I could not have looked at the chances of an eternal separation without having seen an asylum open to her. . . . If you use her kindly you may do what you please, & by piqueing her or annoying her you will do nothing, for she has a generous mind & a true woman—that is, regardless of itself and its

F

interests when affection is put in competition with reason, and that reason is at any time to be obtained by gentle usage.

He tells his uncle that if he pursues this course he

will have comfort with the prettiest woman confessedly in London—the poets and painters would say more.*

So all his plans adjusted, he resigned himself to the inevitable climax which was approaching to his affairs, in the knowledge that the transfer was for the ultimate advantage of his favourite; and though in her heart of hearts he reigned supreme for many a day; and wiled away under the delusion that he, Greville, would follow in six months at furthest, she sailed for foreign shores in her mother's charge, escorted by the talented artist Gavin Hamilton, with his wife and daughter as companions, arriving at Naples on the day on which she attained her twenty-first birthday.

She bade adieu to the quiet life of her little London home, where she had made the best use of the limited allowance of her much cared for co-partner, managing his domestic arrangements with the most praiseworthy economy, as attested by her housekeeping books, which she kept with scrupulous accuracy. She was materially assisted by her homely and industrious mother, who was in herself a capital cook, personally serving many a pleasant repast which redounded both to the host's and her own credit. An interesting specimen of the minuteness with which Emma kept her household accounts is to be found in the following copy of a page from her daily expenses. The memorandum itself is the size of a school exercise book. On the first leaf is made the entry, " Day acct. book, Oct. 27th, 1784, Emma Hart;" on the next leaf :—

Money paid, &c.

Oct. 27 & 28.		s.	d.
,, 27 Baker's Bill, one week ..		4	11
,, 27 Butter Bill, one week ...		5	0
,, 27 Butcher		7	8½
,, 27 Wood		1	0
., 28 Pidgeons		2	0
,, 29 Mold Candles		2	3

* The Morrison MSS.

HER ARRIVAL AT NAPLES.

		£	s.
Oct. 29	Gloves	1	6
	Letters	0	4
	Coach	1	0
	Apples	0	2½
	Poor man	0	0½
	Mangle	0	5
,, 30	Tea	12	0
	Suger	9	9
	Butcher	5	4
	Scotch gaze (gauze)	0	6
,, 31	Porter	0	2
	Eggs	0	4
Nov. 1	Magazines	1	0
	Cotton and needles	0	9

So on in succession come the miscellaneous necessaries of domestic life, such as "cotton for mending stockings, 2d,, parsley, bellman, nutmegs, snuff, oranges, muffins;" and oh, people of to-day, take note that tea, one hundred years ago, cost twelve shillings a pound. The entry which occurs the oftenest is "muffins," an old Hawarden institution which has not collapsed with time, for in all friendly interchange of civilities the inevitable muffin makes its appearance at every hospitable table in that interesting village.

The only one mention of a piece of extravagance on the part of careful Emma is an entry of £2 12s. 6d. for a gown.

With equal clearness and precision did she make note of all moneys received. The amount most frequently appearing is £1, so that the poor little housekeeper never had a very large sum to disburse. Greville was in the right when he remarked that her expenses were not very great.

This very interesting relic of a dead hand is the property of Mr. Alfred Morrison, Fonthill House, Wiltshire, who is also the possessor of two little packets which contain her hair; they lie as she made them up herself, as presents, just one hundred years ago. One is inscribed in her own characteristic handwriting, " Emma's hair, cut the tenth of Agoste, 1790, presented to her dear, dear Sir William ;" and the other, her gift after she had acquired the right to bear his name, " Hair of Emma Hamilton, for my dear Sir William, 1791."

As Emma planted her foot on the soil of Italy she took her step on the first rung of the social ladder, which led her to the pinnacle of popularity and notoriety. Before her lay the homage of princes and men of genius, the friendship of queens, and the companionship of the cream of the fashionable world. The winning girl, who had fascinated the clever man of position, was received by him on her arrival at Naples with the extreme of ceremony and courtesy. He took her and her mother to the British Embassy, resigning to them the best apartments, until the workmen had finished the decoration of the rooms overlooking the sea which he had hired for them in accordance with Greville's suggestion that she should have a separate establishment. She was supplied with a private carriage and a staff of servants, and there was likewise a boat placed at her service, manned by men wearing her own livery.

Her appearance at this time was that of a lovely, lithe, girlish form, her face radiant with happiness and good-humour, and her hair a crown of glory, which, when loose, completely enveloped her with its superabundance—its colour dark chesnut. At subsequent garden parties she frequently appeared with her hair let down, touching her heels, Sir William remarking that she walked about in her hair, so completely did it conceal her.

Veni, vide, vincas, might truthfully have been adopted by her as her motto. From the moment that she was first introduced into Neapolitan society she won all hearts; her incomparable loveliness, rare dramatic and musical genius, added to her fascinating and *distingué* manners, gathered around her a host of ravished worshippers, to Sir William's intense pride and satisfaction. Her beauty soon drew all eyes in her direction, and whenever she appeared in public her carriage was immediately surrounded by an admiring crowd, eager to give evidence of their appreciation of the charms of the pretty English stranger; and great was the commotion and emulation among the numerous artists as to which could obtain a sitting for her portrait. With great fidelity she kept Mr. Greville informed of the sensation she created; she took child-like pleasure in telling him how much she was honoured and fêted. All her letters denote large powers of observation, and are written with great simplicity. Her extra good heart, which was untainted by the deluge of flattery that fell upon her, really enjoyed the praise which her beauty and kindness drew forth.

In simple justice to a memory that for seventy-five years has been pur-

PLATE II.-- ATTITUDE OF LADY HAMILTON, FROM A DRAWING BY REHBURG

HER BEAUTY ATTRACTS CROWDS.

sued with cruel malignity, it is only right to show the facts as they actually occurred. Ignorance of genuine transactions, and reckless assertions so long continued, have founded a prejudice against a woman who was really gifted with a splendid character, and who certainly did not seek to be other than virtuous; the fault lay with those who are never reckoned in the summing up.

The next letter (from which extracts only are taken) which bears directly on the tale, is dated April 30th, 1786. At the commencement she mentions that she arrived at Naples on April 26th, and, continuing, she alludes to its having been her birthday. "You have a true friend in Sir William, & he will be happy to see you, & to do all he can to make you happy; and for me, I will be everything you can wish, for I find it is not either a fine house, or a fine coach, or a pack of servants, or plays or operas, can make me happy, it is you that have it in your power either to make me very happy or very miserable. I respect Sir W^m· I have a great regard for him, as the uncle and friend of you, and he loves me, Greville, but he can never be anything nearer to me than your uncle and my sincere friend. He never can be my lover. You do not know how good Sir W^m· is to me; he is doing everything he can to make me happy; he as never dined out since I came hear, & endead, to speke the truth, he is never out of my sight; he breakfasts, dines, sups, and is constantly by me looking in my face; I can't stir a hand, a legg, or foot but what he is making it as graceful or fine, and I am sorry to say it, but he loves me now as much as ever he did *Lady Bolingbroke*; endead I am sorry, for I canot make him happy; I can be civil and oblidging, and I do try to make myself as agreable as I can to him, but I belong to you, Greville, and to you only will I belong, & nobody shall be your heir appearant. You do not know how glad I was to arrive hear the day I did, as it was my birthday, & I was very low spirited. Oh God! that day that you used to smile on me, & *stay at home*, & be kind to me, that that day I should be at such a distance from you! But my comfort is, I rely on your promise, & September or October I shall see you; but I am quite unhappy at not hearing from you; no letter for me yet, Greville, but I must wait with patience. We have had company most every day since I came; some of S^r· W^m·'s friends. The are all very much pleased with me, & poor S^r· W^m· is never so much pleased as when he is pointing out my beauties to them; he thinks I grown much more ansome than I was; he does nothing all day but look at me & sigh.

Yes, last night we had a little Concert, but then I was low, for I wanted you to partake of our amusement.

"Sir Thomas Rumbold is hear with his son, who is dying of a decline; it is a son he had by his first wife, & poor young man, he can't walk from the bed to the chair, & Lady Rumbold, like a tender-hearted wretch, has gone to Rome to pass her time there with the english, & as took the coach & all the english servants with her, & left poor Sr Thomas hear with his heart broken waiting on is sick son; you can't think what a worthy man he is, he dined with ous, & likes me very much, & every day as brought a carridge or phæton, which he as bought hear, & carries me & my mother & S^r W^m out, & shows ous a deal of civclities, for you are to understand I have a carridge of Sir W$^{m.'s}$ an english one, painting, & new Livereys, & new coach men, foot men, &c., the same as Mrs. Damer had of her own, for she did not go with it, for if I was going abbout in is carridge the would say I was either his wife or mistress, therefore, as I am not, nor ever can be either, we have made a very good establishment. I have very good apartments of 4 rooms, very pleasant, looking to the sea. Our Boat comes out to-day for the first time, & we shall begin to bathe in a day or two, & we are going for one day or two to Caserta. I was at Paysilipo yesterday. I think it a very pretty place. Sir W. as give me a camel's shawl, like my old one. I know you will be pleased to hear that, & he as given me a beautiful gown, cost 25 guineas, India painting on wite sattin, & several little things of Lady Hamilton's, & is going to by me some muslin dresses, loose, to tye with a sash, for the hot wether, made like Turkey dresses, the sleeves tyed in fowlds with ribbon, & trimmed with lace; in short, he is allways contriving what he shall get for me. The people admires my english dresses, but the blue hat, Greville, pleases most; Sr W. is quite inchanted with it. Oh, how he loves you. He told me he had made is will & left you everything belonging to him; that made me very happy for your sake. Pray, my dear Greville, do write me word if you want any money. I am afraid I distressed you, but I am sure Sir W. will send you some, & I told him he must help you a little now, & send you some for your gurney hear, & he kissed me, & the tears came into is eyes, & he toald me I might comand anything, for he loved ous boath dearly." *

Poor dupe! The tears might well arise if he felt the treacherous part he was playing, for Greville had never intended to go to Naples. There is no

* The Morrison MSS.

trace of vice or wickedness in Emma's ill-spelt letter, and it is sad to find that she had so strongly attached herself to the cynical man of the world who, in the future day, when her need came, forgot the efforts she had made to assist him, and even attempted to defraud her. What intense gratification it must have yielded him to find his future prospects fall in so entirely with his designs. Sir William had decoyed the girl to Naples, beguiling her with the promise that Greville would follow as soon as business arrangements would permit his absence from England. He had no such intention, and did not even write to her in spite of her repeated petitions for "just one line." Meanwhile, correspondence between uncle and nephew was not neglected; and in the next letter we learn how King George the Third's faithful servant (Greville) planned to keep his Majesty in good humour.

> My dear Hamilton,
>
> I write this on the subject of commissions. You are naturally very obliging; but when the moment passes, you omit doing what you intend, merely from want of recollection, till the moment elapses. I wrote you several letters on the subject of reeds for Hautboys & Clarinets, which you told me you would not forget, though you thought it an useless commission, being as good in London; but the King has repeatedly mentioned your forgetfulness, & has asked Fisher who you was civil to, & he said you had sent them. But you must write me a few lines expressing your sorrow that those you sent had not reached me, and that you should send another parcel, & desire me to present them, and add some proper civilities to the giver of the commission; and my brother will be in waiting, & I shall send the letter to him, by which you will get out of the scrape. These little fiddle-faddle things are mountains at our Court.

Mr. Greville was truly a veritable exponent of the saying, "Men were deceivers ever." In the course of this same letter he reverts to his cast-aside friend, who was breaking her heart for him across the sea. "Emma's passion is admiration, and it is not troublesome, because she is satisfied with a limited sphere, but is capable of aspiring to any line which would be celebrated."*

In the girl's next letter we find her still faithful to her distant love, and Sir William had made no further advances in her affections. Certain it is that her conduct was most proper for some time after her arrival in Naples,

* The Morrison MSS.

and many a better woman than Emma might have fallen before the temptations by which she was assailed. The following piteous lines will surely be read with sympathy:—

NAPLES, *July the 22nd*, 1786.

MY EVER DEAREST GREVILLE,

I am now writing to beg of you for God's sake to send me one letter, if only a farewell. Sure I have deserved this for the sake of the love you once had for me. Think, Greville, of our former connexion, & don't despise me. I have not used you ill in any one thing. I have been from you going of six months, & you have not wrote *one letter* to me, enstead of which I have sent *fourteen* to you. Pray, lett me beg of you, my much-loved Greville, onely one line from your dear, dear hands, & you don't know how thankful I shall be for it, for if you knew the misery I feel, oh! your heart would not be entirely shut up against me, for I love you with the truist affection, & don't lett anybody sett you against me. Some of your friends, or your foes, peraps—I don't know what to stile them. I know the have long wisht me ill; but, Greville, you never will meet with any body that has a truer affection for you than I have, & I only wish it was in my power to show you what I could do for you. As soon as I know your determination, I shall take my own mesures if I don't hear from you, & that you are coming according to promise. I shall be in england by cristmass at farthest. Don't be unhappy at that. I will see you once more for the last time. I find life is insuportable without you. Oh! my heart is intirely broke. Then, for God's sake, my ever-dear Greville, do write to mee some comfort. I don't know what to do. I am now in that state I am incapable of anything. I have a language master, a singing master, &c., &c. But what is it? If it was to amuse you, I should be happy. But, Greville, what will it avail me? I am poor, helpless, & forlorn.

She then referred to Sir William, and in the wisdom she had gained by experience, she said he wasn't going to live with her for a little while, and then, perhaps, send her to England; that she respected him, and she would not allow him to place her in a false position. She continues:

If I have spirits I will tell you something concerning how we go on that will make my letter worth paying for. Sir W^{m.} wants a picture of me the size of the *Bacante* for his new appartments, & he will take that picture of me in the black gown of Romney's, & I have made the bargain with him that the picture shall still be yours if he will pay for it, & he will; & I have wrote to Romney to send it. Their is two painters now in the house painting me. One picture is finished. It is the size of the *Bacante*, setting in a turban & turkish dress; the other is in a black rubin (Rubens?) hat, with fethers, Blue silk gown, &c., &c.; but as soon as these is finished there is two more to paint me & Angelaca (Kauffman?), if she comes, & Marchmont is to cut a head of me for a ring.

Greville answered this letter, and though the receipt of his handwriting, and the wafer which his lips had pressed afforded her much pleasure, yet the pleasure had its alloy in the advice he gave her to yield to his uncle's wishes. She indignantly retorted that she would not answer him on such a subject— that he could not know the pain it gave her to read those lines, and that if she was with him she would murder him and herself also to repay him for his advice. Her letter closes with a very important postscript—" Pray write, for nothing will make me so angry, & it is not to your interest to disoblige me, for you don't know the power I have hear." Her final words are--" If you affront me, I will make him marry me. God bless you for ever."

CHAPTER VI.

GREVILLE'S CONCERN ON HEARING EMMA'S RESOLVE TO RETURN TO ENGLAND. HER GRAPHIC DESCRIPTION OF VESUVIUS IN ERUPTION. THE DUTCH COMMODORE GIVES AN ENTERTAINMENT IN HER HONOUR.

At this point she resolved to return to England, and Sir William wrote to his nephew that in the event of her taking such a step, he would make provision for her, so as to maintain her in comfortable circumstances; for he had become greatly attached to her, and was wishful that he could make impression on her affections; but as she steadily resisted his advances, arrangements were made that within a few months she should carry out her expressed intention and leave Naples. This was far from pleasant news to the self-considering Greville, and in replying to his uncle, on October 24, 1786, he lays before him the reasons for his having disbanded his establishment. "You are well aware," he says "that I was losing myself by secluding myself from the world, my finances gradually diminished, and my incumbrances increased. I had no option but to bury myself for life, or to resume my situation in the world. Your kindness to me, and a partiality to Emma, made you, before you left England, offer your assistance, in case of an event which you knew would not be long delayed; and your letters, bearing direct avowal of the continuance of those sentiments when absence might have obliterated a slight impression, made me accept your offer to receive Emma; your proposed provision exceeds your promise. . . . But you have now rendered it possible for her to be respected and comfortable, & if she has not talked herself out of the true view of her situation, she will retain the protection and affection of us both. For after all, considering what a charming creature she would have been if she had been blessed with the advantages of an early education, & had not been spoilt by the indulgence of every caprice. I never was irritated by her momentary passions, for it is a good heart which will not part with a friend in anger,

EMMA'S PROPOSED RETURN TO ENGLAND.

& yet it is true that when her pride is hurt by neglect, or anxiety for the future, the frequent repetition of her passion balances the beauty of the smiles. If a person knew her, and could live with her by an economy of attention—that is, by constantly renewing little attentions—she would be happy & good-tempered, for she has not a grain of avarice or self-interest. On the contrary, she has a pleasure in sharing her last shilling. Knowing all this, how infinite have been my pains to make her respect herself . . ." In laying his case before his uncle, and tendering his "considerate" advice, he had mainly one issue in view—the ridding himself of a bar to his own advancement in life; and he greatly dreaded Emma's return and the annoyance which she might bring to him when she discovered that he had played her falsely. He therefore requested his uncle to impress upon her that if she carried out her threat of returning, it could no longer be on the old familiar terms. He continued his letter—"If she will put me on the footing of a friend, which she says I have always assumed, she will write to me fairly on her plans; she will tell me her plans, & her future comfort shall be my serious concern. But she must not think that I can resume the close connexion & live as I did with her. In the first place, I cannot afford it, & in the next it would keep me out of the world, & would ruin me & herself; whereas, if she acts wisely & kindly to herself & to me, she will take up a new line, live independent & consult me as a friend, & either settle for life or adopt any line which she shall see is favourable & agreeable. She has conduct & discernment. I have always said that such a woman, if she could control her passions, might rule the roast & chuse her station. You see that the line you have adopted & placed her in she has followed up, & it therefore requires mere management at present. I think her return in the spring may be well settled, but I should be much embarrassed if it happened before the middle or end of May; & I will write to you again fully on the subject." He advises his uncle to continue his attentions to Emma, in the assurance of ultimate success, as it was his opinion that it was not in the power of any woman to withstand a long siege: but in the event of her determined return, he adds—" The plan I propose is to make Mr. Romney her trustee, & vest your grant in him for her benefit, & I will consider further and write to you when I have formed my opinion, & it will be much better that the plan is generally discussed & approved before it is executed. It is her peace and comfort, and not those of caprice or convenience which

LADY HAMILTON.

I consider."* Up to this stage in the story Emma had only entertained very natural gratitude to her benefactor for the luxuries and comforts with which he had surrounded her; but then, bracing herself to meet the inevitable, and realizing that Greville had abandoned her, she resigned herself to circumstances, and determined to regard him in future only as a friend who would take an interest in her daily doing. The next letter he received from her was more of a diary, for she had it four months in hand, which will account for its unusual length. It is without date, but was apparently written about 1789:—

NAPOLI.

Altho' you never think me worth writing to, yet I cannot so easily forget you, & whenever I have had any particular pleasure, I feel as though I was not right till I had communicated it to my dearest Greville; for you will ever be dear to me, & though we cannot be together, lett ous correspond as friends. I have a happiness in hearing from you & a happiness in communicating my little storieys to you, because I flatter myself that you still love the name of that emma that was once so dear to you, & but for unfortunate evils might still have claimed the first place in your affections, & I hope still you will never meet with any person that will use you ill. But never will you meet with the sincere love that I shewed you. Don't expect it, for you cannot meet with it. But I have done; only think of my words. You will meet with more EVILS than ONE, & as Sir William says, that one is the Devil. We have been at Sorrento on a visit at the Duke de Saint Maitre for ten days. We are just returned, but I never spent a happier ten days except Edg . . re Road. In the morning we bathed, & returned to a fine sumer house, where we breakfasted. But first, this sumer house is on a rock over the sea that looks over Caprea, Ischea, prochida, vesuva, portice, paysilipo, Naples, &c , &c., &c., & the sea all before ous, that you have no idea of the beauties of it. From the little Paradise after breakfast we viewed the Lava running down 3 miles of vesuvua, & every now & then black clouds of smoak rising in the air had the most magnificent apearance in the world. I have made some drawings from it, for I am so used to draw now, it is as easy as a b c; for when we are at Naples we dine every day at Villa Emma, at Paysilipo, & I make two or three drawings.

---

* The letter from which these extracts are taken is very lengthy, embracing much of the plans between Mr. Greville and Sir William concerning Miss Hart. The document itself is among the valuable Morrison MSS.

HER GRAPHIC DESCRIPTION OF VESUVIUS.

Sir William laughs at me, & says I shall rivel him with the mountains now. After breakfast I had my singing lesson, for Sir W^m· as took a master into the house, but he is one of the best masters in Italia. After my lesson, we rode on asses all about the country, paid visits, &c., & dined at 3, & after dinner sail'd about the coast; returned for the Conversazione. We had Sir W^m·'s band of musick with ous, & about dark the concert in one room, & I satt in a nother & received all the nobility, who came every night whilst we was there. I sung generelly 2 songs & 2 buffos. The last night I sang fifteen songs. One was a recatitive from a opera at St. Carlos. The beginning was "*Luce bello sio vadore,*" the finest thing you ever heard, that for ten minutes after I sung it their was such a claping that I was obliged to sing it over again, & I sung after that one with a tambourine in the character of a young girl with a raire (rarce) show, the pretiest thing you ever heard. In short, I left the people at Sorrento with their heads turned. I left some dying, some crying, & some in despair. Mind you, this was all nobility, as proud as the devil, but we humbled them. But what astonished them was that I should speak such good Italian, for I paid them; I spared none of them, tho' I was civil & oblidged everybody. . . . We are going up Vesuvua to-night, as there is a large eruption, and the lava runs down allmost to Porticeo. The mountain looks beautiful. One part there is nothing but cascades of liquid fire—Lava, I mean—red hot, runs into deep cavern, that it is beautiful; but I fancy we shall have some very large eruption soon, as large as that of '67. I wish we may dine to-day at 2 o'clock, so sett off at four. We shall get on our asses at Porticeo, & arrive at the top just at dark, & so be at Naples abbout 2 o'clock to-morrow morning. Sir W^m· is very fond of me & very kind to me. He as now got nine pictures of me & 2 a painting. Marchant is cuting my head in stone; that is, Camea for a ring. There is a nother man modeling me in wax, & a nother in clay All the artists is come from Rome to study from me, that Sir W^m· as fitted up a room that is called the painting room. Sir W^m· is never a moment from me He goes no where without me. He has no diners but what I can be of the party; nobody comes without the are civil to me. I now live upstairs in the same appartments where he lives, & my old appartments is made the music rooms, where I have my Lessons in the morning, & our house at Caserta is fitting up eleganter this year, a room making for my musick, & a room fitting up for my master, as he goes with ous. Sir W^m· says he loves nothing but me, Likes no person to sing but me, & takes delight in all I do & all I say, so we are happy. Sunday morning—We was last night up Vesuvus at twelve o'clock, & in my life I never saw so fine a sight. The lava runs about 5 miles down from the top, for the mountain is not burst, as ignorant people says it is; but when we got up to the Hermitage there was the finest fountain of liquid fire falling down a great precipice, & as it ran down it sett fire to the trees & brushwood, so the mountain looked like one entire mountain of fire. We saw the lava surround the poor Hermits' house & take possession of the chapel, notwithstanding it was covered with pictures of saints and other religious preservitaves against the fury of nature. For me I was inraptured & could have staid all night there, & I have never been in charity with the moon since, for it looked so pale & sickly, & the red hot lava served to light up the moon, for the moon was nothing to the lava. We met the Prince Royal on the mountain, but his foolish tutors onely took him up a little whay, & did not let him stay 3 minuets; so when we asked him how he liked it, he said, "*Bella ma poca roba*," when if the had took him five hundred yards higher he would have seen the noblest, sublimest sight in the world; but, poor creatures, the were frightened out of their sences & glad to make a hasty retreat. O I shall kill myselfe with laughing. Their has been a prince paying us a visit. He is sixty years of age, one of the first families here, & as allways lived at Naples, & when I told him I had been to Caprea, he asked me if I went there by land. Only think what ignorance!

I must tell you I have had great offers to be first whoman in the Italian Opera at Madrid, where I was to have six thousand pound for 3 years. But I would not engage, as I should not like to go into Spain without I knew people their, & I could not speak their language, so I refused it; & a nother reason was that Galini as been hear from the Opera house of London to engage people, & tho' I have not been pursuaded to make a writen engagement, I certainly shall sing at the Pantheon & Hanover Square, except something particular happens, for Galini says he will make a subscription concert for me if I won't engage for the opera. But I wish'd to consider of it before I engage. Sir W^m says he will give me leave to sing at Hanover Square on the conditions Galini as proposed, which is 2 thousand pounds. Sir William as took my master into the house, & pays him a great price, on purpose that he shall teach no other person. . . . I have my French master; I have the Queen's dancing master 3 times a week; I have 3 lessons in singing a day, morning, eight o'clock, before diner, and the evening, & people makes enterest to come

THE DUTCH COMMODORE'S ENTERTAINMENT.

hear me; my master goes to England with ous. O, then I give up one hour in the day to reading the Italian, there is a person comes a purpose; & for all this their is now five painters & 2 modlers at work on me for Sir W^m, & their is a picture going of me to the Empress of Russia. But Sir William as the phaeton at the door after I have had my first singing lesson & dancing, & he drives me out for 2 hours, & you will say that's right, for as I study a deal it is right that I should have exercise. But last night I did a thing very extraordinary. We gave yesterday a diplomatic diner, so after diner I gave them a Concert; so I sent the coach and my compliments to the Banti,* who is first whoman at St. Carlos, & desired her to come & sing at my concert, so she came, and there was near sixty people; so after the first quartett I was to sing the first song. At first I was in a little fright before I began, for she is a famous singer, & she placed herself close to me; but when I begun, all fear whent awhay, & I sung so well that she cried out, Just God, what a voice, I would give a great deal for your voice. In short, I met with such applause that it almost turned my head. The Banti sung one song after me, & I assure you everybody said I sung in a finer stile than her. Poor Sir W^m was so inraptured with me, for he was afraid I should have been in a great fright, & it was of consequence that evening, for he wanted to shew me to some Dutch officers that was their, that is with a sixty gun ship and a Frigate. The Comodore, whoes name is Melville, was so inchanted with me, that tho' he was to depart the next day, he put it off, & give me a dinner on board that realy surpasses all description. First Sir W^m, me, and mother, went down to the . . . where the Long boat was waiting, all man'd so beautiful. There was the Comodore & the Captain, & four more of the first officers waited to conduct ous to the ship. The 2 ships was drest out so fine in all the collours, the men all put in order, a band of musick, & all the marrine did their duty; & when we went on board twenty pieces of cannon fired. But as we passed the Frigate she fired all her guns, that I wish you had seen it. We sett down thirty to dine, me at the head of the table, mistress of the feast, drest all in virgin wite, and my hair in ringlets reaching all most to my heals. I assure you it is so long that I really looked and moved an angel, Sir W^m said so. That night there was a great Opera at St. Carlos in honor of the

---

* The wife of Banti, the dancer. She was formerly a pupil of Signor Piozzi, who married Mrs. Thrale. Though an exquisite singer, and an actress surpassing her predecessors in dignity, feeling, and grace, her want of application exasperated her master, and he abandoned his task

King of Spain's nameday, so St. Carlos was illumanated & every body in great galla. Well, I had the finest dress made up on purpose, as I had a box near the Queen. My gown was purple sattin, peticoat trimd with crepe & spangles, my cap lovely, from Paris, all wite fethers; my hair was to have been delightfully drest, as I have a very good hair dresser. But for me, unfortunately, the Diner on board did not finish till half-past five english; then the Comodore & Sir W^{m.} would have another bottle to drink to the *belle ocche* of the lovliest whoman in the world, as the called me at least. I whispered to Sir W^{m.} and told him I should be angry with him if he did not get up to go, as we was to dress & it was necessary to be at the theatre before the Royal party, so at least the put out the Boat to offer a salute from the 2 ships of all the guns. We arrived on shoar with the Comodore and five princapal officers, & in we all cram'd into our coach which is large. We just got in time to the Opera. The Comodore went with us, & the officers came next, & attended my box all the time, & behaved to me as tho' I was a Queen.*

From the pen of the favoured *protégé* of Sir William we get an insight into her own life. Her voluminous correspondence flowed with the ease of conversation, and we fail to find in it the attribute of artfulness; nay, rather the openness of truth is eminently to the fore. The secret of Emma's success with womankind lay in the fact that she aped not their courtly manners, but adhered to her rustic naturalness, which formed a pleasing variety in their midst, and aroused no ill-feeling against her, which assuredly would have been the case had she assumed any superior airs or displayed any pretensions. Her line of conduct was kind, open, and simple, which suited the court ladies better than if any attempt had been made to imitate their higher tone. Among the great ladies with whom she became a favourite was another famous beauty, whose history is equally as interesting as her own, Elizabeth, Duchess of Argyle, once the celebrated Elizabeth or Betty Gunning; indeed it was entirely due to her Grace's good offices that Sir William married her. All classes alike admired the beautiful Emma, the priesthood even looking with reverence on her heavenly face, comparing her to the Virgin as depicted in their masterpieces of painting. One night Sir William made her put a shawl over her head, and cast up her eyes Madonna-wise, her saintly expres-

* The Morrison MSS.

ELIZABETH GUNNING, DUCHESS OF HAMILTON

SHE PREPARES TO RETURN TO LONDON.

sion so touched a priest who was present that the tears came into his eyes, and he told her that God had sent her for a special purpose. Her shawls had become worn out from the frequent use she made of them in her performances, and she wrote to ask Mr. Greville if he would coax an old friend named McPherson to give her another, which it is presumed he did, as in a letter written later she desires him to thank Mr. McPherson. Early in the year 1791, she intimated to her correspondent that Sir William and herself would be in England during the summer, and, accustomed as she was to being the observed of all observers, she desired only a quiet reception in England. She says:—

> We come for a short time, and that time must be occupied in business, and to take our last leave. I don't wish to atract notice. I wish to be an example of good conduct, and to shew the world that a pretty woman is not allways a *fool*. All my ambition is to make Sir W^m· happy, and you will see he is so. Sir W^m· will lett you know on what a footing we are here. On Munday last we gave a concert and Ball at our house. I had near four hundred persons; all the foreign ministers and their wives, all the first ladies of fasshion, foreigners and Neapolitans; our house was full in every room, and I had the Banti, the tenor Cosacelli, & 2 others to sing; Sir W^m· dressd me in wite sattin, no culler about me but my hair and cheeks. I was without powder, as it was the first assembly we had given publicly. All the ladies strove to outdo one another in dress and Jewels. But Sir W^m· said I was the finest jewel amongst them. . . . Think then, after what Sir W^m· as done for me, if I should not be the horridest wretch in the world not to be exemplary towards him. Endead I will do all I can to render him happy. We shall be with you in the spring, and return hear in Nov^r, & the next year you may pay ous a visit; we shall be glad to see you. I shall allways esteem you for your relationship to Sir W^m· & having been the means of me knowing him. As to Sir W., I confess to you I doat on him, nor I never can love any other person but him; this confession will please you, I know."

The artlessness of her final words is almost amusing, for the position of affairs had reached a point that was never intended by Mr. Greville. Sir William had resolved to marry the girl, and we may easily imagine the feel-

* The Morrison MSS.

ings of Emma's old lover when he realised the likelihood of being ousted from his prospective possessions by the very woman whom he intended to frustrate such an event.

Throughout all her correspondence we read her earnest wish to be good. That she ever failed in her endeavour should be laid at the door of those who led her feet in wrong paths; she was formed for better things.

CHAPTER VII.

MME. LE BRUN PAINTS EMMA'S PORTRAIT. SHE SITS FOR HER PORTRAIT TO SIR THOMAS LAWRENCE. HER LETTER TO ROMNEY, AND HIS REPLY. THE MARRIAGE OF SIR WILLIAM AND EMMA.

ABOUT this time, owing to the disturbed state of affairs in France, a lady artist of repute, by name Mme. Le Brun, sought refuge on the Neapolitan shores. Ever ready to patronize merit, partly out of kindness, and partly to add to his stores one more delineation of the pretty face that was daily growing more dear to him, Sir William commissioned the exiled lady to paint a portrait of his intended wife, for which she was to receive £96; the attitude to be reclining on the seashore in the character of a Bacchante. As the picture progressed, Emma protested against the freedom of figure drawn by the artist, who accordingly painted a leopard skin as thrown over the form. Sir William eventually sold this picture for three times the amount that he paid for it, which caused great discontent to Mme. Le Brun, who considered herself underpaid when she heard the amount realised; but she did not reflect that the winsome Emma's celebrity would greatly enhance the value of the portrait. It was at least an ungracious act on her part to attribute paltry selfish motives to a man of position, who gave her, as an exile, her first commission, and introduced her to families of standing.

SIR W. HAMILTON.
From a sketch by C. Grignion.

When we further learn that our Sir Joshua Reynolds was content to take fifty guineas as remuneration for his conception of the Bacchante, we cannot think the lady was underpaid. Sir William had waited upon the French lady immediately upon her arrival at Naples, and he exerted himself to do the honours, and invited her to accompany his party to the "Madonna de l'Arca," which for its originality distinguishes it above all other festivals. Madame has left us a record of the fête, and her own bad behaviour, in these words: "The square in front of the church was covered with stalls containing sweets, cakes, and images of the Virgin, and groups of people in the different costumes of their cantons, some richly embroidered with gold. All the crowd entered the church to hear mass; Sir William Hamilton, Mrs. Hart and myself placed ourselves near a little chapel, where was a picture of the Virgin as black as ink. The peasantry, both male and female, continually knelt before it to solicit some favour, or return thanks for one; they expressed their wishes in so loud a voice that we could hear their petitions quite easily. First a handsome man, with bare throat, came to return thanks for his child's restoration to health. After him came a woman, who scolded the Madonna furiously for allowing her husband to ill-treat her. I was suffocating with laughter, and Sir William had to continually remind me to restrain my feelings." Sir William had a small casino on the shore at Caserta, where his guests frequently dined. He used to amuse himself by throwing coppers into the water for which the boys of the place dived. Here Mme. Le Brun drew two cherubs' heads on the panel of a door, and when she visited Lord Warwick's house in England she renewed acquaintance with them, as Sir William had cut them out of the door and brought them to England. According to the same lady, "nothing was more curious than to watch the facility which Mrs. Hart had of expressing in her features either joy or sorrow, or of imitating different persons. One moment she would be a delightful Bacchante, with animated eyes and hair in disorder; then, all at once, her face would express sorrow, and you saw a beautiful repentant Magdalen." When painting her portrait as the Sybil, several exalted ladies were present. Madame arranged a shawl round the head of her beautiful subject in the form of a turban, one end of which fell in graceful drapery, and the ladies pronounced her exquisitely lovely. She painted a third portrait in which the sprightly Emma was depicted dancing to the accompaniment of a tambourine.

Mme. Le Brun received the command of the Queen of Naples to attend at the palace and take the portraits of herself and her two daughters. The second one, Louisa, who married the Grand Duke of Tuscany, was very ugly,

SIR THOMAS LAWRENCE PAINTS HER PORTRAIT.

and made such dreadful faces, that it was quite against the wish of Madame that she finished her picture. However, she entertained a high opinion of her Majesty, who in the exercise of charity would frequently mount five flights of stairs. One day while the Queen was sitting to Madame, her Majesty was so overcome by the heat that she fell asleep, and ere long the artist herself was a similar victim to atmospheric influence.

So, 'mid revellings and fêtes the days passed pleasantly along, until Sir William and his fiancée departed for England in the spring of the year 1791, which visit would terminate in the important ceremonial that gave her the title by which she will be ever known while a historian pens Britain's history—Lady Hamilton.

During their short stay artist vied with artist in the endeavour to delineate her pretty features; rightly conjecturing that her beauty and celebrity would add lustre to the work of each accomplished knight of the brush. We find Sir Thomas Lawrence writing to Mr. Lysons, delighted at the prospect of an introduction to her ladyship that was to be, and exulting in the pleasure he was likely to derive from it.

OLD BOND ST., *Thursday.*

D^{R.} SIR,

A particular friend of mine promised to get me introduced at Sir William Hamilton's, to see this wonderful woman you have doubtless heard of—Mrs. Hart. He has succeeded, but unfortunately made an appointment for that purpose on Sunday morning next, at half-past ten. What shall I do? I hear it is the most gratifying thing to a painter's eye that can be, and I am frightened at the same time with the intimation that she will soon be Lady Hamilton, and I may not have such another opportunity. . . .

It was in this limited time that he drew the profile chalk drawing which is in the British Museum, signed " Emma, 1791." The head is enveloped in a gauze turban, and the sketch has an unfinished appearance.

Lawrence painted a full-length portrait, eight feet upright, of Lady Hamilton, which is in the possession of his Grace the Duke of Abercorn at his London residence, Hampden House. It was exhibited at Somerset House in 1803. The lady is portrayed seated in an arbour or cave, on a semi-circular seat or stone, along the top rail of which there twines a spray of ivy. Through the opening of the arbour is shown a perspective of trees; her left arm lies on the ivy-entwined rail. The face is three-quarters turned to her own right shoulder, looking upwards; the eyes large and dark; complexion, a soft and rich tint; lips full and sweet; the hair wavy; a thick and long light brown tress falls over her right arm into her lap in rich profusion. The dress is white, with a gold cincture, and gold embroidery surmounts the half-high bodice. Across her knee is thrown a drapery of dark grey, lined with pale pink silk; one white shoe is visible. From the absence of rings, we may infer that the picture was painted at the time referred to in Lawrence's letter, one or two weeks before her marriage, at which time the artist would be twenty-two years of age.*

Her old friend, Romney, was naturally one of the favoured few to whom she vouchsafed sittings during her brief and important visit to England. Writing to his friend Hayley, he says—"At present, and the greatest part of the summer, I shall be engaged in painting pictures from the divine lady, I cannot give her any other epithet, for I think her superior to all womankind. I have two pictures to paint for the Prince of Wales." Again, anterior to the wedding ceremony, which was close at hand—" I dedicate my time to this charming lady. There is a prospect of her leaving town with Sir William for two or three weeks. They are very much hurried at present, as everything is going on for their speedy marriage, and all the world following her and talking of her, so that if she had not more good sense than vanity, her brain must be turned. The pictures I have begun are 'Joan of Arc,' a 'Magdalen,' and a 'Bacchante' for the Prince of Wales, and another I am to begin as a companion to the 'Bacchante.' I have also to paint a picture of 'Constance' for the Shakespeare Gallery." The picture of "Constance" was never begun. It has been written that Romney at this juncture fretted on account of a coldness in her manner towards him; but his trouble was merely the natural resentment that any one might feel at being slighted by a friend who had made a rise in life; however, at their next meeting she showed him every attention, which greatly cheered his downcast spirits, and proved his grievance to have been imaginary. After a brief interval, he again addressed the companion with whom he loved to correspond,†

* The description of this picture is inserted by the kind permission of his Grace the Duke of Abercorn.
† Hayley.

LADY HAMILTON.

and who was invariably the repository of his inmost thoughts. "In my last letter," he says, "I told you I was going to dine with Sir William Hamilton and his lady. In the evening of that day there were collected several people of fashion to hear her sing. She performed, both in serious and comic, to admiration, both in singing and acting; but her 'Nina' surpasses everything I ever saw, and I believe as a piece of acting nothing ever surpassed it. The whole company were in an agony of sorrow. Her acting is simple, grand, terrible, and pathetic. My mind was so much heated that I was for running down to Eartham, to fetch you up to see her." Then comes his last letter before the marriage. "She performed in my house last week, singing and acting before some of the nobility with the most astonishing powers. She is the talk of the whole town, and really surpasses everything both in singing and acting that ever appeared. Gallini offered her two thousand pounds a year and two benefits if she would engage with him, on which Sir William said pleasantly that he had engaged her for life." These outpourings to the friend who knew him best betray no other sentiment than sincere admiration for the girl, and in no correspondence of his does there appear the faintest allusion to friendship of any warmer character. In furtherance of this assertion a letter is here inserted, written by Lady Hamilton on her return to Naples, to the fatherly painter who cared so much for her. It plainly bears out the statement that his interest in her was mainly such as tended to her good:—

  MY DEAR FRIEND,

       I have the pleasure to inform you we arrived safe at Naples. I have been received with open arms by all the Neapolitans of both sexes, by all foreigners of distinction. I have been presented to the Queen of Naples by her own desire. She as shown me all sorts of kind and affectionate attentions. In short, I am the happiest woman in the world. Sir William is fonder of me every day, and I hope he will have no cause to repent of what he has done, for I feel so grateful to him that I think I shall never be able to make amends for his goodness to me. But why do I tell you this? You know me enough. You was the first dear friend I opened my heart to. You ought to know me, for you have seen and discoursed with me in my poverty and prosperity, and I had no occasion to have livd for years in poverty and distress if I had not felt something of virtue in my mind. Oh, my dear Friend! For a time I own, through distress, my

virtue was vanquish'd; but my sense of virtue was not overcome. How gratefull now, then, do I feel to my dear, dear husband, that as restored peace to my mind, that as given honer, rank, and, what is more, innocence and happiness. Rejoice with me, my dear Sir, my friend, my more than father. Believe me, I am still that same Emma you knew me. If I could forget for a moment what I was, I ought to suffer. Command me in anything I can do for you here. Believe me, I shall have real pleasure. Come to Naples, and I will be your model—anything to induce you to come, that I may have an oppertunity to show my gratitude to you. Take care of your health for all our sakes. How does the pictures go on? Has the Prince been to you? Write to me. I am interested in all that concerns you. God bless you, my dear Friend. I spoke to Lady Southampton about you; she loves you dearly. Give my love to Hayley. Tell him I shall be glad to see him at Naples. As you was so good as to say you would give me the little picture with the black hat, I wish you would unfrill it and give it to Mr. Dutens.* I have a great regard for him. He took a deal of pains and trouble for me; and I could not do him a greater favour than to give him my picture. Do, my dear Friend, do me that pleasure, and if there is anything from Naples command me. We have a many English at Naples—Ladys Malmesbury, Malden, Plymouth, Carneigee, Wright, &c. They are very kind and attentive to me. They all make it a point to be remarkably civil to me. You will be happy at this, for you know what prudes our Ladys are. Tell Hayley I am always reading his *Triumphs of Temper*. It was *that* made me Lady Hamilton; for God knows I had, for 5 years, enugh to try my temper, and I am affraid if it had not been for the example Serena taught me, my girdle would have burst; and if it had I had been undone, for Sir William more minds temper than beauty. He therefore wishes Mr. Hayley would come, that he might thank him for his sweet-tempered wife. I swear to you I have never been once of humour since the 6th of last September.†
God bless you.—Yours,   E. HAMILTON.

The letter, in its rustic openness, is a distinct evidence that the companions of what might be called her worst days were men who used their best endeavours to direct her life in a proper course. She appreciated and

---

* The Rev. L. Deutens, one of the witnesses to her marriage.
† Her wedding day.

thanked them for the goodness they had instilled into her, and in the day of her triumph she invited them to visit her and see her success, assigning to their guiding hands the credit of her attaining so brilliant a position. The respectful tone of Romney's reply is additional evidence to quash the accusation of too great familiarity having at any time existed, for this is his response:—

MY DEAR LADY,
What must you think of my neglect of answering your kind letter? Do not accuse me of ungratitud. I wish I could express myself as I felt at the perusal of it to find your happyness so compleat. May God grant it may remain so till the end of your days. You may be assured that I have the same anxiety that Sir William and yourself should continue to think well of me, and the same desire to do everything in my power that may merit your esteem. I have waited till I could give you some account of the picter of Cassandra, and some other of the pictures you were so kind to sit to me for. The Cassandra is at last gone to the Shakespere Gallery—it suits.

The King and Royal Family saw it. I hav never heard from the Prince of Wales till a few days ago Mr. West called and said the Prince desired him to look at the Picture for his Royal Hiness, they are near finished. The lively one I have made to suit Calipso. I am anxious to know what you would wish me to do with the picture with a Bonnet, as you have not mentioned it in your letter. Mr. Crawford has expressed a great desire of possessing it in prefference to the other. I shall wait for your instructions. I sent, as your ladyship required, the picter in Black to du 'Ton (Deutens). I was lead into a thing that has given me uneasyness, I was solicited so very strongly for a letter of recommendation to your Ladyship that I was not able to get off. The person was then in Italy, but was not informed who he was. I hope your Ladyship will forgive me for taking such a liberty, and that nothing unpleasant happened.*

A very natural letter, containing nothing but what is courteous. Allusion is made in Lady Hamilton's letter to the good influence she felt from the poem of Hayley, *The Triumphs of Temper*. Nor was she alone in her grateful

* The Morrison MSS.

acknowledgment of the beneficial effects of this composition, for the mother of a large family wrote to the poet that she was beholden to it for a complete reformation in the character of her perverse daughter, who, by ambition to emulate Serena (one of his characters), became most docile and tractable. In 1804, Hayley was engaged in writing the life of his intimate friend, Romney; indeed, it was at the suggestion of Lady Hamilton that he undertook the task. He wrote to ask her to furnish a list of the pictures Romney had painted of her, with their dates, so that he could insert them in his work, adding, " You were not only his model, but his inspirer; and he truly and gratefully said that he owed a great part of his felicity as a painter to the angelic kindness and intelligence with which you used to animate his diffident and tremulous spirits to the grandest efforts of art." In concluding the same letter, he invited her to visit him at his seaside home, calling himself " an old hermit." He told her he had three pretty ladies to show her, who were well worth a visit if the old hermit were not. The three pretty ladies were portraits of herself as "Cassandra," "Serena," and "Sensibility."

The marriage with Sir William Hamilton took place in Marylebone Church, on September 6, 1791, and in order that the ceremony should be complete in legality, she signed the register with her correct baptismal name, " Amy Lyon," though the announcements went forth to the world, through the medium of the society papers, in the name by which she was better known—" Miss Hart." The witnesses were the Marquess of Abercorn and the Rev. L. Deutens.

CHAPTER VIII.

QUEEN CHARLOTTE REFUSES TO RECEIVE LADY HAMILTON AT COURT. HORACE WALPOLE'S SARCASM ON HER MAJESTY'S ACT. MARIE ANTOINETTE SHOWS HER MUCH CIVILITY AT THE COURT OF FRANCE.

IN the height of her ambition, Lady Hamilton fondly hoped that Queen Charlotte would confer the crowning touch to her happiness, and allow her to be presented at Court before her return to Italy. The prim little German lady used her usual firmness in refusing this request. Though personages of high estate exerted their persuasive powers to induce Her Majesty to relax in favour of the indulged beauty, still she declined to honour the aspirant. It can only be said she was right. In this and many another act which has obtained for her the charge of severity the Royal lady really deserves all praise. No easy task had she set herself when she undertook to clear and purify the Court of the wantonness which had been openly permitted and encouraged during the reigns of the two preceding Georges—such scandal as the German Platens and Schwellenbergs following their admirer, the second George, in their sedan chairs in the park, or appearing at the opera seated on either side of him, facing a public so accustomed to such scenes that it totally disregarded the glaring impropriety of their conduct—the Court could only be compared to a hotbed of corruption. Possessing many disagreeable qualities, and disliked for her austere discipline, the Queen of George III. was, in the main, a homely, right-living woman.

Horace Walpole, the king of satirical penmen, mentions Emma in a letter to his fair correspondents, the Misses Berry, who were absent in Italy, and whom he kept advised of the leading topics which stirred London society. In August, 1791, he wrote:

> I shall fill my vacuum with some lines that General Conway has sent me, written by whom I know not, on Mrs. Harte, Sir William Hamilton's pantomime mistress or wife, who acts all the antique statues in an Indian

shawl. I have not seen her yet, so am no judge; but people are mad about her wonderful expression, which I do not conceive, so few antique statues having any expression at all, nor being designed to have it. Here are the verses :—

ATTITUDES: A SKETCH.

To charm the sense, the taste to guide,
Sculpture and Painting long has tried.
Both called ideal beauty forth;
Both claimed a disputable worth,
When Nature, looking down on Art,
Made a new claim and showed us Mistress Harte.
All of Corregio's faultless line,
Of Guido's air and look divine;
All that arose to mental view
When Raphael his best angels drew;
The artist's spell, the poet's thought,
By her to beauteous life is brought.
The gazer sees each feature move,
Each grace awake, and breathing love;
From parts distinct, a matchless whole—
She finds the form and gives the soul.

Critically indisposed to be pleased with her exhibitions, he owned himself enraptured with her grace and singing, after meeting her at the house of the Duke of Queensberry, which concession he felt bound to report to his two absent fair friends. His letter bears date August 23, 1791:

On Saturday evening I was at the Duke of Queensberry's (at Richmond *s'entend*) with a small company, and there were Sir William Hamilton and Mrs. Harte, who, on the 3rd of next month, previous to their departure, is to be made Madame l'Envoyée à Naples, the Neapolitan Queen having promised to receive her in that quality. Here she cannot be presented, where such over-virtuous wives as the Duchess of Kingston and Mrs. Hastings, who could go with a husband in each hand, are admitted. . . . But I forgot to retract and make the *amende honorable* to Mrs. Harte. I have only heard of her attitudes, and those in dumb show I have not yet seen. Oh! but she sings admirably, has a fine strong voice, is an excellent buffa, and an astonishing tragedian. She sang Nina in the highest perfection; and there her attitudes were a whole theatre of grace and various expressions.

This rhapsody from the most sarcastically severe man of his age, or, indeed, of any age, meant genuine praise; and excellent must the performance have been to have earned *his* commendation, when he went prepared to ridicule what he termed "the Nymph of the Attitudes." One more word he gives on September 11, 1791 :—"Sir William Hamilton has actually married his gallery of statues, and they are set out on their return to Naples. I am sorry I did not see her attitudes, which Lady Di. (a tolerable judge) prefers to anything she ever saw." Horace Walpole might rightly query the precedence allowed to a lady with two husbands over a lady with none to the *entrée* at the Court of prudent Queen Charlotte. When we consider that she excluded her daughter-in-law from her assemblies in consequence of her undue levity, we cannot expect that she would unbend her rigidity in favour of an equally lively stranger.

Chagrined as the bride was by her Majesty's decision, she soon forgot her annnoyance in the cordiality of her reception at the Court of France. Marie Antoinette was most condescending in her kindness, and although harassed with exceeding anxiety and trouble, owing to the Revolutionary disturbance, she contrived to show every civility to the new Ambassadress, and on her departure for Italy, she entrusted her with an autograph letter to her sister, the Queen of Naples. Daughters of Marie Theresa of Austria, the Neapolitan Queen had a much larger share of personal beauty than Marie Antoinette; her mind was of a superior mould, almost masculine. In the chatty memoirs of Sir Nathaniel Wraxall, we find his impressions of these sister queens. Of the French Queen he writes:—"Her personal charm consisted more in her elevated manner, lofty demeanour, and graces of deportment, than in her features or countenance, which wanted softness and regularity; she had, besides, weak, or rather inflamed eyes, but her complexion, which was dazzling, aided by youth and all the decorations of dress, in which ornaments she displayed great taste, imposed on the beholder." Of the lady who ruled the Court of Naples, he observed:—"Though neither possessing beauty of face nor loveliness of person, yet was she not absolutely deficient in either respect. She is the only Queen whom I ever saw weep in public before a crowd of both sexes assembled in her own Palace on a gala day. The Festival on which I was presented to her happened to be the anniversary of the loss of her eldest son, who expired exactly a year before, in 1778; he was a very fine boy, of promising expectations, to whom his mother was passionately attached. The ignorance of the Neapolitan physicians, as it was believed, had caused his death; for being seized with violent sickness and pain, from which an emetic, promptly administered, might have relieved him, they had the imprudence to bleed him, and brought on fatal convulsions. Such was the Queen's distress at the recollection of the event which had taken place on this painful anniversary, that she was unable to repress her emotion. In the Presence Chamber of the Palace at Naples she stood under a canopy, her right hand held out to the nobility as they approached to kiss it, holding in her left a handkerchief with which she perpetually wiped her eyes that were suffused with tears, an involuntary testimony of her maternal tenderness." From Sir Horace Mann we learn the curious circumstances of her marriage:—"Her eldest sister, Joanna, had been betrothed to Ferdinand at the age of twelve, but she succumbed to an attack of smallpox while very young, and the honour was transferred to her next sister, Josefa, who, with great reluctance, was to be married in 1767. The affectionate girl keenly felt the impending separation from her family. She descended into the vault of the Capuchin Church to bid farewell to her dead father, whose remains were there interred, and though at the time seriously indisposed, she remained for several hours weeping and praying; her illness increased, malignant smallpox showed itself, and Josefa, the bride-elect, died on the day on which it had been arranged she should have set out for Florence on her way to Naples. She, in turn, was replaced by her sister Maria Caroline, whom the fates permitted to culminate the marriage." Of her royal consort it was written, that he was so wanting in delicacy and sense as almost to approach madness, and, at the time of his marriage, his education was not more advanced than that of an ordinary boy of twelve.

On the return to Naples, the "Attitudes" of Lady Hamilton were resumed, and so enchanted was her enamoured spouse that he commissioned Frederick Rehburg (historical painter to the King of Prussia at Rome) to execute drawings of the whole of the exquisite *tableaux vivants* as portrayed by his wife. These were engraved, and published in book form, by Thomas Pirolis, called *Lady Hamilton's Attitudes*, and are reproduced in this volume.

Every character which Lady Hamilton attempted fitted her with equal ease, and the grace she displayed while performing excited the admiration of all who were fortunate enough to be present. The celebrated Shawl Dance owes its origin to her inventive faculty; and it is admitted to have been

PLATE III.— ATTITUDE OF LADY HAMILTON, FROM A DRAWING BY REHBURG.

executed by her with an elegance far surpassing that with which it has ever been rendered on any stage in our theatres. About this time another tribute of praise was laid at her feet from the pen of Mr. Richard Payne Knight :—"I frequently see and hear from Lord Moira. He is among the most constant and fervid of your admirers; he never writes without saying something in your commendation. The having heard you sing he reckons an epoch in his life, and often says that you gave him ideas of the power of expression in music which he would never otherwise have conceived."

Lady Hamilton was welcomed back among the people to whom she had endeared herself by many a good-natured act. Mme. Le Brun records that after her marriage Sir William brought her back to Naples, and she became as grand a lady as could be. Within a fortnight after her arrival she was honoured by an invitation to dine at the Palace of Caserta. Lady Malmesbury, who was present, mentioned the meeting in a letter to her sister, Lady Elliott :—" Lady Hamilton really behaves as well as possible, and quite wonderfully, considering her origin and education. The Queen has received her very kindly as Lady Hamilton, though not as the English Minister's wife, and I believe all the English here mean to be civil to her, which is quite right."

CHAPTER IX.

GREVILLE CONSIDERS SIR WILLIAM THE RIGHT PARTY TO PROVIDE FOR "LADY HAMILTON'S *PROTEGEE.*" SIR WILLIAM'S ILLNESS; EMMA ASSISTS HER GRANDMOTHER.

Up to this period (the year 1792) little Emma—the child that had accompanied her mother to Parkgate in 1784—was in the custody of a Mr. and Mrs. Blackburn, to whom Mr. Greville had made an annual allowance of £65 to cover the cost of her care. From the date of Sir William's marriage, his crafty nephew considered him to be the rightful party to bear the burden in future, and he lost no time in informing his uncle of the existence of what he transparently called "Lady Hamilton's *protégée*," in order that Sir William might at once pay the amount due for one half-year's keep to the Blackburns. He therefore wrote Sir William, early in January, 1792 :—

DEAR HAMILTON,
I have taken a liberty with you, and I communicate it to you instead of Lady H., because I know it would give her some embarrassment, and she might imagine it unkind in me so soon to trouble you with her *protégée*. I had settled the midsummer half year, and I intended to have done the same at Xmas if I could have kept my account at Mr. Hoare's within bounds. I have overdrawn him £150, and my next receipt is in May. It will not therefore be taken ill of you that I have given Blackburn an order on Messrs. Ross and Ogilvy for £32. 10s. od. in this form—

£32 . 10 . 0   *Jan.* 10, 1792.
Please to pay to Mr. Blackburn or bearer thirty two pounds, 10/ on account of Sir Wm Hamilton, the particulars of which demand I have transmitted to him at Naples.   C. F. G.

I do not mean this necessary step to be concealed from Ly. H., but I should be sorry that she considered it unkindly. You will know better than me that an early decision should be taken about her. Blackburn says she has grown, and that she has been evidently more anxious since Mrs.

Cadogan visited her. The age of curiosity is, however, near at hand, and her future plans should be settled and communicated. As every part of her history has been stated to you, there can be little difficulty to decide. The natural attachment to a deserted orphan may be supposed to increase from the length of time she has been protected. I have avoided any such sentiment by having only found the means to indulge so amiable a sentiment in Ly. H. If I could have done so longer, I would; and if I could have taken care of her for life I should have personally seen the progress of it. I had full confidence in Mr. Blackburn & in Mrs. B.'s discretion, and as Mrs. Cadogan saw her situated to her satisfaction, I had only to ensure the continuance of her residence with these good people until her plans in life could be settled.

I enclose the amount that you may see the particulars of what I have allowed her; which I daresay you will continue till her plans are decided on. I cannot have an opinion of what that plan should be, but that which is most agreeable to Ly. H. will be best, and I know that she will consider your attention on this subject as additional proof of your kindness . . .
ever affectionately yours,
C. F. G.

The wily Greville, playing on the devotion of Sir William to his young wife, thought that the child would be sent for to Naples; but Sir William would seem to have considered the consequences that might accrue from such a move, and for two years at least Sir William remitted the payments for her charge. No doubt her mother wished to have her near her, for in 1794 we find her asking Greville to devise a scheme how she "could situate poor Emma."

This young girl was kept in ignorance of her real relationship to Lady Hamilton, and obtained her own living as companion or governess, as may be inferred from a letter which will appear later.

In the winter of 1792, Sir William was seized with an alarming illness, which at one time had all appearance of a fatal termination. During his convalescence his wife was troubled on behalf of her old grandmother, to whom she had made an annual allowance ever since she had sufficient means. Unable to hold converse with her sick husband on monetary affairs, she had recourse to Mr. Greville to solicit the advance in a letter which discloses the genuine affection she felt for her husband:—

LADY HAMILTON.

CASERTA, *Dec.* 4, 1792.

DEAR SIR,
    I have the pleasure to inform you that Sir William is out of danger, and very well, considering the illness he as had to battle with. He as been 15 days in bed with a billious fever, and I have been almost as ill as him with anxiety, apprehension, and fatigue, the last, endead, the least of what I have felt, and I am now doubly repaid by the daily progress he makes for the better. Luckily, we are at Caserta, were his convalescence will have fair play, and I am in hopes he will be better than ever he was in his life, for his disorder has been long gathering, and was a Liver complaint. I need not say to you, my dear Mr. Greville, what I have suffered; endead, I was almost distracted how such extreme happiness at once to such misery that I felt your good heart may imagine. I was eight days without eating or sleeping. I have great obligations to the English ladies and Neapolitans. Altho' we are 16 miles from Naples, Lady Plymouth, Lady Dunmore, & several others sent twice a day, & offered to come & stay with me; & the King & Queen sent constantly morning & evening the most flattering messages. But all was nothing to me. What could console me for the loss of such a husband, friend & protector? for surely no happiness is like ours. We live but for one another. But I was too happy. I had imagined I was never more to be unhappy. All is right. I now know myself again, and I shall not easily fall into the same errors again, for every moment I feel what I felt when I thought I was loseing him for ever. Pray excuse me, but you, who love Sir William, may figure to yourself my situation at that moment. I will trouble you with my own affairs, as you are so good as to interest yourself about me. You must know I send my Grandmother every cristmas twenty pounds, & so I ought. I have two hundred a year for nonsense, and it wou'd be hard I cou'd not give her twenty pounds when she as so often given me her last shilling. As Sir W^m is ill, I cannot ask him for the order, but if you will get the twenty pounds and send it to her, you will do me the greatest favour; for if the time passes without hearing from me, she may imagine I have forgot her, and I wou'd not keep her poor old heart in suspense for the world; & as she as heard of my circumstances (I don't know how), but she is prudent; therefore, pray lose no time, & Sir W^m shall send you the order. You know her direction, "Mrs. Kidd, Hawarden, Flintshire." Cou'd you not write to her a line from me, or send to her & tell her by my order, & she may write to you and send

me her answer; for I cannot divert myself of my original feelings. It will contribute to my happiness, and I am sure you will assist to make me happy. Tell her every year she shall have twenty pound. The fourth of November last I had a dress that cost twenty-five pounds, as it was gala at court, & believe me I felt unhappy all the while I had it on. Excuse the trouble I give you, & believe me your sincere,

EMMA HAMILTON.

Sir W^{m.} writes you a few lines."

Greville faithfully executed his commission, for in a letter, dated January 30, 1793, Sarah Kidd acknowledged the receipt of £20. Grateful Emma! carrying to her stately home in a distant land the needs of her humble relative. Before Mrs. Kidd's acknowledgment reached her she was in receipt of a letter from Mrs. Burt, of Chester, who had chaperoned her on her first journey to London. The communication was to advise her of the very straitened circumstances of her grandmother, the lady being in ignorance that assistance had been forwarded, to which Lady Hamilton made reply, addressing her epistle to "Mrs. Burt, at Mr. Roberts', No. 16, upper John Street, Marlebone, London." It was worded as follows:—

CASERTA, NEAR NAPLES, dec^{her.} 26th. 1792.

MY DEAR MRS. BURT,

I Receved your very kind Letter this morning, & am surprised to hear my poor dear grandmother can be in want, as I left her *thirty pound* when I Left england, besides tea, sugar, & several things, & it is now five weeks since I wrote to a friend of ours, &, endeed, a relation of my husband's, † to send twenty pounds more, so that my Grandmother must have had it on cristmas day, you may be sure I shou'd never neglect that dear tender parent, who I have the greatest obligations to, & she must have been cheated or she never cou'd be in want; but you did very Right, my dearest friend, to send her the four Guines, which I will send you with enterest & a thousand thanks; endeed I Love you dearly, my dear Mrs. Burt, and I think with pleasure on those happy days I have pass'd in your Company. I onely wait for an answer from our friend with the account of my grandmother's having Receved her twenty pounds, and I will then send you an order on him for your money, & I send a piece of Silk to make you a Gown. We send it in the ship Captain newman, who sails

* The Morrison MSS.   † Mr. Greville.

for england this month, but my next Letter I will send you a bill of Loading. I wrote you a Long Letter Last march, but I am affraid you never got it, which I am sorry for, as their was a Long account of my reception at the Court of naples; endead the Queen has been so Kind to me I cannot express to you, she as often invited me to Court, & her magesty & nobility treats me with the most kind and affectionate regard. I am the happiest woman in the world; my husband is the best & most tender of husbands, & treats me & my mother with such goodness & tenderness; endeed I love him dearly. If I cou'd have my dear grandmother with me how happy I shou'd be; but god's will be done, she shall never want, & if she shou'd wish for any thing over above what I have sent, Let her have it, & I will repay you with entrest & thanks. You see, my dear Mrs. Burt, in a year & 2 months she will have had fifty pounds, theirfore I have nothing to Lay to my charge. I write to Mrs. Thomas, who lives on the spot,* & who I hope will see she is kindly used. I enclose this in a friend's Letter to save you the postage, which is very dear. I will write to you as soon as we have Receved the answer that the twenty pounds are receved, & I then will say more about Mr. Connor. My dear mother desires her best Love to you & your Brother, & pray present my Compliments to him, & when you write to Mitchell say every thing that's kind from us to him. Miss Dodsworth—Mrs. Greffor now—is brought to bed, & the King was Godfather, & made her a present of a Gold watch set in pearls, twelve Sylver Candlesticks, & Sylver tea board, & Sylver Coffey pot, Suger Basen, &c., &c. She is a very good wife, and Mr. Greffor is a good man, & the King is very fond of him. When the Court is at Caserta we go with them, and I see Mrs. Greffor often. Sir William is now on a shooting party with the King. The Queen is at Caserta, & our family is now there, we onely Come to naples for a few days. I am now at Caserta; we have a good many english with us, the duchess of ancaster, Lord & Lady cholmondly, Lady plymouth, Lady webster, Lady Forbes, &c., &c., they all dined with me yesterday. I expect Sir William home to-night. God bless you, my dear Mrs. Burt, and thank you for all your goodness. Write soon, & believe me your ever true and affectionate friend, Emma Hamilton.

Direct—For Lady Hamilton, at Naples.

Mrs. Burt had been the intimate friend of Emma's mother, and, at her

* Mrs. Thomas, her old mistress, at Hawarden.

request, she conducted Emma up to London on her first journey; but, despite the intimacy, we may infer, from the way in which Lady Hamilton alludes to Mr. Greville, that Mrs. Burt was not aware of his former relations with her. Nor was her grandmother the only recipient of her unbounded generosity. Her uncle, Thomas Kidd, who had been in the employment of Mr. Hancock, colliery proprietor, at Hawarden, as labourer on the tramway used for the coal wagons, retired from work, from disinclination to exert himself, before he was by any means a very old man. In consequence of his near relationship to her dear mother, Lady Hamilton made her uncle an allowance of 10s. a week, which was supplemented by his old master and distant relative, Mr. Hancock. On his withdrawal from active service, he bestowed himself on Richard Reynolds, his nephew, spending his little income on everything but board and lodging. Lazy and idle, he would go out into a croft behind the house, and lie on his back in the sun until its scorching rays peeled the skin off his face. Hearing that he had burdened Richard Reynolds, and made no effort to recoup him, Lady Hamilton sent her cousin Richard £20, saying "it must be the last, for if she supplied all the wants of her needy relatives, it would absorb all Sir William's income."

CHAPTER X.

THE QUEEN OF NAPLES ADMITS LADY HAMILTON TO CLOSE FRIENDSHIP. SHE FINDS HER PIN MONEY TOO LIMITED FOR HER REQUIREMENTS. HER RECEPTIONS AT THE EMBASSY.

LADY Hamilton's affectionate disposition was sorely tried by the serious illness of her indulgent husband, and though she expressed herself as overcome with anxiety, apprehension and fatigue, she adds, that she felt fatigue in the lesser proportion. Her ideas are beautifully put forth as considering herself too happy; and she wisely saw the chastening hand which taught her not to place dependence on happiness as imperishable.

In June, 1793, we find her writing from Caserta to her quondam friend, Greville, giving an insight into the court-life at Caserta, and the familiar footing on which she was received by the King and Queen of Naples. Her letters are invaluable social records, and the intelligible easy flow of thought is wonderful in a woman whose early years were neglected.

CASERTA, *June 2nd*, 1793.

I should have answered your kind letter sooner, but I have not had time to write to any of my friends these five months, which I am sorry for, as they may accuse me of ingratitude, which if they do, it will be a wrong accusition, for I litterally have been so busy with the english, & the Court, & my home duties as to prevent me doing things I had much at heart to do.

for political reasons we have lived eight months at Caserta, that is, making this our constant residence, & going twice a week to town to give dinners, Balls, &c., &c., &c., returning here at 2 or 3 o'clock in the morning, after the fatigue of a dinner of fifty, & ball & supper of 3 hundred. Then to dress early in the morning to go to Court to dinner at twelve o'clock, as the Royal family dine early, & the have done Sir W^{m.} & me the honner to invite us very, very often. Our house at Caserta as been like an inn this winter, as we have had partys that have come either to see the

environs or have been invited to Court. We have had the Duchess of
Ancaster several days. It is but 3 days since the Devonshire familly as
left us, & we had fifty in familly for four days at Caserta. 'Tis true we
dined every day at Court, or at some Casino of the King's, for you cannot
imagine how good the King & Queen as been to the principal english who
have been here, especially to Lord & Ly. Palmerston, Cholmondleys, Ly.
Spencer, Ly. Besborough, Ly. Plymouth, & Sir J. & Lady Webster, and I
have carried the ladies to the Queen very often, as she as permitted me to
go to her very often in private, which I do; and the reason why we stay
now here is, that I have promised the Queen to remain here as long as she
does, which will be till the tenth of July. In the evenings I go to her, and
we are *tête-à-tête* 2 or 3 hours. Sometimes we sing. Yesterday the King &
me sung duetts for 3 hours. *It was but bad, as he sings like a king*. To-day
the Princess Royal of Sweden comes to Court to take leave of their
Majesties. Sir W. & me are invited to dinner. She is an amiable
Princess, & as lived very much with us. We have given her several
dinners, balls, &c., for she loves dancing dearly. The other ministers'
wives have not shew'd her the least attention, because she did not pay
them the first visit, as she travels under the name of Countess of Wasa.
In consequence, the Queen as not asked them to dinner to-day, & her M^y.
told me I had done very well in waiting on her R.H. the moment she
arrived. However, the ministers' wives are very fond of me, as the see I
have no pretentions, nor do I abuse of her Majesty's goodness, as she
observed the other night at Court, at Naples. We had a drawingroom in
honner of the Empress having brought a son. I had been with the Queen
the night before *alone, en famille*, laughing, singing, &c., &c.; but at the
drawingroom I kept my distance, & paid the Queen as much respect as
tho' I had never seen her before, which pleased her much; but she shew'd
me great distinction that night, & told me several times how she admired
my good conduct; & I only tell you this to show & convince you I shall
never change, but allways be simple & natural. You may immagine how
happy my dear, dear Sir William is, & I can assure you if ever I had any
little teasing caprice, it is so intirely gone that neither Sir William nor me
remembers it, and he will tell you the same. Endead, you cannot imagine
our happiness—it is not to be described. We are not an hour in the day
seperete. We live more like lovers than husband & wife, *as husbands &
wives go now a days*. Good Lord deliver me! and the english are getting as
bad as the italians, & some few excepted. I study very hard, & have made

great progress in French & musick, & I have had all my songs set for the violo, that Sir William may accompany me, which as pleased him much; so that we now study together. The english garden is going on very fast. The King & Queen go there every day. Sir W^{m.} & me are there every morning, at seven o'clock; sometimes dine there, & allways drink tea— in short, it is *Sir W^{m.'s} favorite child*, & boath him & me are now studying botany—but not to make ourselves pedantical prigs to show our learning, like some of our traveling neighbors, but for our own pleasure, . . ."

The intimacy between the Queen of Naples and Lady Hamilton daily increased. According to Sir Nathaniel Wraxall, they dressed in the same colours, and Lady Hamilton had the *entrée* at all times, unannounced. In the autumn of the next year, her ladyship sat down to congratulate Mr. Greville on his appointment to the Vice-Chamberlainship. In the opening of her letter it is amusing to note the mistake she makes in her reading of the man's character. Capable of great self-control when required to play a part to serve his ends, his obsequious fawning on his uncle, and plausible fidelity in executing commands by which he lost nothing, were merely undertaken to secure for himself a sure and firm standing in the dead man's shoes. The day came when Emma knew him at his just worth.

CASTELLAMARE, Sept^{bre} 16th. 1794.

I congratulate you, my dear Mr. Greville, with all my heart, on your appointment to the Vice chamberlainship; you have merited it, and all your friends must be happy at a change so favorable, not only for your pecuniary circumstances, as for the honner of the situation. May you long enjoy it, with every happiness that you deserve, *& I speak from my heart.* I don't know a better, honester, or more aimable worthy man than yourself, and it is a great deel for me to say, for whatever I think, I am not apt to pay compliments.

My dear Sir William as had the disorder that we & all Naples have had since the eruption, a violent diarea, that reduced him to so very low an ebb that I was very much alarmed for him, notwithstanding I thought I shou'd have gone with him; but, thank God, we are here as happy as possible in the Queen's palace, enjoying every comfort & happiness that good health, *Royall favour, & domestic happiness* can give us. So much so, the

* The Morrison MSS.

HER LIMITED PIN MONEY.

other day, the aniversary of our marriage, Sir W^m told me he loved me better than ever, & had never for one moment repented. Think of my feelings in that moment, when I could with truth say the same to him. I gave here that day a little fête. Lord and Lady Plymouth, &c., &c., came down here, and I never saw Sir William nor never was so happy myself. I tell you this because I know you will rejoice at it. I will write soon, and send to you to settle with Mrs. Hackwood, but all the things were spoilt, and I had no right to pay for them, but I will setle it, and pray go and tell her so. For the other affair, I will write to you fully, & as this is a letter of congratulation, nothing shall disturb our happy ideas. I wish you could send me an english riding hat, very fashionable, but I desire you to put it to Sir W^m.'s account. We have company to-day from Naples, & I cannot write more than that I am, my dear Mr. Greville, ever sincere & affectionate friend,

EMMA HAMILTON.

P.S.—Mother's love to you. She is the comfort of our lives, and is our housekeeper. Sir W^m doats on her. Give my love to the Col.

R^t Honb^le Chas. Greville, London.*

In gratitude for services as housekeeper and nurse, Sir William subsequently left Mrs. Cadogan an annuity of £100 per annum. The English ladies, either resident or *en passant*, always remembered in a kind way her motherly offices to them, and spoke of her as an unassuming old body, making each one comfortable in an unobtrusive way. Sir William made his wife an allowance of £200 a year for pin-money, to cover the cost of dress for herself and mother, charities, and any other monetary outlets. Not too large a supply of pocket-money where there were so many demands on it. In fact, she admits as much in the letter which will be given later. The records of her personal purchases are very simple, and her wants most modest for the wife of an ambassador. Her dress was more noticeable for its simplicity than its magnificence. If extravagance could ever be laid at her door it was under the form of hospitable entertainment. Seeing that she was kept so short of funds, where was the opportunity to lay up the nest-egg for the inevitable future which would deprive her of his support and income? Sir William's expensive tastes in the acquiring of works of art would likewise

* The Morrison MSS.

LADY HAMILTON.

prove a drain on the funds. Her letter is an amusing exposition of the difficulty she found in making ends meet.

CASERTA, Dec^{br} 19, 1794.

I have only time to write you a few lines by the Neapolitan Corriero, who will give you this; he comes back soon, & pray send me by him some Ribbands & fourteen yards of fine muslin work'd for a gownd, or fine leno; ask any lady what leno is, and she will tell you; & pray pay Hackwood's & put it down to Sir William's account with his banker. He told me I might, for I have so many occasions to spend my money that my 2 hundred pounds will scarcely do for me; a constant attendance at Court, now once & generally twice a day, and I must be well dress'd; you know how far 2 hundred will go. To-day we expect the prince Augustus from Rome, he is to be lodged in the Pallace here, & with us in town to-morrow. We have a great dinner at Court for the Prince, the Queen invited me last night herself, & I carried Lord Bristol to her, & we pass'd four hours in an enchantment. No person can be so charming as the Queen, she is everything one can wish, the best mother, wife, and friend, in the world. I live constantly with her, & have done so, intimately, for 2 years, & I never have in all that time seen any thing but goodness and sincerity in her; and if ever you hear any Lyes about her, contradict them; and if you should see a cursed book, written by a vile French dog, with her character in it, don't believe one word. She sent it me last night, and I have been reading the infamous calomny, & put myself quite out of humer that so good & virtus a princess should be so infamously described.

Lord Bristol * is with us at Caserta. He passes one week at Naples, & one with us. He is very fond of me, and very kind. He is very entertaining, & dashes at everything, nor does he mind King or Queen when he is inclined to show his talents. I am now taking lessons from Willico, & make a great progress, nor do I slacken in any of my study's. We have been here three months, & remain 4 or 5 months longer. We go to Naples every now and then. I ride on horseback. The Queen has had the goodness to supply me with horses, an equery, & her own servant in livery, every day; in short, if I was her daughter she cou'd not be kinder to me. I love her with my whole heart. My dear Sir William is very well, & as fond of me as ever, & I am, as women generally are, ten thousand times fonder of him than I was, & you would be delighted to see how happy we

---

* Lord Bristol was the third of the three sons of "sweet Molly Lepel."

are; no quarrelling, nor crossness, nor caprices. All nonsense is at an end, & every body that sees us are edified by our example of congugel & domestick felicity. Will you ever come & see us? You shall be received with kindness from us boath, for we have boath obligations to you for having made us acquainted with each other. Excuse the haist with which I write, for we are going to Capua to meet the Prince Augustus. Do send me a plan how I could situate poor Little Emma, poor thing, for I wish it.

E. HAMILTON.*

The Lord Bristol, to whom allusion is made in the foregoing, was Earl of Bristol, one of the many persons of distinction by whom they were surrounded, a man brimful of eccentric humour. He was Lord Spiritual as well as Lord Temporal, for besides holding his peerage he was Protestant Bishop of Derry. One day, being wishful to see over the Monastery of the Grande Chartreuse, he applied, but at an inconvenient hour, for the Society were at dinner. On the porter informing him that no one could be admitted while the brotherhood were at meals, he handed in a letter to the abbot from a neighbouring Roman Catholic bishop, who had given him the letter of introduction, wherein, out of courtesy, he alluded to his lordship as "his brother, the Bishop of Derry," albeit their tenets of faith disagreed. Immediately the introduction was delivered, the doors flew open, and the whole body of monks advanced to meet him, falling down on their knees for his blessing, which he, without undeceiving them, gravely bestowed. The brethren were ignorant where Derry was located, and, relying on the fraternal testimonial, thought he was a Roman Catholic bishop. When the monks were better informed, they doubted the efficacy of his benedictions. He was overburdened with fun, and an ardent admirer of Emma, to whom he dedicated many poetic effusions, one of which runs thus:—

> Ah, Emma, who 'd ever be wise
> If madness be loving of thee.

Mr. Greville would seem not to have troubled himself to execute the little commissions Lady Hamilton required, for we find her reproaching him with the omission in a letter of April 19, 1795 :—†

You never answered my letter by the last courier, nor sent what I

* The Morrison MSS.   † Ibid.

wanted, so I will not trouble you with any more commissions, but try to find out somebody else *who will be more attentive to me*. My ever dear Queen as been like a mother to me since Sir William as been ill. She writes to me four & five times a day, & offered to come & assist me. This is friendship. I have seen letters that the King of england is not pleased with this Court & Sir William, because they did not leave Castilescala with them. Sir W^{m.} did all he could, and he does not care wether they are pleased, as they must be very ungrateful to a minister like him that as done so much to keep up good harmony between the 2 Courts, & as done more business in one day than another wou'd in ten, owing to the friendly footing he is on here with their Majesties & Ministers, so if they are out of humer, they may be; but between you & me I have spoke a great deal to the Queen about the consequence it is to them to have a person of Castilescala's abilitys, & being beloved in England, there; & I believe he will return, from a letter I had from the Queen this morning; & yesterday she said they wou'd do their utmost; but I can assure you Sir W^{m.} did all he cou'd to have him kept in England, so don't let them blame the best & most worthy man living, for they have no minister like him.

I have had Lady Bath with me here 2 days. I carried her to the Queen. She is very shy, but she took a great fancy to me, as I put her at her ease, & did the honners of a Ball for her that she gave at Naples. She envited all the Neapolitan ladies of the first distinction, & I was to present them; & she took a nervous fit, & wou'd not come out of her room for 3 hours. At last I got her out, & brought her into the room between me & Lady Berwick; & I carried the ladies, who were dancing, one by one to her in a corner, & she took such a liking that we are very great friends. Sir James seems a worthy good man; but Sir W^{m.} says he wou'd not have her with all her money. However, I like her, for I think she as a great deal of good about her. You was to have married her, I think I heard. However, the Queen was very civil to her, as she is to every body I carry to her.

I have had a very bad billious fever this winter—near dying—but it was owing to fatigue when Prince Augustus was with us, dancing, supping, &c., &c. Send me some news, political & private; for, against my will, *owing to my situation here*, I am got into politicks, & I wish to have news for our dear, much loved Queen, whom I adore. Nor can I live without her, for she is to me a mother, friend, & everything. If you cou'd know her as I do, how you would adore her, for she is the first woman in the world. Her

SHE TRIES TO HELP A FRIEND.

talents are superior to every woman in the world, & her heart is the most excellent, & strictly good & upright; but you say it is because we are such friends that I am so partial, but ask every body that knows her. She loves england, & attached to our ministers; & wishes the continuation of the war as the only means to ruin that abominable french consul.*

Her next letter to Mr. Greville was written by the desire of her husband, who lay in bed suffering under an attack of bilious fever. He requested Mr. Greville to make apologies to the King, through his brother, the Hon. Robert Fulke Greville, and to explain that his indisposition prevented his writing personally; that, under existing political circumstances, he would not trust his secretary, but would himself communicate when his health would allow him. As a postscript, she requests him to forward her a few modest purchases by the courier on his return to Italy. " Pray send me by this courrier 2 or 3 pieces of the finest sprig'd muslin for gownds, & twelve fine muslin handkerchiefs, & 2 pieces of plain clear muslin. Don't fail, for I want them. Put them down to Sir $W^{m.'}$ account with Ross & Ogilvy. Excuse this haist, as I don't leave my dear Sir William's room a moment."

These letters were quickly followed by another, its tenour being to endeavour to obtain a vacant post for a necessitous friend. With her invariable promptitude, she sent private intimation of its having become void, urging a speedy application before it could truthfully be retorted that the situation was given away, as she was urging the request before the news of the vacancy would reach official quarters.

CASINO MERALA, SOTTO, St. ELMO,
SATURDAY, 16th of May, 1795.

DEAR SIR,

I have only time to say 2 words is the courrier is going of. Sir James Douglas died yesterday, & Macauley thinks there is a possibility of his getting the Consulship with enterest, which would set his affairs a little to right. If it is possible, do help him by speaking to somebody in power. Do you know Lord Grenville? 2 words to him would do, & they cannot make an excuse that it is given away, as they don't know of poor Sir James' death, so pray do your utmost, for I wish of all things that poor Macauley may get it; and do, for God's sake, pay Mrs. Hackwood my

* Napoleon.

debt. I wrote to you in Jany last to beg of you to do so, yet I am afraid my letters never got to you. Get the money from Ross & Ogilvy, & let it be done immediately, though she does not deserve it, as the things were all spoilt, & I never cou'd make use of any one thing.

We go to-morrow to Caserta for ten days, as the Queen has beg'd to see me. Sir W^m as not as yet seen their Majesty's since his illness, therefore to-morrow we dine at Actons', & go to Court in the evening, were Sir W^m. will be received with open arms by all. This air as done him a great deal of good, and he is better than he as been for some years. The Queen as offered me to go to her Pallace of Castellamare, which I believe we shall in the summer; in short, we are so happy. Our situation here is very flattering in the public character, and in private we are models for all husbands and wives. This will give you pleasure I am sure. Remember me to the Col., tho' he never thinks of me. Is the Princess of Wales handsome? How can red hair be handsome? . . .*

The colonel, to whom she so often wishes to be remembered, is her nephew by marriage, Robert Fulke Greville, brother of her heedless deputy, who gave her so much anxiety over Mrs. Hackwood's unpaid account; in fact, in a letter dated September 21, 1795, we find the commission still unexecuted—her own blind good nature could not realise unwillingness in others. We read in the same letter the first allusion to approaching troubles, and she speaks of her own indisposition resulting from want of rest. The best of everything loses its savour in course of time, and the energetic woman expresses her weariness of Court gaieties.

We have not time to write to you, as we have been 3 days & nights waiting to send by this Courier letters of *consequence* for our Government. They ought to be gratefull to Sir William & *myself* in *particular*, as my situation at this Court is very *extraordinary*, & what no person as as yet arrived at; but one as no thanks, & I am allmost sick of grandeur. We are tired to death with anxiety, & God knows were we shall soon be, & what will become of us if things go on as they do now. Sir W^m. is *very* well, I am not; but hope when the cold wether comes on, & we go to Caserta, I shall be better. Our house, breakfast, dinner, & supper is like a fair, and what with attendance on my adorable Queen, I have not one moment for writing or anything comfortable, I, however, hope soon to get

* The Morrison MSS.

quiet, & I then will write you fully. Pray settle Hackwood's account, Sir W^m desires it, & send me by the bearer a Dunstable hat & some ribbands, or what you think will be acceptable. Pray do you never think on me? He is our courrier, so pray do not spare him. In haist, ever your sincere

EMMA HAMILTON.

I have now to-night an assembly of 3 hundred waiting.

It was due to the intimacy between the Queen of Naples and Lady Hamilton that her ladyship obtained, in 1796, an insight into the letter of the King of Spain, declaring his intention to make war against England, and desert the allies. Fully alive to the danger this meant to the British nation, she took a verbatim copy of the document, and, to ensure its safe delivery, despatched it to the English Minister in London by a courier, herself defraying all expenses, which Government never recouped. Thanks to her step, forewarned was forearmed; and instructions were accordingly sent to Sir John Jervis to strike a stroke, if he found the opportunity, against either the arsenals or fleets of Spain.

CHAPTER XI.

NELSON—HIS BOYHOOD; HE TAKES TO THE SEA; HIS YOUTHFUL LOVE AFFAIRS; HIS MARRIAGE.

THE next year brought the British fleet into the vicinity of Naples; and at this point Lord Nelson, who will play a prominent part in the story, must be introduced.

About a couple of miles from Burnham Market Station lies a village named Burnham Thorpe. In the year 1755, the Rev. Edmund Nelson (who for eight

BURNHAM THORPE RECTORY, THE BIRTHPLACE OF LORD NELSON.

years previously had held the rectory of Hillborough) was instituted to the rectory of Burnham Thorpe, on the presentation of Horace Walpole. The wife of the Rev. Edmund Nelson was Catherine, daughter of Dr. Suckling, prebendary of Westminster and rector of Woodton, Norfolk. Her grandmother had been sister to Robert Walpole, first Earl of Orford, and it was owing to Mrs. Nelson's connection with the house of Walpole that her

NELSON'S BOYHOOD.

husband received the benefice of Burnham Thorpe. The old rectory nestled at the foot of a rising ground, environed by aged elms and beeches, and in close proximity babbled a brooklet spanned by a piece of timber as a foot-bridge. The way from the rectory to the church was over this brook and across a meadow, until a narrow lane was reached which ran parallel with the village street. There was no roadway to the sacred edifice, which stood on a slightly elevated ground, almost surrounded by trees, behind some farm buildings belonging to an old moated manor house. An ordinary field gate, with a stile adjoining, gave admission to the footpath, which lay along a good stretch of grassy upland, flanked at one spot by clumps of aged thorns, leading to the churchyard, confined within crumbling walls. For forty-six years the Rev. Edmund Nelson was the respected rector of the church, and on the 29th day of September, in the year 1758, was born unto him his sixth child and fifth son, the future Admiral Horatio Nelson, the entry of whose birth appears in the parish register as follows:—" Horatio, son of Edmund and Catherine Nelson, born September 29th, baptised October 9th, priv., pub., November 15th, Rector, Edmund Nelson." The fragile condition of the infant necessitated immediate baptism, and the certificate shows that the child was privately baptised on October 9th, and publicly received into the Church on November 15th. His sponsors were Horatio, second Lord Walpole, of Wolferton, the Rev. Dr. Hamond, and Mrs. Joyce Pyle. His noble godfather's christian name was given to him at the font.

As the little lad advanced in years, he received his early education from a schoolmaster named Noakes, of Downham, at which time the embryo admiral wore a green coat, and not unfrequently employed his schoolmates to send a stream of water from the pump on the market place, on which he floated paper boats. In his young days, he once engaged in a trial of strength with a lad named Fish, on the margin of the aforesaid brook, which was much wider and deeper than at present. The result of the tug-of-war was to the disadvantage of young Nelson, who was ignominiously cast into the water. As a youth, he was exceedingly generous, kind-hearted, and tenderly affectionate, with special care for dumb animals. Going one day on an errand to the shoemaker's, he accidentally jammed a pet lamb between the doorpost and the door. He wept with distress when he found he had occasioned pain to the little creature.

When Nelson was between nine and eleven years of age, he twice accompanied his father to church, to act as witness to marriages. The first occasion on which he thus signed his name, he did so in a carefully-rounded, schoolboy hand; but on the second time he put a little more dash into it, and wrongly subscribed his christian name, for he wrote "Horace Nelson," thus showing that he was more frequently called Horace than Horatio by his relatives. The precise rector, however, corrected the error, for in the register the "ce" is erased, and "tio" written above in the big characters which mark the father's caligraphy.

An anecdote is told of Nelson's school days which gives a forecast of the high sense of honour which pervaded his whole career. He and his brother, William, had set off for school on their ponies, but finding that a great deal of snow had fallen, they returned home. William told his father that the snow was too deep for them to venture. The father replied that if such were the case they need not go, "but," he added, "make another attempt. I will leave it to your honour." The boys accordingly started again, meeting with many difficulties which might have afforded excuse for returning home, but to the remonstrances of William the younger boy replied: "We have no excuse; remember, brother, it was left to our honour." Nothing he liked better than the performance of any act that entailed an amount of risk or enterprise. One Christmas Eve he laid a wager that, despite a snowstorm that was raging, he would go within a given time from the rectory to the churchyard and back again, bearing evidence of the accomplishment of his task by bringing a sprig from a low, bushy yew tree (which yet stands and bears berry) that grew on the south side of the church near the tower. The distant churchyard and dreary surroundings far from the road have already been described. As the time in which he ought to have returned was far exceeded, his relatives grew anxious, and went in search of him. It was well that they did so, for he had sunk into deep snow, and had he not been rescued he would have lost his life.

When Horatio was only nine years old, he sustained an irreparable loss in the death of his good mother, which occurred in the year 1767. Her remains were interred in the chancel of the church at Burnham Thorpe. This estimable lady had been the mother of eleven children, eight of whom were living at the period of her decease. This sad occurrence was the occasion of the recall home of Horatio, who was pursuing his studies at the High School, at Norwich, under the supervision of the Rev. Mr. Symonds, then Head Master.

NELSON TAKES TO THE SEA.

After a year's residence at home, young Nelson was sent to the Paston Grammar School, at North Walsham. In the garden of the master, the Rev. Mr. Jones, there grew some remarkably fine pears, for which every boy naturally craved; but none was sufficiently venturesome to attempt to secure them; seeing which, Horatio Nelson, then about eleven years of age, volunteered to brave the danger and obtain them. Therefore, one night he was lowered from the window of his dormitory, by means of sheets tied together, and, at considerable personal risk, he returned with the coveted fruit. He had achieved the feat merely because no other would undertake it, and divided the spoil among his schoolfellows, reserving none for himself, saying he had only taken them because everyone else was afraid. Great was the indignation of Mr. Jones when he missed his fruit, on which he set great store; so much so, that he offered a reward of five guineas for information that would convict the culprit. But the delinquents duly recognised the honour which is proverbial among thieves, and refused to betray their confederate. The limited income of the country rector prohibited a prolonged course of education for Horatio, and after a couple of years he was once more recalled home to Burnham Thorpe, the centre of his affection in later days, where, on his return from sea, he would sit beneath the beech and elm trees, in company with his father, in the rectory garden. Alas! not a vestige of the old home or its appurtenances remains—save the pump!

The lad's wishes now turned seaward, and, to further his views, he applied to his uncle, Maurice Suckling, R.N. In his influential position he yielded to the desires of his nephew—albeit he feared the delicacy of his constitution would prohibit a nautical career; however, he granted him a berth in his own ship, and gave him his start in life. A sailor was sent to convey him to the vessel. On his arrival his uncle was absent, and the unknown boy remained a whole day and night on deck without anyone addressing a word to him. To the close of his life he remembered those hours of lonely anguish and the cruel reception. His age at that time was only twelve years. His, early experience caused him to be particularly considerate to his young midshipmen as they first arrived on his vessels.

The first voyage was an expedition to the North Pole. On his return to England he passed a brilliant examination, and was promoted to the rank of lieutenant in the Royal Navy. He then took part against the Spanish colonies, and was prominent in the defence of Jamaica against the French fleet. Bivouacing one day in the forests of Peru, to give the handful of men he commanded time to dress their wounds and bury their dead, he fell asleep at the foot of a tree. An enormous serpent glided under his cloak, coiled itself round his leg, and stung him in the foot. The antidotes supplied by the Indians saved his life, but his constitution retained permanent symptoms of the mortal poison. Admiral Cornwallis brought him back to England, nursing him with the care of a parent more than of a commander. His health reinstated, he sailed next year for Quebec, and here he nearly allowed a fleeting passion to wreck his career. Having become enamoured of a beautiful Canadian girl of inferior rank to himself, he was on the point of quitting the service and marrying her when the squadron received orders to return to Europe. His officers, vexed at his foolishness, carried him off by force, and so saved him committing himself and blighting his splendid prospects. At the conclusion of the American war, in 1783, Nelson returned home in command of the "Albemarle" frigate. On his arrival in England he was paid off. He deemed it prudent to economise on his half-pay, and therefore crossed to France, taking lodgings at St. Omer's, where, however, he remained long enough to fall in love with the daughter of an English clergyman, a Miss Andrews, on whose beauty and accomplishments he was never weary of expatiating. His limited income prohibited the expenses attached to a matrimonial alliance, for he felt he could not provide an establishment suitable to his professional rank and the lady's position; he, therefore, made an appeal to his worthy uncle, William Suckling, Esq., laying his case before him in these terms:—

Jan. 14, 1784.

MY DEAR UNCLE,

There arrives a time in a man's life (who has friends) that either they place him in life in a situation that makes his application for anything further totally unnecessary, or give him help in a pecuniary way if they can afford and he deserves it. The critical moment of my life has now arrived, that either I am to be happy or miserable—it depends solely upon you. You may possibly think I am going to ask too much. I have led myself up with hopes you will not—till this trying moment. There is a lady I have seen of good family and connections, but with a small fortune, I understand. The whole of my income does not exceed £130 per annum. Now I must come to the point. Will you, if I should marry, allow me yearly £100 until my income is increased to that sum either by employment or any other way. A very few years I hope would turn something up if my friends will but exert themselves. If you will not give me the above sum, will you exert yourself with either Lord North or Mr. Jenkinson to get me a guardship, or some employment in a public office where the attendance of the principal is not necessary, and of which they must have such numbers to dispose of. In the Indian Service I understand (if it remains under the Directors) their marine force is to be under the command of a Captain in the Royal Navy—that is a station I should like. You must excuse the freedom with which this letter is dictated: not to have been plain and explicit in my distress had been cruel to myself. If nothing can be done for me I know what I have to trust to. Life is not worth preserving without happiness, and I care not where I may linger out a miserable existence. I am prepared to hear your refusal, and have fixed my resolution if that should happen; but in every situation I shall be a well-wisher to you and all your family, and pray they or you may never know the pangs which at this moment tear my heart. God bless you, and assure yourself I am,

Your most affectionate and dutiful nephew,
HORATIO NELSON.

This uncle, William Suckling, was Chairman of the Board of Customs at this time, and he immediately fell in with the young lover's request, and indulgently increased his income by the gift of £100 per annum. But for some cause he did not marry the lady for whom he ventured so much, and in consequence he became so depressed and low-spirited that another uncle, the Captain Maurice Suckling before mentioned, who held the post of Comptroller of the Navy, obtained from the first Lord of the Admiralty the appointment to the "Boreas," of 28 guns, on the Leeward Island Station, by which step he was aroused and diverted to better things. He sailed away to meet his matrimonial fate at Nevis, one of the West India islands. After Nelson's death, Lady Hughes (whom he had taken to the West Indies in that voyage of 1784) wrote some pleasing reminiscences to his brother-in-law, Mr. Bolton, regarding his care of and goodness to the lads who sailed under him. Thus she expressed herself: "It may reasonably be supposed that among the number of thirty there must be timid as well as bold. The timid he never rebuked, but always wished to shew them he desired nothing of them that he would not instantly do himself; and

I have known him say: 'Well, sir, I am going a race to the masthead, and beg I may meet you there.' No denial could be given to such a wish, and the poor fellow instantly began his march. His lordship never took the least notice with what alacrity it was done, but when he met in the top began speaking in the most cheerful manner, and saying how much a person was to be pitied that could fancy there was any danger or even anything disagreeable in the attempt. After this the timid youth led another, and rehearsed his captain's words. How wise and kind was such a proceeding! In like manner he went every day into the schoolroom, and saw them do their nautical exercises, and at twelve o'clock he was the first upon deck with his quadrant"—what an excellent example of punctuality for the youngsters. Nelson himself saw to the proper provisioning of his vessels consistent with economy, and studied the health of all under his command. His hour for rising was four or five o'clock, and for retiring ten o'clock. He breakfasted never later than six, and during the middle watch he would send to invite the lads to breakfast with him when relieved. At table he would enter into their boyish jokes, and be the most youthful of the party. He invariably allowed some of them to accompany him, even on visits of ceremony. At dinner he invited in turn every officer of the ship, treating them with polite hospitality. Like all great men, Nelson had a keen appreciation of the value of time; and whatever work he undertook to do was done heartily. When Dr. Scott became his translator of the foreign letters, which fell into Nelson's hands in the prizes taken in battle, the doctor would grow weary of his work, while his chief laboured on incessantly; they both occupied arm chairs having deep pockets, into which the assistant would thrust a parcel of unopened letters, for he was unable to cope in his powers of endurance with Nelson, who would not have ceased his work until he thought he had inspected every document.

Lady Hughes was wife of the Commander-in-Chief of the Leeward Islands. The cost of the escort of this lady and her *suite* upon Captain Nelson might be named at a pretty high figure, but the lady's sense of obligation was limited to the presentation of a silver ladle for a tea caddy!

Soon after his arrival at his station, he formed an attachment to a young widow, the niece of the President of Nevis. She had lost both parents at a tender age, from which time her uncle had undertaken the charge of her. Her name was Frances Herbert Woodward. She became the wife of a physician of Nevis, of Scotch descent, who had formerly practised as an apothecary at Coventry—a Dr. Nisbet—who died eighteen months after marriage, leaving her with a little son called Josiah.

Finding his admiration of the young widow reciprocated, he again appealed to his indulgent uncle, William Suckling, for the means to enable him to ask for the lady's hand, saying that his doing so would make a couple happy who would pray for him for ever. "Don't disappoint me," he pleads, "or my heart will break." Again the generosity of the uncle was bestowed upon the ardent lover. On March 11, 1787, the marriage took place in Figtree Church, Nevis. The Duke of Clarence, afterwards William the Fourth, was then sailing under Nelson's orders as Captain of the "Pegasus," and honoured the ceremony with his presence; himself giving the bride away by his own special desire. The Duke ever retained a pleasing memory of that period of service.

Ten days after the wedding the elated and happy bridegroom wrote to a friend, Captain Lockyer, "I am married to an amiable woman, that far makes amends for everything. Indeed, until I married her, I never knew happiness; and I am morally certain she will continue to make me a happy man all the rest of my days."

CHAPTER XII.

NELSON'S INTRODUCTION TO LADY HAMILTON. SHE USES HER INFLUENCE WITH THE QUEEN OF NAPLES IN THE INTEREST OF THE BRITISH FLEET. THE BATTLE OF THE NILE.

IN the July of the same year, the newly-married couple returned to England, and when the "Boreas" was paid off in November, Nelson and his wife settled at Burnham Thorpe. Here he devoted his time to rustic sports, in which he was anything but an adept; indeed, when he killed a partridge, his friends considered it a remarkable occurrence. Shooting, as he practised it, was ominous to those in his vicinity, for he carried his gun at full cock, and whenever a bird arose, he let fly without putting the fowling piece to his shoulder. During his five years' retirement on half pay, he gave much attention to his kitchen garden, and exercised himself with his spade, digging as hard as any paid gardener. At other times he would go bird-nesting with his wife as companion. Still his heart was out at sea, and he longed to win fresh laurels. He made frequent applications for a ship, and though the Duke of Clarence supported him by his recommendation to Lord Chatham, no regard was paid to his desires until the year 1793, when he was appointed to the "Agamemnon," and sailed for the Mediterranean to join Lord Hood. It is not necessary for this story to follow minutely the naval career of Lord Nelson, which does not bear directly on the narrative. On July 12, 1794, he received an injury to his eye from a shot scattering some sand into it during an attack on San Francisco. After much suffering, he lost the use of that eye.

His crew on the "Agamemnon" was partly composed of men from his native place, whom he had imbued with the same ardent wish to serve their country that was so deeply embedded within his own breast.

One other engagement must be mentioned, for in an attack on Santa Cruz, Teneriffe, in 1797, he was wounded in the right elbow by a shot. His life was providentially saved by his stepson, Josiah, who had accompanied him. On this disastrous night the Admiral received his wound soon after the detachment had landed. The shock caused him to fall to the ground, where, for some minutes, he was left to himself, until Mr. Nisbet, missing him, had the presence of mind to return. After some search in the dark, he found his brave stepfather lying in his blood, with his arm shattered, and apparently lifeless. Young Nisbet applied his handkerchief as a tourniquet to the Admiral's arm, and carried him on his back to the beach, where he obtained the assistance of some sailors, and got him on board the "Theseus." On laying him in the small boat his stepson placed his hat over the shattered arm, lest the sight of the gushing blood should increase the sufferer's faintness. Had it not been for this young man's presence of mind on this occasion, Nelson must undoubtedly have perished. That night, at ten, the arm was amputated. Immediately after he began his official letter, and finished it by eleven. The next day he wrote to inform his wife, closing with the remark, "I know it will add much to your pleasure in finding that your son, Josiah, under God's providence, was instrumental in saving my life." The painful operation of amputation having been performed in the night, some mistake was made in taking up the arteries, which afterwards caused him most excruciating pains, and he had to return home for advice. The surgeon who performed the operation asked if he should embalm the arm or send it to England to be buried. Nelson answered, "Throw it into the hammock of the brave fellow who fell beside me,"—an ordinary seaman!

In the year 1793, Lady Hamilton had first seen Nelson, on the occasion of his being sent by Lord Hood with despatches to Sir William to obtain troops for Toulon.

The introduction of Nelson to Lady Hamilton was effected by her husband, who, being a man of penetration, had discerned the great promise and ability of the Commodore. Though it was not his custom to invite any of the officers of the fleets to reside at the Embassy, he waived his rule in favor of the new favorite. In giving the necessary instructions he thus addressed his wife—"The Captain I am about to introduce to you is a little man, and far from handsome; but he will live to be a great man. I know it from the talk I have had with him. Let him be put in the room prepared for Prince Augustus (son of George the Third.)" Nelson's first impression of the woman whose life would be so interwoven with his own is contained in a letter to his wife—" Lady Hamilton has been wonderfully kind and good to Josiah (his wife's son). She is a young woman of amiable manners, and who does honor to the station to which she is raised." Lady Hamilton, with her invariable good nature, had been exceedingly kind to Josiah Nisbet, who had accompanied his step-father on the Neapolitan expedition, making much of the young man, driving him about in her handsome carriage, and inviting him to her crowded receptions; Nelson duly recounting to his wife the welcome her son was receiving—which welcome the youth totally ignored in a few months, when he vehemently protested at a public dinner against the too profuse attentions of his step-father to Lady Hamilton, his violent conduct necessitating his removal from the table by his brother officers. His excitement was afterwards condoned on the plea of inebriety.

On June 8, 1798, hearing of the departure of Bonaparte from Toulon, Earl St. Vincent detached Nelson with a squadron to pursue the French fleet. After steering as far as Alexandria, and coming upon no trace of the enemy, greatly to his mortification, he returned to the Italian shores. The French Revolution had a most direful effect upon Naples at this juncture. The Directory, determined to revolutionize Italy, prepared to make an attack upon that country. The English fleet at this point found their store of provisions rapidly diminishing, and their fresh water exhausted. A compact had been entered into between France and Italy that not more than two English men-of-war vessels should be allowed in Italian waters at the same time. If the fleet returned to Gibraltar to re-victual, they would in all probability lose the French ships, therefore Nelson sent a letter by one of his captains (Troubridge) to Sir William Hamilton requesting him to obtain the necessary permission for the fleet to enter the Bay of Naples, or any other Sicilian port, for the purpose of provisioning, &c. This messenger arrived at the Embassy at six o'clock in the morning. Sir William and Lady Hamilton at once arose, and proceeded to the residence of the Minister, Sir John Acton, who convened a council, the King of Naples being present. While this conference was taking place, Lady Hamilton sought the Queen's apartment, her Majesty being still in bed. To her Lady Hamilton explained the position of the English fleet, and urged the Queen to write instructions in accordance with Nelson's request, for she was well aware that any command of Caroline of Naples would be more honoured than that of her feeble-minded husband. At first the royal lady was reluctant to interfere, saying that the King and his ministers would decide in council; but, on the earnest representations of her petitioner that dire calamity would accrue to her kingdom

LADY HAMILTON

HER INFLUENCE BENEFITS THE BRITISH FLEET.

should the result be a refusal, and moved by the supplicating entreaties poured forth by Lady Hamilton, who was kneeling by her bedside, she at last consented. A pen was immediately placed in her hand, and, at the dictation of her clear-headed companion, she wrote the order, directed to all the Governors of the Two Sicilies, "to receive with hospitality the British fleet, to water, victual, and aid them." At eight o'clock the council broke up, and the elated ambassador's wife was summoned to join her husband. From the expression on the faces of the King, Sir John Acton, and Sir William, she quickly learnt that the conclave had ended in failure, and that they felt they could not break the compact with France. She said nothing while the King was present, but on the way home she told the two gentlemen that she had anticipated the result, and provided against it, and to their astonishment and delight she produced the important document. In communicating to Nelson the decision of the council, Sir William Hamilton was proudly desirous that his clever wife should receive all credit for the great feat she had successfully performed; he, therefore, left it to herself to forward the Queen's command; and to signify that the achievement was hers solely, and that as such it should be recognised, he added to his letter: "You will receive from Emma herself what will do all the business, and procure all your wants." In forwarding the order to Nelson, Lady Hamilton begged that her royal mistress should be as little committed as possible. To which Nelson made reply, that he had received the precious order, and that if he gained a battle, it should be called Lady Hamilton and the Queen's, for to them he would owe his success, as without the order he had determined to return to Gibraltar. Anticipating disappointment, a woman's wit manœuvred. According to the laws of Naples, when a Queen Consort became mother of an heir she was entitled to a voice in the council. This right Maria Caroline had exercised from the date of her acquiring it. Lady Hamilton knew this. At the end of one of Nelson's letters to the Commanders of any of His Majesty's ships, dated "Syracuse, 22nd July, 1798," informing them of the route he intends to take in pursuit of the enemy, Lady Hamilton has made a note: "The Queen's letter, privately got by me, got him and his fleet victualled and watered in a few days." The book which contained Nelson's letters was long in the possession of Lady Hamilton. On July 23, 1798, Nelson wrote to Sir William to inform him that the fleet was unmoored, and that they were only waiting for the wind to blow from the land so that they could go out of that most delightful harbour

(Syracuse) where their present wants had been most amply supplied, and every attention shown them. With fair wind, therefore, they renewed the search for the French fleet, which search culminated in the glorious battle of the Nile, just ten days from their departure from Syracuse. What a different tale would history have told had that order never been obtained. Entering keenly into the grave importance of the part she had played in refitting the expedition, Lady Hamilton was in a state of the highest nervous tension, awaiting the result of the enterprise, and she became very excited and anxious.

During the evening of August 1, 1798, Nelson was struck in the forehead with a piece of langrage shot, or piece of iron, the skin being cut by it at right angles, it hung down over his face, covering his eye, and rendering him blind. Captain Berry caught him in his arms as he exclaimed : " I am killed, remember me to my wife." On being carried below, the surgeon immediately attended to him, but he said : " No, I will take my turn with my brave fellows." The pain was so intense that Nelson felt convinced the wound was mortal. However, after his head was dressed, he went upon deck led by Captain Berry, in order to see one of the French vessels, " L'Orient," which had taken fire, and subsequently exploded. After which fearful catastrophe, Nelson was induced to go to bed.

During the brilliant attack on the French, " L'Orient " was commanded by Admiral Brueys, who was wounded by an early discharge of grape-shot, followed by a cannon-ball, which cut him in two. His Flag Captain, Louis Casabianca, was struck down immediately afterwards. " L'Orient " took fire, and the English ships in the vicinity retreated in order to be beyond the consequences of the inevitable explosion. The sailors on the doomed ship flung themselves into the sea, and they implored Casabianca to allow them to remove him ; as he was unable to move his shattered limbs he rejected their kindly offers. They then tried to induce his son, a boy of twelve years of age, to accompany them ; the lad who was devotedly attached to his father, clung to the mangled form, and refused to be separated from his loved parent. The generous seamen were therefore forced to abandon the child to his awful fate, and in self-preservation they unwillingly quitted the pitiable couple. Faithful unto death—the heroism of that child has caused his memory to become a lasting by-word of filial devotion !

" L'Orient " soon after blew up with an explosion that was heard for

THE BATTLE OF THE NILE.

miles, and made the very land tremble as far as Rosetta; her masts, cannon, and spars falling in a storm of fire. The tremendous explosion was followed by a silence no less awful. A French historian, who witnessed the battle of the Nile, declared it to be the most complete sea victory since the invention of gunpowder. As soon as the conquest was secured, Nelson sent orders through the fleet to return thanksgiving in every ship for the victory which the Almighty had vouchsafed to His Majesty the King. The French at Rosetta, who beheld the engagement, were at a loss to understand the stillness of the fleet during the performance of this solemn duty. It affected the prisoners, officers as well as men, and graceless and godless as the officers were, some of them remarked that it was no wonder that order was preserved in the British navy when the minds of our men could be impressed with such sentiments in a moment of dire confusion.

Captain Hallowell, of the "Swiftsure," afterwards presented Nelson with a coffin made out of the mainmast of the unfortunate "L'Orient," telling him that when he had finished his course of glory in this world he could be buried in one of his own trophies; and so it came to pass. Every article used in the construction of the coffin was a relic of "L'Orient;" the nails were made from spikes taken from the mast. A paper was pasted in the bottom of it containing the following certificate: "I do hereby certify that every part of this coffin is made of the wood and iron of 'L'Orient,' most of which was picked up by His Majesty's ship, under my command, in the Bay of Aboukir. 'Swiftsure,' May 23, 1799."

The following letter accompanied the gift:—

    THE RIGHT HON. LORD NELSON, K.B.
    MY LORD,
        I send you a coffin, made of part of " L'Orient's " mast, that when you are tired of this Life you may be buried in one of your own Trophies, but may that period be far distant is the sincere wish of your obedient and much obliged servant,

                                BEN. HALLOWELL.

    " SWIFTSURE," *May* 23, 1799.

Nelson highly appreciated the gruesome gift, and for some time it stood upright against the wall of his cabin, with the lid on, behind the chair on which he sat at dinner. One day he found his officers looking at it, " You may look at it, gentlemen," he said, "as long as you please, but depend on it none of you shall have it."

Gillray, the famous caricaturist of the period, made Nelson's great victory the subject of one of his clever squibs, entitled: "Extirpation of the Plagues of Egypt, Destruction of the Revolutionary Crocodiles; or, the British hero cleansing the mouth of the Nile." The great fight was fought on the days of August 1, 2, and 3, in the year 1798. Returning to Naples suffering severely from his wound, and his health shattered, Nelson was received by Sir William Hamilton with great hospitality, and tenderly nursed by his kind-hearted wife.

The best account of the rejoicings at the Embassy is to be gathered from the *Autobiography* of Miss Cornelia Knight, afterwards Lady Companion to Princess Charlotte. Miss Knight had been committed to the care of the British Minister at Naples by her dying mother. Sir William was then absent, but she remained with Mrs. Cadogan. She considered there was perfect propriety in joining that family circle, and thus she writes of Lady Hamilton. "The house was the resort of the best people of all nations, and the attentions paid to Lord Nelson appeared perfectly natural. He always spoke of his wife with the greatest affection and respect, and I remember that shortly after the battle of the Nile, when my mother said to him that no doubt he considered the day of that victory as the happiest of his life, he answered, "No, the happiest was that on which I married Lady Nelson."

At the Embassy Nelson obtained every attention that a good nurse could devise, for he suffered intense pain from the wound in his forehead, while his general health also was seriously impaired. When he received his medal to commemorate the victory of the Nile, he turned to Lady Hamilton and hung it round her neck, in acknowledgment of the important service she had rendered to the fleet. It was of gold, beautifully set in crystal, and depicted the setting sun, the position of the fleets, and a medallion likeness of Nelson. The workmanship was that of Kuchler. Whilst Haydn, the great musician, was writing his D Minor Mass (No. 3) at Vienna, news was brought him of the victory of the Nile. He was then at work on the "Benedictus," and so elated with the news that he at once inserted in the score the well-known fanfare of triumph (on the chord of B flat) which occurs towards the end of the movement. The Mass is usually called "The Imperial," but by many "The Nelson" Mass.

A LETTER FROM NELSON'S FATHER.

At this period a beautiful letter, written by the Rev. Edmund Nelson, in reply to an old friend, the Rev. Brian Allot* (who had sent a congratulatory epistle to the old gentleman after the battle of the Nile), bears testimony to the high esteem in which the thoroughly religious clergyman held his brave son. It is dated October, 1798 :—

SIR,
My great and good son went into the world without fortune, but with a heart replete with every moral and religious virtue ; these have been his compass to steer by, and it has pleased God to be his shield in the day of battle, and to give success to his wishes to be of service to his country. His country seems sensible of his services, but should he ever meet with ingratitude, his scars will plead his cause, for at the siege of Bastia he lost an eye ; at Teneriffe an arm ; on the memorable 14th of February he received a severe blow on his body, which he still feels ; and now a wound on his head. After all this, you must allow his bloom of countenance must be faded, but the spirit beareth up yet as vigorous as ever. On the 29th of September he completed his 40th year, cheerful, generous, and good ; fearing no evil, because he has done none ; an honour to my grey hairs, which with every mark of old age creeps fast upon me.

Lord Nelson's flag was now removed to the " Vanguard ;" his old vessel, the " Agamemnon," having gone into dock in October, 1796, to be refitted. There was not a mast, yard, or sail, or any part of her rigging, but what was obliged to be repaired, the whole being so cut to pieces with shot—her hull had long been held together by cables served round.

The Admiral continued to be the guest of Sir William Hamilton, and the following letter to his wife shows how naturally and unreservedly he kept her informed of his position in that household :—

NAPLES, 11*th December*, 1798

I have not received one line from England since the 1st of October. Lord St. Vincent is in no hurry to oblige me now ; in short, I am the envied man, but better that than to be the pitied one. Never mind, it is my present intention to leave this Country in May. The poor Queen has again made me promise not to quit her or her Family, until brighter prospects appear than do at present. The King is with the Army, and she

* The Rev. Brian Allot was Rector of Burnham, in Norfolk.

is sole Regent; she is, in fact, a great King. Lady Hamilton's goodness forces me out at noon for an hour. What can I say of hers and Sir William's attention to me. They are, in fact, with the exception of you and my good father, the dearest friends I have in this world. I live as Sir William's son in the house, and my glory is as dear to them as their own; in short, I am under such obligations as I can never repay but with my eternal gratitude. The improvement made in Josiah by Lady Hamilton is wonderful; your obligations and mine are infinite on that score; not but Josiah's heart is as good and as humane as ever was covered by a human breast. God bless him—I love him dearly, with all his roughness.

Yours, &c., &c.,

NELSON.

On his reinstatement to health he returned to his vessel. Troubles grew thick and fast round the Court of Naples, and it was deemed advisable that the Royal Family should ensure their safety by flight, a difficult matter to accomplish with the eyes of the populace watching their every movement. The army had been defeated. Nelson did not entertain much respect for their capabilities, for he observed of them: "The Neapolitan officers did not lose much honour, for God knows they had not much to lose."

PLATE IV.—ATTITUDE OF LADY HAMILTON, FROM A DRAWING BY REHBURG.

CHAPTER XIII.

LADY HAMILTON ASSISTS THE FLIGHT OF THE ROYAL FAMILY OF NAPLES; THE EXECUTION OF CARACCIOLO.

A PRIVATE conclave was held, among the Queen, Nelson, and the Hamiltons, deciding that they should try to make good their retreat to Palermo, a movement requiring the utmost caution, for a suspicion of the project would have led to their immediate destruction. Here again Lady Hamilton was to the fore with heart and hand. Southey, truthfully endowing her with the merit of removing the Royal Family of Naples, and their most valued treasures, to a place of safety, says:—" Lady Hamilton arranged everything for the removal of the Royal Family. This was conducted on her part with the greatest address, and without suspicion, because she had been in habits of constant correspondence with the Queen. It was known that the removal could not be effected without danger, for the mob, and especially the Lazzaroni, were attached to the King, and as at this time they felt a natural presumption in their own numbers and strength, they insisted that he should not leave Naples. Several persons fell victims to their fury. Among others was a Messenger from Vienna, whose body was dragged under the windows of the Palace in the King's sight. The King and Queen spoke to the mob, and pacified them, but it would not have been safe, while they were in this agitated state, to have embarked the effects of the Royal Family openly. Lady Hamilton, like a heroine of modern romance, explored, with no little danger, a subterraneous road leading from the palace to the seashore. Through this passage the Royal treasures, the choicest pieces of painting and sculpture, and other property, to the value of two millions and a half, were conveyed to the seaside, and stowed safely on board the English ships. On the night of the 21st of December, 1798, at half-past eight, Nelson landed, brought out the whole Royal Family, embarked them in three barges, and carried them safely through a tremendous sea to the 'Vanguard.'" An accident nearly betrayed the flight. A bell was inadvertently touched which would have caused the sentry on duty to answer the summons, but Lady

Hamilton, with great presence of mind, hastened to the man, and apologised for unintentionally making the noise, and requested him to avoid disturbing the family. By this quickness of action discovery was averted, and the fugitives continued their flight. Notice was then given to the British merchants that they would be received on any ship in the Squadron. Their property had previously been embarked in transports. Two days were passed in the Bay for the purpose of taking such persons on board as required an asylum. On the night of the 23rd the fleet sailed. They had hardly set sail when a tremendous hurricane arose; Nelson declared it was the most fearful storm he had ever seen at sea. As they had gone on board without any personal attendant, it devolved on Lady Hamilton to wait upon the illustrious invalids. The goodnatured lady had both the will and the way to turn her hand to any work that was required, and being a capital sailor, she passed from one to another endeavouring to soothe their sufferings, and bestowing cheerfully on each what comfort she could.

A sad episode occurred in connection with the flight. The little Prince Albert, a boy of seven years, was so debilitated by the seasickness that he was unable to combat the attack, and succumbed. He was unremittingly attended to by Lady Hamilton, but no effort could save him, and he died in her arms on the evening of December 25. Lord Nelson, writing to Earl St. Vincent on December 28, 1798, says, in allusion to the distressing occurrence :—

> On the 25th, at 9 a.m., Prince Albert, their Majesties' youngest child, having eaten a hearty breakfast, was taken ill, and at 7 p.m. died in the arms of Lady Hamilton; and here it is my duty to tell your Lordship the obligations which the whole Royal Family, as well as myself, are under on this trying occasion to her Ladyship. They necessarily came on board without a bed, nor could the least preparation be made for their reception. Lady Hamilton provided her own beds, linen, &c., and became *their slave;* for except one man, no person belonging to Royalty assisted the Royal Family, nor did her Ladyship enter a bed the whole time they were on board. Good Sir William also made every sacrifice for the comfort of the august Family embarked with him.

The refugees landed at Palermo in a state of great prostration, taking with them the dead body of their darling child, and to sympathise at his funeral was the first attention which those in this noble island could give to the Royal personages who sought the shelter of their shores.

On January 31, 1799, Nelson received a letter from Thomas Leyland, Esq., then Mayor of Liverpool, informing him that the Common Council had conferred on him the Freedom of the Town; to which he returned the following letter of thanks:—

"VANGUARD," PALERMO, 31st *January*, 1799.

TO THOMAS LEYLAND, ESQ., MAYOR OF LIVERPOOL.

SIR,

I am this day favoured with your letter, conveying to me the unanimous Resolution of the Common Council of Liverpool to honour me with their Thanks, and also the Freedom of their Town. I beg you will assure those whom, from this moment, I am to call my Brother-Freemen, that my future exertions shall never be wanting to approve myself worthy of the high honour conferred me by the Representative body of the second Sea Port in the Kingdom; and believe me, with the highest respect, your much obliged and obedient servant,

NELSON.

The Hamiltons had forwarded to England, in the October of 1798, much of their most cared for property, but dared not risk exciting any suspicion of an intended flight, hence much was left behind and destroyed by the furious mob that broke into the Embassy. Owing to an accident to the vessel, they were sufferers to the extent of several thousand pounds. Nelson had managed to save some vases and pictures by placing them on board a transport.

On the 10th of June, 1799, the King of Naples wrote to Nelson, begging him to return to Naples with the Squadron, and describing to him the condition of his kingdom; and in conformity with his wishes, he and the Hamiltons set sail in the "Foudroyant" for Naples on June 13.

Much opprobrium has been cast upon Nelson and Lady Hamilton concerning the death of the traitor Caracciolo, which took place in the end of June. Like so many of the cruel and reckless assertions which have been levelled against their fair fame, it falls to the ground on investigation, and proves unmerited when tested to the core. Captain Brenton, in his *Naval History of Great Britain from 1783 to 1822*, gives the following warped account of the occurrences in connection with this execution:—"At the last fatal scene, she (*i.e.* Lady Hamilton) was present, and seems to have enjoyed the sight, while the body was yet hanging at the yardarm of the frigate. 'Come,' said she, 'come Bronté,'* let us take the barge, and have another look at poor Caracciolo.' The barge was manned, and they rowed round the frigate, and satiated their eyes with the appalling spectacle." On the appearance of the publication, the fabrication was indignantly denied by a man named John Mitford, one of Nelson's seamen, in a strong letter to the *Morning Post*. On receiving the lie direct, Captain Brenton endeavoured to vindicate himself in the second edition of his work, asserting, with withering contempt, that there could be no truth in his critic, "as he lived over a coal shed in some obscure street near Leicester Square." It is difficult to define why poverty and truthfulness could not be combined in the same structure, but when it is shown how twisted were Captain Brenton's ideas of humanity in general, it is not a matter of wonder that he should pervert the conduct of a lady against whom he was prejudiced. Poor John Mitford found a supporter in Commodore Sir Augustus Collier, of the "Foudroyant," from which vessel Captain Brenton had stated the barge was manned. This gentleman, in good sound English, denounced the tale as "an arrant falsehood," and numerous eye-witnesses arose, who gave totally different versions to that of the literary Captain. Caracciolo had been an Admiral in the service of King Ferdinand, but deserted to assist the Republicans, and fired at both Neapolitan and English ships. As a traitor he earned his fate. To evoke sympathy he has been represented as an old man, but his age was forty-seven years when he died. The following account of the execution, and its weird finale, is from the pen of an eye-witness who had been one of the refugees in the flight from Naples, and who was on board the "Foudroyant" during the whole transaction.

"In the year 1799, being then on my travels, and having long and at various times been a sojourner at Naples, and on terms of intimacy with Sir William Hamilton and his lady, and also with Lord Nelson, I was a frequent guest at their tables. Lord Nelson's flagship, the 'Foudroyant,' was then lying in the Bay of Naples, off Portici, about four miles from where I was staying; and on the 29th of June in that year I went on board Lord Nelson's

* Captain Brenton was premature in giving him his title, and therefore the speech attributed to Lady Hamilton is open to question, as Nelson had not yet been created Duke of Bronté.

ship to pay a morning visit, and had scarcely reached the deck when Lady Hamilton accosted me with 'Well, Mr. ——, we have most important news for you. That arch-traitor, Caracciolo, is taken. He was found concealed in a ditch, and is now on board this vessel awaiting his trial, which Lord Nelson has appointed to take place at one o'clock to-day. Will you be there?' I told her ladyship that I had particular business to attend to, and that I must go on shore, but that I would return again in time to be present if possible. Shortly afterwards, I quitted the vessel; and when I again went on board I saw Lord Nelson, who told me that the trial had commenced, and that he did not understand Italian himself, neither had he any English officer on board who did, and he wished me to go below and see how the proceedings were going on. I did so immediately, and on entering the Ward-room below I found the Court Martial was sitting. It was composed of Neapolitan officers—the Count de Thurn, who acted as president, and four others of inferior rank and station. The Count was known to be an implacable enemy of Caracciolo, and then held the office of Admiral which the Prince Caracciolo had so recently filled. I had been in the room a few minutes only when strangers were ordered to withdraw, upon hearing which I bowed to de Thurn, the President, to whom I was well known; but the only recognition he vouchsafed was a repetition of the words, 'Strangers are ordered to withdraw.' On leaving the Ward-room I told Lord Nelson what had happened. Soon after, the doors were opened, and a report was made to the British Admiral that Caracciolo had been found guilty, it being understood that two of the Neapolitan officers were for his immediate execution, and two others for respiting him until the King's pleasure could be known, but that the President had given the casting vote for the sentence to be carried into effect at five o'clock that afternoon. The captains and officers of the British Fleet, then on board the 'Foudroyant,' were speaking strongly and openly against the decision, when Nelson, who had ratified and confirmed the sentence, without which it could not be carried into effect—the sole government of the country being *de facto* vested in the Commander of the British Fleet—became agitated and irritated, and insisted on their putting an end to the conversation and not interfering. Shortly afterwards, whilst several of the officers, with myself, were pacing the deck, waiting for the dinner hour, Caracciolo was brought up from below, chained and guarded, to be transferred to the 'Minerva,' a Neapolitan frigate, where the execution was to take place. On seeing the officers and myself, to most of whom he was perfectly well known, he threw himself into a supplicating attitude, and, almost kneeling, implored for mercy, and said, in Italian, 'I have not been fairly tried,' or words to that effect. But no notice, under the circumstances of the case, could be taken by any officer not supreme in command, and he was hurried away by the officer who had him in charge. At the appointed hour, five o'clock, whilst at dinner with Lord Nelson, Sir William and Lady Hamilton, and several captains of the navy, the report of a gun was heard, and Lady Hamilton, instantly starting up from the table with a wine glass in her hand, exclaimed, 'Thank God, that gun announces the doom of a traitor.' The King of Naples, who had been invited, and was hourly expected on board Lord Nelson's ship, arrived from Palermo about eight or ten hours after the event; but on hearing of the fate of his friend and companion (to whom he was warmly attached, and whose life he, no doubt, would have spared had time been allowed him), and that no effort had been made to save him, he was so much hurt and mortified that he declined the invitation, and proceeded at once to his Sitio, or Royal Palace, in the island of Procida. Ten or twelve days after the execution of Caracciolo had elapsed, and several ineffectual attempts having been made to induce the King of Naples to abandon his resolution and to come on board, Lady Hamilton volunteered her services. They were accepted, and her ladyship went off in the Admiral's barge accompanied only by her usual attendants and a boat full of musicians, and, syren like, returned in triumph with the King, who slept on board that night. The following morning the King rose at the earliest dawn of day, and went into the gallery of the state cabin which had been appropriated to His Majesty's use, and approached the window to bathe his head in cold water, as was his custom, and whilst in the act of ablution, being then in his nightclothes only, he beheld from the window the dead body of Caracciolo floating upon the water, with his hands clasped as if in the attitude of prayer, and being immediately seized with the utmost terror and alarm, he ran into the cabin of Sir William Hamilton, and, dragging him out of bed, exclaimed, 'Monsieur Hamilton, *venite chi, venite chi*,' nor did he release his grasp until he had pointed out to Sir William the cause of his excitement, and added, 'Monsieur Hamilton, Monsieur Hamilton, *ho veduto, ho veduto*, Caracciolo.' Sir William Hamilton, who possessed at all times great coolness and tact, replied, 'Yes, your Majesty, it is true that it is Caracciolo, and it is also true that he was a great traitor to your Majesty; but he was, nevertheless, a sincere Christian, and he now appears in that attitude to supplicate, at the hands of your Majesty, those rites of sepulture which the offended laws of his country have denied to him—a Christian burial.' Orders were instantly given to get the body on board. It was sewed up in a hammock, a Catholic priest was procured, and it was conveyed to Castellamare, where the Catholic

SIR WILLIAM HAMILTON
(*From an old Drawing*).

ceremonies were performed, and the body was then interred. That having been done, the King remained on board the 'Foudroyant' as the Admiral's guest."

After Caracciolo's body had been hung at the fore-yard-arm of the Neapolitan frigate "La Minerva," it was taken down, weighted with shot, and carried a considerable distance into the Bay of Naples, where it was sunk. Before the King had seen the corpse, a fisherman who had been with his boat in the Bay, came to the "Foudroyant" and assured the officers that Caracciolo had risen from the bottom of the sea, and was coming as fast as he could to Naples, swimming half out of the water. When the body was rowed ashore for burial, the coxswain of the boat took back the shot with a portion of the skin still adhering to the rope by which they were fixed. They were weighed by Captain Hardy, who ascertained that the body had risen and floated with the immense weight of 250 lbs. attached to it. Captain Brenton was one of the inventive band who scattered broadcast aspersions against Lady Hamilton. He puts into her mouth the words: "Haul down the flag of truce, *Bronté*, no truce with rebels." Whereas Nelson was not created Duke of Bronté until the following August. He furthermore stated that in her last moments she uttered agonising screams of repentance for her act of cruelty; that the Prince was ever before her eyes; she could not endure to be in the dark, &c., but according to the testimony of a lady,[*] who for many years lived with Lady Hamilton, and who scarcely ever quitted her room during the last few weeks of her life, the screams and remorse existed only in the imaginative brain of the vindictive writer, and she was never known to have mentioned the Prince's name! The late Lord Northwick was one of those who rushed into the King's cabin to see his cause of alarm, and when he looked through the window, he saw Caracciolo lying with his face upturned and his eyes wide open. While in command of an armed force he had fired upon a ship bearing the colours of his sovereign, and all must agree that as a traitor he merited his doom! Earl Spencer wrote in reference to Nelson's conduct of affairs at Naples, that "the intentions and motives by which all his measures had been governed had been as pure and good as their success had been complete." Misfortunes, and a common asylum in Sicily, increased the attachment between the Queen of Naples and Lady Hamilton. In the midst of the friendly intercourse between Lord Nelson and the Hamiltons, his heart was with his home, as we gather by the following letter to his wife, in whose hands he placed the whole of the splendid allotment of ten thousand pounds awarded to him by the East India Company for the very great and important services he had rendered the Company, in the ever-memorable victory he had obtained over the French fleet on the 1st, 2nd and 3rd of August,

[*] Horatia, Nelson's adopted daughter, afterwards Mrs. Ward.

1798. His instructions to Lady Nelson relative to its disbursement run as follows :—

NAPLES, 14*th July*, 1799.

MY DEAR FANNY,

I have to thank you sincerely for your letters. I rejoice that you gave Mr. Bolton the money, and I wish it made up to £500. I never regarded money, nor wanted it for my own use; therefore, as the East India Company have made me so magnificent a present, I beg that £2,000 of it may be disposed of in the following manner: five hundred pounds to my father; five hundred pounds to be made up to Mr. Bolton, and let it be a *God-send*, without any restriction ; five hundred to Maurice, and five hundred to William. And if you think my sister, Matcham, would be gratified by it, do the same for her. If I were rich I would do more, but it will very soon be known how poor I am except my yearly income. I am not surprised at my brother's * death ; three are now dead, younger than myself, having grown to man's age. My situation here is not to be described, but suffice it to say, I am endeavouring to work for good. To my father, say everything which is kind. I love, honour, and respect him as a father, and as a man, and as the very best man I ever saw. May God Almighty bless you, my dear father, and all my brothers and sisters, is the fervent prayer of your affectionate

NELSON.

Lady Nelson grumbled much at these distributions, and on her discontent reaching the ears of old Mr. Nelson, the high-spirited old gentleman declined his share, and his name does not appear in the list of those who accepted the gifts.

* The Rev. Suckling Nelson, died in April, 1799.

CHAPTER XIV.

REJOICINGS IN HONOUR OF NELSON. SIR WILLIAM BEECHEY'S PORTRAIT OF OLD MR. NELSON. JOSIAH NISBET IN TROUBLE. NELSON AND THE HAMILTONS RETURN TO ENGLAND.

THE anniversary of the battle of the Nile was celebrated in Naples with great rejoicing, the King dining with Lord Nelson; the Queen and Royal family were still resident at Palermo. A letter to Lady Nelson will better describe the *fête* :—

NAPLES, *4th August*, 1799.

Thank God all goes well in Italy, and the kingdom of Naples is liberated from thieves and murderers. But still it has so overthrown the fabric of a regular government that much time and great care are necessary to keep the country quiet. The 1st of August was celebrated here with as much respect as our situation would admit. The King dined with me; and when His Majesty drank my health, a Royal Salute of twenty-one guns was fired from all His Sicilian Majesty's Ships of War, and from all the Castles. In the evening there was a general illumination. Amongst other representations, a large vessel was fitted out like a Roman galley; on its oars were fixed lamps, and in the centre was erected a rostral column with my name; at the stern were elevated two angels supporting my picture. In short, my dear Fanny, the beauty of the whole is beyond my powers of description. More than 2,000 variegated lamps were suspended round the vessel. An orchestra was fitted up, and filled with the very best musicians and singers. The piece of music was in a great measure to celebrate my praise, describing their previous distress—" but Nelson came, the invincible Nelson, and they were preserved and made happy again." This must not make you think me vain; no, far, very far from it, I relate it more from gratitude than vanity. I return to Palermo with the King to-morrow. May God bless you all. Pray say what is true, that I really steal time to write this letter, and my hand is ready to drop. My dear father must forgive my not writing so often as I ought, and so must my brothers, sisters, and friends. But believe me your affectionate

NELSON.

MARIA CAROLINE, QUEEN OF NAPLES
FROM A PICTURE GIVEN BY

Accordingly, accompanied by the King of Naples and the Hamiltons, he steered for Palermo, where the Queen received them at the port, publicly embracing Lady Hamilton, at the same time placing round her neck a miniature portrait of herself set with diamonds, which formed the words, "*Eterna Gratitudine;*" and, a little later on, she forwarded to her residence two coachloads of splendid dresses, about the value of £3,000, to recoup her for the losses sustained in the flight from Naples. On the second day after their return to Palermo, the King informed Nelson of his intention to create him Duke of Bronté; and upon the receipt of that honour he wrote at once to apprise his venerable father. His greatest pleasure in earning distinction was to share it with his relatives, and as each honour was tendered to him he divided it amongst those most nearly connected with him in exceeding generosity. His letter is thus worded :—

PALERMO, *Aug.* 15, 1799.

MY DEAR FATHER,

His Sicilian Majesty having created me a Duke by the title of Bronté, to which he has attached a Feud of, it is said, about £3,000 a-year to be at my disposal, I shall certainly not omit this opportunity of being useful to my family, always reserving a right to the possessor of having one-third of the income for the payment of legacies. It shall first go to you, my dear father, and in succession to my elder brother and children male, William the same, Mrs. Bolton's boys, Mrs. Matcham's, and my nearest relations. For your natural life the estate shall be taxed with £500 a-year; but this is not to be drawn into a precedent that the next heir may expect it. No, my honoured father, receive this small tribute as a mark of gratitude to the best of parents from his most dutiful son,

NELSON.

To his friend and business agent, Mr. Alexander Davison, he wrote the same day: "You will observe in a part of the King's letter an observation is made that this present could not hurt my delicate feelings; that is, I might have before received money and jewels, but I rejected them as became me, and never received one farthing for all the expenses of the Royal Family on board the 'Vanguard' and the 'Foudroyant.' This I expect from the Board of Admiralty, and that they will order me a suitable sum. It has been honour, and not money, which I have sought, nor sought in vain." Blind expectations which were never realised, for the Board of Admiralty never refunded to either Lord Nelson or Lady Hamilton any expenses incurred for national glory.

On September 3, 1799, the anniversary of the day on which the news of the battle of the Nile was received at Naples, a magnificent entertainment was improvised in honour of Lord Nelson and his two friends, the Hamiltons, the invitations being sent out in the name of the young Prince Leopold. The festival took the form of a *fête champêtre*. An almost ludicrous incident in connection with our principal personages is worthy of mention. A temple of Fame was erected, which contained wax figures, one representing Lady Hamilton in the character of "Victory," holding in outstretched hand a wreath of laurel for the decoration of the waxen effigy of the British Admiral, who was being presented to her by her husband, likewise in model. Nelson, Sir William, and Lady Hamilton were received by their Sicilian Majesties on the steps of this temple, and were affectionately embraced by them. The King took the laurel wreath, set with diamonds, from the hand of Victory, and placed it on the head of the veritable Nelson, also decorating Sir William and Lady Hamilton in a similar manner. They wore their leafy coronets during the whole of the entertainment, and anything more foolish than they must have appeared can hardly be presented to the imagination. A plain little man with one arm and one eye, an old man verging on seventy, and a woman rapidly approaching *embonpoint*, walking about in public company so crowned, and smiling in self-consciousness. Some countries set up queer gods! Nelson, at least, might have had the sense to evade appearing to so much disadvantage, and his declining the wreath would have been a precedent for the act of a statesman of our own time, who was quick-witted enough to know that his acceptance of the golden laurels offered by obsequious flatterers would not tend to his aggrandisement. Nelson felt acutely the desire of being loved and admired by all. Kind to every person himself, he accepted too readily the adulation which was forced upon him. Not only did Lady Hamilton acquire influence over the mind of Nelson, but men such as Lord St. Vincent, Captains Troubridge and Ball acknowledged the ascendency she gained over them, not by artful trickery, as stated by her defamers, but by the open generosity of her nature, by her impulsiveness and promptitude in action, for only good and great qualities could have attracted men of repute so undoubtedly high. As Nelson once wrote her, in later days,

SIR W. BEECHEY'S PORTRAIT OF OLD MR. NELSON.

that if she fell down and broke her nose the world would cold-shoulder her, but *he* loved her for her pure goodness of heart.

Affectionate and interesting letters were constantly passing between Lord and Lady Nelson at this time. Those of the husband containing accounts of the various engagements, with grateful mention of the hospitality of Sir William and his talented wife; on the part of Lady Nelson, came home news; and this may be considered an appropriate place to introduce a letter of hers with an interesting anecdote of Sir William Beechey, the eminent portrait painter. The autograph bears the date of the year 1800. "I think you will be surprised when I tell you our good father is sitting for his picture. Sir William Beechey is the fortunate man. You must know it is a profound secret. I went to Sir W. Beechey to ask his price, look at his pictures, and then inquire whether he would go to an invalid. The answer, ' No,' puzzled me ; however, I said, ' sometimes general rules were broken through.' Sir William finding I was rather anxious about this picture said that ' really he never went out to any person except the King and Royal Family ; the Duke and Duchess of York had that instant left the house.' I knew that. ' But, pray, Madam, may I ask who is this gentleman ?' ' Yes, Sir, my Lord Nelson's father.' ' My God, I would go to York to do it. Yes, Madam, directly.' He was as good as his word, and has been here twice. I think the likeness will be an exceedingly good one. I don't know whether the picture is for you or for me. . . . The picture is for you, I hear this morning."

When at sea, Nelson never forgot the poor of his home in Norfolk, and they were ever substantially remembered at festive seasons. In directing his winter gift to the poor of his native place, he wrote : " Fifty good large blankets of the very best quality, and they will last for seven years at least. This will not take from anything the parish might give. I wish enquiry to be made, and the blankets ordered of some worthy man. They are to be at my father's disposal in November."

There is no doubt that at this juncture Lady Nelson received injudicious reports from her son, Josiah, concerning the intimacy existing between her husband and his fair hostess, which caused her to put the inquiry to him as to when they should see him at home, and to express her determination to join him at Naples, unless there were a probability of his immediate return.

Truth to tell, it would seem to have been the mission of Captain Nisbet to carry trouble to all with whom he came in contact. We find Rear-Admiral Duckworth, on June 17, 1800, sending to the young officer's step-father the following exposition of the miserable differences between himself and his subordinates on the vessel under his command. "The near connection Captain Nisbet bears to your lordship must ever make me interested that no disgrace should attach itself to him. I therefore felt great concern to find on his arrival, that he and his officers were at daggers drawn; the Surgeon about three months under arrest, writing for a court martial on his Captain; the first Lieutenant with a string of complaints which he signified his intention of sending to your lordship, that must (to say the least of them) quite destroy Captain Nisbet's reputation." In order to avoid the scandal of a public investigation, Rear-Admiral Duckworth considerately effected a compromise between the disputants, and the surgeon was released; but he told Lord Nelson that there could be no second opinion as to the desirability of the parties being separated, and as the vessel was likely to be paid off, he would suggest that a few months residence with Lady Nelson would correct the young man's foibles.

About this time Lord Nelson gave a ball to commemorate the capture of the "Guillaume Tell" (the only French vessel that had escaped at the battle of the Nile), and also to celebrate the marriage of the Prime Minister at Naples. A postscript in a letter from Nelson to Admiral Goodall, concisely reports the event: "Acton is married to his niece, not fourteen years of age, so you hear it is never too late to do well. He is only sixty-seven." On the occasion of the ball, as the barge containing the Princesses arrived, a lieutenant officiously assisted one of the young ladies to step on Lord Nelson's vessel; but so awkward were his efforts, that he and the royal lady fell into the water. The latter, on being rescued, gave way to a furious outburst of temper, which Lady Hamilton kind-heartedly soothed, and she retired with the poor girl to change her clothes and re-deck her for the festival.

The appointment of Lord Keith as Commander-in-Chief deeply galled Lord Nelson, for he had not anticipated that any one would be placed over him after Lord St. Vincent's retirement, therefore he determined to return to England as soon as he could obtain the requisite permission from the Admiralty. Until such leave arrived, he joined Lord Keith at Leghorn, accompanied him to Palermo, and was for some months employed cruising between that station and Malta. In departing for Malta, on April 24, 1800, he had on board Sir William and Lady Hamilton; the latter suffered so severely from bilious fever that the course of the vessel was altered for a day to give relief to the invalid.

Sir William Hamilton had applied for leave of absence to visit his property in Wales, adding that if he could not obtain this favour, for which he had asked more than once, he should be obliged to tender his resignation. No notice whatever was taken of this application at the time, but, when he least expected it, a letter arrived from the Foreign Office informing him that his request was granted, and that Sir Arthur Paget was to succeed him as Minister. He felt deeply hurt, but made no complaints, and when Sir Arthur (" the inevitable Paget," the Queen of Naples dubbed him) arrived, there was mutual amiability between the two gentlemen, and Sir William did his best to give him all confidential information likely to be of service to him. Sir William wrote to a friend: "Twenty-seven years service—having spent all the king's money, and all my own, besides running into debt, deserves something better than dismission." Lord Keith had sent to advise the Queen of Naples to depart for Vienna, and she determined to join the Hamiltons on part of their journey to England. Sir William felt great regret at leaving the Two Sicilies. Mount Vesuvius, Pompeii, and the antiquities which he had made his study, and which had become part of his life—all had to be left. He was really beloved by the people of the country, and a sensible Neapolitan nobleman was heard to say, that during the thirty years Sir William had resided at that court he had never injured any one, but had always employed his influence to benefit the deserving. As Lord Nelson was about to return to England, he received an order from Lord Keith directing him to convey the Queen of Naples, her family and suite, on board his vessel the "Alexander," to which he had been transferred; the illustrious party were joined by the Hamiltons, and Nelson set sail for Leghorn. The Queen was here detained, in consequence of the French having entered Marengo. A report was circulated that the enemy were advancing, the populace, gaining courage and confidence in the knowledge of Nelson's presence among them, broke into the arsenals and seized the weapons. *En masse* they surrounded the palace, demanding to be led against the French. The poor Queen was terrified, and knew not what to do, but Lady Hamilton coolly stepped out on to the balcony, and by her eloquence induced the people to return the weapons to the arsenal, and quietude was restored. From Leghorn the party proceeded by land to Ancona; Sir William was very ill indeed, and frequently declared he should die by the way. At Castel San Giovanni, the coach in which were Lord Nelson, Sir William and Lady Hamilton, was overturned; Sir William and his lady being hurt, but not dangerously. The wheel was repaired, but broke again at Arezzo. As the Queen of Naples was two days' journey ahead of them, and news arriving that the French army was rapidly advancing, it was decided that the Hamiltons and Nelson should proceed to overtake the royal party, leaving Mrs. Cadogan and Miss Knight with the broken carriage, as being of less consequence if taken by the army. At length they reached Vienna in safety. Whenever Lord Nelson appeared in public, a crowd collected; his portrait was hung up as a sign over shops; and milliners gave his name to particular dresses. He was the subject of general ovation. As in Italy, Sir William and Lady Hamilton immediately became the centre of a talented circle. Artists and musicians craved the honour of introduction to them. Haydn was an occasional guest, quiet and unobtrusive in manners, modest and sensible in conversation. He set to music some verses, composed by Miss Knight after the battle of the Nile, which were descriptive of the blowing up of "L'Orient":—

> Britannia's leader gives the dread command;
> Obedient to his summons, flames arise:
> The fierce explosion rends the skies,
> And high in air the pond'rous mass is thrown.
> The dire concussion shakes the land:
> Earth, air and sea united groan.
> The solid Pyramids confess the shock,
> And their firm bases to their centres rock.

Haydn himself accompanied Lady Hamilton on the piano when she sang the Ode; the effect of his master touch, and the lady's splendid vocal delivery, was sublime. He was staying at that period with Prince Esterhazy, conducting the famous concerts given by that nobleman at his magnificent palace in Hungary. The prince had avowed his intention of giving up these concerts, and told Haydn that the next would be the last. It was an unusually fine performance, and at the conclusion Haydn introduced a finale at once so touching and melancholy that it drew tears from the eyes of many among the audience. During the last movement, the performers one by one left the orchestra; as each player finished his part he blew out the candle fixed to his desk, took up his music, and made his exit. The conductor, finding himself beating time in silence, cast around glances of dismay, and hurriedly snatching up his score left the orchestra also. The impressive performance so touched the prince that he abandoned the idea of discontinuing the concerts. Setting aside the curious incidents which are said to have suggested the "Farewell Symphony" to Haydn, the composition itself is full of interest, and may fairly take rank with the best of the great composer's less important orchestral works. The circumstances under which it is usually played cause its performance to be particularly affecting.

Haydn was greatly attached to Austria's Imperial family. He received his death stroke while seated at his pianoforte singing his own composition of the national prayer, "God Save the Emperor," known to us as "the Austrian Hymn."

Sir William had despatched his valuable treasures to England by sea, consigning them to the custody of his effusive nephew, who, faithful and considerate to no man but himself, wrote to a fair correspondent, Lady Caroline Cawdor, on September 23, 1800, a letter in which he laid bare his ungracious sentiments towards his beneficent uncle, and his unwillingness to render a service to the friend who had shown himself so worthy of grateful attention. He wrote: "I am still expecting Sir William Hamilton, and have the pleasure to be charged with the trouble of his effects just arrived, and to be landed next Monday, but this will not be the most troublesome part of my occupation when they arrive." At Leghorn, the Queen of Naples handsomely acknowledged her obligations to Lord Nelson and the Hamiltons by valuable gifts. That of Lady Hamilton was a diamond necklace, with the cyphers of the royal giver and her four children, and ornamented with their hair. After being *fêted* and entertained by the *élite* of the Austrian capital, and receiving every civility at the hands of the Imperial family, the English travellers prepared to resume their homeward journey. It had been the earnest desire of the Queen of Naples that Lady Hamilton should accept a pension of £1,000 per annum; but this Sir William declined, as he felt assured that the English Government would recoup them for losses sustained in foreign service. On September 27, 1800, therefore, he, his wife, Lord Nelson, and the little band of fellow-travellers bade farewell to their illustrious friends, and continued their progress, arriving at Prague next day. The hotel at which they put up was splendidly illuminated in honour of Lord Nelson; the host, however, charged for the lights in the bill, which Nelson good-humouredly paid. On the 2nd of October they reached Dresden, where they were received by Mr. Elliot, the British Minister. From an early age, Emma was particularly partial to the fatted meats of this world, holding that good eating was the height of human enjoyment; and in consequence, at table, she never spared its viands, which she despatched with every appearance of rude health. At one of the crowded assemblies in Dresden, Lady Hamilton expressed a wish to go to court. The Electress had determined to ignore her, which fact was known to Mrs. Elliot, the Minister's wife, who endeavoured to dissuade her ladyship from presenting herself, adding that she must not expect much merriment at the entertainments given by the Elector, and that they were singularly devoid of animation owing to his giving neither dinners nor suppers. The outspoken Emma exclaimed: "What, no guttling?" The cloven foot must show itself; complete good-breeding can never be the result of after-life education; neglected early years carry their brand to the end.

There was at this time a lady resident in Dresden named Mrs. St. George, better known as Mrs. Trench, who kept a diary, afterwards published as *The Remains of Mrs. Trench*. From these pages we gather a very graphic description of the doings of the notable birds of passage, and with what disfavour she regarded the principal lady of the party. A beauty, and a refined beauty herself (to judge by Romney's beautiful picture of her), she may have viewed the visitor as a trespasser in her own privileged circle. "Lady Hamilton," she writes, "is bold, forward, coarse, assuming and vain, her figure colossal, but, excepting her feet, which are hideous, well-shaped. Her bones are large, and she is exceedingly *embonpoint*. She resembles the bust of Ariadne. The shape of all her features is fine, as is the form of her head and her ears; her teeth are a little irregular, but tolerably white; her eyes bright blue, with a brown spot in one, which, though a defect, takes nothing away from her beauty and expression. Her eyebrows and hair are dark, and her complexion coarse. Her expression is strongly marked, variable, and interesting; her movements in common life ungraceful; her voice loud, though not disagreeable. Her mother, Mrs. Cadogan, is what one might expect. After dinner we had several songs in honour of Lord Nelson, sung by Lady Hamilton; she puffs the incense full in his face, but he receives it with pleasure, and snuffs it up cordially. The songs all ended in the sailor's way, with "hip, hip, hurra," and a bumper with the last drop on the nail, a ceremony I had never heard of or seen before." The comments on Lady Hamilton's rapacious appetite were equally unrestrained.

Though Mrs. Trench was usually severe whenever she elected to sit in judgment on the captivating ambassadress, for once she relaxed and meted out praise of the clever woman thus:—"October 7, 1800, Dresden. We breakfasted with Lady Hamilton, and saw her represent in succession the best statues and paintings extant. She assumes their attitudes, expression, and drapery with great facility, and swiftness, and accuracy. Several Indian shawls, a chair, some antique vases, a wreath of roses, a tambourine, and a few children, are her whole apparatus. She stands at one end of the room with a strong light to her left, and every window closed. Her hair is short, dressed like an antique, and her gown a simple calico chemise,* very easy, with loose sleeves to the wrist. She disposes the shawls so as to form Grecian, Turkish, and other drapery, as well as a variety of turbans. Her arrangement of the turbans is absolute sleight of hand, she does it so quickly, so easily, and so well. It is a beautiful performance, amusing to the most ignorant, and highly interesting to lovers of art. Each representation lasts ten minutes. . . . After showing her attitudes, she sang, and I accompanied her." These displays were a source of everlasting enjoyment to the exponent herself, and she performed them with equal pleasure either in the most fashionable London houses, before the Queen and Court at Naples, or before one single admirer, failing a larger audience.

On October 5, we find Mrs. Trench went, by Lady Hamilton's invitation, to see Lord Nelson dressed for Court. On his hat he wore a large diamond feather, or ensign of sovereignty, given him by the Grand Signior; on his breast the Order of the Bath, the order he received as Duke of Bronté, the diamond star, including the sun or crescent, given him by the Grand Signior, three gold medals obtained by three different victories, and a beautiful present from the King of Naples, which consisted of His Majesty's picture, richly set and surrounded with laurels, which sprang from two united anchors at the bottom, and support the Neapolitan crown at top; on the back was the

* A sort of tea-gown, to judge from Rehburg's sketches.

Queen's cypher, which turned so as to appear within the same laurels, and was formed of diamonds on green enamel. In short, Lord Nelson was a perfect constellation of stars and orders. The Sultan's aigrette, or plume of triumph, referred to, was an artificial plume, formed of thirteen fingers covered with diamonds. They were intended to represent the thirteen ships taken and destroyed in battle. The centre diamond, and the four surrounding it, were estimated at an immense sum, and there were at least three hundred diamonds of smaller size.* The reversible miniature of the King of Naples had been given to Lord Nelson by the Queen just before landing at Leghorn; the device surrounding it was executed in large diamonds, and was, therefore, of great pecuniary value. The design was her Majesty's own idea.

Mr. Elliot foretold a future for his fair guest which however was not realised. He prophesied that Lady Hamilton would play a great part in England, and captivate the Prince of Wales, whose mind, he remarked, "was as vulgar as her own." Mrs. Trench said Lady Hamilton acted her songs, which she considered vulgar in the extreme; a decidedly opposite view to that expressed by an equally competent judge, Horace Walpole, who thought that, while singing, her attitudes were a whole theatre of grace. The *Edinburgh Review* for October, 1886, deals with Mrs. Trench's perverted though amusing representations, by sensibly comparing them with the letters of Lady Minto at Vienna, from whence the *voyageurs* had but just departed, who reported upon them in a more friendly and natural tone. The extract from the *Review* which bears on the comparisons is in these words: "The pictures of Nelson at Dresden and Vienna are not reconcilable; but Lady Minto knew the man well, and Mrs. St. George (or Trench) did not know him at all. It must be allowed that to the mere spectator Nelson's ordinary behaviour in the company of Lady Hamilton would be regarded as an outrage, yet it was an outrage of which neither of them was conscious. We do not believe in the 'arts' of Lady Hamilton. It was unfortunate for both of them that two characters so unsophisticated ever came together; and it is pitiable to read some of the simple, homely, and wife-like letters of the lady who was the chief sufferer in the result." The remarks made by Lady Minto, English Ambassadress, are found in a letter to her sister Lady Malmesbury:

* Among Lady Hamilton's papers at a later date was found a Turkish Manuscript with seal affixed, supposed to have accompanied this gift. The following is a literal translation:—"Our honourable and dear friend Nelson, Chief Admiral of the Maritime Forces of England—a man of the highest consideration among the Christian followers of the Messiah. May his end be happy!"

"I don't think Nelson altered in the least; he has the same shock head of hair, and the same honest, simple manners; but he is devoted to Emma. He thinks her quite an *angel*, and talks of her as such to her face and behind her back, and she leads him about like a keeper with a bear. She must sit by him at dinner to cut his meat, and he carries her handkerchief."

It was with little regret on both sides that the travellers departed from Dresden, Lady Hamilton having received a slight from the Electress, who refused her the honour of a presentation. At Hamburg, Nelson purchased a lovely lace trimming for a court dress for his wife, and a black lace cloak for a lady who had shewn her kindness during his absence, and which he wished to acknowledge. In spite of the great terms of intimacy on which he and the Hamiltons lived, he was in nowise unfaithful in his allegiance to his wife, and in his simplicity he expressed the hope that on the return to England they would see very much of each other, and often dine together, and that when Sir William and Lady Hamilton went to their musical parties, he and Lady Nelson would go to bed. The scenes of national interest in which Nelson and the Hamiltons had played so serious and important a part had most naturally drawn them together into bonds of considerable friendship and familiarity. These ties were not understood or entered into by the scandal-mongers; Lady Nelson was duly informed of them, and, as might be expected, she awaited his arrival with a feeling of great coolness and reserve.

On the 6th of November, Nelson and his friends arrived at Yarmouth in the mail packet "King George," after a very stormy passage, having crossed the bar only just in time to avoid a tremendous gale, which must have driven them out again to sea for several days. This being the first time that Nelson had returned to England since the battle of the Nile, the populace turned out in crowds to welcome him. They took the horses from his carriage and drew him to his hotel, the Wrestler's Arms. The Mayor and Corporation immediately waited on him to present him with the Freedom of the Town, which had some time previously been voted to him.

By his request, public service was performed in the church to return thanks to God for his safe return home, and for the many blessings he had experienced. As he entered the church the organist played, "See the conquering hero comes." Lord Nelson duly reported his advent to the Admiralty on the day of his arrival at Yarmouth, stating that his health was perfectly re-established, and that he desired to serve again immediately, and they must not consider his journey home from the Mediterranean by land as a wish on his part to retire from active service. On taking his departure from Yarmouth, he instructed his agents to forward to the Mayor £50 for distribution, to the Town Clerk five guineas, and one guinea for the officer.

Upon this occasion, the good people of Norwich presented Lady Hamilton with a beautiful ring, composed of a fine pink topaz, surrounded by fourteen large diamonds, bearing on the inner side the inscription, " Presented to Emma, Lady Hamilton, by the citizens of Norwich, Nov. 6, 1800."* Why did the respectable people of that venerable city select Lady Hamilton to receive this tribute more than any other lady of the party? For no other reason than that she came as an acknowledged benefactress to the English nation, fresh from her share in the transactions that won the battle of the Nile.

The journey from Yarmouth to London was made in Sir William's travelling carriage; they went by easy progress, making only two stages a day. On the way, they called at the house of Lord Nelson's father, but they found he had departed for town. On arriving in London, Nelson wore his full uniform, with three stars and two gold medals. He was immediately recognised, and received with loud huzzas, which he acknowledged by a low bow. The illustrious trio put up at Nerot's Hotel, King Street, St. James.

In the evening, Sir William and Lady Hamilton accompanied Lord Nelson to dine with his father and Lady Nelson. His wife had remained at her hotel, and made no attempt to meet her husband on his homeward progress. Sir William and his lady took up their residence in a house in Grosvenor Square, lent to them by Mr. Beckford, whose wife, Margaret, was related to Sir William. At the return dinner given by Sir William to the Nelsons, they were honoured by the presence of the Duke of Sussex (the Prince Augustus whom they had entertained at Naples), and his wife, Lady Augusta Murray. This lady was a daughter of the Earl of Dunmore, and had been married to the Prince at Rome according to Roman Catholic rites, and again at St. George's, Hanover Square. She had two children by the Prince, but, after her marriage was declared illegal, she refused to live with him.

* This ring became the property of the Rev. Jacob Johnson, of Saxlingham, on the sale of the effects of a member of the Nelson family. On the death of the reverend gentleman, it was purchased by Dr. Mills, of Norwich, who had it inserted in a bracelet as a wedding gift to his sister, Mrs. Philipp Herz, of Frankfort, in whose possession it remains.

CHAPTER XV.

LADY NELSON'S RESENTMENT. THE FONTHILL REVELS: LADY HAMILTON'S IMPORTANT REPRESENTATION OF THE ATTITUDES. MR. BECKFORD'S ECCENTRICITY.

THE imprudent conduct of Lord Nelson himself at this stage was conducive to much of the unhappiness which so soon followed. Hearing comments on his great friendship for Lady Hamilton, and feeling that the obligation he was under to herself and Sir William merited no other, he resented them. He felt keenly the injustice of such reports, and was greatly irritated at the tittle-tattle, and in very obstinacy was to be seen daily in her company, with the full knowledge and desire of Sir William Hamilton, who held his friend in the highest esteem. For two months Lord and Lady Nelson lived together, but not on happy terms. Apparently incited by the reports conveyed to her by her acquaintances, the lady grew to consider herself aggrieved; and, as Nelson's conversation invariably introduced his fascinating compatriot, womanly ire was aroused in the heart of the wife. In spite of constant bickerings, Lord Nelson resided with his wife at lodgings in Arlington Street. The occasion of the outbreak which led to their separation is described in a letter from the legal adviser of his lordship, Mr. W. Haslewood, to Sir Harris Nicolas, which is here inserted in its entirety :—

KEMP TOWN, BRIGHTON, 13*th April*, 1846.

DEAR SIR,

I was no less surprised than grieved when you told me of a prevailing opinion that Lord Nelson, of his own motion, withdrew from the society of his wife, and took up his residence altogether with Sir William and Lady Hamilton, and that you have never received from any member of his family an intimation to the contrary. His father, his brother, Dr. Nelson (afterwards Earl Nelson), his sisters, Mrs. Bolton and Mrs. Matcham, and their husbands, well knew that the separation was unavoidable on Lord Nelson's part; and as I happened to be present when the unhappy rupture took place, I have often talked over, with all of them, but more especially with Mr. and Mrs. Matcham, the particulars which I proceed to relate in justice to the memory of my illustrious friend, and in the hope of removing an erroneous impression from your mind. In the winter of 1800-1801, I was breakfasting with Lord and Lady Nelson, at their lodgings in Arlington Street, and a cheerful conversation was passing on indifferent subjects, when Lord Nelson spoke of something which had been done or said by 'dear Lady Hamilton'; upon which Lady Nelson rose from her chair, and exclaimed, with much vehemence, 'I am sick of hearing of dear Lady Hamilton, and am resolved that you shall give up either her or me.' Lord Nelson, with perfect calmness, said ' Take care, Fanny, what you say; I love you sincerely, but I cannot forget my obligations to Lady Hamilton, or speak of her otherwise than with affection and admiration.' Without one soothing word or gesture, but muttering something about her mind being made up, Lady Nelson left the room, and shortly after drove from the house. They never lived together afterwards. I believe that Lord Nelson took a formal leave of her ladyship before joining the fleet under Sir Hyde Parker, but that, to the day of her husband's glorious death, she never made any apology for her abrupt and ungentle conduct above related, or made any overtures towards a reconciliation.

If she had not carried matters with so high a hand, the painful crisis might never have come; Nelson's heart was in the right place, and he simply submitted to an overbearing will when he agreed to a separation. The sisters of Lord Nelson were aware that he had no alternative, for during the few months that he had been in England he had suffered much irritation at her hands, and a man so accustomed to command was little likely to submit to unreasonable dictation, such as he felt that of his wife to be, and at no time did she receive the sympathy of his relatives. In Naples, Lady Hamilton was equally attentive to all the officers of the fleet. We find Lord St. Vincent writing to thank her for some fan mounts which she had entrusted to his care for Lady St. Vincent and Lady Nelson, concluding his letter with this rhapsody: " Continue to love me, and rest assured of the most unfeigned and affectionate regard of, my dear Lady Hamilton, your faithful and devoted knight, St. Vincent." It was impossible to know this lovable woman without admiring her as a natural result; the admiration that she excited was so general, that harm in it was never looked

AUTOGRAPH LETTER OF LADY NELSON
TO HER HUSBAND, JULY 23, 1798.

My Dearest Husband,
I am now writing opposite to your Portrait—the likeness is great—I am well satisfied with Abbott. Our Good Father was delighted with the likeness.
July 23d
Your Affectionate Wife
Frances H. Nelson

EXTRACT FROM LETTER
FROM LORD NELSON TO MAJOR-GEN VILUTUS, DATED "VICTORY," JANUARY 1, 1805.

"The British Meaning are safer this sentence should be wrote in letters of gold in every Council anchor in Europe."

for. At the same time, abundant proof is to be found that affection had existed between Lord Nelson and his wife, and it is to be regretted that any occurrence should have embittered their relations. The following extract from a letter of Lady Nelson is full of wifely tenderness:—

ROUND WOOD, *July* 23, 1798.

MY DEAREST HUSBAND,

I am now writing opposite your portrait; the likeness is great. I am well satisfied with Abbot. I really began to think he had no intention of letting me have my own property, which I am not a little attached to. Indeed it is more than attachment, it is real affection. It is my company—my sincere friend in your absence. Our good father is delighted with the likeness. The room is very near eleven feet, therefore it stands very well opposite the East window.

In the same year, an equally affectionate communication was forwarded from husband to wife, giving ample evidence that his heart was true to his lawful love, and his companionship with the Hamiltons merely the result of natural gratitude for favours conferred. On October 1, 1798, he writes to his wife:

"Our time here is actively employed, and between business, and what is called pleasure, I am not my own master for five minutes. The continued kind attention of Sir William and Lady Hamilton must ever make you and I love them, and they are deserving the love and admiration of all the world. The Grand Signior has ordered me a valuable diamond;* if it were worth a million, my pleasure would be to see it in your possession. My pride is being your husband, the son of my father, and in having Sir William and Lady Hamilton for my friends. While these approve of my conduct, I shall not feel or regard the envy of thousands. Could I, my dearest Fanny, tell you half the honours which are shown me here, not a ream of paper would hold it. On my birthday, eighty people dined at Sir William Hamilton's, one thousand seven hundred and forty came to a ball, where eight hundred supped. A rostral column is erected under a magnificent canopy, never, Lady Hamilton says, to come down while they are at Naples. A little circumstance has also happened which does honour to the King of Naples, and is not unpleasant to me. I went to view the magnifi-

* The Sultan's mother also presented Nelson with a golden rose, set with diamonds, valued at £1,000.

cent manufactory of china. After admiring all the fine things, sufficient to seduce the money from my pocket, I came to some busts in china of all the royal family. These I immediately ordered, and when I wanted to pay for them, I was informed that the King had directed whatever I chose should be delivered free of all cost—it was handsome of the King,"

On the 24th of September, 1799, he reposes full confidence in his wife, and his placing in her hands the sum voted to him by the Court of Directors of the East India Company testifies that he had no intention of abandoning his household. To these gentlemen he wrote:—

Sep. 24, 1799.

GENTLEMEN,

Please to pay the ten thousand pounds, so generously bestowed upon me by the East India Company, to my wife, Frances Herbert Nelson, and her receipt shall be considered the same as if given by myself, I have the honour to be, with the greatest respect, your obliged

NELSON.

Lady Nelson would not seem to have been as precise in her domestic arrangements as was compatible with comfort. We find Lord Nelson constantly making remarks in regard to the incorrectness of her linen list, and the careless way in which his belongings were scattered or missing. From St. Helens, April 3, 1798, he writes: "I cannot find my black stock and buckle. I find the weights for your scales are on board this ship." On the 5th: "Pray, my dear Fanny, did you put up the three Portugal pieces—*joes*? If you did, they cannot be found. . . . . My black stock and buckle has not yet appeared, nor are the keys of my dressing-stand sent." And again, on the 7th of April: "My dearest Fanny, I have looked over my linen, and find it very different to your list in the articles as follows: thirteen silk pocket handkerchiefs, only six new, five old. Thirteen Cambric ditto; I have sixteen. Twelve cravats; I have only eleven. Six Genoa velvet stocks; I have only three. You have put down thirty huckaback towels; I have from 1 to 10, 11 is missing, from 11 to 22, that is Nos. 12 to 21; therefore there is missing No. 11, 22 and to 30—ten in all. I only hope and believe they have not been sent." Nelson mildly drew attention to the

THE FONTHILL REVELS.

discrepancies, which certainly did not represent very businesslike or comfortable tendencies.

In the December of the year 1800, Lord Nelson, accompanied by his inseparable friends, the Hamiltons, proceeded to Bath to visit Mr. William Beckford (Sir William's relative), at Fonthill Abbey, of great renown, who provided a series of entertainments in their honour commencing on December 20, 1800. The mornings were spent in seeing the house, the paintings and library, and such out-door excursions as the weather permitted; in the evening the company were delighted with a vocal display on the part of Lady Hamilton and Madame Banti, who exercised every charm of voice. The citizens of the good city availed themselves of his presence among them to organise a festival in his honour. On Tuesday, the 23rd of December, the festivities were transferred from the Mansion House to the seat of Mr. William Beckford. The following description of the weird and brilliant scene which took place on that occasion is gathered from *The Gentleman's Magazine*, April, 1801 :—

The Company being assembled by five o'clock, a number of carriages waited before the mansion house to receive them. The several parties as arranged for each took their places. Lord Nelson was loudly huzzaed by the multitude as he entered the first coach. They all proceeded slowly and in order, as the dusk of the evening was growing into darkness. In about three-quarters of an hour, soon after having entered the first great wall which encloses the Abbey woods, the procession passed a noble Gothic arch. At this point the company were supposed to enter the Abbot's domain, and thence upon a road winding through thick woods of pine and fir, brightly illuminated by innumerable lamps hung in the trees, and by flambeaux moving with the carriages, they proceeded between two divisions of the Fonthill volunteers, accompanied by their band, playing solemn marches, the effect of which was much heightened by the continued roll of drums placed at different distances on the hills. What impression at this dark hour—the blaze of light partly stationary and partly moving, as reflected from the windows of carriages, or gleaming on the military armour, together with the music echoing through the woods— what impression, I say, this *ensemble* of light, sound, and motion must have made on those who could quietly contemplate it all at a distance, may be left to the imagination without any attempt to describe it. The company,

132   LADY HAMILTON.

on their arrival at the Abbey, could not fail to be struck with the increasing splendour of lights and their effects, contrasted with the deep shades which fell on the walls, battlements, and turrets of the different groups of the edifice. Some parts of the light struck on the walls and arches of the

THE FONTHILL REVELS.
From an old Pen and Ink Drawing.

Great Tower, till it vanished by degrees into an awful gloom at its summit, over which, mounted on a flag of sixty feet, the broad sheet (the Admiral's flag, in compliment to Lord Nelson) of colours could at some moments be discerned by catching lights mysteriously waving in the air. The parties, alighting by orderly succession from their carriages, entered a groined Gothic hall through a double line of soldiers. From thence they were received into the great saloon, called the Cardinal's parlour, furnished with rich tapestries; long curtains of purple damask hung before the arched windows; ebony tables; chairs studded with ivory, of various but antique fashion; the whole room in the noblest style of monastic ornament, and illuminated by lights in silver sconces. At the moment of entrance they sat down at a long table occupying nearly the whole length of the room (fifty-three feet), to a superb dinner, served in one long line of enormous silver dishes, in the substantial manner of the antient abbeys, unmixed with the refinements of modern cookery. The tables and sideboards glittering with piles of plate and a profusion of candlelights, not to mention a blazing Christmas fire of cedar and the cones of pine, united to increase the splendour, and to improve the *coup d'œil* of the room. It is needless to say, the highest satisfaction and good humour prevailed, mingled with sentiments of admiration at the grandeur and originality of the entertainment. It should not be omitted that many of the artists whose works have contributed to the embellishment of the Abbey, with Mr. Wyatt* and the President of the Royal Academy at their head, formed a part of the company. The gentlemen with the distinguished musical party before mentioned, and some prominent characters of the literary world, formed altogether a combination of talent and genius not often meeting at the same place. Dinner being ended, the company removed upstairs to the other finished apartments of the Abbey. The staircase was lighted by certain mysterious living figures at different intervals, dressed in hooded gowns, and standing with large wax torches in their hands. A magnificent room, hung with yellow damask, and decorated with cabinets of the most precious Japan, received the assembly. It was impossible not to be struck, among other objects, with its credences (or antique buffets), exhibiting much treasure of wrought plate, cups, vases, and ewers of solid gold. It was from this room they passed into the Library, fitted up with the same elaborate taste. The Library opens by a large Gothic screen into the Gallery. This room, which when finished will be more than two hundred and seventy feet long, is to have that length completely fitted up and furnished in the most impressive monastic style. A superb shrine, with a beautiful statue of St. Anthony

* Mr. Wyatt was the designer of Fonthill.

in marble and alabaster, the work of Rossi, placed upon it, with reliquaries studded with brilliants of immense value, the whole illuminated by a display of wax lights on candlesticks and candelabras of massive silver gilt, exhibited a scene at once strikingly splendid and awfully magnificent. The long series of lights on either side resting on stands of ebony enriched with gold, and those on the shrine, all multiplied and reflected in the great oriel opposite, from its spacious squares of plate glass, while the whole reflection narrowed into an endless perspective as it receded from the eye, produced a singular and magic effect. As the company entered the gallery, a solemn music struck the ear from some invisible quarter, as if from behind the screen of scarlet curtains which backed the shrine, or from its canopy above, and suggested ideas of a religious service—ideas which, associated as they were with so many appropriate objects addressed to the eye, recalled the grand chapel scenes and ceremonies of our antient Catholic times. After the scenic representation, a collation was presented in the Library, consisting of various sorts of confectionery served in gold baskets, with spiced wines, &c., whilst rows of chairs were placed in the great room beyond, which had first received the company above stairs. A large vacant place was left in front of the seats. The assembly no sooner occupied them than Lady Hamilton appeared in the character of Agrippina, bearing the ashes of Germanicus in a golden urn, as she presented them before the Roman people, with the design of exciting them to revenge the death of her husband, who, after having been declared joint Emperor by Tiberius, fell a victim to his envy, and is supposed to have been poisoned by his order, at the head of the forces which he was leading against the rebellious Armenians. Lady Hamilton displayed with truth and energy every gesture, attitude, and expression of countenance which could be conceived in Agrippina herself, best calculated to have moved the passions of the Romans on behalf of their favorite General. The action of her head, of her hands, and arms in the various positions of the urn; in her manner of presenting it before the Romans, or of holding it up to the Gods in the act of supplication, was most classically graceful. Every change of dress, principally of the head, to suit the different situations in which she successively presented herself, was performed instantaneously with the most perfect ease, and without retiring or scarcely turning aside a moment from the spectators. In the last scene of this most beautiful piece of pantomime, she appeared with a young lady of the company, who was to personate a daughter. Her action in this part was

so perfectly just and natural, and so pathetically addressed to the spectators as to draw tears from several of the company. It may be questioned whether this scene, without theatrical assistance of other characters and appropriate circumstances, could possibly be represented with more effect. The company, delighted and charmed, broke up at eleven o'clock to sup at the Mansion House. On leaving this strange nocturnal scene of vast buildings and extensive forest, now rendered dimly and partially visible by the declining light of lamps and torches, and the twinkling of a few scattered stars in a clouded sky, the company seemed, as soon as they had passed the sacred boundary of the great wall, as if waking from a dream, or just freed from the influence of some magic spell. And at this moment that I am recapitulating to you in my mind the particulars of the description I have been writing you, I can scarcely help doubting whether the whole of the last evening's entertainment were a reality or only the visionary coinage of fancy.

The extraordinary genius of William Beckford was indeed capable of conceiving this weird entertainment. A few years later, soured, selfish, and morose, he enclosed himself within the walls of his vast estate, and though the narration of the following anecdote is a divergence from the real story, it will serve to demonstrate the change which took place in the character of the host of that gorgeous assembly. A gentleman of means and education (a relative of our popular artist, Mr. W. P. Frith), residing at Bath, was most wishful to obtain an entrance into Fonthill, the sanctuary of art, and, *faut de mieux*, made a bet with a friend that, in spite of all difficulties, he would do so. No tradesman was ever admitted inside the gates, which were closely guarded. However, on a lucky day, the entrance was neglected for a few moments, and in he stepped unnoticed. On he walked, steering for a high tower known as "Beckford's Folly." Suddenly a voice hailed him, asking how he got there, and what he wanted. He saw an old man with a spade, whom he at once concluded was the gardener, and to whom he replied that he had heard of the beauty of the place, and, finding the gates open, had walked in. Instead of ordering him out, the old fellow offered to show him grounds and house, making answer to the gentleman's expressed fear that Mr. Beckford would not be pleased, "Oh, he's known me all my life, and he lets me do pretty much as I like." The acres of well-kept greenhouses were enchanting, and, to a man of artistic cultivation, the house unveiled untold treasures. Five o'clock arrived, and the guide finished the exhibition by an invitation to the stranger to dine with him, acknowledging himself as monarch of all he surveyed—Beckford *in veritas !* The dinner was sumptuous, the conversation elevating and thoroughly enjoyable, until the hour of eleven was reached. As the clock struck, the host rose and left the room. He was immediately replaced by a footman, who began to extinguish the lights. On expressing his wish to see Mr. Beckford to thank him for his hospitality, the guest received for answer: "Master's compliments to you, sir, and he desired me to say that, as you found your way in by yourself, so you may find your way out; and he hopes you'll take care of the bloodhounds, which are let loose in the grounds at night," which message was delivered with grim courtesy. Out went the interloper into the midnight air, and as the door closed upon him his courage forsook him—the warning regarding the bloodhounds assumed gigantic proportions, and he climbed into the branches of the first available tree, and awaited, with untold mental anxiety, the coming dawn. He won his bet, but he said that not for fifty millions would he pass such another night.* *The Gentleman's Magazine* for December, 1821, records that "the public are not allowed to view this as they are most other mansions; and if a traveller more curious than the rest perchance gains admittance within the *chevaux de frise*, he is immediately expelled by force of arms." Samuel Rogers mentions that he received an invitation from the recluse to pay him a visit, and on reaching the gates he was informed that neither his carriage nor horses could be admitted, and he entered *solus*.

In taking up the thread of the tale, we find Lord Nelson in London, and, after many painful scenes with Lady Nelson, he took a final leave of her, emphatically saying, as he quitted her, "I call God to witness there is nothing in you or your conduct I wish otherwise." This interview was on the occasion of his departure for Plymouth to join the Channel Fleet under Lord St. Vincent. When Nelson hoisted his flag on the "San Josef," the *Naval Chronicle* says, "it was cheered by the whole Fleet." He appointed his faithful friend Hardy, who had sailed with him in the Mediterranean encounters, to be Captain of the "San Josef." From London to Southampton he was accompanied by his brother, the Rev. William Nelson. From the latter port he wrote a few lines to his wife, giving her one more chance to reconsider her decision :—

* A more lengthy account of this adventure is to be found in Mr. Frith's *Autobiography*.

NELSON'S LAST LETTER TO HIS WIFE.

My dear Fanny,
We are arrived and heartily tired; and with kindest regards to my father and all the family, believe me your affectionate

NELSON.

To this the lady never vouchsafed a reply! and so completed the breach between them. Surely it was not within her rights to demand absolutely that he should immediately turn his back upon a kind-hearted couple, in whose house he had been nursed to health and attended upon with unremitting kindness. Had Lady Nelson waited until she knew her good-natured rival more intimately, she might have grown to understand her better; but she met her with all her feathers up, prepared to dislike her. From Italy Lady Hamilton had written to Lady Nelson, giving her one of her own peculiarly graphic descriptions of the honours that were falling fast on her illustrious husband, and kindly undertaking, unsolicited, to give her the information that would be of so much interest to her, at the same time forwarding some prints. To this well-meant effusion the dignified lady did not reply, at which Lady Hamilton simply expressed surprise. Poor woman, who was meant for better things, she received many an unmerited rebuff in her course through life, and invariably from people who were nothing like so pleasant as herself.

Leaving the advances towards reconciliation on the part of Lord Nelson unheeded, his lady could not expect him to renew his overtures. The next, and probably the last, letter he ever wrote his wife, shows painfully the widening of the breach, and how keenly he felt her resentment in unison with her son, to whom he had ever shown the greatest kindness, with but poor result, as he wrote Rear-Admiral Duckworth regarding his stepson, "he has by his conduct almost broke my heart." It is sad to read the unhappiness which runs through the following letter. What a home-coming it had been for the conqueror after his victories!

"St. George," *March* 4, 1801.

Josiah is to have another ship, and to go abroad if the "Thalia" cannot soon be got ready. I have done *all* for him; and he may again, as he has often done before, wish me to break my neck, and be abetted in it by his friends, who are likewise my enemies; but I have done my duty as an honest, generous man, and I neither want nor wish for any one to care what becomes of me, whether I return or am left in the Baltic. Living I have done all in my power for you, and if dead you will find I have done the same, therefore, my only wish is to be left to myself, and wishing you every happiness, believe that I am, your affectionate

NELSON AND BRONTË.

Still silent, the coldly proper woman let matters take their course, and Nelson turned for comfort to the two warm hearts which so deeply sympathised with him. Hearing Lord Nelson complain that he had no longer a house to put his head in, Sir William turned to his wife saying, " Our house is large enough, shall we give him the use of it?" She readily assented, but Nelson cautiously observed that such a proceeding would probably make the world talk, which ought to be avoided. "A fig for the world," replied the knight, " I have lived too long to mind what the world either thinks or says on such matters; so you have no more to do than plant yourself here without further scruple or delay." They could only consider him aggrieved, for had they not met with rudeness at her ladyship's hands? and Sir William Hamilton, feeling that she was an exceedingly disagreeable person, invited Nelson to take up his residence with himself and his wife, and so commenced the combined household, only dissolved by death. A few days after Lord Nelson had arrived at Southampton to join the Channel fleet, he wrote Lady Hamilton a letter which shows how regardless Lady Nelson had been to provide any comforts for her husband's voyage, and his letter is full of complaints at the absence of all necessaries save those supplied by Lady Hamilton: "Jan. 21, 1801. I have not got, I assure you, scarcely a comfort about me except the two chairs which you ordered of Mr. Foxhall. I have wrote her (Lady Nelson) a letter of truths about my outfit." She seems to have worked well for the fate which befell her—lifelong separation from a considerate, generous heart, nor is it a matter of wonder that his legal agent, Mr. Alexander Davison, received the following instructions to notify to Lady Nelson her husband's intention to separate from her :—

April 23, 1801.

MY DEAR DAVISON,

You will, at a proper time, and before my arrival in England, signify to Lady Nelson that I expect, and for which I have made such a very liberal allowance to her, to be left to myself, and without any inquiries from her; for sooner than live the unhappy life I did when last I came to England, I would stay abroad for ever. My mind is fixed as fate; therefore you will send my determination in any way you may judge proper, and believe me ever your obliged and faithful friend,

NELSON AND BRONTÉ.

Though Nelson had a comparatively small income for the expenses of his station, he made his wife an annual allowance of £1,600. Dr. Doran, in his work *In and about Old Drury Lane*, concisely sums up her ladyship's character as "highly virtuous, very respectable, and exceedingly ill-tempered."

CHAPTER XVI.

THE THOMSON LETTERS. IMPORTANT EVIDENCE FAVOURING THE ASSERTION THAT LADY HAMILTON WAS NOT THE MOTHER OF HORATIA.

WE have now to consider a point in the story which is and ever will be a mystery; we may think we read aright, but in the absence of any clue or evidence, it is impossible to decide the question as to the maternity of Nelson's adopted child, Horatia. In the year 1801, there dwelt at 9 Little Titchfield Street, Marylebone, a Mrs. Gibson, whose daughter, Mary, ultimately married, and became a Mrs. Johnstone. In the year 1828, this Mrs. Johnstone received a visit from a Captain Ward, brother to the Rev. Philip Ward, whom Horatia, the child in question, had married in the year 1822. To the Captain was given the following information as to the manner in which the infant was confided to the care of Mrs. Johnstone's mother. "Lady Hamilton," she said, "brought the child to my mother's house in a hackney coach one night, and placed her under her charge, telling her that she should be handsomely remunerated. She was unattended, and did not give the nurse any information as to the child's parents. The nurse declared she was no more than eight days old. This was either in the month of January or February, and Mrs. Gibson said she could never make out why her birthday was kept in October. She remained with the nurse till she was five or six years old. Lady Hamilton constantly visited her, Lord Nelson was frequently her companion, and often came alone and played for hours with the infant on the floor, calling her his own child." In after life, Horatia had lost sight of her nurse, and it was during a visit paid by Captain Ward to his brother's curacy at Bircham Newton, in Norfolk, that a letter arrived from Mrs. Johnstone inquiring after her. At Mrs. Ward's request the Captain called upon her on his return to London, in order to obtain information concerning the parentage and infancy of his sister-in-law, and, if possible, to fathom the mystery which surrounded her birth. The good woman was most wishful to help in the research, and as she had preserved many letters that had been written to Mrs. Gibson relative to her little

LADY HAMILTON'S MEMOIR OF NELSON.

charge, she offered to send them to Mrs. Ward, along with a portrait of her as a child, which Lord Nelson himself had given to Mrs. Gibson; and so there came into Mrs. Ward's possession a series of letters, all written without a date, but they were preserved in their original envelopes, bearing dated postmarks, which serve as a guide to their order. In communicating to Mrs. Ward the result of this interview, the Captain wrote, on September 18, 1828: "I have seen Mrs. Johnstone; she is the little deformed woman whom you recollect. She appeared very much pleased at hearing of you. Although the poor creature was under great affliction, her husband (whom I understand was a most respectable man and comfortably off) was then nearly dead. I have since called twice, and find he is no more, so that probably I may not see her again for some days. I sat with her an hour, and she gave me the following information about yourself, which probably you may have heard before." The information alluded to was concerning the placing of the child with nurse Gibson.

The letters which had been so faithfully preserved were merely instructions to the nurse to take her to see Lady Hamilton, or enquiries as to the little girl's health.

We have now arrived at a stage at which the most serious attention must be bestowed on the considerations that will follow, for upon their study will devolve the decision as to whether Lady Hamilton was the mother of Horatia, or whether Nelson bore *undue* love for the wife of his hospitable and unsuspecting friend during that friend's lifetime. Upon one letter rests the almost universally accepted opinion that such was the case; but after the perusal of succeeding arguments, may Nelson's name be cleansed of that foul stain!

To explain the reasons for exonerating Nelson from the onus of the odious charge, it is necessary to introduce subsequent events. After the death of the great naval commander, Lady Hamilton took into her house a man named Harrison, who, under her directions, compiled a memoir of the late Admiral. During the progress of the biography, she lodged and fed him and his family; but he ill-requited her kindness by abusing his confidential position, and abstracting many of her private papers, which, at a later period, in the year 1814, he published without her knowledge, entitled *Letters of Lord Nelson to Lady Hamilton;* and to make the book of a savoury nature, he assisted it by the insertion of some correspondence which has never been within the province of anyone to examine or test as to genuineness, for this reason—the letters were sold at auction by Phillips, in New Bond Street, in the year 1817, after their publication in the anonymous book of 1814, and were purchased by Mr. Croker; but, strange to say, every one of them was abstracted, and he never obtained possession of them. Now, why were they tampered with, unless there was something uncanny about them that a stranger's keen inspection would detect? The man who could basely avail himself of a trusted post to rob his patroness, and publish his ill-gotten gains to her detriment, was capable of any treachery to make his book saleable.

When Lady Hamilton heard what he had done, she called him a "wretch," and he was certainly worthy of the epithet. An example is given to show how he manipulated the documents, and made offensive additions in his publication that never existed in the originals. On August 1, 1803, Nelson *actually* wrote a most staid business-like letter to Lady Hamilton, and at the commencement of one paragraph he says:—

> Hardy is now busy hanging up your and Horatia's picture, and I trust soon to see the other two safe from the Exhibition. You will not expect much news from us. We see nothing.

So runs the original, but in the anonymous work it has this malicious addition:—

> Hardy is now busy hanging up your and Horatia's picture, and I trust soon to see the other two safe from the Exhibition. I want no others to ornament my cabin. I can contemplate them, and find new beauties every day; and I do not want anyone else.

Many similar examples could be given. Suffice it to say that the messages to "Mrs. Thomson," or ultra affectionate expressions to Lady Hamilton, are not to be found in *original* documents; they were the savoury additions to genuine letters already alluded to and exemplified. What wonder, then, that the manuscripts disappeared? Would not their comparison with the printed missives have led to exposure?

The second series of what may be called "The Thomson Letters" was unheard of until the production of Pettigrew's *Life of Nelson*, in which they made their first appearance. They are supposed to anticipate the advent of the mysterious little stranger, and by outpourings of wild delight to betoken the birth as having taken place at the end of January, 1801. These notes were written to convey that Nelson acted as the agent for a Mr. Thomson to Mrs. Thomson, who could only be reached through the medium of Lady Hamilton, but that in reality there were no such persons, the two correspondents being the sole actors.

To explain the circumstances under which they were placed in Pettigrew's work, it must be known that, a few years previously, Sir Harris Nicolas had given to the literary world a most painstaking compilation of *Lord Nelson's Letters and Dispatches*; he had received from Mrs. Ward (Horatia) the loan of Lady Hamilton's notes to Nurse Gibson, and these, with the aforenamed statement of Mrs. Gibson's daughter, he entered in his voluminous work in a summary entitled "Miss Horatia Nelson Thompson"; and as *he* questioned the authenticity of the letters published in 1814, he held, from his remaining documents, that Lady Hamilton was not the mother of Horatia. These letters to the nurse, and the statement of her daughter, thus obtained circulation, and would serve to supply dates whereon to frame the spurious compositions of the later biography. As some readers may be unfamiliar with the extracts which have so thoughtlessly been accepted as genuine, it will be as well to place a few so that they may be compared with Nelson's well-known concise style, with which they are totally at variance. On January 21, 1801, Nelson, according to Pettigrew's *Life of Nelson*, vol. ii, p. 645, writes:—

> I sincerely hope that your very serious cold will soon be better. I am so much interested in your health, that pray tell me all. I delivered to Mr. —— Mrs. Thomson's message and note; he desires me, poor fellow, to say he is more scrupulous than if Mrs. T. was present. He says he does not write letters at this moment, as the object of his affections may be unwell, and others may open them.

Now in the full letter which Pettigrew has inserted in vol. i, p. 411, there is nothing relative to the "Thomson" fiction, the portion of the composition relative to Lady Hamilton's health is merely these few words,

> I sincerely hope that your very serious cold will soon be better. I am

so much interested in your health and happiness that pray tell me all. You have had a large party ; . . . . .

This shows how the fabrications were placed *in printing*, which were not in original MSS. The offensive extracts to be found in Pettigrew's *Life of Nelson*, vol. ii, p. 645, &c., are dated to correspond with genuine letters as if they had been enclosed with them, but that slip letters, having neither customary beginning nor ending should be dated, seems but an additional reason to doubt them. Furthermore, the letters from Lady Hamilton to the nurse show that the child must have been in existence, and was old enough to be taken out, in the beginning of February, so that the *anticipations* of this "Thomson" letter are in arrears! On January 24, 1801, Pettigrew has it, "Pray tell Mrs. Thomson her kind friend is very uneasy about her, and prays most fervently for her safety."

So these vapid rigmaroles continue, without beginning or end, until February 1, when we are asked to believe that poor Nelson wrote this outrageous effusion : —

MY DEAR LADY,
I believe poor dear Mrs. Thomson's friend will go mad with joy. He cries, prays, and performs all tricks, yet dare not show all or any of his feelings. He has only me to consult with. He swears he will drink your health this day in a bumper; and d—— me if I don't join him in spite of all the doctors in Europe, for none regards you with truer affection than myself. You are a dear, good creature, and your kindness and goodness to poor Mrs. T. stamps you higher than ever in my mind. I cannot write, I am so agitated by this young man at my elbow. I believe he is foolish ; he does nothing but rave about you and her. I own I partake of his joy. I cannot write anything.

Is it credible that this vagary emanated from the same man who, on January 28, 1801, wrote his friend Mr. Davison, "Either as a public or private man I wish nothing undone which I have done."

In giving to the world the defamations that were to blast the reputation of one of England's noblest characters, Pettigrew should unquestionably have annexed his authority, and placed beyond contention that they were traced to an absolutely genuine source. Not the faintest clue is given as to how he became possessed of them, and they as mysteriously disappeared when his foul mission was accomplished. His bare word was no guarantee of their genuineness. Records of such grave import should have been backed by incontestable evidence of authenticity. In spite of the taunts levelled at him through the medium of literary papers, Pettigrew remained singularly silent. In very indignation he has been accused of having forged them himself, but there are no grounds to suppose this. May he not have been—nay, was he not—the victim of an imposition which seems only to have been at his service for the destruction of the honoured memory of a good man?

When Sir Harris Nicolas was engaged upon his task, he continuously advertised for the loan of letters bearing on the subject in hand; no man could have made more effort to that end; yet *he* had no knowledge of their existence, and it may be asserted with certainty, that if the letters that nurse Gibson had so faithfully preserved had never been published, the world would never have received the dubious inanities which found their headquarters in Pettigrew's mischievous work.

In furtherance of the assertion that the information gleaned from Mrs. Gibson's relics fixed the dates for the Pettigrew letters, it can be shown that in all the new "extracts" which he introduced, the name is spelt "*Thomson*." On every occasion when Nelson wrote Horatia's surname it *invariably* appears as "*Thompson*"; to wit, the codicils to his will; his first letter to the little girl, headed "Miss Horatia Nelson Thompson"; and in the following instructions, in his writing, found among Mrs. Gibson's collection, the envelope containing which was dated 19th November, 1802:—

MRS. GIBSON, 9 LITTLE TITCHFIELD STREET, MARYLEBONE.
Mrs Gibson is desired on no consideration to answer any questions about Miss Thompson, nor who placed her with Mrs. G., as ill-tempered people have talked lies about the child.

Would Nelson spell the child's name "*Thompson*," and the mother's "*Thomson*"? Most certainly not! It was Lady Hamilton who defectively wrote it "*Thomson*" in her letters to Nurse Gibson, which Sir Harris Nicolas published, and upon which the "*Thomson*" letters were palpably based in the later work.

The copy of the will in favour of Lady Hamilton (see Pettigrew's *Life of*

Nelson, vol. ii, p. 648), bequeathing to her the rental of the Bronté estate failing heirs male, must be rejected as spurious, for it, too, is followed by a sentence in which the fatal "Thomson" is twice repeated. The improbability of Nelson's making such a will is enhanced by the fact that he had already written to his father that it was his intention to bequeath the estates first to him, and in succession (failing heirs) to his elder brother; to the Rev. W. Nelson; to the sons of his sisters, Mrs. Bolton and Mrs. Matcham;* so that Nelson would never make a will *providing for* Lady Hamilton after these conditions. In this supposititious will, this incongruity also occurs: Nelson is made to empower Lady Hamilton to bequeath the estate of Bronté to "any child she may have, in or out of wedlock," while some lines further on contain the assurance, "I rely with the greatest confidence on her unspotted honour and integrity." This insulting innuendo Nelson's? Never!

The same document leaves Horatia all the money he shall die possessed of above the sum of twenty thousand pounds. This testament was dated February 5, 1801; yet in the August of the same year, Nelson wrote Lady Hamilton that he "could only command three thousand pounds"; and again, on September 6, 1803, to Mr. Haslewood, "It is possible that my personal estate, after the disposal of the furniture at Merton, may not amount to four thousand pounds." Where were the twenty thousand?

On February 16, 1801, we find in one of the fictitious letters, "I send you a few lines, wrote in the late gale, which I think you will not disapprove." Now the lines in question were descriptive of the calm succeeding a gale off Cadiz. One trashy verse will suffice to prove that an event which did not take place until 1805—four and a half years later—could not have been anticipated by Nelson in February, 1801 :—

> But hark! I hear
> The signal gun!
> Farewell, my dear!
> The "Victory" leads on!
> The fight's begun!
> Thy picture round this cannon's mouth shall prove
> A pledge—to valour! sent by thee and love!

* *Ante* p. 115.

SPURIOUS VERSES

SAID TO HAVE BEEN WRITTEN BY LORD NELSON ON THE DAY ON WHICH
THE BATTLE OF COPENHAGEN WAS FOUGHT.

Lord Nelson to his Guardian angel

From my best Cable thred I'm forced to part
I leave my Anchor in my Angels heart
Love like a Pilot shall the pledge defend
and for a Buoy his Sanguine Quivering that

Answer of Lord N's Guardian angel

Go where you list, each thought my Angels Soul
Shall follow you from Indus to the Pole
East, west, North, South, our minds shall never part
and my Angels loadstone shall be Nelson's heart
farewell and oer the wide, wide Sea
Bright Glorys course pursue
and adverse winds to Love & me
prove fair to fame and you,

and when the dreaded hour of battle nigh
your Angels heart which trembles at a Sigh
By your Superior Danger bolder Grown
Shall dauntless place itself before your own
happy thrice happy should her fond heart
a Sheild to Valour Constancy & Love

St George April 2nd 1801 9 OClock at night
very tired after a hard fought Battle,

AN AUTOGRAPH LETTER
FROM LORD NELSON TO LADY HAMILTON.

My Dear Lady Hamilton—

I have kissed the Queen letter pray say I hope for the honor of kissing her hand when no fears will intervene, assure her Majesty that no person has her felicity more than yourself at heart, and that the sufferings of her family will be a Tower of Strength on the day of Battle. fear not the event, God is with us, God Bless you and Sir William pray say I cannot stay to answer his letter Ever

yours faithfully
Horatio Nelson

THE FICTITIOUS LETTERS.

In the final verse, the hope of return to Merton is expressed. Nelson had no thought even of purchasing Merton in February, 1801.

Of honoured Nelson's last hours we have a better record than is insinuated by this puerile composition, which was in reality written many a year after the dead hero was laid to rest, with the awful intent of robbing the great death scene of its grandeur.

It is within the reach of any student to satisfy himself that forgeries did exist. If he will analyse the annexed facsimiles—the first, of verses said to have emanated from Nelson—the second, a genuine letter of Nelson's—let him take the name "Nelson" at the beginning of the verses and the finish of the letter, and say were they written by the same hand? Where is the bold dash in the verses with which Nelson invariably finished his N? Let the capital B which commences the lines twelve and seventeen in the poem be compared with that in "Battle" and "Bless" in the letter. Nelson certainly terminated his d's with an upward stroke ending abruptly; but in the verses, though taken upwards, they are brought round in hook form.

Let the reader examine words, which from frequent repetition become characteristic, such as "to" and "of" in each manuscript; let him look at the decided loops to the "f" in the verses, and he will soon convince himself that though a fair (or unfair) imitation, the poetic effusion is spurious. The lithographed verses do not even convey the idea that they were written with the left hand, being too regular and small for Nelson's clearly defined, bold and shaky caligraphy.

The following foot-note is attached to these verses:—"'St. George,' *April 2nd*, 1801. Nine o'clock at night; very tired after a hard fought battle."

Is it necessary to ask whether this was the occupation of the great Admiral on the evening of the momentous day on which the battle of Copenhagen had been fought? There is a letter extant from Nelson to Lady Hamilton bearing the same date, "April 2, 1801. Eight o'clock at night," in which he recounts the contest of four or five hours, and the loss of life which had resulted, naming one esteemed captain in particular; and he concludes by saying, "I am not a little tired, for I have scarcely slept one moment since the 24th of last month." Would he then one hour afterwards (for the time of day is entered in both letter and verse) write trashy poetry? Personally, Nelson had no poetical tendencies. Could we credit such heartlessness to a man of deep feeling such as Nelson undoubtedly was, fresh from the fearful fight in which he had witnessed the scenes of carnage and horror, and the terrible sacrifice of human life ? Perish the thought!

To continue the narrative. Lady Hamilton as a matter of fact did take the infant and give it into the good keeping of Mrs. Gibson early in the year 1801; but that is no proof that the birth had only just taken place; indeed, there is plain testimony that the time fixed by the "Thomson" letters is inaccurate, for in notes from Lady Hamilton to Mrs. Gibson (February 11 and 18) we find directions that the child shall be taken to see her; risks that would not have been permitted to a babe of ten days or a fortnight old. What infant of even the working class would be so recklessly taken out in the keen February weather at so tender an age? The baptismal entry certifies the child's birthday as October 29, 1800—Nelson was no liar—and that it was otherwise rests solely in the statement of Mrs. Johnstone, made to the best of her ability, twenty-seven years after her mother had received her little charge, when Mary Gibson was but a child herself; and as we have shown, upon that statement were the "Thomson" letters concocted. The first letter to the nurse which has been preserved in its original envelope dated February 7, 1801, conveys the idea that the babe had not been seen by Lady Hamilton within a day or two at least; it does not even read like a first letter to a comparative stranger—it seems more fit to consider it as *the first of those that have been preserved.*

DEAR MADAM,
My cold has been so bad, I could not go out to-day, but to-morrow will call on you. Write me by the penny post how the dear little Miss Horatia is. Ever your sincere friend,

E. H.

To further disprove the "Thomson" letters, one containing instructions for the christening may be analysed.*

MY DEAR MRS. THOMSON,
Your dear and excellent friend has desired me to say that it is not usual to christen children till they are a month or six weeks old; and as Lord Nelson will probably be in town as well as myself,

---

* The confusion between the first and third person in this letter betokens it to be a forgery, as Lord Nelson was too well educated to have committed such a mistake.

THE FICTITIOUS LETTERS. 149

before we go to the Baltic, he proposes then, if you approve, to christen the child, and that myself and Lady Hamilton should be two of the sponsors. It can be christened at St. George's, Hanover Square; and, I believe, the parents being at the time out of the kingdom, if it is necessary it can be stated born at Portsmouth, or at sea. Its name will be Horatia, daughter of Johem and Morata Etnorb.* If you read the surname backwards, and take the letters of the other names, it will make, very extraordinary, the names of your real and affectionate friends, Lady Hamilton and myself; but, my dear friend, consult Lady Hamilton. Your friend consults me, and I would not lead him wrong for the world; he has not been very well; I believe he has fretted, but his spirit is too high to own it. But, my dear Madam, both him, you and your little one must always believe me your affectionate,

NELSON AND BRONTÉ.

This letter conveys the desire to postpone the christening until the infant be a month or six weeks old, when he and Lady Hamilton can act as sponsors. Here is another attempt to fix the period of birth as recent (acting on information gathered from the already printed statement of Mary Johnstone). The christening did not take place until two years and three months from this date, and though at that time both Nelson and Lady Hamilton were in town,† neither of them was present at the ceremony, as we find from her ladyship's written instructions to the nurse—" To give the Clergyman a double fee, and the same to the Clerk. The Register of the Baptism to be taken out." In the above letter the child is supposed to be given her name; but she was already known as "Horatia." These lines, written on February 5th, would be received by Lady Hamilton on the 6th, yet on the 7th she wrote to Mrs. Gibson, " My cold has been so bad, I could not go out to-day, but to-morrow will call on you. Write me by the penny post how the dear little Miss Horatia is." Here she is called Horatia, and the nurse knows it, which would not have been the case if Lady Hamilton, confined to the house on the 7th, had only received the name on the 6th.

The transposition of the names into Johem and Morata Etnorb betrays the falsity of the letter; Nelson had neither the talent, time, nor inclination

* Emma and Horatio Bronté.
† The christening took place three days before Nelson was appointed to the command of the Mediterranean Fleet.

to compose verses or transpose words. Nelson wrote his letters as a diary, and when opportunity offered these were forwarded. On February 5th, 1801, we find he has only time to enter in his diary-letter, " We are here all in a bustle from this French squadron having got to sea. So much for our sharp look-out." Yet on this same date the Thomson fiction states that he made his will in favour of Lady Hamilton and Horatia, and wrote the above letter.

The record of baptism is in the Marylebone Register; no parentage is named. It reads thus :—

Baptisms, 1803.
May 13, Horatia Nelson Thompson; B 29 October, 1800.

Want of space prohibits the prolongation of arguments against the genuineness of the unauthenticated letters, but surely sufficient has been said to show that original documents were tampered with by making additions in printing, and that likewise actual forgeries existed. There will, then, be no occasion to dilate at length on the following letter, the crowning infamy, diabolically conceived, to destroy fair fame—written to appear that Nelson sent by hand dishonourable acknowledgement of criminality to the wife of his sincere friend. Its very excess is its own condemnation.

March 1, 1801.

Now, my own dear Wife, for such you are in my eyes and in the face of Heaven, I can give full scope to my feelings, for I dare say Oliver will faithfully deliver this letter. You know, my dearest Emma, that there is nothing in this world that I would not do for us to live together, and to have our dear little child with us. . . . . I love, I never did love any one else. I never had a dear pledge of love till you gave me one, and you, thank my God, never gave one to any one else. I think, before March is out, either you will see us back or so victorious that we shall ensure a glorious issue to our toils. Think what my Emma will feel at seeing return safe, perhaps with a little more fame, her own dear, loving Nelson. Never, if I can help it, will I dine out of my ship, or go on shore, except duty calls me. Let Sir Hyde have any glory he can catch—I envy him not. You, my beloved Emma, and my country, are the two dearest objects of my fond heart—*a heart susceptible and true*. Only place confidence in me, and you never shall be disappointed. I burn all your dear letters, because it is right for your sake, and I wish you would burn all mine—for they can do no good, and will do us both harm if any seizure of them; or the dropping even one of them would fill the mouths of the world sooner than we intend. . . . . I had a letter this day from the Reverend Mr. Holden, who we met on the Continent; he desired his kind compliments to you and Sir William; he sent me the letters of my name, and recommended it as my motto—Honor est a Nilo—Horatio Nelson. May the Heavens bless you.

N. & B.

Monday Morning.

Oliver is just going on shore; the time will ere long arrive when Nelson will land to fly to his Emma, to be for ever with her. Let that hope keep us up under our present difficulties. Kiss and bless *our* dear Horatia. Think of that.

Would Nelson have forwarded this vile composition on the mere "*dare say*" it will be faithfully delivered? Would not the exercise of ordinary common prudence have prevented his entrusting it to mortal hand? What would have been the result if it had *not* been faithfully delivered? Would Nelson have risked it? No! Nelson never wrote that letter! Is the line "I love, I never did love anyone else" the outcome of one who so recently had told Lady Knight that "the happiest day in his life was that on which he led Lady Nelson to the altar." The words "a heart susceptible and true," are quoted from some of the spurious verses, which with the transposing of the name Horatio Nelson into "Honor est a Nilo" betoken them as the inspiration of a more poetic genius than was the gift of poor Nelson, and akin to the "Johem and Morata Etnorb" production, which we have disproved. It is well known that a celebrated literary doctor sent the anagram, "Honor est a Nilo," to Nelson directly after the battle of the Nile, therefore its introduction in this letter betrays its falsity; for Nelson would not have availed himself of surreptitious methods to convey to Lady Hamilton old news of which she had been well aware for at least two years. A natural correspondence under the circumstances would have kept to the point at issue—love, and would not have introduced immaterial matter. It may be asked, how do the words "I never had a dear pledge of love" compare with those in a subsequent letter, genuine or spurious, bearing date May 30, 1804—"Your resemblance is so deeply engraved in my heart that there it can never be effaced, and who knows? Some day I may have the happiness of having a living picture of you." This would insinuate that there had been no offspring; original or counterfeit, one letter contradicts the other. The former document still exists; but the forger's art would be of little avail if of easy detection. Nelson's misfortune in being compelled to use his left hand made his writing no difficult matter to copy. In recent times have not the learned staff of a leading newspaper been the victims of similar fraud? But why say so much? For are not the infamous insinuations contained in this and the "Thomson" letters utterly confuted by one fact alone? Return to the festivities at Fonthill Abbey, held in honour of Lord Nelson, in December, 1800.* It will be remembered that on the twenty-third day of that month Lady Hamilton performed her exquisite attitudes with so much grace and pathos before a vast assemblage of the élite of society that many were affected to tears; her dress during the elegant exhibition consisting only of a calico gown of simple make. Could a performance of such finish, ease and rapidity have been given by a woman, who only six weeks later placed in the hands of a nurse, a child of her own, said to be eight days old? The attitudes under such circumstances could not have been affecting; they would have been repulsive. Each tableau lasted ten minutes. The insinuation of maternity is destroyed by a moment's reflection. Little did the eye-witness of those gorgeous revels think of the important evidence of vindication he was recording as his pen detailed the brilliant scene at the Abbey, and the rapid and classically graceful movements of the principal performer! Of what value then are the so-called "Thomson Letters," which are framed to betoken uneasiness concerning the lady's condition up to January 31, 1801, and elation and mental relief after that date? The idea is preposterous!

A letter from the Rev. William Nelson to Lady Hamilton, written less than three weeks from the date of the child's birth (as fixed by the "Thomson" fiction), is amply sufficient to prove that Lady Hamilton had not been seriously indisposed. He invariably used a tone of obsequious adulation to his fair correspondent so long as he sought her good-natured services. The letter was sent on the completion of a visit to Sir William

Ante, p. 134.

PLATE VI.—ATTITUDE OF LADY HAMILTON, FROM A DRAWING BY REHBURG

and Lady Hamilton, and had she been only slightly invalided, it would have been of the deepest concern to this arch-hypocrite.

February 19, 1801.

MY DEAR LADY,

For I must call you by that name, and feel myself highly honoured in being permitted to do it, I cannot find words to express the grief I feel in leaving London and such amiable society as yours. Indeed, I have been scarcely able to speak a word the whole journey. Your image and voice are constantly before my imagination, and I can think of nothing else. I never knew what it was to part with a friend before, and it is no wonder that my good, my virtuous, my beloved brother should be so much attached to your ladyship after so long a friendship, when I feel so much after so short an acquaintance. May it continue unabated to the latest period of our lives! I hope it will not be very long before we all meet again. We are now at an inn, thirty miles from London, and have just finished our mutton chop. Mrs. Nelson, who thinks of you, and loves you all as much as I do, has this moment given a toast, "Sir William and Lady Hamilton, and Lord Nelson, God bless them," to which I answer "Amen, and Amen." We shall pursue our journey to-morrow morning, and hope to reach home by dinner. We beg to join in kindest regards and good wishes to Sir William. I remain your grateful and affectionate friend,

WILLIAM NELSON.

The hostess has apparently taken an active part in the entertainment of her guests; and the absence of sympathetic expression from the correspondence of the effusive cleric shows there was no foundation for it.

Furthermore, on this same day, February 19, 1801, Sir William Hamilton wrote to inform Lord Nelson that the Prince of Wales had invited himself to dine with them on the following Sunday (the 22nd), for the purpose of hearing Lady Hamilton and Mme. Banti sing together, which would not have occurred had he been informed of any indisposition on the part of the lady. A woman of her time of life could not have been out and about at so early a stage; the very attempt would have thrown her into a serious illness.

Would not Mr. Greville have been concerned about the destruction of his life-long hopes? But there is nothing to show that he was troubled about coming events, or the likelihood of his dethronement. No voice has been raised in anticipation, no pen recorded the probability of her ladyship's condition; and, in dying, her brave confiding husband bequeathed a refutation of all slanders. He, too, doubtless, held the key to the mystery, for he often saw Horatia, and was a man whom it would have been impossible to deceive.

It is to be regretted that Mr. Haslewood, in whom the secret was reposed, did not break confidence, for surely the reputation of Lady Hamilton was of equal importance to that of any other lady. To many the care and affection bestowed through life by Lady Hamilton on Horatia would warrant a belief in the maternal tie; but the character of her ladyship was beyond ordinary appreciation. So large-hearted was she, that she embraced all needy relatives; her devotion to her humble mother was exemplary, and the house over which she presided was the scene of unbounded hospitality; and she could not fail to be true to the trust reposed in her keeping.

On any one of these points might the slanderous tales be doubted. First, that the graceful "attitudes" were performed at so close a date upon the event; second, that a lady living with her husband without intermission should give birth to a child without even his suspicion being excited; third, that the babe remained for some days in a busy household without attracting any attention; fourth, that it was removed within a brief period of its birth by the invalid herself; fifth, that having deposited her burden with its nurse, entailing a perilous night drive in cold weather, she returned—not to her couch—but to preside over the amusements of her guests. Any one of the foregoing points would be difficult to successfully surmount, but that all five should have been accomplished is to credit superhuman achievements.

THE SEAL OF LORD NELSON, A PORTRAIT OF LADY HAMILTON, USED BY LORD NELSON WHEN WRITING TO HER LADYSHIP.

CHAPTER XVII.

NELSON'S REGARD FOR HORATIA. "EMMA HAMILTON" OF THE FOUNDLING HOSPITAL.

AFTER so clearly disproving Lady Hamilton's relationship to Horatia, it is not out of place to state that there is no absolute reason to believe that Nelson was the *actual* father. He called her "his child," but very sympathy for the unfortunate circumstances of the little creature's birth would make his most tender nature compassionate the babe, and the very intensity of his feelings induce him to be all the world to it, and take it into his generous heart as his very own. Nelson always wrote of her as his adopted daughter, and in writing *to* her as "My dear Child," and signing himself "Your Father," meant nothing; he could scarcely say "My dear *adopted* Child," &c. Captain Hardy, Nelson's constant companion, never thought she was the veritable daughter of his Chief, and when Lady Hamilton said that such was the case, it was Hardy's opinion that she asserted it in order to strengthen Horatia's claim for a pension. At Merton she told friends that it was a child whom Nelson had adopted out of generosity, and this certainly bears out the statement that Mr. Haslewood wrote, "If he gave the name it would destroy the happiness of a happy and united family." Lady Hamilton's reputation reinstated, there is no difficulty in believing that the adoption of Horatia was the charitable act of a God-fearing man.

On January 14th, 1804, Nelson wrote to the little Horatia, apparently in reply to a letter she had written to him. There are letters of Lady Hamilton's with the child's writing across them, and they are sufficiently advanced to further the assertion that she was older than the period assigned by the "Thomson" letters. Nelson's reply, in like manner, seems to be suited for an older child than three years.

The attempt no doubt gave exceeding pleasure to the receiver, and drew from the loving man the following response:—

MY DEAR HORATIA,
I feel very much pleased by your kind letter, and for your present of a lock of your beautiful hair. I am very glad to hear that you

> are so good and mind everything that your governess and dear Lady Hamilton tell you. I send you a lock of my hair, and a pound-note to buy a locket to put it in, and I give you leave to wear it when you are dressed and behave well; and I send you another to buy some little thing for Mary * and your governess. As I am sure that for all the world you would not tell a story, it must have slipt my memory that I promised you a watch, therefore I have sent to Naples to get one, and I will send it home as soon as it arrives. The Dog I never could have promised, as we have no Dogs on board Ship. Only I beg, my dear Horatia, be obedient, and you will ever be sure of the affection of
>
> NELSON AND BRONTÉ.

Mrs. Ward said that instead of a dog, he sent her a locket with a dog engraved upon it,† so considerate was he for his dear child's pleasure, and so wishful to gratify every desire.

On March 14th, 1804, he wrote home instructions for the protection of the Nile, a stream running through his grounds, as the little girl was about to take up her permanent residence with Lady Hamilton.

> I also beg, as my dear Horatia is to be at Merton, that a strong netting, about three feet high, may be placed round the Nile, that the little thing may not tumble in. . . . I shall, when I come home, settle four thousand pounds in trustees' hands for Horatia,‡ for I will not put it in my own power to have her left destitute, for she would want friends, if we left her in this world. She shall be independent of any smiles or frowns.

On April 2nd, 1804, he wrote in much distress of mind, the little circle in whom his affections were centred having been indisposed—

> I have, my dearest beloved Emma, been so uneasy for this last month, desiring most ardently to hear of your well-doing. Captain Capel brought me your letters sent by the "Thisbe," from Gibraltar. I opened, opened—found none but December, or early in January. I was in such an agitation. At last I found one without a date, which, thank God,

---

* Mary Gibson, afterwards Mrs. Johnstone.
† This locket is now in the possession of Mrs. Raglan Somerset.
‡ What had become of the codicil, February 5, 1801, in which Dr. *Pettigrew* provided for her by leaving her all that he (Nelson) would die possessed of above £20,000?

"EMMA HAMILTON" OF THE FOUNDLING HOSPITAL.

told my poor heart that you was recovering, but that dear little Emma was no more! and that Horatia had been so very ill; it quite upset me. But it was just at bed time, and I had time to reflect and be thankful to God for sparing you and our dear Horatia. I am sure the loss of one, much more both, would have drove mad. I was so agitated as it was, that I was glad it was night, and that I could be by myself. Kiss dear Horatia for me, and tell her to be a dutiful and good child, and if she is, that we shall always love her. You may, if you like, tell Mrs. G——* that I shall certainly settle a small pension on her. It shall not be large, as we may have the pleasure of making her little presents; and, my dearest Emma, I shall not be wanting to everybody who has been kind to you, be they servants or gentlefolks.

The child "Emma," to whom reference is made in the above letter, died in a convulsive fit very suddenly. It does not necessarily follow that she was any relative to Lord Nelson or Lady Hamilton; in fact there is not much expression of concern regarding the death of the infant; the words: "I am sure the loss of one, much more both, would have drove mad," signify Lady Hamilton or Horatia, both of whom had been seriously indisposed. The child most probably was one of their numerous Godchildren in whom they invariably took an interest, and she does not appear in any other document, so that the notion of relationship may satisfactorily be dispelled. There was at this time another "Emma Hamilton" in existence, and as this child is traceable, its history may serve to carry out the assertion that the "little Emma" whose death was referred to was merely connected by spiritual ties.

Among Lady Hamilton's papers a few years later, which passed among her effects that she made over to a gentleman who rendered her pecuniary assistance,† was found the following document :—"Mrs. Sarah Snelling takes the liberty to acquaint Lady Hamilton that the child 'Emma Hamilton' (which she received from the Foundling Hospital) is well and much grown. May 20, 1801. Gogmore Lane, Chertsey, Surrey." If no further enquiry were made, it might easily be set down that this was the same child, but, on searching the records of the Foundling Hospital, it appears that the child "Emma Hamilton" was received at that institution in April, 1801, being then six weeks old. She was put out to nurse with Mrs. Sarah

* Nurse Gibson. † Alderman Smith.

Snelling of Chertsey, who was one of the hospital staff of nurses under the supervision of the hospital doctor of that district. To the present day children are still sent to that locality. This Emma was apprenticed by the Governors of the Charity in the year 1816, and therefore could not be the same Emma to whom Lord Nelson made reference. The date of the birth of the Emma of the Foundling Hospital was about the middle of February, 1801—three weeks after Horatia's appearance. It is important that readers should know that in those days it was the fashion for people of rank and wealth to visit the Foundling Hospital constantly; to stand sponsors for the children, and to be responsible for the charge of a certain number near their country seats. Lady Hamilton was one of those who took a great interest in that valuable institution, and particularly in the children, and like many other of the visitors who were the members of noble families, she gave her name to children, and so became interested in their well being. This custom at last gave rise to difficulties, through foundlings making unfounded claims, and so it was discontinued. There is certainly nothing to show that either the good Lord or Lady was connected with the child by any closer tie; nor yet to any child in the institution. May not that other Emma have been merely a *protégée*? especially as there is no reference to her in the well preserved letters of all parties concerned. They both had a great partiality for children, and loved the patronage of sponsorship. May not Lady Hamilton, in the kindness of her heart, have made the same mistake as misguided Queen Caroline, and taken too much interest in other people's children, which brought her into much the same discredit?

Mrs. Cadogan at this time was residing with Lady Hamilton, as also were different relatives of Lord Nelson, such as his sister, Mrs. Bolton's daughters Eliza and Anne, and his niece Miss Charlotte Nelson, the daughter of his brother the Rev. William Nelson (of whom more hereafter). In a letter from Sir Gilbert Elliot to his wife, dated August 26, 1805, he says—

> I went to Merton on Saturday, and found Nelson just sitting down to dinner surrounded, by a family party of his brother the Dean, Mrs. Nelson, their children, and the children of a sister; Lady Hamilton at the head of the table, and mother Cadogan at the bottom. He looks remarkably well and full of spirits.

It does not appear feasible that these various relatives would have continued in residence in a house whose owner could have been considered wanting in social propriety. Miss Charlotte Nelson had shown much kindness to little Horatia, which greatly gratified the absentee, and he sent her a letter to thank her for her goodness to his favourite, for his heart went forth to all who extended the hand of friendship to his little pet, and he felt bitterly the dread that she should ever receive a slight. On the 19th of April, 1804, he wrote to his niece—

> I thank you very much for your letters of January 3rd and 4th, and I feel truly sensible of your kind regard for that dear little orphan, Horatia. Although her parents are lost, yet she is not without a fortune, and I shall cherish her to the last moment of my life; and curse them who curse her, and Heaven bless them who bless her! Dear innocent! she can have injured no one.

On the same day he wrote to Lady Hamilton—

> I am pleased with Charlotte's letter; and as she loves my dear Horatia, I shall always like her. What hearts those must have who do not! But, thank God, she shall not be dependent on any of them.

On the 30th of May he wrote to Lady Hamilton—

> I wish I could but be at dear Merton to assist in making the alterations. I think I should have persuaded you to have kept the pike and a clear stream; and to have put all the carp, tench, and fish that muddy the water into the pond; but do as you like, I am content. Only take care that my little darling does not fall in and get drowned. I begged you to get the little netting along the edges, and particularly on the bridges.

The next two documents came into the possession of Horatia in a remarkable manner. During her residence with Mrs. Matcham (one of Nelson's sisters), in 1815, directly after the death of Lady Hamilton, Mr. Coutts, the banker, made a communication to Mr. Matcham that he had some papers of importance in his keeping, deposited by the Duchess of Devonshire, who had received them from Lady Hamilton before her decease. As she had been requested to take charge of them for Horatia, she preferred to place them with Mr. Coutts for safe custody, for she was going abroad. As will be seen, they were written by Lord Nelson in case of the worst happening, and sent to Lady Hamilton for the benefit of the child when he would be no more. He must ever have lived in sight of death. The first of the two letters was written off Toulon, October 21st, 1803, evidently anticipating an engagement:—

> My Dear Child,
> Receive this first letter from your most affectionate Father. If I live, it will be my pride to see you virtuously brought up, but if it pleases God to call me, I trust, to Himself, in that case I have left dear Lady Hamilton your Guardian. I therefore charge you, my dear child, on the value of a Father's blessing, to be obedient and attentive to all her kind admonitions and instructions. At this moment I have left you, in a Codicil dated the 6th of September, 1803, the sum of four thousand pounds sterling, the interest of which is to be paid to Lady Emma Hamilton, your Guardian, for your maintenance and education. I shall only say, my dear child, may God Almighty bless you, and make you an ornament to your sex, which I am sure you will be if you attend to all dear Lady Hamilton's kind instructions; and be assured that I am, my dear Horatia,
> Your most affectionate Father,
> NELSON AND BRONTÉ.

This was penned to a child not yet three years old, incapable of reading or understanding, to be held in trust for her, knowing that death might be his lot at any hour, and wishful that the idol in whom his heart's best love was centred should, in the day when his place among men would be vacant, think of him in that future with all the love for which his great heart yearned.

In the codicil to his will, in which he requested Lady Hamilton to undertake her guardianship, he says:—" This request of guardianship I earnestly make of Lady Hamilton, knowing that she will educate my adopted child in the paths of religion and virtue, and give her those accomplishments which so much adorn herself, and, I hope, make her a fit wife for my dear nephew, Horatio Nelson, who I wish to marry her if he proves worthy in Lady Hamilton's estimation of such a treasure as I am sure she will be."

Knowing that after his death she would have no claim to his title and estates, but that, failing issue, his nephew would in due course possess them, his earnest wish was that the marriage between the two young people should take place, and so she would obtain the position the law did not give her by right of inheritance.

The second of the two letters in the hands of Mr. Coutts was the last he ever wrote to her, written on the morning of the eventful October 19, 1805, the day which gained to England the victory of Trafalgar, and cost him his life. He took his pen as he received word that the combined fleets of the enemy were seen to be coming out of port, giving his last act before that momentous battle to the darling of his heart :—

"VICTORY," *October* 19th, 1805.

MY DEAREST ANGEL,

I was made happy by the pleasure of receiving your letter of September 19th, and I rejoice to hear that you are so very good a girl, and love my dear Lady Hamilton, who most dearly loves you. Give her a kiss for me. The Combined Fleets of the Enemy are now reported to be coming out of Cadiz; and therefore I answer your letter, my dearest Horatia, to mark to you that you are ever uppermost in my thoughts. I shall be sure of your prayers for my safety, conquest, and speedy return to dear Merton, and our dearest good Lady Hamilton. Be a good girl, mind what Miss Connor* says to you. Receive, my dearest Horatia, the affectionate Parental Blessing of your Father,

NELSON AND BRONTÉ.

Still keeping the child in mind, and acting under the influence of the dread foreboding which hung over him all that fateful day, he added the memorable codicil to his will, "I also leave to the beneficence of my country my adopted daughter, Horatia Nelson Thompson, and I desire that she will use in future the name of Nelson only." Sacred legacy, shamefully ignored! Having written thus far concerning the birth and childhood of Horatia, the subject shall be for the present abandoned, and the continuation of the story resumed.

In the April of 1801, Mrs. Cadogan revisited her old home at Hawarden, and sojourned for a few days with relatives and friends both in Chester and

* Lady Hamilton's cousin, who became Horatia's governess.

Liverpool. The house at which she remained in Chester was that of Mrs. Burt, her long-standing friend, and it was during this residence that she sat for her portrait to the lady's son, an artist of fair repute. The *pose* selected was that of sitting by an old-fashioned upright piano! In announcing his capabilities, Mr. Burt used the following form of advertisement :—
"From the facility that extensive practice has given to his pencil, he can take the likeness in half an hour, and afford the coloured profiles at ten and sixpence each."

Mr. Burt visited Parkgate weekly as a drawing master; his mode of conveyance was one of those old-fashioned hobby horses then in vogue,* the wheels being specially made for him out of wooden barrel hoops for lightness. The house he rented at the seaside village was opposite the "Chester Arms." As he strolled on the shore in an evening, he amused himself by picking up pebbles, which he inserted in the ground in front of his modest abode; with the black ones he embedded the name "Nelson," making a background of yellow stones. This work of art still remains.

Bidding adieu to her friends, Mrs. Cadogan proceeded to Manchester on the matter of business which had brought her north, the calling on Mrs. Blackburn, who had reared Emma's first child, and interrogating her upon the question of undertaking a similar office for the little Horatia. Her endeavours must have been futile, for the little girl was not removed from the charge of her nurse, Mrs. Gibson.

Most writers on the subject of Lady Hamilton have given Preston as the place of her birth, an error which doubtless arose from her ladyship's defective penmanship, in the following way. During the absence of Lord Nelson from Palermo, in 1799, Lady Hamilton, who was perfectly competent to act as his deputy, was empowered by him to open all letters and despatches, Sir William's serious indisposition prohibiting any exertion. Certain envoys had been sent to consult his lordship on the condition of affairs at Malta, whom she received. Hearing from them that the Maltese in a state of hungry desperation were about to join the French in any attempted attack they might make, and that they were rising from sheer starvation, she at once bestirred herself to avert this; she went to the port, purchased grain from several captains, and hired

---

* The precursor of the bicycle, a seat upon two wheels, propelled by the feet acting upon the ground.

vessels to convey it to the suffering people. These transactions were effected by a loan of money obtained by the energetic patriot, and although her services enabled Captain Ball to hold his position in Malta, yet not one penny was ever refunded to Lady Hamilton. What wonder is it, then, that in a very few years this generous woman was found to be without substance, when she had personally to repay this loan? In recognition of the valuable services rendered to the Maltese in their time of sore distress, the Emperor Paul of Russia wrote her with his own hand a very flattering letter, and conferred upon her the decoration of a cross of the order of the Petite Croix, together with the title and insignia of the Lady of Malta of the Honorable Order of the Petite Croix. To be correctly enrolled, it was necessary for the Heralds' College to have information concerning her parentage; and it is probably due to her very illegible handwriting that the letter N has been converted into Pr—anyone conversant with her letters will readily understand how easily the mistake could be made by a person to whom her writing was unfamiliar. It was not an intentional act, as has been suggested, for the purpose of eluding her relatives, for they were in full cognizance of her social position. Lord Whitworth, the Minister at St. Petersburg, received the Imperial commands to write to George the Third and ask that she might be permitted to wear the order. Here then was the recognition by a foreign power of deeds worthy of honour, yet her own countrymen have endeavoured to prove that she never assisted the Maltese, and that her having done so was the invention of her own brain.

CHAPTER XVIII.

MERTON PLACE. GILLRAY'S CARICATURES. NELSON OBJECTS TO PAY FEES FOR HONOURS CONFERRED. NELSON'S FATHER ACKNOWLEDGES LADY HAMILTON'S KINDNESS. THE HOUSEKEEPING ACCOUNTS OF THE COMBINED HOUSEHOLD.

IN the March of 1801, Nelson sailed for the Baltic, where the fleet lay under Admiral Sir Hugh Parker, Nelson being second in command. About this time he wrote Lady Hamilton an amusing letter relative to his brother. He says:—

> You read, of course, my brother's letter; and if you like to have Mrs. Nelson up, say that I will pay their lodgings, and then you can have as much of her company as you please; but Reverend Sir you will find a great bore at times; therefore he ought to amuse himself all the mornings, and not always dine with you, as Sir William may not like it. They can have a beefsteak at home, for some people may say that Sir William maintains the family of Nelson, which would vex me.

To meet the expenses of this trip to London, Nelson instructed Mr. Davison to remit Mrs. William Nelson £100, and at the same time he advised his brother not to trespass too much upon Sir William's hospitality. The wisdom of Lord Nelson in his estimate of his brother's undesirable companionship may be inferred from a few lines written by Sir William to Nelson, April 16, 1801, when the acquaintance was recently formed: "Your brother was more extraordinary than ever. He would get up suddenly and cut a caper; rubbing his hands every time that the thought of your fresh laurels came into his head."

Later, in the year 1801, feeling the slights to which he was subjected by the Admiralty, he longed to quit the service and retire to a home of his own; he therefore requested Lady Hamilton to act as his deputy, and purchase for him a small estate to be in readiness for his next return to England—he

THE PURCHASE OF MERTON PLACE. 165

yearned to be quit of turmoil and vexation, and longed for quiet and rest. Like the celebrated Similis under Trajan, who retired into the country to enjoy its repose, Nelson might declare that he had been many years on earth, but only lived four for himself. Writing from off Boulogne he intimated to Lady Hamilton his desire that she should act on his behalf. She

LADY HAMILTON
(*From a Miniature painted in 1801, in the possession of Miss Holtby, York*).

promptly set about the inspection of saleable property, resulting in the purchase of a small estate called "Merton Place," in Surrey. His letter ran as follows.

August 15*th*, 1801.

MY DEAREST EMMA,

From my heart I wish you could find me out a good comfortable house, I should hope to be able to purchase it. At this moment I can only command £3000; as to asking Sir William, I could not do it. I would sooner beg. Is the house at Chiswick furnished? If not, you may fairly calculate at £2000 for furniture; but if I can pay as you say, little by little, we could accomplish it. Be careful how you trust Mr.———. All must be settled by a lawyer. It is better to pay £100 than to be involved in law.

On the 16th of October, 1801, Sir William Hamilton wrote to Lord Nelson to acquaint him that he and his wife had taken up their residence at Merton Place.

> MY DEAR LORD,
> We have now inhabited your Lordship's premises for some days, and I can now speak with some certainty. I have lived with our dear Emma several years. I know her merit, have a great opinion of the head and heart that God Almighty has been pleased to give her, but a seaman alone could have given a fine woman full power to choose and fit up a residence for him without seeing it himself. You are in *luck*, for in my conscience I verily believe that a place so suitable to your views could not have been found, and at so cheap a rate, for if you stay away three days longer I do not think you will have any wish but you will find it completed here; and then the bargain was fortunately struck three days before an idea of peace got abroad. Now, every estate in this neighbourhood has increased in value, and you might get a thousand pounds for your bargain. The proximity to the Capital, and the perfect retirement of this place, are for your Lordship two points beyond estimation; but the house is so comfortable, and furniture clean and good, and I never saw so many conveniences united in so small a compass. You have nothing but to come and enjoy it immediately. You have a good mile of pleasant dry walk around your own farm. It would make you laugh to see Emma and her mother fitting up pig-styes and hen-coops, and already the canal is enlivened with ducks, and the cock is strutting with his hens about the walk, &c., &c.

What an admirable testimony to a wife's worth. This letter is distinct evidence that Sir William's mind was untainted by the malicious whisperings in regard to his wife and Lord Nelson, in fact, he incited him to admire the woman whom he himself so thoroughly appreciated and esteemed. What a valuable record to set against that infamous production that credits this true friend with writing to this woman as "My dear Wife!"

Horatia was often at Merton, and also at Sir William's house in Piccadilly, and no doubt he was perfectly satisfied. They seem to have been

NELSON'S ANXIETY CONCERNING HIS FATHER.

happy in their united home, revelling in its rural pleasures with all the joyousness of simple children. On October 20, 1801, Nelson sent a merry letter to Lady Hamilton in answer to some proposition she had made to row him—very likely on the canal in the grounds:—

> How I should laugh to see you, my dear friend, rowing in a boat—the beautiful Emma rowing a one-armed Admiral! It will certainly be caricatured! Well done, farmer's wife! I'll bet your turkey against Mrs. Nelson's; but Sir William and I will decide. Hardy says you may be sure of him, and that he has not lost his appetite. You will make us rich with your economy.

Childish letter, and innocent enough in all faith!

As soon as all domestic arrangements were complete, his love and regard for his father manifested itself in his desire that the old gentleman, who was afflicted with asthma, and suffering from partial paralysis, should become a permanent inmate of his home, and this wish he communicated to Lady Hamilton, adding, "If he remains at Burnham he will die; and I am sure he will not stay in Somerset Street (Lady Nelson's). Pray let him come to your care at Merton. Your kindness will keep him alive, for you have a kind soul." Had they been a guilty pair would Nelson have planned to place his virtuous father where he would be a daily witness of their delinquencies?

Agreeably to his wish the invitation was sent to the old gentleman, and on November 2, 1801, his son received the following reply to his solicitations:—

HILLBOROUGH

MY DEAR HORATIO,

I have to acknowledge many kind and polite invitations from yourself and Lady Hamilton to visit Merton, which it is my intention to accept before my winter residence commences at Bath. My journey to London is very slow, not only from infirmities, but by necessary and pleasing visits with my children, whose kindnesses are a *cordial for old age* such as few parents can boast of. After finishing some necessary business in town, if convenient to your family, I shall, with the highest gratification a fond parent can receive, pass a time with you. I am, with all proper regards to the family at Merton,

Yours, most affectionately,
EDMUND NELSON.

Old Mr. Nelson eventually arrived, and paid a most agreeable visit, to which he afterwards gratefully referred. In the February of 1801, on the sixth day, there appeared a caricature from the pen of the eminent James Gillray, in reference to the absence of Lord Nelson from the lady of his admiration. It was entitled "Dido in despair," shewing the interior of Sir William Hamilton's sleeping apartment, the open window displaying the British Fleet sailing away, the Admiral's flag-ship the last to leave. This prospect is too affecting for Lady Hamilton, she has forsaken her slumbering lord, and with tearful eyes and outstretched arms is manifesting anguish at her hero's departure. She is satirised as a lady of huge proportions and exaggerated rotundity, a scrap-book of her attitudes lies on the sofa, and below the plate appears this parody :—

> Ah where, and ah where is my gallant sailor gone?
> He 's gone to fight the Frenchman for George upon the Throne,
> He 's gone to fight the Frenchman, to lose t' other arm,
> And left me with the old Antiques to lay me down and cry.

A companion print appeared on February 11, containing the portrait of Sir William Hamilton as "A Cognoscenti contemplating the beauties of the Antique." The quaint figure of the diplomatist and antiquarian, clad in out-of-date garments, is peering through his spectacles at a damaged head of the beautiful Lais; busts, &c., are scattered about. On the wall is a clever caricature of Sir William as Claudius (the venerable collector had the reputation of a *bon vivant*), a picture of Mount Vesuvius in eruption, and sketches of Lord Nelson as Marc Antony, and Lady Hamilton as Cleopatra, pledging her admirer in a glass of gin. A few years later, the same ingenious but vulgar draughtsman executed a parody on the "Attitudes" of Rehburg, grotesquely portrayed, and titled, "A new edition, considerably enlarged, of Attitudes, faithfully copied from Nature, humbly dedicated to the Admirers of the Grand and Sublime, 1807." So they fell a prey to the pen of the able caricaturist, a penalty which attaches itself to notoriety!

On the 2nd of April, 1801, was fought the memorable battle of Copenhagen. Although Nelson was the leading spirit in this engagement and victory, he again had to encounter mortification by the withholding of medals to commemorate the conquest. He wrote—"I long to have the medal for

PLATE VII.—ATTITUDE OF LADY HAMILTON, FROM A DRAWING BY REHBURG.

NEWS OF THE VICTORY OF COPENHAGEN.

Copenhagen, which I would not give up to be made an English duke." The medal had certainly been promised to him, and he severely felt the slight.

We have the authority of Sir Nathaniel Wraxall for an account of his visit to the house of Sir William Hamilton on the evening of the day on which the news of the victory of Copenhagen reached London. He says:— "Intelligence of the glorious victory obtained by the English fleet under Lord Nelson before Copenhagen arrived in London on Wednesday, the 15th of April, 1801. Sir William Hamilton then resided opposite the Green Park in Piccadilly. About ten o'clock that evening, I went to his house with Sir John Macpherson. We found assembled there the Dukes of Gordon and Queensberry, Lord William Gordon, Monsieur de Calonne, Mr. Charles Greville (Sir William's nephew), the Duke de Nöia, a Neapolitan nobleman, Mr. Kemble, the celebrated comedian, and his wife, the Rev. Mr. Nelson, and some other persons. Lady Hamilton, inspired by the recent success of Lord Nelson against the Danes, of which victory he had transmitted to her with his remaining hand all the particulars as they occurred from the 1st up to the 8th of April, the day when the despatches came away, after playing on the harpsichord, and accompanying it with her voice, undertook to dance the Tarantelle.* Sir William began it with her, and maintained the conflict, for such it might well be esteemed, during some minutes, when, unable longer to continue it, the Duke de Nöia succeeded to his place; but he, too, though near forty years younger than Sir William, soon gave in. Lady Hamilton sent for her own maid servant, who, being presently exhausted, was relieved by another female attendant, a Copt, perfectly black, whom Lord Nelson had presented to her on his return from Egypt." A rare feat to dance down these hale persons six weeks after an *accouchement!*

On the 22nd of August, 1801, Nelson beheld for the first time his new home, purchased by deputy, the country residence in which he sought to take refuge from the worries of active service in the fleet. Morton Place has long since been dismantled, but its locality may be found by going up the High Street at Merton (which lies to the east of the turnpike) until the Abbey Road is reached, at the south of which, adjoining the road, was Nelson's residence, the "dear Merton," so lovingly longed for, which he had taken on Lady Hamilton's recommendation without even seeing it. Writers have

* A Neapolitan dance. Horace Walpole describes its performance by the Neapolitan Minister's wife in London, Countess Castelcicala.

attributed to her undue extravagance in making unnecessary alterations about the house, but these allegations are without foundation. She acted under Nelson's instructions, all changes being well considered with an eye to

THE SEAT OF THE LATE ADMIRAL LORD NELSON, MERTON, SURREY
(*From an old Sketch*).

the utmost economy. In 1803, in resuming command in the Mediterranean, he wrote to Lady Hamilton regarding the said alterations:

> I would not have you lay out more than is necessary on Merton. The rooms and the new entrance will take a deal of money. The entrance by the corner I would have certainly not done; a common white gate will do for the present, and one of the cottages which is in the barn will do for a temporary lodge. The road can be made to a temporary bridge, for that part of the Nile* one day shall be filled up. Downing's canvas awning will do for a passage. For the winter the carriage can be put in the barn, and giving up Mr. Bennett's premises will save £50 a year, and another year we can fit up the coachhouse and stables, which are in the barn. The footpath should be turned. I will show Mr. Haslewood the way I wish it done.

* The grounds had been laid out under Lady Hamilton's supervision. The Nile was an artificial stream, so named in memory of the great naval victory.

Lord Nelson directed his London agent to pay Lady Hamilton whatsoever she would require for the expenses of Merton, adding—"She will not be extravagant." The internal decorations do not appear to have caused much outlay. Lord Minto leaves this record :—"Not only the rooms, but the whole house, staircase and all, are covered with pictures of her and him of all sizes and sorts, and representations of his naval actions, coats of arms, pieces of plate in his honour, the flagstaff of 'L'Orient,'" &c.; all inexpensive, and though the hanging of their trophies and portraits held them up to the scorn of the critical Lord, it destroys the accusation of extravagance, as the adornments were already in their possession. The river Wandle lay adjacent, and in it Lord Nelson and Sir William often threw their lines. The stream was praised by Izaac Walton for its "fishful qualities." The whirr of mills and factories, and the stir of busy life, have frightened away the trout. This happy country home, where he anticipated so much bliss, dwelling in unanimity with his two amiable friends in forgetfulness of the vexations and annoyances caused to him by jealousy, only knew him for one year and a half. Many a line he wrote to the friends who knew him best, in which he commented on the injustice done to him by the Admiralty, and complaining how little of right he expected from them. Sir Harris Nicolas, in the preface to the third volume of *Lord Nelson's Dispatches and Letters*, introduces the following remark which endorses Nelson's own expressions of discontent at the jealousy which prompted men to act to his detriment : " Death, it has been said, canonizes and sanctifies a great character; but neither a death the most glorious, nor a life the most honourable, has prevented Nelson's integrity and motives from being suspected and aspersed, chiefly, it is painful to remark, by men of his own profession."

To his friend, Alexander Davison, Lord Nelson wrote, in the year 1797, date May 27, and from the matter contained in the letter, it is easy to conceive the rancour which filled his breast when he was made aware of another squadron lying in wait for the prey for which he and his captains had worked. His indignation was the very natural result of injustice. Thus runs his letter:—

> We hear of a squadron laying wait within Sir John Jervis' command for to take those rich ships which otherwise would fall into our hands. It is impossible to conceive the ill-blood it has created in this fleet—leave us so inferior to the enemy, and one of our *Task-Masters*, attempting to rob us of

our harvest, but leaving us very *handsomely* to spend our blood in opposing so superior a force.

To the same friend he wrote on January 28, 1801, resenting the notice he had received from Sir Isaac Heard, Garter King at Arms, that he should conform to a monetary imposition from certain State officials, else he could not be credited with the hardly-earned dignities which had been conferred upon him.

> Pray tell Sir Isaac Heard that I cannot afford to pay for any honours conferred upon me. They are intended to do honour to this country, and to mark the gratitude of his Sicilian Majesty to his faithful ally our Gracious King, in my person, his faithful servant. As far as relates to the personal trouble of Sir Isaac, or any other friend, I am not backward in payment by thanks or money, as the case requires; and for personal trouble I have already paid £41, and have had no answer relative to the Imperial Order of the Crescent. Sir Isaac is bound in honour to follow up this application; for my wish is to have all my honours gazetted together, but paying those fees to Secretaries of State, Earl Marshals, &c., &c., without which I am told the King's orders will not be obeyed, it would in my opinion be very wrong to do it. I could say more on this subject, but I think it better not at present.

The preceding letter is a very sensible remonstrance against the tax levied by officials connected with the bestowal of State honours. Many a man has been ridiculed for attempting his own aggrandisement *sub rosa;* but in high quarters it is an extortion that each party receiving honours for work well done shall pay for the distinction. Little wonder that the man who owned to having only £3,000, which he wished to invest in a home, should resent and decline to pay the imposition!

As the time arrived when he wished to retire from the service he spoke bitterly of the pension he would receive, saying that if they gave him less than they had bestowed on the *rich* Lord St. Vincent he would not have much to thank them for—he felt his labours merited at least an equality.

On October 20, 1801, he wrote to Lady Hamilton :—

> The Rev. Dr.* likes going about. Only think of his wanting to come up with an Address of Thanks! Why the King will not receive him,

* Nelson's brother, the Rev. W. Nelson.

though he is a Doctor; and less for being my brother, for they certainly do not like me.

In July, 1802, Lord Nelson, Sir William and Lady Hamilton, Dr. Nelson and his nice little wife, of whom everybody spoke well, started on a tour in South Wales, visiting several large cities, towns, and private estates, in their course. The whole expedition was a triumphal progress, save at Blenheim, the seat of the Duke of Marlborough, where they met with a most unpleasant and unlooked-for rebuff. Instead of courteously receiving the travellers, the Duke ordered refreshments to be supplied to them in the grounds, without making his appearance, at which slight they were highly incensed, and left the park without partaking of anything. As they made their exit, Emma denounced the insult in her own peculiar and expressive vocabulary: " Nelson shall have a monument to which Blenheim shall be but a pig-sty." However, this uncalled-for snub was soon cast into the shade, as every city, borough, and town vied with the others to do honour to the notable visitors, and all country houses of note on the road extended right heartily the hand of friendship and hospitality.

At Gloucester the bells were rung upon their arrival. The cathedral and other objects of interest were inspected. Preferring the passage to Monmouth by way of the river Wye instead of by land, a vast concourse of people attended them to the boats; that which Lord Nelson was to occupy being tastefully decorated with laurels. The shore was lined with spectators, guns were fired, and other manifestations of delight displayed. At Brecon, he was warmly greeted by the farmers; and at Milford the reception was most enthusiastic. Here Sir William visited his tenants, whom he had not seen for many years. At Haverfordwest, Nelson was drawn through the streets by the populace in a most triumphant manner; and at Swansea he received the same attention from a body of seamen. At Ross, a triumphal arch was erected for him to pass through; and at Hereford he received the Freedom of the city, enclosed in a box made out of an apple-tree—the produce and pride of the county. So on, through towns and cities too numerous to mention in detail, until they reached Althorp, where Earl Spencer accorded them a genuine welcome.

In the summer of 1802, Elliston, the player, received a letter from a friend, a Mr. Gore, written from Tenby, in which he made mention of seeing the tourists, and his thoughts thereon found vent thus :—

> I was yesterday witness to an exhibition which, though greatly ridiculous, was not wholly so, for it was likewise pitiable, and this was in the persons of two individuals who have lately occupied much public attention. I mean the Duke of Bronté, Lord Nelson, and Emma, Lady Hamilton. The whole town was at their heels as they walked together. The lady is grown immensely fat and equally coarse, while her "companion in arms" has taken to the other extreme—thin, shrunken, and to my impression in bad health. They were evidently vain of each other, as though the one would have said, " This is the Horatio of the Nile," and the other, " This is the Emma of Sir William." Poor Sir William, wretched, but not abashed, he followed at a short distance, bearing in his arms a *cucciolo*,* and other emblems of combined folly. You remember Hogarth's admirable picture, " Evening,"—it somewhat illustrates the scene I would describe. This distinguished trio are just concluding a summer tour; but at Blenheim I understand they encountered a rebuff which must have stung the hero to the quick.

On the 5th of September they reached Merton, and several waggons were laden with the costly and splendid presents which had been offered to them. Lady Hamilton wrote to Mr. Davison that they had had a most delightful tour, which would cause some of Nelson's enemies to "burst with envy."

Lord Nelson experienced a severe blow during the year 1802 in the loss of his father, who died at Bath, in the seventy-ninth year of his age. The venerable clergyman was a typical old gentleman of the last century. His letters to Lady Hamilton teem with respect, and distinctly prove that this Christian teacher had no thought of any equivocal relations between her and his son.

A very interesting letter from the worthy minister exemplifies that Lady Hamilton was held in high esteem, not only by himself, but also by other members of his family :—

December 13, 1801.

My Dear Horatio,

The little addition that you are likely to make to your landed property will, I hope, bring some further pleasure and domestic

* A little dog.

comfort, such as the real comfort of a private and independent life must consist of, and every event which you are so good as to communicate to me, which is likely to increase your happiness, adds a prop to my declining life; and the little incidents, even of indifference, which Lady Hamilton politely communicates to me, are at all times very acceptable. Your sister's daily life in watching my infirmities, and rendering them as easy as in her power, I feel with delight. She is, as usual, cheerful, often regretting not having been able to see you, and even still she and Mr. M. (Matcham) meditate a visit to Merton for a day or two, to wait upon Lady Hamilton and yourself, if the weather is tolerably good, and she herself can prudently undertake such a journey five or six weeks hence when the bairns are all returned to their several academies. The box came safe, so did the plaid—very handsome. Lady Hamilton will accept my thanks for her care about it, to whom, with Sir William, present my respects, as also to the whole party.

I am, my dear, your affectionate father,
EDMUND NELSON.

This good clergyman saw nothing to resent in his son's residing with the Hamiltons, neither did his daughters, which is sufficient evidence that Lady Nelson's overbearing conduct did not receive their countenance. They recognised that her action had left their brother no alternative. It was arranged that old Mr. Nelson should take up his permanent abode at Merton in May, 1802; but his demise in the preceding month frustrated the filial scheme. Lord Nelson was mostly absent from his country home, and though he yearned for peace and rural enjoyment, he felt his country had the first claim on his services, and his life became a continued sacrifice of self in his endeavours to add to England's greatness. When he availed himself of his short periods of rest he resided at Merton, and entertained a perpetual succession of visitors. About this time, Lady Hamilton renewed her acquaintance with her old fellow-servant in Dr. Budd's employment, Jane Powell, who had risen to a position of eminence in the theatrical profession. Lady Hamilton had been on a visit to her friend, Mrs. Billington, the actress, and on her return home she received this letter from Mrs. Powell:—

SOUTHEND.

DEAR LADY HAMILTON,
I cannot forbear writing you a line to inform your Ladyship

that I am at this place, and to tell you how much your absence is regretted by all ranks of people. Would to Heaven you were here to enliven this (at present) dull scene. I have performed one night, and have promised to play six, but, unless the houses are better, must decline it. Please to remember me most kindly to your mother, and every one at Merton.

I am, dear Lady Hamilton,
Your obliged
JANE POWELL.

Many old friends found a welcome at Merton—a son of Mrs. Burt, her Chester acquaintance, a young engraver, among the number. Lady Hamilton was very kind to him, and obtained several subscribers for two plates which he engraved and published; one a small portrait of Nelson, the other a large work representing Britannia crowning the bust of Nelson—the head of Britannia was a portrait of Lady Hamilton. Young Burt was a valiant defender of her Ladyship's reputation, and he used to say that the servants at Merton, whom it is natural to infer held a good post of observation, were wont to express great indignation at the scandalous rumours which were rife.

Among other visitors who were entertained at the hospitable house of Lord Nelson was the celebrated Dr. Wolcot, more generally known by his *nom de plume* "Peter Pindar." This eccentric character went to bed one night in an elevated and slightly helpless condition, in which he contrived to set fire to a nightcap belonging to Lord Nelson. Next morning he pinned a paper to it with these lines:—

> Take your nightcap again, my good Lord, I desire,
> For I wish not to keep it a minute;
> What belongs to a Nelson, where'er there's a fire,
> Is sure to be instantly in it.

Alas for those brief merry days! Days in which Nelson lived with the Hamiltons in what the sarcastic Mr. Elliot called a "harmony that consisted of mutual admiration, pleasure of eating and drinking, and the strong rude society manners of the period, all at Nelson's expense;" which statement was as incorrect as every other that he uttered concerning the trio, for Mr. Alfred Morrison has in his possession the original housekeeping books of the

THE ACCOUNTS AT MERTON PLACE.

Merton conjunction, which prove that the accounts were settled by Lord Nelson and Sir William equally, at the rate of £3,000 or £4,000 a year.

Lord Nelson shared the household expenses at the Piccadilly residence as well as at Merton. An extract of one week's expenditure, as shown by a summary drawn up by Mr. White, the butler, will serve to demonstrate the amount of outlay in the combined household; and, furthermore, it is existing proof that Sir William paid his half down to the very penny. The servants would seem to have been remunerated each quarter. One or two entries in the book warrant that statement; such as "for three months' wages, £2 12s. 6d., to Phillis Thorpe," the housemaid at Merton. As an entry in her favour occurs more than once, this Phillis Thorpe was, no doubt, one of the extinct race of good old-fashioned servants, who comfortably performed their duties for the reasonable recompense of ten guineas per annum. There seems to have been two coachmen—one for Sir William and the other for "Milady"—besides another old coachman, named Caetano, an antiquated individual who accompanied them from Italy. The expenses are far less interesting than those incurred at Paddington Green, when the girlish house-keeper had much contrivance to eke out her limited allowance with a satisfactory result.

Weekly acc^{t.} of the R^{t.} Honble Sir Wm. Hamilton and the R^{t.} Honble Lord Vis^{ct.} Nelson, from the 1st to the 8th Nov^{r.}, 1802.

	£	s.	d.
Mr. Stinton, Grocer ...	8	14	8
Mr. Coleman, Fishmonger	2	15	9
Mr. Wyld, Cheesemonger ...	2	2	2½
Mr. Scott, for Brown Stout ...	1	10	0
Mrs. Bethell, for Fruit to Merton ...	1	7	0
W. Richard, for Turnpike	0	11	2
Mr. White, Lemons and Cakes to Merton	0	10	6
Mr. Gadd, Baker	0	6	3
Mr. Cummins, for Washing	0	5	3½
Mr. Allard, Greengrocer	0	2	11
Mr. Lucas, for Milk	0	2	2
Mr. Pascoe, for Malt, Hops, and Sugar	12	0	0
Mr. Hammers, for Barley ...	8	8	6
To do. 2 more bills ...	3	13	6

LADY HAMILTON.

	£	s.	d.
Mr. Pascoe, for Malt and Hops	9	0	0
Mr. Greenfield, Butcher, at Merton	8	19	5
Mr. Skelton, Baker, at do.	1	14	4
Mr. Cribb, for Vegetables, at do.	1	5	9
Tradesmen and Bills from 1st to 8th Nov^{r.}	£63	9	5
Expended in the Town House from do. to do.	2	0	9
Do. by the Cook at Merton	7	10	0
	73	0	2
Last week's acc^{t.} brought forward	37	16	10½
Total from the 25th Octr. to 8th Nov^{r.}	110	17	0½

12th Nov^r, 1802, Rec^{d.} of the R^{t.} Honble Sir Wm. Hamilton the sum of Fifty-five pounds, eight shillings and sixpence, being the half of the above accounts—by me, T. White (*signed*).

(Paid by Lord Nelson to Mr. White) [*in Nelson's autograph*].

LADY HAMILTON
(*From a Miniature furnished by the Right Hon. W. E. Gladstone, M.P., &c.*)

CHAPTER XIX.

DEATH OF SIR WILLIAM HAMILTON. HIS LEGACY TO LORD NELSON. GREVILLE REALISES HIS EXPECTATIONS. LADY HAMILTON APPLIES FOR A PENSION FROM THE GOVERNMENT.

IN the beginning of the year 1803, Sir William began to show signs of failing health, and as his life gradually ebbed away he found two tender and faithful nurses in his wife and Lord Nelson, who was unremitting in his care and devoted attention, and for the last six weeks of Sir William's life the night watch was kept by the kind-hearted sailor. On April 6, 1803, this brilliant old gentleman passed away, at the ripe age of seventy-three; his hand in that of his wife, and his head on Lord Nelson's breast. Among Lord Nelson's papers was found the following note in the handwriting of the troubled wife:—April 6th. "Unhappy day for the forlorn Emma. Ten minutes past ten dear blessed Sir William left me." The Duke of Clarence received the intelligence from Nelson's hand in these words: "My dear friend Sir William Hamilton died this morning; the world never, never lost a more upright and accomplished gentleman."

Commenting on the severe loss sustained by society in the death of Sir William, the periodicals, then so rare, selected the portrait of Lady Hamilton to adorn their pages, and, as will be seen from the succeeding extracts, not the faintest hint or breath of tarnish sullies the fair fame of the beautiful woman at the very hour fixed upon by her future traducers. The *European Magazine* for June, 1803, says :—" To the lady whose portrait ornaments the present *Magazine*, the sister arts of music and painting have been under considerable obligations. From her affability and attention abroad, her country folks have derived much satisfaction, and to her efforts and exertions in a time of imminent danger from foreign violence and domestic treachery, Royalty has been indebted both for consolation and comfort." After remarking on her unwearied attention to her late husband, the article closes in these words :—" To conclude, we are told that to her relations she is liberal and kind; to those from whom she has at any time received obligations grateful and remembering, and to her friends in general, polite and engaging."

Under the ominous heading "Deaths," in the *Gentleman's Magazine* for April, 1803, is to be found a condensed account of Sir William Hamilton's career, which contains matter of interest. It notifies that the knight died at his house in Piccadilly, which was bought for him by his lady during his own financial difficulties, by the sale of jewels presented to her by a foreign princess, who, in a letter to a foreign sovereign, praises Lady Hamilton in full gratitude of heart as "her best friend and preserver! to whom she was indebted certainly for life, and probably for the crown." It is thus shown that the leading periodicals of the day awarded their tribute of praise for deeds evidently done. All coincide in tone of commendation. The obituary notice continues thus :—"Twelve years ago he married the present Lady Hamilton, and never was an union productive of more perfect felicity. The anxious solicitude, the unwearied attentions, the domestic duties joined to the uncommon talents and accomplishments of Lady Hamilton were sources of the purest happiness to both, as well as of delight to the circle in which they lived. Sir William derived from his lady in his last illness all the consolations of which life was susceptible, and he at length, without a struggle or a sigh, breathed his last in her arms. He had a pension of £1,200 a year on the Irish establishment conferred on him for his long diplomatic services, which ceases with his existence. He has made his nephew, the Hon. Charles Greville (Deputy Lord Chamberlain), his sole heir. His estates near Swansea, which he got by a former wife, amount to £5,000 per annum; these he has left charged with £700 per annum* as an annuity to the present Lady Hamilton during her life. His remains were interred at Milford Haven, in Pembrokeshire."

Later, Lady Hamilton presented to the chapel at Milford a relic from the scenes of glory in their past life—a piece of the wreck of "L'Orient."

During Sir William's illness Lord Nelson had evinced deep concern at the impending result. In a letter to Mrs. Bolton, March 30, 1803, he wrote :—

> Dear Sir William is very, very bad; he can't in my opinion get over it, and I think it will happen very soon. You will imagine Lady Hamilton's and my feelings on the occasion; indeed all London is interested in the fate of such a character.

* The sum left to Lady Hamilton by Sir William was £800 per annum.

Sir Wm. Hamilton, K.B.

To this Lady Hamilton added a postscript :—

> I have only to say, dearest Mrs. Bolton, Sir William was so ill yesterday, he could not live we thought; to-day he is better; I am worn out, but ever yours affectionately,
>
> E. H.

To Captain Murray, Lord Nelson wrote on April 2, 1803 :—

> We are on the eve of losing dear Sir William, I much doubt his holding twenty-four hours longer. Our dear lady is dreadfully afflicted.

To his sincere and intimate friend, Mr. Alexander Davison, of St. James Square, he wrote on the day of Sir William's decease :—

> MY DEAR DAVISON,
> Our dear Sir William died at ten minutes past ten this morning, in Lady Hamilton's and my arms, without a sigh or struggle. Poor Lady Hamilton is, as you may expect, desolate. I hope she will be left properly, but I doubt.
> Ever yours most affectionately,
> NELSON AND BRONTÉ.

These letters breathe natural regret at the loss of a mutual friend. There is not a suggestion that does not read sincerely, nor one line to point that he congratulated himself that one bar to his happiness was removed. In like manner did the lady bewail her lord. On the 13th of April, Nelson, writing again to Captain Murray, says : " Lady Hamilton is very low." It must not be supposed that Sir William had been in ignorance of the floating rumours concerning the intimacy existing between his wife and his friend, but the noble old man totally ignored the wicked whisperings, and in dying gave his trusted and attached wife the assurance that for the years she had borne his name she had never caused him one hour's unhappiness. One week before he died he bequeathed her picture to Nelson in these words—so full of import, so full of confidence and sound faith in the man whom society has accused of being his false betrayer : " The copy of Mme. le Brun's picture of Emma in enamel, by Bone, I give to my dearest friend, Lord Nelson, Duke of Bronté, a small token of the great regard I have for his lordship, the most virtuous, loyal, and truly brave character I have ever met with. God bless him, and shame fall on those who do not say ' Amen.' "

A solemn legacy, as though he would defend him from the censures of the world; a lasting testimony to his trust in their fidelity. Nor was he likely to be easily deceived—a clever, keen, and upright, high-minded old gentleman; the friendship was all in accordance with his own desire. Though proud that his wife should be sought after and admired, he was the last man living to connive at his own dishonour. They were in truth what Emma described to Dr. Nelson's wife: "One heart in three bodies." The picture—sacred testament of faith from the man so seriously interested—was bought from Lady Hamilton by George, Prince of Wales, in 1810, and is at present among the treasures of the late Sir Richard Wallace, at Hertford House.

Upon the decease of Sir William Hamilton, Lord Nelson immediately removed into lodgings in Albemarle Street, after which he was in England for a very brief period.

On May 16, 1803, he received his appointment as Commander-in-Chief of His Majesty's Ships and Vessels employed on the Mediterranean Station, and on the 18th he took his departure, rising on that day, in accordance with his usual early habits, at four o'clock in the morning, reaching Portsmouth at half past twelve mid-day, when he immediately hoisted his flag on board the "Victory." In the early part of the year 1803, he wrote a letter of kind advice to Charles Connor, a young cousin of Lady Hamilton, who had just entered the navy. The interest which he showed in each young midshipman caused him to take personal trouble in seeing to their well-doing.

DEAR CHARLES,

As Captain Hillyar has been so good as to say he would rate you Mid., I sincerely hope that your conduct will ever continue to deserve his kind notice and protection by a strict and very active attention to your duty. If you deserve well, you are sure of my assistance. Mr. Scott will furnish you with money to begin your mess, and I shall allow you thirty pounds a year, if it be necessary, which Captain Hillyar will supply you with. And as you from this day start in the world as a man, I trust that your future conduct in life will prove you both an officer and a gentleman. Recollect that you must be a seaman to be an officer; and also that you cannot be a good officer without being a gentleman. I am always with most sincere good wishes, your true friend,

NELSON AND BRONTÉ.

The sound and simply expressed closing lines might probably bear good result if printed and presented to each young aspirant for nautical fame. Into some impressionable heart the important words might sink, and be an incentive to spur the lad to diligent work, so that the thorough knowledge of his profession might enable him to acquit himself with satisfaction in the day when he should rise to command.

A more discriminating chief than Nelson it would have been impossible to find—he equally balanced the scales of justice whenever he was appealed to. A young officer wrote him a letter concerning his superior, to which Nelson replied with an eye to the maintenance of discipline, and yet conciliatory to the complainant. He said :—

> I have just received your letter, and I am truly sorry that any difference should arise between your captain, who has the reputation of being one of the bright officers of the service, and yourself, a very young man, and a very young officer, who must naturally have much to learn ; therefore the chance is, that you are perfectly wrong in the disagreement. However, as your present situation must be very disagreeable, I will certainly take an early opportunity of removing you, provided that your conduct to your present captain be such that another may not refuse to receive you.

Yet one more instance of mercy tempered with justice meted out by the even hand of that clear-seeing man. In every issue he firmly upheld the dignity of authority. A young officer was awaiting a court-martial for misdemeanour, and Lord Nelson received a request from Sir John Warren that he would interfere to prevent it, to which the following reasonable response was sent :—

> The young man must write such a letter of contrition as would be an acknowledgement of his great fault, and with a sincere promise, if his captain will intercede to prevent the impending court-martial, never to so behave again. On his captain's enclosing me such a letter, with a request to cancel the order for the trial, I might be induced to do it ; but the letters and reprimand will be given in the public order-book of the fleet, and read to all the officers. The young man has pushed himself forward to notice, and he must take the consequence. It was upon the quarter-deck, in the face of the ship's company, that he treated his captain with contempt ; and I am in duty bound to support the authority and consequence of every

officer under my command. A poor ignorant seaman is for ever punished for contempt to *his* superiors.

After the departure of Lord Nelson to take charge of the fleet in the Mediterranean, Lady Hamilton paid a succession of visits to his lordship's relatives in Norfolk, during which time the new possessor of her husband's wealth and estates entered into his inheritance, and commenced to dismantle the Piccadilly residence and remove its valuables. An agent named Oliver, whom she had left at 11 Clarges Street to look after her affairs, kept her informed of Mr. Greville's doings, or as he named him "Dei Gracias Mr. Greville." In writing to her ladyship June 8th, 1803, Oliver said:—

> My Lady,
> Mr. Greville came this day at about twelve, and stayed till a quarter past five; he and Francalette have been very busy all the time, Mr. White* only part. He has marked many of the pictures to be taken away, your ladyship's portrait by Angelica Cauffman † (Kauffman) is of the number. Mr. Greville asked me your direction; he will write to you to-morrow, 'tis too late to day. He put on a cheerful mien, and told Sig^m Madre ‡ to be of good cheer.

Immediately after Sir William's death, Lady Hamilton wrote to Mr. Greville asking how long he could permit her to remain in the house in Piccadilly, which had now become his; and also if he would pay her debts, and let her know what she could depend on, so that she might curtail her expenses and establishment at once. The death of Sir William had reduced Lady Hamilton's income to a minimum. His nephew, Charles, had stepped into all his uncle's belongings, charged only with a jointure of eight hundred pounds to be paid to the widow. Sir William's pension of £1,200 ceased at his death.

The following letter from Mr. Greville shows that he had no intention that the reduced lady should receive from him one iota more than she was absolutely entitled to:—

---

* Mr. White was the butler.
† The Marquess of Hertford owns a portrait of Lady Hamilton, by Angelica Kauffman, as "Thalia" in the act of removing her mask.
‡ Mrs. Cadogan, Lady Hamilton's mother.

GREVILLE'S LETTER TO LADY HAMILTON.

Dear Ly. Hamilton,
　　　　　I received your Letter on Monday Morning, after the hour you mentioned in it as being fixt for your departure from Piccadilly, and this was the first notice I had of the day. Dr. Nelson having mentioned his intention of paying his visit to Canterbury, and had left the making apologies for not waiting a drawing Room to me, as it happens, the Queen has appointed one for to-morrow, but it was only known by the *Gazette* of last Night.

　　I saw Mrs. Cadogan on Monday and yesterday, and shall see her presently. I only write to assure you that I take to myself no charge of Cruelty or intentional neglect. You had on Saturday my letter regretting the amount of your Bills, and the impossibility of all being paid, but that I would be able to pay you *on account* what would be required for you before you went. If, with this notice of my wish to accommodate you, you chose to go to another person, I only hope that you will not expect me to allow that you was obliged by me so to do. I will not continue the line of Correspondence in the tone of finding fault as you do with me. I will do all I can to conclude the business for your Ease and Comfort, and I wish you to inform me to whom you have given directions to receive any Sums I may in the Course of a few days pay to your account, either at Coutts' or Elsewhere, as you may direct; and if you will either direct me, or desire Mr. Booth, to prepare a proper receipt for any specified Sum you may want immediately, I will take care it is provided, and I expect to find Mr. Coutts will sell the stock of £7,000 (which will not be sufficient to pay the Bills), and I shall see to paying them without delay.

　　Having written so much on business, I now must request you to inform me how you are, and I hope that the Quiet of the Parsonage will make you Comfortable, and you may be assured that I will do all in my power to promote your good plans, which will lead to an independence which neither the flattery nor dissipation of the Fashionable World brings with it. My kind Compliments attend the party, believe me, Dear Lady Hamilton,
　　　　　　　　　　　　　　Sincerely yours,
　　　　　　　　　　　　　　　　　　C. F. G.

Wednesday, *June* 8, 1803.

Nothwithstanding his protestations and desire to be of service, the heir was not disposed to be so generous as he wished to appear. It will be noticed that he proposes to advance money to her *on account*, which words he underlines, lest she should delude herself with the belief that it was possible for him to be openhearted enough to start her solitary course free and unincumbered by debts incurred while she was his uncle's wife. The cold and calculating man not only intended to keep her strictly within the limits of her allowance, but even endeavoured to reduce it by deducting the value of a tax. When this reached the ears of Lord Nelson, he broke out in righteous indignation against the mean and selfish man, who, in the possession of all that once had been the poor lady's, should attempt to render her circumstances more straitened by withholding a portion to meet a tax. In a letter dated August 31, 1804, Nelson wrote to her concerning the extortion:—

> Mr. Greville is a shabby fellow! It never could have been the intention of Sir William but that you should have had the seven hundred pounds a year neat money; for, when he made the Will, the Income Tax was double to what it is at present, and the estate which it is paid from is increasing every year in value. It may be law, but it is not just; nor in equity would, I believe, be considered as the will and intention of Sir William. Never mind! Thank God you do not want any of his kindness, nor will he give you justice! I may fairly say all this, because my actions are different, even to a person who has treated me so ill.* As to ——, I know the full extent of the obligation I owe him, and he may be useful to me again; but I can never forget his unkindness to you. But I guess many reasons influenced his conduct in bragging of his riches and my honourable poverty; but, as I have often said, and with honest pride, what I have is my own; it never cost the widow a tear, or the Nation a farthing. I got what I have with my pure blood from the Enemies of my Country. Our house, my own Emma, is built upon a solid foundation, and will last to us when his house and lands may belong to others than his children. I would not have believed it from any one but you.

It may be gathered in the foregoing that Mr. Greville had been making insidious comparisons between his own financial position and that of the absent hero, which roused the spirit of resentment in the breast of the poorer man, and caused him to refer to his comparatively limited means as being

---

* This refers to his own ample allowance to his wife, who had so embittered his life.

PLATE VIII. - ATTITUDE OF LADY HAMILTON, FROM A DRAWING BY REHBURG.

more meritorious than the wealth of the individual who was attempting to defraud the widow. Galling enough it must have been for the poor lady to retire from the luxuriant surroundings, and have to part from the beautiful valuables and works of art collected by her late husband.

On August 26, in the year 1803, we find Lord Nelson wrote a letter to Lady Hamilton in which he dwelt on the expected happiness he hoped to derive from his residence at Merton — short-lived happiness when attained, for from the day on which Sir William Hamilton died until Nelson sailed to take charge of the Mediterranean fleet, only six weeks elapsed, and when next he returned to his coveted home, on August 19, 1805, after an absence of two years and three months, his visit was of very brief duration, only three weeks and four days, when he left never again to return. Lord Nelson was, therefore, only in the company of Lady Hamilton for two periods—one of six weeks, the other twenty-five days, after her husband's death. As the widow of his sincere friend, there could be no impropriety in her acting as his housekeeper, and superintending the establishment and its necessary alterations. After her round of visits she settled at Merton, where she received the letter to which allusion has been made : —

> This letter will find you at dear Merton, where we shall one day meet, and be truly happy. I do not think it can be a long war, and I believe it will be much shorter than people expect ; and I shall hope to find the new room built, the grounds laid out neatly but not expensively, new Piccadilly gates, kitchen garden, &c. Only let us have a plan, and then all will go on well. It will be a great source of amusement to you, and Horatia shall plant a tree. I dare say she will be very busy. Mrs. Nelson or Mrs. Bolton, &c, will be with you, and time will pass away until I have the inexpressible delight of arriving at Merton. . . . I feel all your mother's kindness, and I trust that we shall turn rich by being economists. Spending money to please a pack of people is folly, and without thanks. I desire that you will say everything kind from me to her, and make her a present of something in my name. . . . How could you afford to send Mrs. Bolton a hundred pounds ? It is impossible out of your income. I wish Mr. Addington would give you five hundred pounds a year, then you would be better able to give away than at present ; but your purse, my dear Emma, will always be empty, your heart is generous beyond your means.

With so many needy relatives who made constant demands on her kindness, the late ambassador's widow found her income sadly below her requirements. She, therefore, petitioned the government to allow her a pension on the ground of the important services she had rendered to the fleet when in Italian waters. At the same time Lord Nelson requested the Queen of Naples to second these claims, relying on her Majesty's full knowledge of her ladyship's efforts, that she would support her friend in what was a matter of vital interest to her. In July, 1803, he wrote to Lady Hamilton:—

> You will readily believe how rejoiced I shall be to get one of your dear excellent letters, that I may know everything which has passed since my absence. I sincerely hope that Mr. Booth has settled all your accounts. Never mind, my dear Emma, a few hundred pounds, which is all the rigid gripe of the law, not justice, can wrest of you. I thank God that you cannot want (although that is no good reason for its being taken from you); whilst I have sixpence you shall not want for fivepence of it! But you have bought your experience that there is no friendship in money concerns, and your good sense will make you profit of it. I hope the minister has done something for you. But never mind, we can live on bread and cheese. Independence is a blessing; and although I have not yet found out the way to get Prize-money—what has been taken has run into our mouths—however, it must turn out very hard if I cannot get enough to pay off my debts, and that will be no small comfort.

Lady Hamilton had already endeavoured to obtain pecuniary reward for the assistance she had rendered, and Mr. Addington actually went so far as to acknowledge that she *had* claims on her country, but beyond that he never advanced. In 1802, Lady Hamilton wrote to Mr. George Rose, Vice-President of the Board of Trade, one of the few friends who remained staunch when the world turned its cold shoulder towards her. Her letter will demonstrate her fidelity to her mother country, and proves her to have been above narrow-minded feelings. Despite the bitter ignoring of national obligations, the patriotic woman never regretted the use to which she had put her keen wits. Thus she expressed herself:—

> I hope you will call on me when you come to town, and I promise you not to bore you with my own claims; for if those that have power will not do me justice, I must be quiet, and in revenge to them I can say, if ever I am a minister's wife again, with the power I had then, why I will again do

the same for my country as I did before; and I did more than any ambassador did, though their pockets were filled with secret service money, and poor Sir William and myself never got even a pat on the back.

Not even thanks did they receive, though they had kept up good feeling between the Court of St. James and the Court of Naples during most critical times, and in her high-souled absence of revenge, the lady declared that should Sir William ever again be an ambassador, and herself in circumstances where she could benefit her native land, she was prepared to do so. The poor lady possessed a fine disposition, which rose superior to rebuffs that would have crushed many another. On December 24, 1803, she appealed to Sir William Scott (afterwards Baron Stowell), elder brother of Lord Chancellor Eldon, a kind-hearted gentleman, who owned that it was "difficult, or rather impossible, to withstand the request of a woman backed by her tears." Through him Lady Hamilton hoped to reach higher powers. She wrote:—

> If you, my dear Sir William, will beg of Mr. Addington to think of me, and may I hope he will think favourably, for without his assistance I shall be in great embarrissement. Lord Nelson has told me that he is good, great we know he is. My relation, the Duke of Queensbury, has told me that he means well, and will give me his protection. You, Sir, are his friend, and can say something to him for me. I could convince him I did much to serve my Country. *When I was in power* I never thought on myself, and now, my husband dead, our dear friend, the glorious Nelson, far away, I have nobody, for I live so retired, I don't try to make friends.

She was indeed leading a life proper at all points, seeking no notoriety, and quietly superintending the changes at Merton, under the directions of its rightful owner. When Lord Nelson purchased the estate he declared which ever outlived the other — either Sir William or his wife — should be the inheritor at his own decease. To Sir William Scott, Lady Hamilton sent in the same year a present with kind consideration, and a little note in its company:—"Dear Nelson was saying you could not get any good port at South End; may I beg your acceptance of half a dozen of mine." Good-natured soul; while she had anything to give, she gave! Finding the Government silent to her appeal, Lord Nelson placed at her disposal the sum of £1,200 per annum. It will be remembered that Lady Nelson enjoyed £1,600 a year.

CHAPTER XX.

NELSON'S UNPROFITABLE ESTATE OF BRONTE. HIS PLANS FOR HORATIA.
HIS GREAT CHARITY. FAREWELL TO MERTON.

THE estate of Bronté, in Sicily, had been anything but a profitable gift to Lord Nelson. It had formerly belonged to an hospital, but he found it impossible to gather his rents, and in disgust determined not to invest any further sum upon it, and so he expressed himself to Mr. Abraham Gibbs, a merchant of Palermo, at the same time requesting him to find a responsible party who would endeavour to collect the rents on his behalf.

"VICTORY," OFF TOULON, 11th *August*, 1803.

MY DEAR SIR,
    I yesterday received your truly friendly letter of July 5th with much pleasure, and I shall be truly thankful if you will have the goodness to put my Bronté estate in a train, that if I cannot receive the value of it, and have done with it, that at least I may receive the full rental regularly, for I never will lay out another sixpence on it, but am content to pay a certain sum for the attention of some respectable person to receive the rents and remit them to London. As you are so good as to offer to attend to this serious concern to me, I will enter at large into the subject. I told Graefer* on first setting out that I would give up two years rent for fitting up a house and improving. I paid more attention to another Sovereign than my own, and therefore the King of Naples' gift of Bronté to me, if it is not now settled to my advantage, and to be permanent, has cost me a fortune, and a great deal of favour which I might have enjoyed, and jealousy which I should have avoided. I repine not on those accounts; I did my duty to the Sicilifying my own conscience, and I am easy. It will be necessary before you can take any steps beyond inquiry, to know from Sir John Acton what has been done, and what is intended. All that I beg is that the just thing may be done immediately, and that I may have it permanent. I shall never again write an order about the estate.

* Mr. Graefer was his agent in charge of Bronté.

The name Bronté is the Greek word for "thunder." The name of Cyclops, who in fabled lore forged the thunderbolt of mighty Jove, was Bronté, and his residence Etna.

This estate is one of the only two country houses in Sicily. Nelson's achievements are celebrated by picture and memorial in every corridor. The property is under the management of the Hon. A. N. Hood, who has redeemed it from the wretched plight in which it was when bestowed as a reward of merit. He has built farmhouses and bridges, and astonished the natives by the introduction of traction engines, laid out roads, and secured prosperity where once there was nothing but penury. The vineyards are some of the best in Sicily, and all devices for making wine are carried on with every modern improvement. The wine is good and cheap. When bearing the burden of wine, the Sicilians accompany their work by an outpouring of their national talent, "song," which has a very beautiful effect.

While absent on the Mediterranean service, Nelson received a communication from an old clergyman, who had known him as a boy, by name Dr. Allot, Dean of Raphoe, and brother to the Rev. Brian Allot, one time Rector of Burnham. In his reply, he made mention of his wish that in death he should lie by his worthy father in their village churchyard at Burnham. He wrote :—

> I remember you, dear Sir, most perfectly at Burnham, and I shall never forget the many little kindnesses I received from your worthy brother, with whom I was always a great favourite. Most probably I shall never see dear, dear Burnham again, but I have a satisfaction in thinking that my bones will probably be laid with my Father's in the Village that gave me birth. Pardon this digression ; but the thought of former days brings all my Mother into my heart, which shows itself in my eyes. May Heaven, my dear sir, long preserve you in health for the sake of your family and friends, and amongst the latter allow me to place the name of your very faithful servant,
>
> NELSON AND BRONTÉ.

The great man's soul in the midst of his arduous duties contained an overflow of attachment for the home of his young days, and he frequently expressed the desire to be buried amid the scenes where the hours of his childhood had been passed. It seems incredible that the man who could write such feeling, pious letters, should deserve the stigma which has attached itself to his name. Who shall be his judge? Dr. Scott said he was a thorough clergyman's son, and never got up or went to bed without kneeling down to say his prayers.

In the May of 1804, Lady Hamilton sent him a present of a cup on which was painted her portrait, which, according to the recipient, was not the least in the world like her; but he would not use it, he said, for if it were broken it would distress him.

Lord Nelson paid the most accurate attention to all the stores, having in view the economising of the public funds. On one occasion a bag of bread, said to contain 112 lbs., fell by accident into the sea, owing to the boats pitching in consequence of a heavy swell; he directed that it should be carefully examined on its recovery, that it should be wiped, and, if possible, saved for further use; and also he caused a strict enquiry to be made in order to find if any blame attached itself to any individual, and if so, the loss should be charged to his growing wages.

On his birthday, September 29, 1804, he wrote home to Lady Hamilton expressive of his desire to rest at Merton. "Forty-six years of toil and trouble!" he said, "how few more the common lot of mankind leads us to expect; and, therefore, it is almost time to think of spending the few last years in peace and quietness."

As it was his intention to remove the little Horatia from the charge of her nurse, he authorised his solicitor, Mr. Haslewood, to pay her an annuity, to commence from the date on which she delivered up her nursling, to which end he wrote as follows:—

"VICTORY," *May 16th,* 1805.

It is my desire that Mrs. Gibson is given an annuity of twenty pounds a year, when that she gives up my adopted daughter, Horatia Nelson Thompson, to the guardianship of my dear friend, Lady Emma Hamilton, and promises not to have anything more to do with the child, either directly or indirectly; and I leave my estate chargeable with this annuity.

NELSON AND BRONTÉ.

On the same day he addressed a formal letter to Lady Hamilton, requesting her to undertake the trust he confided to her, and hoping to find the child fully at home on his return to England, for he was daily growing more anxious for repose and quietude.

"VICTORY," AT Sea, *May 16th,* 1805.
MY DEAREST LADY HAMILTON,
As it is my desire to take my adopted daughter, Horatia Nelson Thompson, from under the care of Mrs. Gibson, and to place her under your guardianship, in order that she may be properly educated and brought up, I have, therefore, most earnestly to entreat that you will undertake this charge ; and as it is my intention to allow Mrs. Gibson as a free-will offering from myself (she having no claim upon me, having been regularly paid for her care of the child), the sum of twenty pounds a year for the term of her natural life, and I mean it should commence when the child is delivered to you. But should Mrs. Gibson endeavour, upon any pretence, to keep my adopted daughter any longer in her care, then I do not hold myself bound to give her one farthing, and I shall most probably take other measures. I shall write to Mr. Haslewood upon your telling him that you have received the child, to settle the annuity upon Mrs. Gibson ; and if you think Miss Connor disposed to be the governess of Horatia, I will make her any allowance for her trouble which you may think proper. I again and again, my dearest friend, request your care of my adopted daughter, whom I pray God to bless.

I am ever, for ever, my dear Lady Hamilton,
Your most faithful and affectionate,
NELSON AND BRONTÉ.

Therefore the good nurse, who had really loved the child and conscientiously reared and guarded her, parted from the little creature with sorrow in her heart, and handed her over to the lady who would place her in a better position—and from that date commenced the nurse's pension. It was owing to this stipulation of Lord Nelson that Mrs. Gibson and her daughter, who had been Horatia's playmate, lost sight of her, and only by chance did the daughter hear of her in after life. The break between them had been complete ! No member of Lord Nelson's family was overlooked, each in turn became the recipient of his unlimited generosity. A stone was placed by his desire over the grave of his brother Maurice, and he took upon himself the burden of the widow's debts, forwarding the requisite instructions to Lady Hamilton in one of his beautifully characteristic letters.

Although I cannot well afford it, yet I could not bear that poor blind Mrs. Nelson should be in want in her old days, and sell her plate; therefore, if you will find out what are her debts, if they come within my power, I will certainly pay them. Many, I dare say, if they had commanded here, would have made money, but I can assure you for the Prizes taken within the Mediterranean I have not more than paid my expenses. However, I would rather pinch myself than the poor soul should want. Your good angelic heart, my dearest beloved Emma, will fully agree with me everything is very expensive, and even we find it, and will be obliged to economise if we assist our friends, and I am sure we shall feel more comfort in it than in loaded tables, and entertaining a set of people who care not for us. An account is this moment brought me that a small sum is payable to me for some neutral taken off Cadiz in May, 1800, so that I shall not be the poorer for my gift. It is odd, is it not?

Overflowing with genuine charity; yet the world scornfully sneered at his asking whether there were a nice church at Merton, adding, that they "must set a good example to the humbler parishioners." The man never commenced or ended a duty without earnest and heartfelt prayer, and the holy sentiments which he transmitted to Lady Hamilton are such palpable evidence of the purity of their acts, as living unselfishly for others, that the best should be thought of them and not the worst. To soothe their neighbours' trouble and care—what a groundwork for the accusation of extravagance which was raised with cruel malignity in the day when death deprived the widowed lady of the hospitable hand that had been her support. So many necessitous relatives to help, educate, and forward in life, these were the drains on the exchequer.

A Mrs. Ullock, daughter of the Rev. Mr. Lancaster, of Merton, wrote to Sir Harris Nicolas, when he was compiling the *Dispatches and Letters of Lord Nelson*. Her correspondence contained a most truthful and feeling tribute to the private life of Lord Nelson at Merton :—

In revered affection for the memory of that dear man, I cannot refrain from informing you of his unlimited charity and goodness during his residence at Merton. His frequently expressed desire was that none in that place should want or suffer affliction that he could alleviate, and this I know he did with a most liberal hand, always desiring that it should not

THE BARBS OF SLANDER.

be known from whence it came. His residence at Merton was a continued course of charity and goodness, setting such an example of propriety and regularity that there are few who would not be benefited by following it.

This testimonial from the hand of a clergyman's daughter, who lived as a neighbour, and who must have intimately known Lord Nelson and Lady Hamilton, is a record of much importance, for it plainly shows that good-living people thought the lady's position in his lordship's house had nothing about it that savoured of impropriety. To the present day, there is a broad seat in the vestry of Merton Church which is called "Nelson's Bench." Throughout all the career of Lord Nelson and Lady Hamilton, detractors surrounded them from the hour of their first acquaintance to their closing days. In the year 1800, the poor lady, smarting under some cruel aspersions which had reached her ears, poured forth her troubled mind to Mr. Greville, in a letter dated February 25 :—

> We are more united and comfortable than ever, in spite of the infamous Jacobin papers, jealous of Lord Nelson's glory, and Sir William's and mine. We do not mind them. Lord Nelson is a truly virtuous and great man, and because we have been fagging and ruining our health and sacrificing every comfort in the cause of loyalty, our private characters are to be stabbed in the dark. First it was said Sir William and Lord Nelson fought; then that we played and lost. First, Sir William and Lord Nelson live like brothers; next, Lord Nelson never plays; and this I give you my word of honour. So I beg you will contradict any of those vile reports. Not that Sir William and Lord Nelson mind it; and I get scolded by the Queen and all of them, for having suffered one day's uneasiness."

What power the evil tongue has to blight the happiness of a fellow creature! Merited or unmerited, who can resist feeling the barbs of calumny? Lady Hamilton, in the zenith of her power, and in the height of her happiness, was sorely hurt by the undeserved shafts levelled at her husband and his great friend.

Poor Nelson was not without his own personal annoyances and vexations. For using, in the guidance of the fleet, his own clear head, which never failed him, instead of waiting for or obeying the orders of distant powers, he earned the disfavour of the Admiralty and expressed his dissatisfaction to Mr. Davison, who seems to have been the recipient of all the hero's concerns, told to him with unconstrained openness. He wrote :—

> Ah! my dear friend, if I have a morsel of bread and cheese in comfort, it is all I ask of kind Heaven until I reach the estate of six foot by two, to which I am fast approaching. I had the full tide of honour, but little real comfort. If the War goes on, I shall be knocked off by a ball or killed with chagrin. My conduct is measured by the Admiralty by the narrow rule of law, when I think it should have been done by common sense. I restored a faithful Ally by breach of orders; Lord Keith lost a Fleet by obedience against his own sense. Yet as one is censured the other must be approved. Such things are. I am satisfied, my dear Sir, you would have been truly happy to have paid the Prize money as soon as possible; but when the requisites are to be got from abroad, and especially if envy steps in, it makes it more difficult.

To his brother William he wrote, "My situation here is not to be envied, and I hope soon to be released from it." To another intimate friend, Lieutenant-Governor Locker, of Greenwich Hospital, he said, "I forgive from my heart my envious enemies."

It is not a matter of wonder that his tender nature rebelled under the slights and attacks of the Government, and yearned to escape from their vexations and return home.

The love of the people, who full well appreciated his splendid qualities, must have acted in a soothing and salutary manner on his ruffled feelings. He walked in public invariably surrounded by a crowd of hearty admirers; his weather-beaten face and form was hailed with a cheer of rejoicing whenever he sallied forth.

In the August of 1805, directly after his return from the Mediterranean, Lord Minto met him in Piccadilly surrounded by a concourse of the populace, and Nelson seemed to enjoy his position in a very kindly way. "I met Nelson," said the aforesaid lord, "in a mob in Piccadilly, and got hold of his arm, so that I was mobbed too. It is really quite affecting to see the wonder, and admiration, and love, and respect of the whole world, and the genuine expression of all these sentiments at once from gentle and simple the moment he is seen. It is beyond anything represented in a play or a poem of fame."

His residence in his coveted home was of brief duration, for in less than one short month the toiler went back to his work. According to Southey, Captain Blackwood called at Merton on September 2, 1805, to inform Lord Nelson that the combined fleets had put into Cadiz, knowing of what vital interest it would be to the man who had unceasingly pursued them. Later in the day, Lady Hamilton found him moodily pacing one of the walks which went by the name of the Quarter-deck.* She at once perceived that he was low-spirited and uneasy, and questioned him. He smiled and tried to pass it off, saying: "No, I am as happy as possible." Her ladyship replied that she did not believe him, and she would tell him what was the matter with him: that he was longing to get at those French and Spanish fleets, for he considered them his own property, and would be miserable if any man but himself did the business, for he had the right to them as the price and reward of his long watching and two years' uncomfortable situation in the Mediterranean; and she finished her oration saying, "Nelson, however we may lament your absence and your so speedily leaving us, offer your services immediately to go to Cadiz, they will be accepted, and you will gain a quiet heart by it." He looked at her for a few moments in silence, and then the overflowing heart burst forth—"Brave Emma, good Emma! If there were more Emmas there would be more Nelsons; you have penetrated my thoughts, I wish all you say, but was afraid to trust even myself with reflecting on the subject. However, I will go to town." He went accordingly next morning, accompanied by her ladyship and his sisters. They left him at the Admiralty, and continued their way to Lady Hamilton's house, 11 Clarges Street, where they awaited the result of his interview. In a short space of time they received a note from him to inform them that his old ship the "Victory" was telegraphed not to go into port, and begging that they would prepare everything for his speedy departure. Fatal bidding, what it cost her! Nelson, ever pliable in her hands, had resolved at once to offer his services, and bitter though the coming separation from friends, relations and home, he yielded up all to accomplish the perfect performance of a glorious naval victory and subjugation of a hated foe. Deeply, too, did Lady Hamilton regret his enforced absence after so short a stay in the home she had rendered so charming. Her letter to Lord Nelson's niece, Lady Bolton, is pitiful in its distress:—

* Each walk had its name; one was the Poop, and so on.

LADY HAMILTON.

September 4, 1805.

My dear Friend,

I am again broken-hearted, as our dear Nelson is immediately going. It seems as though I have had a fortnight's dream, and awake to all the misery of this cruel separation. But what can I do? His powerful arm is of so much consequence to his country. But I do nor can not say more. My heart is broken, &c., &c.

Her personal regard for Nelson, great as it was, became in every way a secondary consideration to the interest she took in his glory and advancement.

Lord Nelson felt so keenly the presentiment that he would never again return home, that, before he quitted London, he called at the shop of Mr. Peddieson, his upholsterer, in Brewer Street, where the coffin presented to him by Captain Hallowell had been sent. He told Mr. Peddieson, with his usual gaiety and good-humour, to get the attestation of its identity engraved on the lid, for, added his lordship, "I think it highly probable I may want it on my return." His last act before leaving his beloved Merton was to steal to the bedside of the sleeping child in whom his heart's great love was centred, and on his knees he prayed—prayed most earnestly. Then taking a painful farewell, full of sad forebodings, he drove from the home he was fated never again to enter. Lord Minto was present at this distressing scene, and thus described the affecting leave-taking, "Lady Hamilton was in tears; could not eat, and hardly drink, near swooning, and all at table. It is a strange picture. She tells me nothing can be more pure and ardent than this flame. Nelson is in many points a really great man, in others a baby."

There died on the 6th of January, 1889, at Merton, a man of great age, named Hudson. In his youth, as a lad of twelve years, he witnessed the departure of our hero, his master, to earn death and fame imperishable. He was employed about the gardens of Merton Place, ran errands, or carried parcels to and from the stage coach. His wife was the daughter of Nelson's gardener, Cribb, and she only shortly predeceased her husband, who reached the patriarchal age of ninety-six years. To the last, he loved to smoke and chat about the Admiral. He lived in one of two cottages, at the bottom of the lane leading down from the "Nelson Arms" at Merton. These cottages were erected by Nelson's orders for the accommodation of his outdoor servants, and they stand to-day the sole remnant of the hero's home, when all else has been dismantled. The mulberry tree which grew on his little grass-plat was planted by the Admiral's direction. Hudson held the door of the chaise and closed it, as his master left. He felt his hand clasped cordially, and heard the parting words of counsel, "Be a good boy till I come back again." The Admiral, he used to say, was greatly beloved at Merton. He would often stop and speak to the boys at play in the street, who hailed his curious little figure with all the more reverence and pleasure because of the fruit and coins with which he was always plentifully supplied for their benefit. Kind, simple heart, carrying into practice the wish expressed to Lady Hamilton, "that he might be loved in his country home." In his brief sojourn he made some faithful friends, knit to him by little deeds of kindness.

On the very morning of the day which witnessed his departure from Merton, as he walked in the grounds, he held a little conversation with Cribb, his gardener, over an anticipated event which was of material interest in Mr. Cribb's family circle. Putting into the man's hand a ten pound note, he told him to buy a christening frock, adding, "If it is a boy, call it Horatio, and if a girl, "Emma." Emma it proved.

He wrote of these twenty-five days as the very happiest of his life. How often does not extreme happiness forerun great sorrow? After the death of Nelson a most pathetic entry was found in his diary, referring to the cause of his country calling him to duty, and compelling him to forsake the retirement for which he had craved, and he fervently trusted that the Almighty Power would preserve him once more to return. Thus did he resignedly bid his farewell to his comfortable home :—

Friday Night, 13th September.

At half-past ten drove from dear, dear Merton, where I left all that I hold dear in this world, to go to serve my King and country. May the great God whom I adore enable me to fulfil the expectations of my country; and if it is His good pleasure that I should return, my thanks will never cease being offered up to the throne of His mercy. If it is His good providence to cut short my days upon earth, I bow with the greatest submission, relying that He will protect those so dear to me that I may leave behind. His will be done. Amen, Amen, Amen.

Saturday, September 14th, 1805.

At six o'clock, arrived at Portsmouth, and having arranged all my business, embarked at the Bathing machines, with Mr. Rose and Mr. Canning.

On the day before his departure, he received a most flattering letter from the father of our loved Queen, His Royal Highness the Duke of Kent, an extract from which will serve to show the very high regard entertained for the great Commander by the exalted writer:—

> If I had the good fortune of seeing your Lordship before you left Town, it was my intention to have said to you how proud I should have felt could I have been thought worthy of being entrusted with the command of the Army that may be employed on any service in which your Lordship might take on yourself that of His Majesty's Naval Forces, being fully convinced that, with such a colleague, there is nothing, almost, that might be undertaken, the issue of which would be doubtful. But alas! since the unfortunate issue of my command at Gibraltar in 1802-3, I appear to have been set quite aside, and I see no prospect of any favourable change occurring. But should such a circumstance, though unexpected, occur, it would be a great satisfaction to me to know that your Lordship would not be averse to having me with you. In the meanwhile, my best and most fervent wishes will ever attend you, and it will be a subject of real pride to me to be considered one of your warmest friends and admirers. With these sentiments, and those of the highest personal regard and esteem,
>
> I remain, my dear Lord,
> Ever yours most faithfully and sincerely,
> EDWARD.

High and low equally idolised him, and even on the occasion of his embarkation at Portsmouth, on the 14th of September, he did not use the ordinary landing place, but pushed off in a small boat from the part of the shore apportioned to the bathing machines, in order to elude the populace; all to no purpose, for their vigilant eyes were on the alert for his appearance, and they rushed to bid him "God speed." Southey describes "a crowd collected in his train, pressing forward to obtain a sight of his face; many were in tears, and many knelt down before him, and blessed him as he passed. England has had many heroes, but never one who so entirely possessed the love of his fellow-countrymen as Nelson.

All men knew that his heart was as humane as it was fearless; that there was not in his nature the slightest alloy of selfishness or cupidity; but that, with perfect and entire devotion, he served his country with all his heart, and with all his soul, and with all his strength; and therefore they loved him as truly and as fervently as he loved England. They pressed upon the parapet to gaze after him when his barge pushed off, and he was returning their cheers by waving his hat. The sentinels who endeavoured to prevent them from trespassing upon this ground were wedged among the crowd, and an officer who, not very prudently upon such an occasion, ordered them to drive the people down with their bayonets, was compelled speedily to retreat, for the people would not be debarred from gazing till the last moment upon the hero—the darling hero of England. It was not in Nelson's nature to witness such affection in his countrymen unmoved, and he touchingly exclaimed to Captain Hardy, 'I had their huzzas before—I have their hearts now.'"

Upon a stone at Southsea beach rests one of the anchors of the good ship "Victory," with an inscription which records that it was near that spot that Lord Nelson embarked.

CHAPTER XXI.

THE BATTLE OF TRAFALGAR. NELSON'S MESSAGE TO THE FLEET.
DEATH IN THE HOUR OF GLORIOUS VICTORY.

RAPIDLY nearing his great end, Nelson wrote to his bosom friend, Mr. Davison, with whom he ever corresponded without the slightest tinge of reserve, and to whom he invariably turned with a desire to relieve his overladen mind. He felt that the crisis was quickly approaching, and even though his constitution was undermined with the wear and tear and anxieties of the last few years, he was determined to be in at the death after his long, long chase; and thus anticipated the probabilities of coming events :—

> Day by day, my dear friend, I am expecting the Fleet to put to sea—every day, hour, and moment, and you may rely that, if it is within the power of man to get at them, it shall be done; and I am sure that all my brethren look to that day as the finish of our laborious cruise. The event no man can say exactly; but I must think, or render great injustice to those under me, that, let the Battle be when it may, it will never have been surpassed. My shattered frame, if I survive that day, will require rest, and that is all I shall ask for. If I fall on such a glorious occasion, it shall be my pride to take care that my friends shall not blush for me. These things are in the hands of a wise and just Providence, and His will be done! I have got some trifle, thank God, to leave to those I hold most dear, and I have taken care not to neglect it. Do not think I am low-spirited on this account, or fancy anything is to happen to me; quite the contrary,—my mind is calm, and I have only to think of destroying our inveterate foe.

The bond between the Admiral and his men was keenly felt by both. Nelson loved his sailors, and, in return, his sailors idolized him. After his death they spoke of him as "Saint Nelson." A Captain Duff was appointed

NELSON'S DIFFICULTIES WITH THE ADMIRALTY.

to H.M.S. "Mars." The unfortunate officer fell at Trafalgar, a cannon ball struck off his head, and as his body fell in the midst of action, it was covered with a spare flag until it could receive attention. In writing home to his wife on October 10, 1805, his remarks will be found to bear out the assertion of the great affection existing between the chief and his subordinates. He said:—" I am sorry the rain has begun to-night, as it will spoil my fine work, having been employed for this week past to paint the ships à la Nelson, which most of the fleet are doing. He is so good and pleasant a man that we all wish to do what he likes without any kind of orders. I have been myself very lucky with most of my Admirals, but I really think the present the pleasantest I have met with," &c., &c.

The ensuing letter demonstrates Nelson's difficulties with the Admiralty, which so frequently find mention in his correspondence. It is in reply to Dr. Sewell, Judge of the Vice-Admiralty Court at Malta, relative to his having taken the sole charge of the detained Spanish vessels out of the hands of the agent whom Nelson had appointed on behalf of the Crown, acting on instructions from the Admiralty in England.

"VICTORY," *October 11th*, 1805.

DEAR SIR,

I am just honor'd with your letter of August 26th, the Admiralty in England seems to have been very ill-advised to give me orders to do that which they had no legal authority for doing, and if I had not complied with what you conceive their illegal Order, and that I should have been liable to be called to a very severe account. I have wrote a very strong letter to the board upon the subject, and requested that if they have given me an improper Order, that they will say so, in order that I may clear myself from the contempt with which I am treated by obeying their Orders, and if they are right, that both for the dignity of the Admiralty and the maintenance of their just rights, they will take proper measures upon the occasion. I have been only an Instrument, but I will not submit tamely to be put wrong by them, or any power on earth. I took no step except that of preserving the property without their Lordships' Orders, and for the obeying of which it seems very cruel that I am to be treated in the manner I have been. The Ministers at Home seem not to have known what each other was ordering. I feel, my Dear Sir, very much obliged by your good wishes, and I hope and expect that very soon I shall have an opportunity of getting at the Gentry from Cadiz.

They cannot stay there much longer, and I hope it will be such a blow as will go far towards humbling the pride of Bonaparte.

I am, my dear Sir, ever with the Highest Respect,
Your most faithful and obedient Servant,
NELSON AND BRONTÉ.

Dr. Sewell.*

The important period is fast approaching in this little history which in one day gave to the British nation a supreme victory and an irreparable loss; a conquest over a great enemy, and a hero's death! Two frigates had been sent out in search of the French fleets, and, pending the result of their quest, preparations were made on board the different vessels in anticipation of an engagement, which now was imminent. While his servant was occupied in transferring his valuables between decks for greater security, Nelson opened his desk to write to the loved ones at Merton, so dearly cherished. To them he gave his latest thoughts, and penned his latest messages, through which will be read the foreboding of evil which haunted him, and which escaped in spite of the effort he made to conceal his depression and feign gaiety.

"Victory," *October* 19, 1805.
Noon. Cadiz, E.S.E., 16 Leagues.

My dearest beloved Emma,
The dear friend of my bosom. The signal has been made that the Enemy's Combined Fleet are coming out of Port. We have very little wind, so that I have no hopes of seeing them before to-morrow. May the God of Battles crown my endeavours with success; at all events I will take care that my name shall ever be most dear to you and Horatia, both of whom I love as much as my own life. And as my last writing before the Battle will be to you, so I hope in God that I shall live to finish my letter after the Battle. May Heaven bless you prays your
NELSON AND BRONTÉ.

October 20*th*.

In the morning we were close to the mouth of the Straits, but the wind had not come far enough to the westward to allow the Combined Fleets to weather the shoals of Trafalgar; but they were counted as far as forty sail

* From MSS. in the possession of Mr. Robert Griffin.

AUTOGRAPH LETTER OF LADY HAMILTON.

WRITTEN FROM CANTERBURY TO LORD NELSON, OCTOBER 8, 1805. RETURNED UNOPENED TO LADY HAMILTON. NELSON WAS DEAD ON ITS ARRIVAL.

Dear Husband of my Heart you are all in this world to your Emma — may god send you victory & Home soon to your Emma. Hurotia & paradise meeting for when you are there it will be paradise my own Nelson my god prosper you & preserve you for the sake of your affectionate Emma

of Ships of War, which I suppose to be thirty-four of the line and six frigates. A group of them was off the Lighthouse of Cadiz this morning; but it blows so very fresh, and thick weather, that I rather believe they will go into the harbour before night. May God Almighty give us success over those fellows, and enable us to get a peace.

In the above transcript of the letter it will be noticed that he began on the 19th, continued on the 20th, and it was left open to record the result of the fight, for the original ends abruptly on the top of the third page. The precious document was found open on his desk when the hand that had penned it was cold in death. Captain Hardy brought it to England along with other treasured relics, and delivered them to Lady Hamilton. As has been said, the letter ends on the top line of the third page in an abrupt manner; below it, written in a hurried and irregular fashion, diagonally across the sheet, are a few words in Lady Hamilton's writing, which read, "Oh miserable, wretched Emma," and below, on another line, "A glorious and happy Nelson." This interesting historical memento is preserved in the British Museum.

Who would not sympathise with the bereaved recipient of the treasured letter? The poor woman who had only so recently sent him her best wishes for his speedy and safe return in these words:—

> Dearest Husband of my Heart, you are all in this world to your Emma. May God send you victory, and home soon to your *Emma*, *Horatia*, *and paradise Merton*, for when you are here it will be paradise, MY own Nelson. May God prosper you and preserve you for the sake of your affectionate Emma.*

Nelson was no more when this letter arrived; Captain Hardy returned it unopened.

On the morning of October 21, a lieutenant on board the "Victory" presented himself at Nelson's cabin door with the intention of laying before him a fancied grievance, but he paused on seeing his lordship on his knees writing, and being unwishful to disturb him, withdrew without making his presence known. When his commander arose from his knees, he simply communicated some official business to Lord Nelson, as he could not bring

* Autograph, among the papers of the late Joseph Mayer, Esq., F S.A.

himself to mention his own affairs at so solemn a moment. It was afterwards discovered that the work upon which Lord Nelson had been engaged was an entry in his private diary which took the form of the following sublime prayer. At the same time he wrote the Codicil to his will, in which he bequeathed to his country's consideration the two loved beings who, before the sun had set that self-same day, were deprived of his loving care for ever :—

THE PRAYER OF LORD NELSON.

MONDAY, *October 21st*, 1805.

At daylight saw the Enemy's Combined Fleet from East to E.S.E.; bore away. Made the signal for Order of Sailing, and to prepare for Battle. The Enemy with their heads to the Southward. At seven, the Enemy wearing in succession.

May the Great God whom I worship grant to my Country, and for the benefit of Europe in general, a great and glorious Victory; and may no misconduct in anyone tarnish it; and may humanity after Victory be the predominant feature in the British Fleet. For myself, individually, I commit my life to Him who made me, and may His blessing light upon my endeavours for serving my Country faithfully. To Him I resign myself and the just cause which is entrusted to me to defend. Amen, Amen, Amen.

CODICIL TO LORD NELSON'S WILL.

October the twenty-first, one thousand eight hundred and five, then in sight of the Combined Fleets of France and Spain, distant about ten miles.

WHEREAS the eminent services of Emma Hamilton, widow of the Right Honorable Sir William Hamilton, have been of the very greatest service to our King and Country to my knowledge, without her receiving any reward from either our King or Country :—First that she obtained the King of Spain's letter, in 1796, to his brother the King of Naples, acquainting him of his intention to declare War against England; from which Letter the Ministry sent out orders to then Sir John Jervis to strike a stroke if opportunity offered against either the arsenals of Spain or their Fleets. That neither of them was done is not the fault of Lady Hamilton. The opportunity might have been offered. Secondly, the British Fleet under my command, never could have returned the second time to Egypt had not Lady Hamilton's influence with the Queen of Naples caused letters to be wrote to the Governor of Syracuse that he was to encourage the Fleet being supplied with everything should they put into any Port in Sicily. We put into Syracuse, and received every supply, went to Egypt, and destroyed the French fleet. Could I have rewarded these services, I would not now call upon my Country, but as that has not been in my power, I leave Emma, Lady Hamilton, therefore, a Legacy to my King and Country, that they will give her an ample provision to maintain her rank in life. I also leave to the beneficence of my Country my adopted daughter, Horatia Nelson Thompson; and I desire she will in future use the name of Nelson only. These are the only favours I ask of my King and Country at this moment when I am going to fight their Battle. May God bless my King and Country, and all those who I hold dear. My relations, it is needless to mention; they will of course be amply provided for.

NELSON AND BRONTÉ.

Witness HENRY BLACKWOOD.
T. M. HARDY.

The disregard which this codicil received at the hands of the King and country can only be looked back upon with a thrill of horror, written as it was in the midst of such awful surroundings, the last effort of a doomed hand, the *only* favour requested by the glorious Commander who personally directed that great sea fight, and who fell a sacrifice in his supreme endeavour to increase the renown of the British nation. How could England ignore the last message sent home by its hero who conquered in death?

Nelson lost, in the service of the British Government, an arm, an eye, and eventually his life, besides carrying on various parts of his body the marks of severe wounds; maimed and disfigured he walked through life, and yet his only petition for reward was left ignored. His solicitude for the welfare of his best loved ones caused him to make his dying bequest so full of simple faith in his countrymen. He justly considered that they for whom he provided had a claim on his country when the sacrifice of his life was the withdrawal of their support. His wish should have been regarded as a sacred charge; ways and means come easily to those who have the will to do, and no excuse can palliate the fact that his legacy was unfulfilled.

After writing the codicil, he gave his time and thoughts wholly to the superintendence of his gallant and well-disciplined men; he passed to and fro among them, encouraging and inspiring them to deeds of energy by kindly, spirited words. As he walked on the poop with his friend Captain Blackwood, he suddenly said that he would give the fleet a signal, adding "Don't you think there is one still wanting?" These words were scarcely uttered when forth he sent to his fleet his final signal, soul-inspiring, impressive, and now the national by-word, "England expects every man to do his duty." The shout with which it was received from all those on the various vessels was sublime, telling by its power how keenly the message had sunk into their brave hearts, bringing before each the remembrance of home, and acting as an incentive and reminder that in their hands lay the credit of that day's fight. What wonder that such a spur, coming at that momentous hour, should cause each to put forth his best endeavour, and that the Battle of Trafalgar was added to the list of England's conquests!

After the despatch of the signal, Lord Nelson turned to Captain Blackwood, and said, "Now I can do no more; we must trust to the Great Disposer of all events, and the justice of our own cause. I thank God for this great opportunity of doing my duty." About half-past eleven, Captain Blackwood was ordered to go on board his own vessel, and, as he prepared to depart, Nelson, still pursued by the foreboding of evil which hung over him in spite of all efforts to cast it off, said, with earnestness, "God bless you, Blackwood, I shall never speak to you again." Prophetic farewell!

The shout with which the fleet had received his message was hardly exhausted when the Admiral gave orders to make the signal, "Close action," and to keep it up. The signal was hoisted, and there it remained until it was shot away.

At twenty-five minutes past one, Nelson received his death wound while walking amidships above his cabin; a ball that was fired from the enemy's mizentop struck him on the left shoulder and entered his chest. He fell forward on his face on exactly the same spot where his secretary, Mr. John Scott, had fallen an hour previously, and with whose blood Nelson's own clothes were bespattered. "They have done for me at last," he exclaimed, "they have shot my backbone through." The Rev. Alexander John Scott, chaplain on board the "Victory," was engaged in the cockpit, which was rapidly filling with wounded and dying men. The carnage on the "Victory" was terrific. The effect of the scene of agony filled his mind with so much

LORD NELSON.
FROM A MINIATURE BY JACKSON.

THE DEATH OF NELSON.

horror that it haunted him like a shocking dream for years afterwards. He never talked about it. Lord Nelson was tenderly carried below, his clothes stripped off, and a sheet placed over him. While this was being effected he said to his chaplain, "Doctor,* I am gone; I told you so." Then, in a low and most earnest manner, he added, "I have to leave Lady Hamilton and my adopted daughter, Horatia, as a legacy to my country." Though undergoing so much intense agony himself, yet he was keenly sympathetic with the sufferings of those near him. A poor wounded seaman lay close to him on a pallet awaiting amputation, and in the prevailing bustle around the fallen Commander, some person in the crowd hurt the injured sailor. Weak as Nelson was, he sharply turned his head, and rebuked the man for not having more humanity and care for the sufferer. A few moments later he was heard to say, "How dear is life to all men." The pain became so intense that he said he wished he was dead, but he added, "Yet one would like to live a little longer." After a pause of a few moments, still in the same low tone, he was heard to say, "What would become of poor Lady Hamilton if she knew of my situation?" He frequently asked for Captain Hardy, to whom he was much attached. When the Captain presented himself, it was to congratulate his chief on the result of the terrible engagement—victory! The combined fleets had given in. The two old friends conversed whenever the agonising pains permitted it, each holding the other's hand. In his failing strength he uttered brief sentences: "Don't throw me overboard, Hardy"; "Take care of my dear Lady Hamilton, Hardy, take care of poor Lady Hamilton. Kiss me, Hardy." The Captain knelt down and kissed the dying hero on the cheek, and heard him murmur, almost inaudibly, "Thank God, I have done my duty." Hardy knelt again, and kissed him on the forehead. Nelson, feeling the caress, said, "Who is that?" to which the Captain replied, "It is Hardy." "God bless you, Hardy," said his lordship. Hardy then ascended to the deck, and never saw him again in life.

Presently Lord Nelson turned towards his chaplain and said, "Doctor, I have *not* been a *great* sinner," and he begged him to see that all his effects and his hair were taken to Lady Hamilton; and again he repeated his impressive injunction, "Remember that I leave Lady Hamilton and my daughter, Horatia, as a legacy to my country," presently adding, "Never

---

* Although Lord Nelson always called him Doctor, he did not receive his degree until after the battle of Trafalgar.

forget Horatia," after which he became speechless, and at half-past four that great soul passed into eternity.

In allusion to the national loss sustained in the death of Nelson, Southey uses these splendid words of tribute: "He cannot be said to have fallen prematurely whose work was done; nor ought he to be lamented who died so full of honours, and at the height of human fame. The most triumphant death is that of the martyr, the most awful that of the martyred patriot, the most splendid that of the hero in the hour of victory, and if the chariot and horses of fire had been vouchsafed for Nelson's translation, he could scarcely have departed in a brighter blaze of glory. He has left us, not indeed his mantle of inspiration, but a name and an example which are at this hour inspiring hundreds of the youth of England—a name which is our pride, and an example which will continue to be our shield and our strength. Thus it is that the spirits of the great and the wise continue to live and to act after them."

The day after the death of Lord Nelson, the body was placed in brandy and spirits of wine, holding a strong solution of camphor and myrrh, to preserve it for interment in England.

The predominant dying thought of Nelson was akin to that of King Charles the Second, "Take care of poor Lady Hamilton," "Take care of poor Nell." Kindred characters; neither ever abused her power, each unspoilt by her rise in life, using only her magnetic influence in kindly feeling and sympathy for her fellow creatures. What wonder is it that both king and conqueror bequeathed such women to the consideration of others, who had ever been thoughtful and solicitous to console, comfort, or add pleasure to the lives of those who sought their assistance. It could never be laid to the charge of either woman that she made a base use of her position.

CHAPTER XXII.

THE FUNERAL AT ST. PAUL'S. NELSON'S MEMORY AFFECTIONATELY HONOURED. THE REV. EARL SHOWS HIS HAND. *PUNCH* SPEAKS HIS MIND.

BAD weather delayed the homeward course of the "Victory," and on the 11th of December she arrived at the Nore. The body was removed from the cask in which it had been preserved, and the ball, which had passed through his spine and lodged in the muscles of his back, was extracted. A large quantity of gold lace, pad, and lining of the epaulette, with a piece of the coat, was found attached to the ball, the lace of the epaulette as firmly embedded as if it had been inserted into the metal while in a state of fusion. On its removal from the "Victory," the body was apparelled in the uniform dress of the late Admiral, and laid in the coffin which had been presented to its occupant by Captain Hallowell some years previously, and which, with sad foreboding, he had instructed his upholsterer to set in order and hold in readiness for his reception before he left England. The coffin was placed within another one so richly ornamented that it was asserted to be the most superb ever seen in Europe. On the 22nd of December it was conveyed in a yacht to Greenwich, accompanied by a procession of boats; there it lay in state for three days, after which it was removed to the Admiralty, where it lay in state until January 9, 1806, when it was interred in St. Paul's Cathedral at public cost. The selection of St. Paul's was in deference to the expressed wish of Nelson himself, as he had desired that his resting place should be within that sacred edifice if honoured by a public funeral. He had an aversion to Westminster Abbey, alleging as his reason that he had heard an old tradition when a boy, that Westminster Abbey was built on a spot where once existed a deep morass, and he thought it likely that the lapse of time would reduce the ground on which it now stands to its primitive state of swamp, without leaving a trace of the Abbey.

The spot selected for his interment was in the middle aisle of the Cathedral, immediately beneath the centre of the dome. The sarcophagus and pedestal were brought from Wolsey's tomb-house at Windsor, and they were the same which the great cardinal had prepared for himself in the reign of Henry the Eighth. The ceremony accompanying the interment was impressive beyond the power of description. The magnitude of the attendant procession may be judged from the fact that although the first part entered the choir at two o'clock in the afternoon, the whole did not reach the choir until four. Evening advanced, and increased the solemnity of the scene. Most of the service was performed by torchlight; the dome was lighted for the first time, and was comparable only in its religious character to the annual illumination at St. Peter's, grand and awe-inspiring in the extreme.

The final anthem was singularly appropriate. Verse: "His body is buried in peace," and the chorus: "But his name liveth evermore."

The flags of the "Victory" were deposited in the grave, save one, which the sailors, with unanimous accord, rent into a thousand shreds to carry away as a relic of the dead hero. The ceremony was concluded a little before six, but the cathedral was not entirely vacated till past nine. The car on which the coffin had been borne was modelled after the hull of the "Victory." While the body lay in state, Caroline Princess of Wales and her retinue paid it a visit, and remained a considerable time. The Dukes of York, Kent, Sussex, and Cambridge attended the obsequies. The four vergers of St. Paul's Cathedral who had the exclusive property of the body of the church, are said to have made more than a thousand pounds by the daily admissions to see the preparations for the funeral of Lord Nelson; the door-money was taken as at a puppet-show, and for several days amounted to more than forty pounds each day. After the obsequies the public, for a charge of a shilling a-piece, were permitted to enter the enclosed spot directly over the body, from whence they could see the coffin. Miss Berry, the friend of Horace Walpole, was an eye-witness of the funeral procession; she decries the arrangements as wanting in much that might have been imposing. In her journal, dated January 13th, she writes: "Never was a mob so decent, so quiet, so serious, or so respectful. The officers were all put into mourning coaches, and therefore could not be distinguished; and the men who had been on the "Victory" during the engagement, instead of surrounding or following the funeral car, were marshalled by themselves in another part of the procession, without music, without officers, without any naval accompaniments whatever. Although few in number, and thus separated from everything that would have added consequence to their appearance, such was the impression that their serious, quiet, decent deportment made on the multitude, that they were repeatedly and almost continually cheered as they passed along. What a deep and lasting impression would the whole of this ceremony have made on the minds of the spectators had the naval part of the procession, as well as the military, been conducted on foot; had the companions of his glory and his danger, exposed to the regards of their grateful and admiring country, immediately surrounded the car which bore his remains; had the whole been accompanied by appropriate music, one band taking up the melancholy strain when another dropped it, and had the passage of the procession been marked by the solemn tolling of the different bells. I will not talk of the disproportions and perfect bad taste of the funeral car, because good taste in forms I never expect here; but I did expect sufficient good taste in moral feeling not to have entrusted the conduct of such a ceremony, the tribute of such a nation to such a chief, as a job to the Herald's Office and their hireling undertakers. The only moment when the mind most disposed to enthusiasm could for a moment indulge it (I speak not of the ceremony in St. Paul's, which I did not see) was that in which the funeral car passed Charing Cross. Here nothing could be seen on every side but pyramids of heads, and every head uncovered from respect to the object on which every eye was bent. One general feeling pervading a great multitude must ever tend to the sublime." Haydon, the artist, saw the procession and expressed himself in a very similar manner as regarded the carrying out of the funeral arrangements. In his *Life* are introduced a few reminiscences of Nelson which will be read with interest: "I remember that after the battle of the Nile, when quite a child, I was walking with a school-fellow near Stonehouse, when a diminutive little man, with a green shade over his eye, a shabby well-worn cocked hat, and buttoned-up undress coat approached us. He was leaning on the arm of a taller man in a black coat and round hat (I should think this must have been poor Scott*). As he came up my companion said, " There's Nelson." " Let us take off our hats," said I. We did so, and held them out so far that he could not avoid seeing us, and as he passed he touched his own hat, and smiled. We boasted of this for months. Just before he embarked the last

* Lord Nelson's secretary, who lost his life at Trafalgar.

time I saw him again with the same man passing by Northumberland House. He had been to Dollond's to buy a night-glass, for I casually called there and saw his address written by his own hand, and his glass on the counter. I saw his funeral, which, as a clever foreigner said, showed the nation's generosity, and its utter want of taste. Instead of employing the first artist of the day, I believe Ackermann, of the Strand, designed the whole thing. At the conclusion of the Funeral Service in the cathedral, the old flag of the "Victory" was torn into a thousand shreds, each of which was carefully preserved by its fortunate owner as a relic of the hero. Lascelles Hoppner brought me home a fragment which I religiously kept until it was irretrievably lost in the confusion of my ruin. The lead coffin, in which Nelson's body was brought home was cut up into pieces, and distributed among the different ships to be preserved also as relics."

Charles Lamb, writing to Hazlitt after the death of Nelson, regretted him in these words: "Was n't you sorry for Lord Nelson? I have followed him in fancy ever since I saw him walking in Pall Mall (I was prejudiced against him before), looking just as a hero should look, and I have been very much cut about it indeed. He was the only pretence of a great man we had, nobody is left of any name at all."

The Rev. A. J. Scott, Lord Nelson's chaplain, returned to England in charge of the corpse, and sat up with it every night for more than a week whilst it lay in state at Greenwich, and so emaciated and distressed was his appearance at the funeral, that many persons who saw him there said "he looked like the chief mourner." He was remembered in Lord Nelson's will by a legacy of £200, "bequeathed to my friend, the Reverend Alexander Scott," and he was also the recipient of a mourning ring, the design of which was both beautiful and appropriate. It was a plain thick gold hoop with the Duke and Viscount's coronets in coloured enamel, and simply inscribed within, "Lost to his country, Oct. 21, 1805."

The first monument erected to his memory was so remarkable that it deserves special mention. As soon as the news of the victory of Trafalgar arrived at Cork, Captain Watson, Commander of the Sea Fencibles, proceeded at once to erect an arch with the assistance of the men under his command and a few masons. This extraordinary feat was accomplished in five hours. The arch stands on a high hill, and can be seen at sea from a considerable distance. It has a marble tablet, bearing the following inscription :—" This arch, the first monument erected to the memory of Nelson after the Battle of Trafalgar, was sketched and planned by Captain Joshua Rowley Watson, R.N., and built by him and twelve hundred of the Sea Fencibles then under his command (assisted by eight masons). It was erected, in five hours, on the tenth of November, 1805." In the area in front of the Liverpool Town Hall is a superb group of bronze statuary, supposed to be the largest in the kingdom, erected to commemorate the death of Nelson. His friend, Mr. A. Davison, raised an obelisk in white freestone at his seat, Swarland Hall, with an inscription to the effect that it was erected not for public service (which was a duty to England), but for private friendship. This obelisk stands close to the great road between Morpeth and Alnwick. The bullet, with lace, epaulette, &c., embedded, was subsequently presented to Her Majesty, and lies at Windsor. Among the relics of Trafalgar which are there preserved, is a piece of the foremast of the "Victory," which had been pierced by a large shot. Upon it stands a bust of Lord Nelson, executed by the celebrated and accomplished sculptress, Mrs. Damer, at the request of the Duke of Clarence. Although Mrs. Damer had arrived at the advanced age of eighty years, she undertook the commission, and completed the colossal bust in bronze a few days before her death. After the victory of the Nile, when Lord Nelson had become the object of universal regard, Mrs. Damer offered to present to the city of London, at her own cost, a bust of his lordship. This gracious offer from the talented lady was gladly accepted, and Nelson gave her many sittings. On one occasion he asked her how he could repay her for her trouble in taking his bust, and the honour she was doing him, to which she replied, " Give me one of your old coats." He answered, " I will give you the one I value most highly." It was that which he had worn during the battle of the Nile, dirty and dusty, and covered with hair powder, just as he had taken it off, with the traces of the labour of the day upon it.

Mrs. Damer, finding her health to be rapidly failing, left instructions that as she was unable to present the bust herself, she wished her nephew to take her place and convey it to the Duke of Clarence, and also to ask his acceptance of the treasured coat, and she desired that the presentation should be made as soon as possible after her death. The Duke of Clarence therefore appointed a day on which to receive the legacy at Bushey, where he then resided, and in accepting it he placed the bust on the stump of the " Victory's" mast, which has since been transferred to Windsor; but the coat he ordered to be enclosed in a glass case, and forwarded to Greenwich Hospital, as being its most fitting resting place, where it can now be seen in the Painted Chamber.

The coat and waistcoat worn by Nelson at Trafalgar were brought home by Captain Hardy, and delivered to Lady Hamilton, in accordance with his dying request that all his belongings should be handed to her. At the time when her circumstances became seriously involved, she parted with a considerable amount of her portable property to Alderman Smith, who came forward and made her an advance of money wherewith to pay off her most pressing creditors; the coat and waistcoat were among the articles consigned from the one to the other. Some years later, a proposition was mooted to solicit subscriptions in order to purchase these relics from the Alderman's widow, and place them at Greenwich as national trophies. His Royal Highness the Prince Consort generously found the whole amount asked by the lady, namely, one hundred and fifty pounds, and handsomely presented the garments to the Hospital at Greenwich, where they also lie in the Painted Chamber, in company with the coat worn in the fight of the Nile.

Government voted splendid gifts to the relatives of Lord Nelson. His widow received £2,000 per annum for life; each of his sisters, namely, Mrs. Bolton and Mrs. Matcham, were granted £15,000; and his brother, the Rev. William Nelson, was elevated to the peerage. To the earldom was attached an annual income of £5,000, and £99,000 wherewith to purchase an estate called Stanlynch, in Wiltshire, which name was to be changed to that of Trafalgar.

Total disregard was paid to Nelson's last wish that the nation should remember the child that he had loved so well. His dying request, that whatever recompense his country should consider him entitled to might include the child of his adoption, was allowed to lie in abeyance. The death of Nelson was a terrible shock to Lady Hamilton. She constantly upbraided herself with the reflection that it was owing to her counsel that he went forth, never to return. When the sad intelligence was first communicated to her, she was perfectly overcome, lying prostrate, beyond consolation, heartbroken, and refusing to be comforted. As the minute guns boomed, and the muffled bells of St. Paul's and the Abbey tolled their dire announcement to the lone woman that the remains of the sailor hero were being consigned to

their resting place, she wept bitterly. In one day her glory departed, her power and greatness were all in the past, and the path that lay before her was hard to tread, and month by month it became a downward progress, her life embittered by cares and troubles, her future one weary struggle. For three weeks after she first received the dreadful news she was entirely confined to her bed, but in the midst of her own sore distress the unselfish beauty of her character came prominently to the front. The death of Nelson had brought his sister, Mrs. Bolton's, family into straitened circumstances, for he had ever been most considerate for their necessities, and generous in his gifts to assist them. Knowing that Mrs. Bolton's means would be very limited, and unable from indisposition to write herself, she commissioned her mother, Mrs. Cadogan, to communicate with the Right Hon. George Rose, Vice-President of the Board of Trade, and to represent their needs. In spite of her humble origin, and dependent position in early life, this unassuming woman does not appear to have been wholly illiterate, which is a natural inference when the subjoined specimen of her penmanship and composition is taken into consideration :—

November 9, 1805.

Lady Hamilton's most wretched state of mind prevents her imploring her dear good Mr. Rose to solicit Mr. Pitt to consider the family of our great and glorious Nelson, who so gallantly died for his country, leaving behind his favorite sister with a large family unprovided for. Her Ladyship is confident you will exert every nerve for these good people, as a mark of your true and real attachment to our lamented hero. Mr. Bolton was ever much esteemed by his brother-in-law, and had it pleased the Almighty to have spared Lord Nelson to his family, he meant to have made them independent. They at this moment surround her Ladyship's bed, bewailing their sad loss and miserable state. Lady Hamilton, whose situation is beyond description, only prays that you, good sir, will do all you can for this worthy family; it will be the greatest relief to her mind. This is written by the mother of the most to be pitied Lady Hamilton, who begs leave to subscribe herself Mr. Rose's

Most obedient and very humble servant,

MARY CADOGAN.

P.S.—If Mr. Rose would condescend to acknowledge this, it would be a comfort to her just now.

Poor, considerate woman! How little Lady Hamilton then imagined that her own burdens would so shortly be hard to bear.

Expressions of sympathy flowed in from every source, accompanied by offers of service. A few lines from the letter of condolence sent by a friend of Nelson's of many years' standing, Richard Bulkeley, Esq., show that Lady Hamilton's position at Merton was perfectly understood, and that there was nothing to resent. He says:—

> You have lost what must be irreparable to you, that which any woman in any age and situation would have been proud to possess, a friend who, in all his actions, was governed by the purest feelings, and whose mind was incapable, under any circumstances, of forgetting those who had in the slightest degree marked kindness towards him. To you, therefore, who had served and SAVED him when no common exertions would have availed, it was quite natural that his attachment should have been (as it was) the most tender and unbounded.

Recovering from the prostration into which she had been thrown by the sad event, she exerted herself to reply to the numerous correspondents who had been neglected during her indisposition. One letter, in the possession of Mr. Robert Griffin, written to the poet Hayley, acknowledging his condolence, is another evidence that former relations between her, Romney, and his life-long friend, Hayley, had been based upon proper lines, and that the sole aim of these two men had been to improve her well-inclined nature:—

CLARGES STREET, *Jan.* 29*th.*

MY DEAR RESPECTED FRIEND,

I have been so ill, so very ill, and I am *So Broken Hearted* that I can scarcely hold my pen to thank you for your Delightful and Consoling letter. Yes, it is consoling to find a true and sincere friend at this moment when I have lost the most virtuous, the Truest, the Bravest, and Sincerest of friends, and to you I am indebted for this glorious man's Love and Regard, for if I had never read your *Triumphs of Temper*, I should never have been the wife of Sir William Hamilton, nor should I have had an opportunity of cultivating those talents which made the great and immortal Nelson think me worthy of his Confidence, and which made Him say now this last time He went forth to fight His Country's Battles: "Brave Emma, Heroic Emma, you encourage me to go forth. If there were more Emmas there would be more Nelsons." These last words still I hear, still I feel, and feel proud when I think I was beloved by Him. To you I therefore owe all my past happiness, but I am now most wretched. I write from bed, and can only say write me a line and say you shall be glad to hear from me again, and shall I send you His last Codicil about me, written the morning of the 21st—the unhappy 21st. I am very sorry that I have promised the Earl Nelson to give him my letters, but none of those in my list, only I beg you to forgive this scrawl, and ever believe me with more gratitude than I can express, your affectionate and grateful,

EMMA.

I will in a few days, when I am able to get up, send you the list of my pictures.

Magnetic influence that had inspired the artist to his best efforts, and the hero to his deeds of highest renown!

To her staunch friend, Mr. Rose, she sent a wail of lamentation deep and earnest. She said:—

My heart is broken. Life to me is not worth having. I lived but for him; his glory I gloried in; it was my pride that he should go forth, and this fatal and last time that he went I persuaded him *to it*.

The new Earl, secure of his prize, was seated at table with Lady Hamilton when he received the welcome news that the coveted Peerage was assigned to him. He then drew from his pocket the codicil to his brother's will bequeathing her to the beneficence of the country she had so advantageously served; he threw the document across the table to her, telling her, with the triumphant taunt of the man in possession of the height of his ambitions, to do what she liked with it. Full well he knew it was valueless to her, nevertheless she had it registered next day at Doctors' Commons.

On December 2, 1805, the Rev. W. Nelson writing to the Rev. A. J. Scott to intimate that he would forward the coffin, the " L'Orient " trophy, to meet the body, adds: " I beg the favour of your transmitting to me by the first safe opportunity such of my dear brother's papers (not of a public nature) as are under your care, and of making for me (with my sincere regards and kind compliments) to Captain Hardy the same request." Again, on December 6,

1805, he says: " It is of the greatest importance that I am in possession of his *last will* and codicils as soon as possible. No one can say that it does not contain among other things many directions relative to his funeral." No such wish to see his brother's remains interred in accordance with any expressed desire, moved him to request for the papers, for he had already conformed to the King's command that the hero be honoured by a public funeral. His aim had self for its centre. How was it that Lady Hamilton was only informed of the codicil when his ends were gained? He was living at her house, and yet treacherously withheld all knowledge from her of the important document in his keeping. That the cruel, unfeeling, and insulting conduct of the Rev. Earl may be more fully understood, an exposition of his previous course of conduct towards Lady Hamilton when their positions were reversed, and he had everything to gain by acting deferentially to her, will show how little he merited the honours which were showered upon him by his impulsive and undiscriminating countrymen; honours which were more the due of the woman at whose bidding the conqueror went forth, than of the servile man who had cringed and fawned at every opportunity in order to achieve self-aggrandisement. Well aware of Lady Hamilton's influence, he constantly solicited her to exert it on his behalf to obtain for him advancement in his sacred profession, to which end he kept her apprised of berths which were likely to become vacant. The following lines will exemplify his tactics:—

> 1801. I am told there are two or three very old lives, prebends of Canterbury in the Minister's gift, near six hundred pounds a year, and good houses. The deans of Hereford, Exeter, Lichfield, and Coventry, York, and Winchester are old men.

Anon he unbosoms his mean aspirations:—

> Now we have secured the Peerage, we have only one thing to ask, and that is my promotion in the Church, handsomely and honourably, such as becomes Lord Nelson's brother and heir apparent to the title. *No put-off with small beggarly stalls.* Mr. Addington must be kept steady to that point. I am sure Nelson is doing everything for him. But a word is enough for your good sensible heart.

Another time he forwarded her half a dozen young apple-trees—Norfolk biffins—throwing veritable crabs to produce apples, as an antecedent to the intimation which followed up his gift, that "he saw by the papers that there was a stall vacant at Durham which he supposed to be worth a thousand a year." On another occasion, he wrote in these disrespectful and unclerical terms concerning Mr. Pitt: "I had a bow from Billy this morning in the Senate House." He subscribed himself her "obliged and faithful servant," called her his "deary," and spent his time on Sunday between morning and evening service in writing jocose and free letters to her, insincerely signing himself her "best and truest friend." His wife and daughter had been frequent visitors and incessant guests with the hospitable lady; the daughter he entrusted to her entire charge for six years, only withdrawing her when his own position was secured. The hue of his cloth had not prohibited contact with a presentable person when protected and in fashion; but to be acquainted, or on familiar terms, with the same woman when bereaved and destitute was not for one instant to be contemplated. But his end was gained; the poor lady was abandoned, and he who had been her most obsequious follower became the first to circulate malicious innuendoes, and traduce her with inveterate malignity.

There was, once upon a time, a Pope who began life as a fisherman. It was not the first Peter but a Pope of a much later date. He vacated his profession, and entered the priesthood, renouncing the pursuit of soles aquatic in favour of angling for souls for the supply of the celestial courts. He took his first degree as a minister of the Church, and so humble was he that he daily ordered his nets to be placed on his dining table, as a reminder of his lowly origin. So through the grades of his upward progress, the nets invariably made their appearance at his principal meal. The great day arrived when he attained the acme of his career, and was elected Pope. From that all important hour the nets were discarded! An intimate friend asked him the reason of their non-appearance; he winked, and made reply, "I've angled my fish, and have no longer a use for my nets!" So with poor Lady Hamilton, she was cast aside when she could no longer be of service; the new Earl had angled his fish, and had no further requirement for his tackle. *Punch*, bearing date January 19, 1850, commenting on the very handsome salaries enjoyed by those fortunate enough to claim alliance with the hero's blood, denounces the recreant Earl, and with biting sarcasm estimates his character in these words: "As for the Earl Admiral's brother, who inherited the profits of Trafalgar, and bobbed in for the coronet that missed the dead—he was in heart and soul as much allied to the sailor as a barnacle upon the copper of the 'Victory' was a portion of her heart of oak. Nevertheless they took Parson Barnacle and gilded his simoniacal head with a coronet, and he—keeping the even tenor of his way—cheated Lady Hamilton, duly robbing the sailor's child, Nelson's orphan, Horatia. Whereon the Prince of Wales wrote letters of sympathy that, like all such epistles from his royal hand, were by no means worth the ink that blotted the paper."

We have stated that Earl William requested Captain Hardy to hand to him Nelson's private correspondence; this accounts for the absence from circulation of Lady Hamilton's letters to the Admiral; therefore the line: "I burn all your dear letters," in the offensive missive commencing "Now, my dear wife," is of no consequence as accounting for the disappearance of *suggested* incriminating letters. By the new Earl's act, correspondence was withheld from publication; it was therefore an easy matter for him who concocted the story of the maternity of Horatia to insinuate that the flames had consumed that which never existed. In like manner did the Earl request Lady Hamilton to give him Nelson's letters to herself. If such correspondence on either side had contained any culpable reference it would have enlightened him, at least, yet it never can be shown that at any time did he ever treat Horatia as the child of his brother.

Nor was Lady Hamilton the only person of whom he endeavoured to get the better. Nurse Gibson was honoured by his attentions. She received a summons from him to attend at his house, and hand him the document which authorised the payment of her annuity of twenty pounds, as arranged by Lord Nelson. She waited on him, but took the precaution to present him with a copy only of the deed. On receiving it, he hurried out of the room, but as quickly returned on finding that it was not the original. He spoke so rudely that his gentle wife interfered, but only to receive insult herself for taking the poor woman's part, and she was forced to withdraw in tears.

The policy of heaping up so much wealth on the relatives of Lord Nelson may well be questioned, when it is considered that he would have felt grateful for a small portion as recompense for his former achievements, and he would not have been heard to complain, in the presentiment of his death, on the morning of his final triumph, that his services had not been requited by the Government of his country, and that he was about to die without

PLATE IX. ATTITUDE OF LADY HAMILTON, FROM A DRAWING BY REHBURG.

possessing the means of performing some acts of kindness and generosity which were among the last of his earthly wishes. Too late to serve the earner's designs came his country's acknowledgment; wreaths were laid upon his coffin, eulogies flowed without limit, monuments rose high to perpetuate his unrivalled memory; but the one trust—the only one which he left to be fulfilled—the succour of his living loved ones, was withheld. With a full knowledge of all the circumstances, he left a reminder to his country to consider it a national obligation to remunerate his able coadjutor in interests vital to the British nation. And are there not in existence letters innumerable from the Lords of the Fleet to her ladyship which prove, without dispute, that with her they corresponded on matters of importance concerning the fleet when in Italian waters? And were not her services acknowledged by a foreign sovereign, the Emperor Paul, who begged that her deeds and his honour to her should be recorded in our archives?

When George, Prince of Wales, as Prince Regent, was appealed to in reference to the fulfilment of Nelson's legacy, he replied, "Did it depend upon me, there would not be a wish or a desire of our adored hero that I should not consider as a solemn obligation upon his friends and his country to fulfil. It is a duty they owe to his memory, and his matchless and unwearied excellence. I hope that there is still in this country sufficient honour, virtue, and gratitude to prompt us to ratify and carry into effect the the last dying request of our Nelson, and by that means proving, not only to the whole world, but to future ages, that we were worthy of having such a man belonging to us."

CHAPTER XXIII.

ENGLAND IGNORES THE LEGACY. DR. SCOTT SYMPATHISES. HIS GRIEVANCE AGAINST EARL WILLIAM. WAS HORATIA OF FOREIGN EXTRACTION?

LOOKING back, it seems inexplicable that Nelson's legacy was not carried into effect, for it reads so clearly that it was his *sole* desire that his charges should be included in the recompense that would be his. The magnitude of the gifts to his relatives does not exonerate the Ministers then in power from the brand of injustice in distributing his earnings according to their discretion, to the disregard of his expressed wishes. That they allowed a female absolutely to sink into poverty, and die amid hard privations, and knowingly withheld reward for services in which uncommon ability had been displayed, is a matter of deep regret. The plea of lapse of time under which the Government resisted the claim was vapid in the extreme. The lady had sufficient means to support her position in life up to the time when she petitioned for remuneration, and would never have sought to place herself as a burden upon the nation except for the failure of all her sources of income—as she herself wrote, she would rather give to her country than take from it. If the pension was withheld on the score of propriety, what can be said of their predecessors in office, who supported and carried through a grant to Mdlle. de Kerouelle, mistress of our graceless Charles the Second, and spy on behalf of His Most Sacred Majesty of France. Let the claims of these two women be taken into consideration, and—their awards. Louise de Kerouelle came ostensibly (craftily) in the train of Henrietta, Duchess of Orleans, as her apparent lady-in-waiting; but her task had been assigned to her by the French King, who was well aware of the susceptible heart of our lively monarch. The woman's beauty was the magnet to attract the amorous King, and, once attached, the conveyance of State secrets to the French Court was of easy moment. The *intrigante* successfully carried her point, inveigled the pliable King into her meshes, and presented him with a son. Without any difficulty arising, the obsequious Government loosed its purse-strings and saddled the country from that time forth with the annual payment of £19,000 to the descendants of the clever Frenchwoman, which sum was enjoyed for generations by the posterity who inherited the honours founded by that wily woman. Emma Hamilton faithfully watched her country's cause with all the earnestness of her uncommonly gifted nature, and it is admittedly owing to her judicious craft that the hero of the Nile was enabled to win for England his supreme victory, and thus leave a signal mark in the history of Britain's naval greatness. At her bidding Nelson went to take his stand in the grand sea fight and conquest at Trafalgar, and though the result of the achievement was to her the cessation of her support and income, yet to the day of her death her claims were merely acknowledged—never recompensed. It is incredible that the bright, beautiful, and good-hearted woman, once the centre and life of a brilliant and cultivated society, should have been allowed to sink from one step to another until she reached the pitiful end that must have been a welcome relief. How she herself felt is told in a letter to Dr. Scott, the chaplain of the "Victory," dated September 7, 1806:—

> My dear Friend,
>
> I did not get your letter till the other day, for I have been with Mrs. Bolton to visit an old respectable aunt of my lord Nelson's. I shall be in town, that is at Merton, the end of the week, and I hope you will come there on Saturday, and pass Sunday with me. I want much to see you—consult with you about my affairs. How hard it is, how cruel their treatment of me and Horatia. That angel's last wishes all neglected, not to speak of the fraud that was acted to keep back the codicil. But enough! when we meet we will speak about it. God bless you for all your attentions and love you showed to our virtuous Nelson, and his dear remains; but it seems those that truly loved him are to be victims of hatred, jealousy, and spite. However, we have innocency on our sides, and we have, and had what they that persecuted us never had, that was *his* unbounded love and esteem, his confidence and affection. I know well how he valued you, and what he would have done for you had he lived. You know the great and virtuous affection he had for me, the love he bore my husband, and if I had any influence over him, I used it for the good of my country. Did I ever keep him at home? Did I not share in his glory? Even this last fatal victory it was I bid him go forth. Did he not pat me on the back, call me brave Emma, and said, "If there were more Emmas

there would be more Nelsons"? Did he not in his last moments do me justice, and request at the moment of his glorious death that the King and Nation will do me justice? And I have got all his letters, and near eight hundred of the Queen of Naples' letters to show what I did for my King and Country, and prettily I am rewarded. Psha! I am above them, I despise them; for, thank God, I feel that having lived with honour and glory, glory they cannot take from me, I despise them. My soul is above them, and I can yet make some of them tremble by showing them how he despised them, for in his letters to me he thought aloud, &c.

It will be observed that Lady Hamilton had been visiting an aunt of Lord Nelson. Without exception, his female relatives cordially welcomed her to their houses, and saw nothing objectionable in her taking charge of his house, insomuch as her position had been supported by her husband, and the combined household commenced in a very natural way, taking circumstances into consideration. Had Lady Nelson remained at her post, how differently transactions might have developed. The letter to the chaplain evinces nothing but propriety. She refers to the minister as to one who knew things as they were: " You know the great and virtuous affection he had for me, the love he bore my husband, and if I had any influence over him I used it for the good of my country." Faithful Emma! Dr. Scott never considered the affection between Nelson and Lady Hamilton as other than Platonic, and surely he ought to know, the keeper of the man's conscience.

The reverend gentleman delayed his reply to her ladyship's letter until October 22, and his correspondence displays the friendly and homely intercourse that existed between him and the neglected lady.

BURNHAM VICARAGE, NEAR SOUTHMINSTER, ESSEX.

MY DEAR LADY HAMILTON!!!

It was my intention always to spend this day and yesterday in London, and, under that idea, supposing we should soon meet, I did not write to you. My dear Lady Hamilton, I am settled here, having no house of my own at Southminster. I have undertaken the additional duty of Burnham, which gives me a good house, and five acres of ground, with a garden besides. I have already got a Cow, a horse, a Cat, and a dog. I have furnished two bedrooms and two sitting rooms, but the house is big enough for a large family,—my establishment consists of a man and his wife, who do everything for me. I bake at home, and make my own milk, &c., &c.; in short, for the first time in my life, I am enjoying all the Comforts, agonies, and miseries of housekeeping. I am employed every day, both Parishes being Populous; but on Sunday I preach three sermons, besides Churchings and Christenings, which abound here. Some of my furniture is of the best, and if I remain I shall improve my establishment by degrees. I am situated about ten miles from South End, but there is a Ferry to cross. I understand, however, that carriages usually pass it; as yet I have not had time to go there myself. The Country here at this season is miserable beyond description, and most dreadfully unhealthy; but it is delightful in the Summer Months, and very healthy. My dear Lady Hamilton, I will be with you on the 29th without fail. Kiss Horatia for me, and tell her so. I prepare myself for remaining here; my books are placed, to the tune of eleven thousand and odd volumes, and, to say the truth, I am not uncomfortable. If Ministry notice me, I shall not mind my expence in settling at this place; and if they do not, it is lucky I have fixed myself. What I most earnestly desire is a stall at St. Paul's—unfortunately it is not worth more than Canterbury, but the *esprit de calcul* does not enter my brain in this case. You, dear Lady Hamilton, will believe me, though the world would not. What is thought of for you? I repeat it, you cannot be forgotten, but you tell me nothing of your prospects. Most truly I can say, as fast as the memory of dear Lord Nelson evaporates from the minds of others, it sinks deeper into that of mine, in which I know you join me.

In the same letter, before concluding, the Rev. A. J. Scott alludes to his having come under the ban of the Rev. Earl Nelson, who had accused him of inserting newspaper paragraphs to his detriment, which Dr. Scott solemnly denied to him; in fact, he also had been the victim of an anonymous assailant, and he concluded that it was the work of the same party who had annoyed the Earl. As he closed, he remarked that he had called regularly on Earl Nelson, though treated by him with indignity, and he would never cease to treat him with respect on account of his bearing the name of Nelson.

From the *Life of the Rev. Dr. Scott*, we gather another fact which lays bare the intense selfishness of the brother of Nelson. Only on the very day on which he sailed on the fatal expedition did Nelson say to Dr. Scott, "You remain quiet, let me get my brother a step, that is all, and you shall have his." The Prebend at Canterbury to which he was looking forward was held by the brother of the departed hero, who, being created an Earl, with the prospect of £10,000 a-year, it was everywhere expected would resign the stall. Dr. Scott's pretensions to it, in the event of his vacating, were founded upon the late Lord Nelson's frequently expressed wishes. The Earl was urged to forego the post by many men of position, including even the Prince Regent; but the grasping man argued with Dr. Scott that his brother meant he should give up the stall only on getting the deanery—that the earldom was in short no *step*. As many of the officers of the fleet were well aware of Lord Nelson's desires, there arose a strong feeling of disapprobation against the Earl. Squibs appeared in the daily papers, and Mr. Fuller, M.P. for Sussex, took up the matter in the House of Commons. The concluding lines of the Bill he introduced were worded thus: " He hoped the representative of that family would also shew some degree of generosity, and comply with the wish expressed by the illustrious founder of the family in his last moments." But no impression could be made on the noble prebendary. The stall was too good a thing to give up, so this anxious matter having hung in doubt for more than a year, distracting Scott's peace of mind and injuring his health, at last ended in disappointment. Dr. Scott had known Lady Hamilton well during the lifetime of Lord Nelson; he considered she had an heroic spirit, great personal attractions, and much cleverness; but, unfortunately, at this period of her history, she fell a victim to her own inordinate vanity, extravagance, and love of society. A friend of the Merton *coterie* was one day hailed from a carriage window in one of the London streets, and he recognised the voice as that of Lady Hamilton, who requested him to return home with her for dinner. Being engaged for that evening, he went down to Merton next day, expecting to find himself the only guest. His astonishment was great on his arrival to see an assemblage of visitors, including Signor Rovedino and Madame Bianchi, whom her ladyship regaled with a sumptuous dinner; and after the ladies had retired, the superb wines of the Merton cellars, gifts of crowned heads, were liberally dispensed by Rovedino as master of ceremonies. The gentleman alluded to was strolling in the garden early next morning before breakfast, when he was joined by his hostess, with whom he remonstrated on the mode of life she was pursuing. She attempted to justify herself by saying, "it was a less expensive plan than

HER FINANCIAL DIFFICULTIES.

taking Horatia to town for singing lessons." Her friend would not admit of her excuse, and at length extorted the confession that her affairs were already in a state of grievous embarrassment. He talked seriously and sincerely with her, and agreed to find means to relieve her. In a few days he re-visited her, and introduced a gentleman who had retired from business, but was well skilled in matters of finance. He undertook to investigate her affairs, and remedy them if possible, on condition she complied with certain conditions. He found that two or three years retirement into Wales, upon a small annuity, would release her from her perplexities. Into Wales she accordingly went, but only for a short term. She returned to London, took lodgings in Bond Street, and was soon again a suppliant for relief from the friends whose advice she had discarded.

Lady Hamilton found herself overwhelmed by her increasing difficulties. The burden of the expenses in connection with the alterations of Merton Place was thrown upon her shoulders. The Earl repudiated all responsibility of clearing the estate, although Lord Nelson had more than once written to both Lady Hamilton and Mr. Haslewood that he never intended her to pay those charges out of the income he allowed her. It was impossible for the poor woman to stem the deluge of bills which flowed in on all sides. Her only income of eight hundred a year was too small to satisfy the besieging creditors who clamoured for payment, and with the alterations to Merton, commenced under Nelson's directions, still going on, she soon became inextricably involved, for the likelihood of the sudden withdrawal of her income had never been fully realised by her. That things soon fell into arrears may be gathered from a letter written by Mrs. Cadogan to her daughter on her birthday, April 26, 1806. Its contents must have had a depressing rather than an elevating influence on its recipient, who was at 11 Clarges Street, Piccadilly, while her mother remained at Merton to superintend the workpeople.

  My dear Emma,

    I pray God send you many happy returns of this day. I have sent you a gown of Sarah Reynolds' making. If I had ten thousand pounds to send you this day I should have been very happy. I have sent Mariann, as I thought she might be of use to you to-day. I am all over with bricks and dust, and stinking paint. Bring no body but your own family on Saturday. You shall have a *Menestra Verde* and one thing roasted. Mariann will tell you how very miserable I have been this week. My dear Emma, I owe Mariann four months wages, which is two guines. I had it not to give her, and she wants shoes and stockings. If you can give Sarah Connor thirty shillings to pay her washerwoman, as she is indetted to her for three months' washing. I have got her washing down here. You must send Mariann as soon as you can in the morning. God bless you, my ever dear Emma.

M. CADOGAN.

Retrenchment was of little avail to satisfy the demands of the army of claimants. The poor woman was gradually reduced to sore straits, until the time came when the last of the united trio found herself unable longer to sustain the expenses of the maintenance of what was to have been their happy home, "Merton Place." The little estate was sold. The property became the prey of the enterprising builder, who speedily dismantled it, and covered the ground with very third rate residences. The usual landmark of a place or person of note was erected, and remains, known as "The Nelson Arms." The district is still named "Nelson's Fields." Ruin, oblivion, and destruction was the portion of all that he held most dear. The sole monument of his cherished home—a public house!

Lady Hamilton sold most of her valuables, and lived for two years at Richmond, residing at Hill Street. From thence she wrote the following letter to Mr. Greville. The Mrs. Greffer to whom allusion is made was the widow of Nelson's agent at Bronté, to whom he had rendered assistance. His death left her in difficulties, and an application to the new Earl Nelson for relief was—as could only be expected from him—declined.

SUNDAY MORNING.

DEAR SIR,

I was on the point of coming to you when I got your note, but I feel sorry to-day I cannot call on you at your house, for I am to meet some of my trustees and my soliciter, at 2 O'Clock, on particular business. As to my dear friend, Mrs. Greffer, it was not any favour she wished for herself, for she wou'd not ask one of the King, and I have taken care to give her such letters for the Queen, and beg'd of Her Majesty by the love she bears or once bore for Emma, by all I have done for her, by the sacred memory of Nelson, by *the charge she has placed in me*, that she will be good to Mrs. Greffer, whom she allways marked with the Royal notice.

I have given her an account of the cruel neglect of the present possessor of dear Nelson's honord titles, estates and honours; neglect to me who was the maker of his family, and neglect to Mrs. Greffer. But why speak of such people?—let it suffice she sails Thursday, and I have done by her as I have done by all that my glorious Nelson thought I wou'd do if he fell. I have fulfilled, and am fulfilling, my dutys daily to his memory. I will not trouble you, therefore, by any request for Mrs. Greffer. It was merely to ask Sir J. Bankes a question to satisfy her on a point. I will call soon to see you, and inform you of my present prospect of happiness. At a moment of desperation, when I thought they neglected me, Goldsmid and my Citty friends came forward, and they have rescued me from distruction. Distruction brought on by *Earl* Nelson's having thrown on me all the bills for finishing *Merton*. Nelson, who attested in his dying moments that I had well served my Country. All these things, and papers of my services and my illtreatment I have laid before my trustees; they are paying my debts. I live in retirement, and the citty are going to bring forward my claims; in short, I have put myself under their protection, and nothing, *no power on earth shall* make me *deviate* from my present system. On Friday next, I come to finsbury Square to Mrs. Goldsmid, and Monday I shall be in Broad Street with Sir John and Lady Perrin for a week, and one of those days I will come to you for a horse, for I have not my horses at present; but I do not want them, friends are so good to me. You will be pleased to hear my mother is well and delighted with my house and small establishment. Horatia is well, and you will, I think, be pleased with her education. Goldsmid has been, and is an angel to me, and his bounty shall never be abused. I hope you will mend as the Spring advances, and if you shou'd ever come to Richmond, pray call and see me, and pray believe me, yours affectionately,

EMMA HAMILTON.*

This is a remarkable letter, insomuch as it contains an allusion to a charge which she had received from her former friend, the Queen of Naples, and seems a connecting link with her other other assertion that Horatia's mother was "too great to be mentioned." The words, "the charge she has placed in me," are underlined to signify that they cover deep meaning. May not the relatives of Horatia have been some high Court personages in whom

* The Morrison MSS.

the Queen of Naples was interested (not necessarily herself), and in the wish to aid, and to conceal a scandal, may she not have confided the secret to those in whose fidelity she had implicit faith. The present Queen of Italy possesses the letters written to the Queen of Naples by Lady Hamilton and Lord Nelson,* but she will not allow their inspection, on the ground that it would give pain to persons living. Her Majesty would scarcely withhold them out of consideration for the descendants of the supposed child of Lord Nelson. The probabilities are more in favour of her shielding a noble Italian family. As a child, Horatia was described as having "a very foreign look." If Nelson and Lady Hamilton held the key to the child's maternity, and had known and cared for the lady in their gay Neapolitan days, the interest they evinced and the adoption of the child are easily understood. One thing is certain, Lady Nelson, Nelson's own wife, never doubted him, and expressed herself to a noble lord as considering marital infidelity an impossible act on the part of Lord Nelson; so also did Captain Hardy, his trusted friend.

The above-quoted letter was written to Mr. Greville at the end of the year 1808, and it will be noticed that Lady Hamilton hoped the coming spring would find his health improved. He made no progress towards amendment, and died on April 23, 1809, at his house on Paddington Green. He was buried in the family vault of the Earls of Warwick, at St. Mary's Church, Warwick, and was succeeded in the inheritance by his brother, The Hon. R. Fulke Greville, subject to the jointure to Lady Hamilton, left her by her husband, of £800 a year.

Business-like, clear-headed, and energetic, Greville had surmounted every obstacle, and carried into effect all the propositions he had laid before Sir William regarding the conversion of Milford into an harbour of eminence. Thoughtful for his future advantage, he had induced his uncle to entrust him with the requisite funds for the furtherance of his gigantic scheme. Other moneys he must have raised, for he worked in earnest, and from the insight which his letters, written in the year 1786, give us into his plans, he was no doubt successful in financing as he proposed. By his personal endeavours he established the Royal Mail; obtained five packets and ran a daily service to Waterford; built his hotel; persuaded the Trinity Brethren to build a light-

* These letters were recently discovered in the Palace of Caserta, and have been placed among the Royal archives at Rome.

house; and induced a colony of American Quaker whale-fishers to emigrate and locate themselves at Milford; besides numerous other enterprises requiring the conception of a master mind, and Milford was started on a foundation that should have led it to the place of eminence among seaports which his great mind had designed, but like many another land of promise, when once the leading spirit which guided its schemes was removed, it gradually collapsed. Yet men of energy might successfully redeem its fallen fortunes, for " there is corn in Egypt still."

LADY HAMILTON AS A "MAGDALEN."
From a painting by Romney, executed at a commission from the Prince Regent.

CHAPTER XXIV.

POOR RELATIONS. LADY HAMILTON MAKES HER WILL. THE DUKE OF QUEENSBURY RELIEVES HER. THE DEATH OF MRS. CADOGAN. YOUTHFUL MEMORIES BETRAY A SECRET.

THE following letter from one of Lady Hamilton's cousins on her mother's side will be read with interest. It is palpably a reply to an invitation, and the reason for declining it is straightforward and amusing. It is addressed to " The Right Hob. Lady Hambleton, hering Cort, Richmond " (Heron Court), and written from Greenwich.

Nov. 17, 1809.

DEAR COUSIN,

I Recvd Yours, and should have been happy had it been in my power to have acted according to your directions, which it is not possible for me to do as I would wish, For I declare my small Cloaths are Scandoulos, and my hat has the Crown part nearly off, but Mr. and Mrs. Ingam has contriv'd it so that what I was in need of they have lent me. I have to inform you that your brother Charles is in Greenwich College, and has been here since the 6th Inst., and when I informed Mr. and Mrs. Ingam that he was here, they have given him a Strong Invitation for to pass what few hours he has to spare to abide at their house, and Mrs. Ingam has got him remov'd from the Hall, where y^r Brother was to an apartment belonging to the Hall where Mr. Ingam is.

From your Affte. Cousn,

THOS. KIDD.

The Thomas Kidd of the disreputable habiliments was the son of the old man aforenamed, and—like father, like son. The young fellow had been apprenticed to a carpenter; when his time expired, he went to Lady Hamilton, and informed her that he had no means wherewith to provide himself with tools. She told him to supply himself, and to direct the bill to be forwarded to her. The young scamp availed himself of this permission, and, in return for her good nature, he caused the ironmonger to present her with an

LADY HAMILTON'S KINDNESS TO HER RELATIVES. 235

account which amounted to £70. Her kindred veritably assisted in bringing about the catastrophe of ruin. Another humble cousin who had arrived in London, desirous of seeing his illustrious relative, wrote his own letter of introduction and presented it personally. He was at once summoned to the drawing-room, and kindly welcomed. Rumours of unsatisfactory conduct on the young man's part had reached Lady Hamilton, and she tendered him good advice. He had with him a complimentary letter from his employer asking him to return to him. After reading it, Lady Hamilton passed it to a lady who was sitting with her, remarking, " Well, there is no gainsaying that." She put her hand into her pocket, and gave the young fellow two guineas. This in the days when money was very, very scarce.

Her prime favourite among her relations was her cousin, Sarah Reynolds, daughter of her uncle, Richard Reynolds, whom she promoted to be housekeeper at Merton Place, and on the dismantling of that happy household, she received from her ladyship a pretty old-fashioned china breakfast service, which still remains in her family. She married a Mr. Newcomb, who had sailed as purser with Lord Nelson. He used to relate that on one occasion the fleet were absent eighteen months, subsisting on salt meat, &c. On arriving at a seaport, the crews purchased and slew some cattle, and so ravenous were they for the taste of fresh meat that they attacked the carcases with their cutlasses, instead of awaiting professional dissection. In the year 1806, Lady Hamilton made a will disposing of her property, mostly in favour of her mother, who was to be succeeded by Horatia; but this she rescinded two years later, by the execution of another testament, of which we give a copy :—

> This I declare to be my last Will and Testament, October the 16th, 1808, Richmond. If I can be buried in St. Paul's, I should be very happy to be near the glorious Nelson, whom I loved and admired. And as once Sir William, Nelson, and myself, had agreed we should all be buried near each other, if the King had (not) granted him a public funeral, this would have been, that three persons who were so much attached to each other from virtue and friendship should have been laid in one grave, when they quitted this ill-natured slanderous world. But 'tis past, and in Heaven I hope we shall meet. If I am not permitted to be buried in St. Paul's, let me be put where I shall be near my dear mother, when she is called from this ungrateful world. But I hope she will live and be a mother to Nel-

son's child, Horatia. I beg that Merton may be sold, and all debts paid, and whatever money shall be left after all debts are paid, I give to my dear mother, and after her death to my dear Horatia Nelson. I also give all that I am possessed of in this world to my dear mother, Mary Doggin or Cadogan, for her use, and after her death to Horatia Nelson. I give them all my ready money, plate, linen, pictures, wearing apparel, household furniture, trinkets, wine, in short, everything I have in the world to my mother during her life, and after her death to my dearest Horatia Nelson. I hope Mr. George Rose will be my executor, and take care of my dear Mother and Horatia ; and if he should not be living, I hope his eldest son will do me this last favour to see justice done to Nelson's daughter. And also I beg His Royal Highness the Prince of Wales, as he dearly loved Nelson, that His Royal Highness will protect his child, and be kind to her, for this I beg of him, for there is no one that I so highly regard as His Royal Highness. Also, my good friend, the Duke of Queensbury, I beg of him, as Nelson beseeched him to be kind to me, so I recommend my dear mother and Horatia to his kind heart. I have done my King and Country some service, but as they were ungrateful enough to neglect the request of the virtuous Nelson in providing for me, I do not expect they will do anything for his child ; but if there should be any Administration in at my death, who have hearts and feelings, I beg they will provide for Horatia Nelson, the child who would have had a father if he had not gone forth to fight his Country's Battles; therefore she has a claim on them. I declare, before God, and as I hope to see Nelson in Heaven, that Ann Connor, who goes by the name of Carew, and tells many falsehoods that she is my daughter, but from what motive I know not, I declare that she is the eldest daughter of my mother's sister, Sarah Connor, and that I have the mother and six children to keep, all of them except two having turned out bad. I therefore beg of my mother to be kind to the two good ones, Sarah and Cecilia. This family, having by their extravagance almost ruined me, I have nothing to leave them, and I pray to God to turn Ann Connor's, alias Carew's, heart. I forgive her, but as there is a madness in the Connor family, I hope it is only the effect of this disorder that may have induced this bad young woman to have persecuted me by her slander and falsehoods. I give all my papers, books, lace, and indeed everything to my dear mother and Horatia Nelson. This I declare to be my last Will and Testament, and do away with other Wills.

                (*Signed*) EMMA HAMILTON, in presence of——.

LADY HAMILTON

HER APPEAL TO THE DUKE OF QUEENSBURY.

Mrs. Bolton, sister of Lord Nelson, wrote a very kind gossipy letter to Lady Hamilton in May, 1806, mentioning, among other things, that she hoped her ladyship would be in favour with the Duke of Queensbury when he died, for she believed he made a new will every week. Fleeting friends followed in the wake of fleeting fortunes; those who had revelled at her entertainments and assisted to bring about the disaster, slunk away, withholding any assistance which it was in their power to give, and which would have enabled the poor woman to stave off the influx of creditors. She wrote in her embarrassment to the old Duke of Queensbury, a relative of her late husband, who, at one time, had been one of her most ardent admirers. Her letter shows how overwhelming were her distresses:—

RICHMOND, *September 4th*, 1808.

MY DEAR LORD AND FRIEND,

May I hope that you will read this, for you are the only hope I have in this world to assist and protect me in this moment of unhappiness and distress. To you, therefore, I appeal. I do not wish to have more than what I have. I can live on that at Richmond, only that I may live free from fear—that everything may be paid. I think and hope that £15,000 will do for everything. For my sake, for Nelson's sake, for the good I have done my country, purchase it (Merton), take it, only giving me the portraits of Sir William, Nelson, and the Queen. All the rest shall go. I shall be free and at liberty. I can live at Richmond on what I have; you will be doing a deed that will make me happy, for lawyers will only involve me every day more and more. Debts will increase new debts. You will save me by this act of kindness; the title deeds are all good, and ready to deliver up, and I wish not for more than will pay my debts. I beseech you, my dear Duke, to imagine that I only wish for you to do this, not to lose by it, but I see that I am lost and most miserable if *you* do not help me. My mind is made up to live on what I have. If I could but be free from Merton, all paid, and only one hundred pounds in my pocket, you will live to see me blessing you, my mother blessing you, Horatia blessing you. If you would not wish to keep Merton, perhaps it will sell in the spring better; only let me pass my winter without the idea of a prison. 'Tis true my imprudence has brought it on me, and villany and ingratitude has helped to involve me, but the sin be on them. Do not let my enemies trample on me. For God's sake then, dear Duke, good friend, think 'tis Nelson who asks you to befriend

EMMA HAMILTON.

Though the Duke refused her request that he should take Merton, he responded so far that he furnished a house for her at Richmond, and allowed her an income which enabled her to keep an equipage. As she enlarged her establishment, relying on the legacies she was led to expect from his Grace, his death increased her perplexities, for the Court of Chancery put a restraint on the payments, owing to the informality of the execution of the documents. He had bequeathed her £500 a year and £1,000. He left twenty-five codicils, written on loose sheets of paper, not one of which was legally attested, although in his Grace's handwriting. In consequence, disputes arose, and Lady Hamilton died without receiving any benefit from his good intentions.

In the summer following the year which brought Lady Hamilton's financial matters to a crisis, Mr. and Mrs. Matcham had sent an earnest entreaty that she, Horatia, and Mrs. Cadogan, would become their guests at their country house; and two years later, when she importuned these genuine friends for assistance, Mr. Matcham made her a gift of one hundred pounds, for she was absolutely without funds for current outlays.

The Dukes de Berri and de Bourbon, having heard of Lady Hamilton's graceful delineations, expressed to Madame Le Brun (who had arrived in England) the pleasure that it would give them to see the celebrated *poses* which for some few years she had declined to exhibit in the Metropolis. Presuming on old acquaintance, the French artist begged her ladyship to give her an evening to gratify the Princes. The good-natured lady acquiesced. Madame Le Brun placed in the centre of her drawing-room a very large frame, enclosed on the right and left by two screens; she arranged the light to fall on the *figurante* as one would light up a picture. When all the guests had arrived, Lady Hamilton portrayed the attitudes inside the frame, as Madame Le Brun herself says, " in a truly admirable manner." She had taken with her Horatia (then a child of about eight years old), who also took part in the *tableaux*. The talented hostess, commenting on the performance, said, " She passed from sorrow to joy, from joy to terror, so splendidly, that we were all enchanted." This was most probably the last exhibition of these charming representations. When Madame Le Brun was in England, after the death of Sir William Hamilton, she left her card at the widow's house. Lady Hamilton immediately entered the room to see her friend of happier days. She was attired in the deepest mourning, and wore

PLATE X.—ATTITUDE OF LADY HAMILTON. FROM A DRAWING BY REHBURG.

DEATH OF MRS. CADOGAN.

an immense black veil. She had cut off all her beautiful hair, to wear it in the prevailing fashion *à la Titus*. At the end of the year 1809 Lady Hamilton returned to London, and took lodgings in Albemarle Street. The year 1810 would seem to have been the climax of her troubles. While beset by angry demands from unpaid creditors, she experienced a severe loss by the death of her mother, who passed away on January 14, 1810, and was interred in a private and quiet manner in a vault under St. Mary's Church, Paddington. The funeral took place on January 20, and the lady was dwelling in the district known as " St. George's, Hanover Square," at the time of her decease.

We may naturally infer that Mrs. Cadogan had a legal claim to the name she bore, and that it was no assumption on her part, for she is mentioned under that cognomen in her daughter's wills and in every legal attestation Lady Hamilton was particularly accurate. The homely old lady had evidently kept no record of her age, as there is no entry under that heading in the register. There is no evidence that she merits the epithets which it pleases some biographers to throw at her, or that she acted as *sage femme* for her daughter whenever circumstances required her attendance, and the only authority for such accusations is the anonymous publication within a few months of Lady Hamilton's death. The wail which went forth when the young girl was suffering from the effects of her youthful folly—" Don't tell my mother what distress I am in "—is sufficient warrant that her mother had not the light character which has been attributed to her. The highest encomiums only can be passed on the filial devotion displayed by Lady Hamilton. In all her successes she placed her mother at her right hand, and though we find that at the Embassy at Naples Mrs. Cadogan preferred to dine in the privacy of her apartments, with one or two intimate friends, rather than to mix with the highborn guests who sat at her daughter's table, yet she unquestionably deserved the kind words spoken of her by all with whom she came in contact, by her homely consideration for each one's comfort, and her own unpretentious conduct. She had been in receipt of an annuity from Sir William Hamilton of £100 per annum, in grateful acknowledgment of the efficient manner in which she had controlled his domestic arrangements.

Among the numerous creditors who beset the sorely tried lady with their claims was her cousin, Cecilia Connor, who had officiated as governess to the little Horatia. The young lady is entitled to sympathy, and under the necessitous circumstances in which the application was made, she certainly worded her request for a remittance with her feelings well under control. The letter is addressed to her ladyship at 16 Dover Street, Piccadilly, and written from Manly Place, Kennington Common :—

> MY DEAR LADY HAMILTON,
>   I take the Liberty once more to address your Ladyship concerning the sum of Thirty Guineas for teaching Miss Horatia Nelson, for which I hold a Voucher signed by your Ladyship. I merely mention this latter circumstance as a proof of your Ladyship's acknowledgement— by no means on the ground of dispute, but as my qualification of Appeal to your Ladyship in the present instance. My future Wellfare constrains me to renew the Solicitation having a Situation of advantage Submitted to me, which I must be compelled with Grief to resign unless your Ladyship supports my views by affording me on Acct. the Sum of ten Pounds between this and next Monday—the time limited to consider the proposal. This is the last resource I have, being denied a character from your Ladyship obliges me to give up the thought of applying any longer for a Preparatory Governess, which I had the Honour of attending on Dear Horatia ; excuse, Dear Lady Hamilton, this familiar term, but it is what I most sincerely feel for you both. Could I forget for a Moment the many obligations me and my family owe to your Ladyship, I hope God will forget me, and he is now the only friend I have. Time will bring forth everything, and then I think your Ladyship will find you have been Misinformed in many circumstances concerning me. Let me, Dear Lady Hamilton, entreat a favourable answer as it will ease my mind greatly. Would that it could relieve my heart from the Sorrow that I feel at being deprived of a Friend and Guardian like you.
>   With due Submission,
>   I remain your Most Grateful and Affectionate,
>   CECILIA CONNOR.
>
>   P.S.—I would not thus intrude on your Ladyship's goodness, but having Washing and other expenses to defray before I go to a situation.

About this time (1811), Michael Kelly relates in his *Reminiscences*, that Lady Hamilton was present at the performance of a new play called " Hearts

LETTER FROM LADY HAMILTON'S DAUGHTER.

of Oak "; a Miss Wheatley, possessing a fine contralto voice, sang with deep feeling a ballad descriptive of a dying warrior. On its being re-demanded, Lady Hamilton, tremulous and agitated, asked her friends to take her home. Next morning, Miss Wheatley received a note, asking her to call on Lady Hamilton, who, after complimenting the young lady on her touching rendering of the melody, said: "The description brought our glorious Nelson to my mind's eye with such terrible truth that at first you overwhelmed me, but now I feel as if I could listen to you for ever." The request that she would repeat the ballad was complied with. The title of the song which caused such strong emotion was "Rest, warrior, rest." This young and promising singer eventually became musical governess to Horatia Nelson.

Towards the close of the year 1811, Lady Hamilton received a very extraordinary letter from her daughter Emily, who had evidently had the facts of her parentage concealed from her. The poor young woman expressed herself well, and keenly felt her position without acknowledged parents or name. The knowledge of her existence would have seriously affected Lady Hamilton's social status, and left her no alternative but to conceal the circumstance, although both mother and child yearned to give each other their rightful affection. The following is a copy of the curious document[*] :—

SUNDAY, . . . *November*, 1811.

MY DEAR LADY HAMILTON,

Mrs. Denis's mention of your name and the conversation she had with you, have revived ideas in my mind which an absence of four years has not been able to efface. It might have been happy for me to have forgotten the past, and to have begun a new life with new ideas; but for my misfortune, my memory traces back circumstances which have taught me too much, yet not quite all I could have wish'd to have known. With you that resides, and ample reasons no doubt you have for not imparting them to me. Had you felt yourself at liberty so to have done, I might have become reconciled to my former situation, and have been relieved from the painful employment I now pursue. It was necessary, as I then stood, for I had nothing to support me but the affection I bore you; on the other hand, doubts and fears by turns oppressed me, and I am determined to rely on my own efforts rather than submit to abject dependance, without a permanent name or acknowledged parents. That I should

[*] This letter is among the Morrison MSS.

have taken such a step shews, at least, that I have a mind misfortune has not subdued. That I should persevere in it is what I owe to myself and to you, for it shall never be said that I avail myself of your partiality or my inclination, unless I learn my claim on you is greater than you have hitherto acknowledged; but the time may come when the same reasons may cease to operate, and then with a heart filled with tenderness and affection will I show you both my duty and attachment. In the mean time, should Mrs. Denis's zeal and kindness not have overrated your expressions respecting me, and that you should really wish to see me, I may (be) believed in saying that such a meeting would be one of the happiest moments of my life, but for the reflection that it may also be the last, as I leave England in a few days, and may possibly never return to it again.

       I remain your
         Devoted and obedient Servant,
              (. . . . .)

Emily would at this period be thirty-one years of age, yet her memory of childhood's days brought back faces which enforced the truth upon her mental vision with painful accuracy. The letter would assuredly have been very trying to Lady Hamilton, whose naturally good heart must have longed to embrace her unacknowledged daughter, but the avowal would entail too much risk, and was therefore left unsaid. Whether mother and daughter ever again met in this world is unknown. From this date the sensitive lady, who so touchingly alludes to the misfortune of her birth, is lost to history.

CHAPTER XXV.

LADY HAMILTON ENDEAVOURS TO OBTAIN A PENSION. HER PETITION TO THE PRINCE REGENT.

LADY HAMILTON had not abated her endeavours to obtain a hearing from the Government in recognition of her aid to the fleet, on which she relied, for her necessities increased daily. The Right Hon. George Rose staunchly rendered her every possible assistance in furtherance of her claims, though he at no time held out any hopes of ultimate success, for he well knew the prejudiced opponents against whom he had to contend, but he manfully exerted himself, both with advice to the lady and consultations with the ministers. He proposed to Mr. Canning to award her the sum of £6,000 or £7,000 out of Foreign Secret Service money, thinking that would be the best mode to recompense her without arousing contention. Lord Grenville ("cold-hearted Grenville," as the sorely tried woman called him) rebutted this suggestion by saying that she could not claim for *secret* service, insomuch as she herself had made it public by talking about it—a quibbling way of evading the grant—the good efforts of her two supporters therefore failed, though a hope was held out to her that the child who lived with her might be afforded a moderate pension. Mr. Rose then proposed that she should draw up a petition for presentation to the Prince Regent, which she did, executing it in her own handwriting. After attributing her difficulties to the expenses in connection with the completion of Merton Place, she said to Mr. Rose:—

> If I had bargained for a reward beforehand, there can be no doubt but that it would have been given to me, and *liberally*. I hoped then not to want it. I do now stand in *the utmost need of it*, and surely it will not be refused to me. I accompany this paper with a copy of what Lord Nelson wrote in the solemn moments which preceded the action in which he fell; and I am still not without a hope that the dying, earnest entreaty of such a man, in favour of a child he had adopted and was devotedly fond of, will be complied with, as well as my own application. . . . . I anxiously

implore that my claims may not be rejected without consideration, and that my forbearing to urge them earlier may not be objected to me, because in the lifetime of Sir W. Hamilton I should not have thought of even mentioning them, nor, indeed, after his death, if I had been left in a less comparatively destitute state.

The petition to the Prince Regent and his Ministers took the form of a narrative. In it she stated that Mr. Canning and Mr. Rose had assured Lord Nelson, on board the "Victory," on the eve of sailing for Cadiz, that the promises made by Mr. Pitt in her favour would be fully realised. When the petition was laid before Mr. Canning, thus worded, he returned it to Mr. Rose, saying he did not know what Mr. Rose had done, but that for himself he had made no such promise, and although he returned the statement on these grounds, he did not consider it lessened her claims, but he deemed it advisable she should be strictly accurate at all points. After conveying Mr. Canning's remarks to Lady Hamilton, Mr. Rose received from her the following reply :—

150 NEW BOND STREET, *March* 4, 1813.

DEAR SIR,
I have been, and am, so ill with anxiety, that I have scarce strength to write. But I had written to you long since, and had enclosed you a copy of my narrative to H.R.H. the Prince Regent, and to his Ministers. I now send you one, and also a letter I sent to Lord Sidmouth, for a kind friend of mine has told me that the reason my claims have not been remunerated was owing to a most infamous falsehood raised against mine honour and that of the brave and virtuous Nelson, which is false, and it shall be made known; for I will appeal to a generous public, who will not let a woman who has served her Country with the zeal I have, be left to starve and insult. You, Sir, who have been ever kind, and ever will be, will, I am sure, read the letter to Lord Sidmouth, and tell me if you approve of it. I am so fatigued with anxiety, and also my situation about pecuniary affairs, that I can only say I am

Yours truly grateful,

E. HAMILTON.

P.S.—Mr. Canning has a short memory, as I have Nelson's letter on the visit to the "Victory," the 14th of September.*

* *The Diaries of the Hon. G. Rose*, by the Rev. L. V. Harcourt.

EMMA, LADY HAMILTON.

HER ENDEAVOURS TO OBTAIN A PENSION.

It will be remarked that she had become cognisant of the rumours regarding the supposed relationship of Lord Nelson and herself to the child who resided with her. This letter contains an absolute denial of the accusation which was making its first circulation seven years after Lord Nelson's death. Her annoyance causes her to threaten that she will appeal to the public, who will deal more generously with her, and protect her from insulting insinuations. The child was twelve years old ere that little ball of slander was started on its blasting course, enlarging itself to such dimensions that now opprobrium is meted out even to her defenders. Repeatedly she besought Ministerial aid on behalf of Horatia, finding it useless to continue applications in her own cause. She urged that the daughter of Mr. Fox, Miss Willoughby, had received a pension of £300 per annum, and that surely the daughter of Lord Nelson, now Miss Nelson, was as worthy of a pension as was the daughter of Mr. Fox, for that gentleman never shed a drop of his blood for his country. Truly, a reasonable argument. Putting all discussion aside as to whether Lady Hamilton's services really merited the recognition of the Government or not, this plain fact can never be ignored, *it was the last and only bequest of our valiant sea king*, the execution of which the Ministers then in power used every endeavour to frustrate. The following narrative is that drawn up for presentation to the Prince Regent, which was returned by Mr. Canning on the grounds already mentioned. The original document was given by Lady Hamilton herself to her old mistress, Mrs. Thomas, to whom she was really attached, and whom she made the recipient of many favours, including her miniature portrait taken at Naples,* and a lady at Hawarden cherishes with the greatest care some remnants of black lace which once adorned a black silk mantle, and the moth-eaten primrose silk lining of a *poke* bonnet,† which, after wearing herself, Lady Hamilton conferred on her former mistress. The narrative is now in the possession of the Misses Rigby, great nieces of Mr. Thomas, of Hawarden.

* By the courtesy of the Misses Rigby, we have the pleasure to insert a copy of this miniature.
† What canonized saint could wish for more?

THE PETITION OF EMMA, LADY HAMILTON, TO HIS ROYAL HIGHNESS THE PRINCE REGENT.

The Memorial of EMMA, LADY HAMILTON, *widow of the late Right Honourable* SIR WILLIAM HAMILTON, *upwards of thirty-seven years Minister at the Court of Naples,*

HUMBLY SHEWETH—

That Your Royal Highness's Memorialist was about thirteen years resident with her said Husband at the Courts of Naples and Palermo, and during that time had the good fortune to conciliate the esteem of the Queen of Naples, which enabled her to effect services of the highest importance to her King and Country, as has in part been made known to the world by the dying declaration of Lord Nelson, register'd as a Codicil to his last Will and Testament, an authenticated Copy of which is annexed, with a more detailed Narrative of services performed, and of expenditures made and losses sustained by Memorialist, as by reference thereto will more fully explain. And the facts therein stated being in Memorialist's power to sustain by numerous other Vouchers, all which will will be found to embrace and prove—

Memorialist's early discovery of the King of Spain's defection from the Coalition in 1796, and intention of joining the French, of which Memorialist gave prompt notice and proof to Government, obtained at a great hazard and forwarded at considerable expense to herself!

Her enabling Sir Horatio Nelson to pursue and destroy the French Fleet in 1798, which neither wou'd or cou'd be attempted but for the aid Memorialist procured him!

Her saving the Royal Family, Court, and Treasures, at Naples, from the French, and thereby the preservation of the two Sicilies!

Her enabling Sir Alexander Ball to hold the Island of Malta, which he could not do but for the prompt supply of Grain provided by Memorialist at her own Expense!

And to effect these important ends will show the necessary Expenses made, and the voluntary losses endured, to no less a Sum than £20,000 of her own, and Thirty Thousand Pounds of her Husband's Property, for no part of which *Services, Expenditures,* and *Sacrifices,* hath Memorialist ever yet received any reward or remuneration whatever!

HER PETITION TO THE PRINCE REGENT.

That Memorialist's Husband died in the Conviction that such Services, Expenditures, and Sacrifices for the public good would not be overlooked by His King and Country, and in proportion to that Conviction did he curtail the provision designed for her, dying satisfied that his Pension *at least* would be continued to Memorialist for life.

In like Sentiments of Conviction died her Friend Lord Nelson, as he testified in the Hour of Death and Victory, who, in committing to Memorialist's care the Chief Object of his Heart, would have made a Suitable Provision if not certain that his only and last invocation to His King and Country at that Awful and Glorious Moment would have full effect.

Memorialist now humbly trusts her Situation and Case to Your Royal Consideration and Justice. Having now lived many years in the just expectancy of remuneration, she has sunk into Embarrassments without a Single Extravagance, which she trusts the beloved and benign Prince of a great, just, and generous nation, will not delay to have removed as to Your Royal Highness shall seem most suited to the occasion.

And Memorialist will in duty pray.

In September, 1791, I went with my Husband thro' France to Naples. At Paris I waited on the Queen, then at the Thuilleries, who entrusted me with the last Letter she wrote to her Sister, the Queen of Naples. This led to an ascendancy in her Majesty's Esteem that I never after failed to exert in favour of every British Interest.

In the Year 1793, when Lord Hood had taken possession of Toulon, and Sir John Jervis was employed upon the reduction of Corsica, the latter kept writing to me for everything he wanted, which I procured to be promptly provided him, and, as his Letters to me prove, had considerably facilitated the reduction of that Island.

I had by this time the King induced, thro' my influence with the Queen, to become so zealous in the good Cause that both would often say, "I had *de Bourbonized them and made them all English*." By unceasing cultivation of this influence, and no less watchfulness to turn it to my Country's good, it happen'd that I discover'd a Courier had brought the King of Naples a private Letter from the King of Spain. I prevailed on the Queen to take it from his Pocket unseen. We found it to contain the King of Spain's resolution to withdraw from the Coalition, and join the French against England. My Husband at this time lay dangerously ill. I

LADY HAMILTON.

prevailed on the Queen to allow my taking a copy, with which I immediately despatch'd a messenger to my Lord Grenville, taking all the necessary precautions for his safe arrival, then become very difficult, and altogether cost me about £400, paid out of my private purse. I shall not detain further by detailing the many less important, altho' useful matters, to which my influence and exertions had given effect from this time until 1798, but merely observe that no exertion of mine was wanting to forward every Object sought, and in which I was always successful, particularly in providing for the Wants of our brave Fleets in those Seas, although at this Period french ascendancy and revolutionary ideas had arrived at such a height in Naples as made it dangerous for the British Minister to go to Court.

It was at this Awful Period, in June, 1798, about three days after the French fleet pass'd by for Malta, Sir William and myself were awaken'd at 6 O'Clock in the Morning by Captain Troubridge, with a Letter from Sir Horatio Nelson, then with his Fleet lying off the Bay, near to Capree, "requesting that the Ambassador would procure him permission to enter with his Fleet into Naples, or any of the Sicilian Ports, to Provision, Water, &c., as otherwise he must run for Gibraltar, being in urgent want, and that consequently he wou'd be obliged to give over all further pursuit of the French Fleet, which he miss'd at Egypt on account of their having put into Malta."

At this time Naples had made peace with France by desire of our Court (Le Comte La Michelle was French Ambassador), one of the stipulations was that no more than two English ships of war shou'd enter into any of the Neapolitan or Sicilian Ports. However, Sir William call'd up General Acton, the Minister, who immediately conven'd a Council, the King present. This was about half-past six. I went to the Queen, who received me in her Bed. I told Her Majesty that now depended on her the safety of the two Sicilies, should the Council decide on negative or half measures, as I fear'd they must do. I told her the Sicilies must be lost if Nelson was not supplied, and thereby enabled to follow the Great French Force that had gone by in that direction but a few days before. Nothing could exceed the alarm with which this Communication inspired her. She said the King was in Council, and wou'd decide with His Ministers. I pray'd and implor'd her on my Knees; she could not withstand my entreaties and arguments. I brought her Pen, Ink, and Paper to the Bed; I dictated and she wrote a positive Order, "directed to all Governors of

HER PETITION TO THE PRINCE REGENT.

the two Sicilies, to receive with hospitality the British Fleet, to Water, Victual, and aid them." In every way this Order, I was well aware, as was the fact, would be more respected than even that of the King. At eight o'Clock the Council broke up. I was called to attend Captain Troubridge and my Husband to our House; the faces of the King, of Acton, and Sir William, too plainly told the determination that they could not then break with France. On our way Home I said I had anticipated the *result*, and *provided* against it; that while they were in Council I had been with the Queen, and had not implored her in vain, producing the Order to their astonishment and delight. They embraced me with patriotic Joy. "It will," said the gallant Troubridge, "cheer to ecstasy your valiant friend Nelson; we shall now be able to pursue and conquer, otherwise we must have gone for Gibraltar." Sir William wrote to Nelson the decision of the Council, but said, "You will receive from Emma herself what will do the business and procure all your Wants!" I enclosed the Order to the Admiral, praying that the Queen may be as little committed in the use of it as the glory and Service of the Country wou'd admit of.

The Admiral's reply, in my hands, says: "That he received the precious order, and that if he gain'd a Battle it shou'd be call'd *Mine* and the *Queen's*, for to you I will owe my success; without this, our returning to Gibraltar was decided on, but I will now come back to you cover'd with Laurel or Crowned with Cypress." The former I had the Glory to witness after his destruction of the French Fleet at Aboukir, where he found them after his having been Water'd, provisioned, and refresh'd by virtue of the order I had so procured. Here I may be allowed to ask, what sum wou'd this Country or its Government have given before that Battle for its attainment, and what less shou'd be given for that instrument which led to it, and without which all hope, all opportunity of success, must have been abandoned? On the 20th September, Nelson return'd to Naples after his glorious victory. I had then inspir'd the Queen with such devotion to our Cause that every desire was granted for the repair of the Ships, taking care of the wounded, and general supply of the Fleet, and I appeal to every Officer, nay, every Seaman of that conquering Fleet, to testify what they witness'd of my unceasing solicitude and indefatigable exertions to reward their valour by every Comfort I could procure them; and, above all, my attentions to their beloved Sick and Wounded Chief, whose invaluable Friendship I ever after had, who to the Hour of his Death did always say he could not have survived but for the manner I cheer'd, nurs'd, and attended him at this time.

The sore evidence that Nelson had now given the French of my influence at the Neapolitan Court urged their Ambassador to sharp complaints for a breach of bad Faith in supplying the British Fleet at *Syracuse*, contrary to Treaty.

At this juncture, while I found the Court flushed with our Victory of the Nile, I suggested to the Queen the benefits and honour that would result by breaking boldly with the French, and to dismiss their Ambassador altogether, and then raise an Army to oppose their threats of invasion.

The Queen, delighted with the proposal, opened it to the King, as I did to Sir William, and to Nelson; the Minister Acton was brought into the Measure, and it was resolv'd on in Council accordingly. In consequence, and totally unexpected to himself, the French Ambassador and his suite were sent off at 24 Hour's notice.

An army of 35,000 men was raised in nearly a month. They marched from St. Germains, under command of General Mack, the King himself in the ranks, on the 21st of November, against a scatter'd and inferior French force, yet so rapidly was this Army destroy'd as to oblige our embarkation at Naples by that Day Month.

The point of policy with the Court was then, "Whether they shou'd put themselves entirely under the French or fly to Sicily under our protection." The many difficulties of getting away, and the uncertainty how a flying Court would be received there, were strong inducements to abide all consequences at Naples. I urged and pleaded the necessity and safety of their coming away. The Queen was almost always with me, and as the French advanced, I placed the Horror of their approach full before her Eyes, and at length prevailed in deciding this important measure, for the King was soon brought over to our side. The difficulties were yet many, and of the most dangerous Complexion; the growth of French principles and rapid march of their Army upon the Capital made it too hazardous to trust the Neapolitans with the plan of getting away the Royal Family, the Court and Treasures.

I, however, began the work myself, and gradually removed all the Jewels, and then 36 Barrels of Gold to our House. These I mark'd as *Stores for Nelson*, being obliged to use every device to prevent the Attendants having any Idea of our proceedings. By many such Stratagems I

HER PETITION TO THE PRINCE REGENT. 251

got those Treasures embarked, and this point gain'd, the King's resolution of coming off was strengthen'd—the Queen I was sure of. The immortal Nelson testifies that all this wou'd never have been effected but for my management and exertions. In his letter to Lord St. Vincent or Lord Spencer, he says on this occasion, " Lady Hamilton seemed to be an Angel dropt from Heaven for the preservation of the Royal Family."

They were indeed unquestionably dear to me, but made entirely so by their perpetual acquiescence to all my wishes in favour of my Country.

Here I humbly submit, if it is not to my Efforts in thus getting away this Royal Family, Court, and Treasures from the French grasp, that Sicily has been preserved from that power.

When the many, I may say the innumerable, hair-breadth risks we ran in our escape are consider'd, it must be obvious that to Cover or Colour our proceedings that we were compell'd to abandon our Houses and all our Valuables as *they stood*, without venturing to remove a single article. My own Private Property thus voluntarily left to effect this great purpose was little, if any, short of £9,000, and Sir William's not less than £30,000, which sum, had he to bequeath, might naturally have been will'd to me in whole or in part!

To shew the caution and secrecy that was necessarily used in thus getting away, I had, on the Night of our Embarkation, to attend the Party given by the Kilem Effendi, who was sent by the Grand Seignior to Naples to present Nelson with the Shahlauh, or Plume of Triumph! I had to steal from the Party, leaving our Carriages and Equipage waiting at his House, and in about fifteen minutes to be at my post, where it was my task to conduct the Royal Family through the Subterraneous Passage to Nelson's Boats by that *moment* awaiting for us on the Shore! The Season for this Voyage was extremely hazardous, and our miraculous preservation is recorded by the Admiral upon our arrival at Palermo.

When in 1799 Lord Keith missed the French Squadron, and Nelson sail'd in quest of them from Palermo, he left me directions to open all Letters and Despatches for him, and to act in his behalf to the best of my power, governing myself by Events.

Sir Alexander Ball was at this time in possession of a part of the Island of Malta, residing at St. Antonio. The French possessed La Valeta.

Sir Alexander sent six natives of Malta Deputies to Nelson at Palermo for a Supply of Grain, their necessity being so great for Provisions that the inhabitants were ready to join any Sortie the French may attempt in the hope of getting reliev'd.

I receiv'd the Deputies, open'd their Dispatches, and without hesitation I went down to the Port to try what could be done. I found lying there several Vessels loaded with Corn for Ragusa. I immediately purchased their cargoes, and engaged the Vessels to go with their loading and the Deputies to Malta. This Service, Sir Alex^r Ball in his Letters to me, as well as to Lord Nelson, plainly states to be " the means whereby he was enabled to preserve that important Island." I had to borrow a considerable Sum on this occasion, which I since repaid, and with my own private money thus expended was nothing short of £5,000, a shilling of which, nor yet the Interest, have I ever yet receiv'd.

The Emperor Paul, the Grand Master, on hearing of this affair, wrote me a letter in his own hand, conferring on me the Cross of the Order, saying, " that I not only saved the Island, but that I was also the Link that kept together the Opponents of the Common Foe!" And I was accordingly invested with the Order with the usual Ceremonies along with Sir Alexander Ball. The Emperor, to show yet further the Value of this service, sent to Lord Whitworth, then Ambassador at Petersburgh, requesting " that this honour might be register'd in the King's College of Arms in my Native Country."

Upon the re-taking of Naples in 1799, Nelson brought us back there, except the Queen; Sir William was yet so ill and feeble as to be unfit for business, and yet less for the active bustle that those times required. From the beginning of June until the middle of August, I was not only Interpreter but Secretary, both to his Secretary and to Nelson. I wrote for them from Morning until Night, translating whole Papers and Documents in various Languages that they neither could do themselves, or procure any one proper to be entrusted with Documents of so secret and Confidential a nature. I had also to manage and control the two Households we were obliged to maintain at Palermo and Naples. And the numerous Letters of Her Majesty to me at this period will prove the manner in which I conducted all these Occupations, and the favorable light in which my attentions to the public Cause was then considered. At this time in particular, but, in fact, for the fourteen years that I was Ambassador's Wife at this Court I might have exercised an Æconomy that wou'd have secured me provision for life; but such Calculations I would have thought a criminal Prudence under the Circumstances in which I was placed. My

HER PETITION TO THE PRINCE REGENT. 253

Sole View was to maintain the dignity of our Royal and beloved Master, to advance His Interests and Wishes ; and to soothe and alleviate the toils of His brave loyal Seamen in a distant Clime. In place of hoarding at such times and occasions, it was my Sole Pride, my Glory, my Ambition, thus to have expended what Private Friendship had bestow'd for my own immediate Comforts and use, as I have already shown ; or, if further Proof be needed, I appeal to His Royal Highness the Duke of Sussex, to all the Nobility, Commanders, to every Briton that witness'd my unceasing Zeal and Efforts for their Comfort and the public good while at the Courts of Naples and Palermo.

When Sir William was recall'd from his Embassy at Palermo in 1800, the Queen determined to travel with us as far as Vienna to see her daughter, then Empress of Germany. Nelson also accompanied us. His Lordship and Sir William were present at my parting with the Queen. At that affecting moment Her Majesty put into my hands a Paper, saying it was the Conveyance of a thousand Pounds a Year that she had fix'd to invest for me in the hands of Friez, the Government Bank at Vienna, THIS she said, "lest by any possibility I should not be suitably compensated for the Services I had render'd, the Monies I generously expended, and the Losses I had so voluntarily sustained for the benefit of her Nation and my own ! "

As I then stood I thought the Acceptance of such a Reward from the Queen, *circumstanc'd* as she was, unworthy a British Heart ; with every expression of respect and gratitude to Her Majesty, I destroy'd the Instrument, *saying*, England was ever just, and to her faithful servants *generous !* and that I would feel it insulting to my own beloved Magnanimous Sovereign to accept of meed or reward from any other hand.

On our arrival in England I did not cease my efforts to serve the Country, and I trust effectually. It was in consequence of my earnest entreaties that Lord Nelson consented in 1801 to go to the attack of Copenhagen, second in command under Admiral Parker. Had he not been there Government must be sensible how very different wou'd have been the result of that memorable Engagement. Again, in 1805, by my representations and entreaties, somewhat against his own notions and presentiments, I prevail'd on him to offer himself to command the Fleet then equiping to go against the combin'd Fleets at Cadiz, which terminated in his last glorious, but fatal Victory of Trafalgar. If either or both those Battles were gained by his Superior Zeal, Vigilance, Skill, and Valour, I *have proof* that he wou'd never have been at the one or the other but at my instance.

It was long after our return to England that Sir William was paid by Government, in which time I sold my Jewels at a heavy loss for his Support. He went on to the end of his life in the full conviction that his Pension would be continued to me, *to a Person* who had gained so many points for the Country and for her Fleets, which he wou'd say was impossible for him or any other man to have gained. In this expectation he was yet more confirmed by the language of his inseparable friend, Nelson, who wou'd ever keep telling him, and indeed all the world, that the Battle of the Nile was *Emma's*, and not his, and also assuring Sir William that he had Mr. Pitt's solemn unequivocal pledge of honor that suitable provision shou'd be made for me, and in corroboration of this fact " I appeal to *the living testimony of Sir Walter Farquar*, to whom that great Statesman, on his Dying Bed, confirmed those promises he had made Lord Nelson on my behalf, with his dying request that they may be fulfill'd by his Successors."

And I also appeal to Messrs. Canning and Rose to state if on behalf of Government they had not reassured his Lordship, on their taking leave of him on board the "Victory" at Portsmouth, the 14th day of September, 1805, upon his last sailing, that the promises made by Mr. Pitt in my favour shou'd be fully Realized.

A disposition more avaricious, and of less love of Country than has been evinced by mine, might well have been buoy'd up by so many flattering pretensions and assurances of publick remuneration with gratitude; and in proportion as Sir William felt their force, as well as his unalterable faith in the justice of the country, so in proportion was his Provision for me lessen'd, so that my title to Publick Reward has thus caused me the loss of private fortune, that without such claim wou'd have been left me by my Husband, who, in his latter moments in deputing Mr. Greville to deliver the order of the Bath to the King, desired he wou'd tell his Majesty that he died in the confident hope that his Pension wou'd be continued for my Zeal and Services.

Time has gone on; thinking that my case could not be overlooked I have felt easy, but the curtailed provision left me by Sir William, under the conviction of its being made an ample one by the Country, has diminished without a semblance of extravagance, and now find myself in Embarrassments, which imperiously press on me to look for Remuneration

THE CONCEALMENT OF THE CODICIL.

for those Services, Expenditures, and losses that I have *recited*, and not alone for immediate Support, but as well for payment of that Support for the time past that I have been waiting in just expectation.

In that expectation being liberally realized I can have nothing but implicit confidence, "As our August Prince was well acquainted with it by Lord Nelson himself, and fully coincided in its Justice."

It may be here expected of me to state why the Codicil to Lord Nelson's Will, bequeathing my Services to the Justice of the Country, was not produced with the will itself.

When Captain Blackwood brought it home he gave it to the present Earl Nelson, who, with his Wife and Family, were then with me, and had indeed been living with me many Months. To their Son I was a Mother, and their Daughter, Lady Charlotte, had been exclusively under my care for Six Years. The Earl, afraid I should be provided for in the Sum that Parliament was expected to grant to uphold the Hero's Name and Family, kept the Codicil in his Pocket until the Day £200,000 was voted for that purpose. *On that day* he dined with me in Clarges Street. Hearing at table what was done, he took the Codicil out, threw it at me, and said, with a very Coarse expression, "that I might now do as I pleased with it." I had it registered next day at Doctors' Commons, where it rests for the National Redemption, &c., &c., &c.

On January 5, 1813, she wrote to Sir William Scott about her petition and the concealment of the codicil by Earl Nelson. The latter gentleman is said by a recent writer to have conferred with the former on the propriety of introducing it directly after the death of Nelson, and that by Sir William's advice it was withheld, but it cannot have been with his sanction that it was not brought forward, else Lady Hamilton would not have written to Sir William Scott in the condemnatory strain about the Earl's deceit, for Sir William would naturally have known that he merited no such attack, and have checked her ladyship in her assertions, instead of which she is found reasserting it to Sir William Scott after a lapse of seven years from the keeping back of the deed, in a tone from which it may be inferred that Sir William did not approve of the Earl's transaction. Thus runs her letter:—

> How much do I esteem and thank you, my dear Sir William, for your kind letter and advice respecting my case. I wish you had been in town

when I sent my narrative to Lords Liverpool and Sidmouth, as I would have been proud to make any alteration you may have recommended. Deprived of that advantage, I thought it best to state the fact of the codicil being kept back, and I assure you I softened the conduct of *Earl Nelson* on that occasion as much as it would allow of. However, in my memorial I did not mention him at all, as you will see by the enclosed copy,* and that will be the document most attended and referred to, and most like what I had occasion to allude to; his lordship may not be further noticed. But if the contrary, I console myself in an honorable adhesion to truth, and if *war* be proclaimed against me, I have not yet let fly the thunderbolt upon his head, nor do I desire to do so unless provoked. To you, my dear Sir, I say what I feel. I have been a fool, and am a victim to my too open heart and soul. All I want now is quiet and comfort, and to be enabled to finish Horatia's education. I would sooner give to my country than take from it. But sure some justice ought to have been done me; I wish not for much. I have had as much of grandeur as a person can have; it is not that makes happiness. But why not make comfortable the woman who exerted herself for her country's good?" . . .

There is a limit to human endurance, and the next petition (which we have recorded) exposed the Earl's treachery.

Owing to Lady Hamilton's adherence to her statement regarding the promise of Mr. Rose and Mr. Canning to Lord Nelson to see her pensioned, they withdrew their support from the petition. Mr. Rose admitted that Lord Nelson had asked *him* to urge her claims, and he thought his lordship might have written hurriedly to her and made himself misunderstood. As a matter of fact, Lord Nelson had, on the occasion of these two gentlemen dining with him on board the "Victory" just before he left England for the last time, asked them to consider his chaplain, the Rev. A. J. Scott, whom he so much respected, and the probabilities are that Lady Hamilton's circumstances were entered upon, albeit Mr. Canning denied it after the lapse of some years. These were the inaccuracies of which her ladyship was guilty, and which caused her to be branded as an inventive genius, incapable of speaking truth under any form, so ready were those whom she designated "her enemies" to enlarge on the smallest transgression or discrepancy. Harassed and impoverished, she found herself unable to sustain the expenses

* This refers to a petition previous to the one copied in these pages.

PLATE XI.—ATTITUDE OF LADY HAMILTON, FROM A DRAWING BY REHBURG.

HER IMPRISONMENT.

of her respectable apartments, and in her distressed position a kindhearted actress named Mrs. Billington opened her sheltering doors at Fulham, and took in the persecuted woman and her little charge, Horatia. As may naturally be expected, her creditors still continued to pursue and worry her, until at length she was placed in the King's Bench Prison, where for some months she was detained. After undergoing these severe measures, she received permission to live "within the Rules," and took up her residence at 12 Temple Place, which relaxation was due to the kindly intervention of Alderman Joshua Jonathan Smith, a liberal-hearted friend, who came forward and paid off her most pressing creditors.

In the *Autobiography of W. Jerdan*, the journalist, we find the following extract, which shows that throughout all her troubles she found sympathisers in men of merit and position, and it is a sad reflection that the earnest endeavours of worthy men were crushed by others who could so easily have awarded her a maintenance. Her detractors and supporters were equally balanced, therefore the fear on the part of the Government that there would be an outcry if the pension were granted was vapid, and—was it not Nelson's dying request?

"Among my curious memoranda about this time," says Jerdan, "is the note of having been taken by my friend, Mr. (Sir F.) Freeling, to see and dine with the celebrated Lady Hamilton, in the King's Bench Prison. She is *embonpoint*, and still a fine woman, full of complaints but too truly founded, of the cruel neglect she received from Government, and the ungrateful return made for her own public services, as well as the dying behests of her glorious sailor. The deep conviction I that day received of the stern inflexibility with which official form can perpetrate and adhere to wrong has never yet been removed by acquaintance with not a few other cases, nor by reparation given for humanity's sake, and the honour of the country, on which the treatment of those whom its Nelson loved is still a shameful stain. Men in their private transactions would shrink from acts of such ignominious ingratitude; but state departments, like corporate bodies or numerous partnerships, have neither feelings nor a nice sense of truth or justice. Mr. Freeling interested himself much with the Government in the cause of Lady Hamilton, but with little if any effect."

Again, we have the sentiment expressed by an officer who served under Nelson, and who was thereby in a position to verify or denounce Lady

Hamilton's assertions regarding the help she had obtained for the fleet in the hour of emergency. In the *Reminiscences* of Lieutenant G. S. Parsons (the gentleman alluded to) we find these lines: "This noble but unfortunate lady has been most grossly calumniated. She served the country with unwearied zeal and activity, and in a greater degree than any female ever before had the power. She was the cause of saving millions of British property from the grasp of the Spanish King in 1795; she enabled Lord Nelson to fight the battle of Aboukir, and kept steady to our interest the fickle and dissolute Court of Naples, from her influence over the daughter of Maria Theresa, then Queen of that place; her generosity and good nature were unbounded; her talents and spirit unequalled."

While living in the ignominious quarters to which unfortunate debtors of bygone times were limited, Lady Hamilton wrote to an old friend, Mr. Thomas Lewis, inviting his company for the next day, August 1, 1813, the anniversary of the victory of the Nile, to her share in which she once more alludes:—

> Do come, it is a day to me glorious, for I largely contributed to its success, at the same time it gives me pain and grief thinking on the dear lamented Chief who so bravely won the day, and if you come we will drink to his Immortal Memory. He could never have thought that his Child and Myself should pass the anniversary of that Victorious day where we shall pass it, but I shall be with a few sincere and valuable friends—all Hearts of Gold, not Pinchbeck—and that will be consoling to the afflicted Heart of your affectionate
>
> EMMA.

It was during her incarceration in the King's Bench that the book appeared which contained the manipulated letters, and others that had been abstracted during her indisposition. It sold speedily, and brought on her devoted head the animadversions of the press, and the condemnation of her friends, who thought they had been published with her sanction. The vicious mind that compiled them, alive to the greed with which the public would devour such a work, made his additions and took his compositions to market, their sale fully realizing his expectations.

CHAPTER XXVI.

LADY HAMILTON TRUE TO NELSON'S TRUST. THE FLIGHT TO CALAIS. HER POVERTY, DEATH, AND BURIAL. DR. BEATTIE'S BEAUTIFUL VERSES ON HER NEGLECTED GRAVE.

DIRECTLY after the death of Lord Nelson, Lady Hamilton was the victim of a similar outrage on her private papers. While physically incapacitated and confined to her bed, letters of a like nature appeared in the daily papers. Her true friend the Hon. George Rose sent her a few words of remonstrance and advice, which she took to heart, insomuch as she had no part in their appearance. Her natural reply will fully justify her:—

CLARGES ST., *Nov.* 29, 1805.

I write from my bed, where I have been since the fatal 6th of this month, and only rose to be removed from Merton here. I could not write you, my dear Sir, before, but your note requires that I should justify myself. Believe me, then, when I assure you I do not see any one but the family of my dear Nelson. His letters are in the bed with me, and only to the *present Earl* did I ever read one, and then only a part. It is true he is leaky, but I believe would not willingly tell anything; but I have been told something like some of my letters have been printed in some daily paper. I never now read a paper, and my health and spirits are so bad I cannot enter into a war with vile editors. Of this be assured, no one shall ever see a letter of my glorious and dear departed Nelson. It is true I have a journal from him ever since he came to Naples to get provisions for our troops in Toulon, when he was in the "Agamemnon"; but his letters are sacred, and shall remain so. My dear Sir, life is broken, life to me now is not worth having. . . . I persuaded him to it; but I cannot go on, my heart and head are gone, only believe me, what you write to me shall ever be attended to. Could you know me you would not think I had such bad policy as to publish anything at this moment. My mind is not a common one, and having lived as a confidante and friend with such men as Sir William Hamilton and dearest glorious Nelson, I feel myself superior to vain tattling women. Excuse me, but I am ill and nervous, and *hurt* that those I value should think meanly of me."

A woman in so prostrate a condition would be totally incapable of giving her attention to the issue of scandalous publications at so early a period of her grief. Her characteristic and amusing vulgarisms involuntarily rise to the surface in her correspondence; they are invariably blurted out in a most natural manner, and would have found no place had her writing been conducted with the thought and caution of an *artful* person. The guardianship of Horatia was attended by many trials owing to the girl's high temper, which was the cause of much anxiety and pain to the already overburdened woman. Though loving the child with intensity, Lord Nelson had during her infancy seen this, and as she grew into girlhood her strong will became more unpleasant to combat and control. Lady Hamilton on more than one occasion framed her reproof in a letter, rightly judging that that form of remonstrance would leave a more lasting impression on the young delinquent, for whom scolding had lost its terrors and took no effect. The following letter is a very sensible reproach, and betokens the earnest desire that the wilful girl should walk in the right path and cultivate amiable ways:—

April 18*th*, EASTER SUNDAY, 1813.

Listen to a kind, good mother, who has ever been to you affectionate (and) truly kind, and who has neither spared pains nor expense to make you the most amiable and most accomplished of your sex. Ah! Horatia, if you had grown up as I wished you, what a joy, what a comfort might you have been to me! For I have been constant to you, and willingly pleased for every manifestation you showed to learn and profit of my lessons, and I have ever been most willing to overlook injuries. But now 'tis for yourself I speak and write. Look into yourself well; correct yourself of your errors, your caprices, your nonsensical follies, for by your inattention you have forfeited all claims to my future kindness. I have weathered many a storm for your sake. But these frequent blows have killed me. Listen, then, from a mother who speaks from the Dead. Reform your conduct, or you will be detested by all the world, and when you shall no longer have my fostering care to shield you, whoe betide you, for you will sink to nothing. Be good, be honourable, tell not falsehoods, be not capricious,

* *The Diaries of the Hon. G. Rose*, by L. V. Harcourt.

follow the advice of the mother whom I shall place (over) you in a school, for a governess must act as a mother. I grieve and lament to see the increasing strength of your turbulent passions. I weep and pray you may not be totally lost. My fervent prayers are offered up to God for you. I hope you will yet become sensible of your eternal welfare. I shall go to join your father and my blessed mother, and may you on your death-bed have as little reproach yourself as your once affectionate mother has! for I can (   ) and say I was a good child. *Can Horatia Nelson say so? I am unhappy to say you cannot.* No answer to this. I shall to-morrow look out for a school for your sake, and to *save you*, that you may bless the memory of an injured mother.

EMMA HAMILTON.

'Look at me now as gone from this world.'

The two phrases alone, "I have been constant to you," and "I have weathered many a storm for your sake," should in themselves have touched a heart not wholly hardened, for young as the girl was, she must have been well aware that she was the cause of many a random shot being levelled at her faithful guardian.

An exemplification of the poor woman's earnest desire to train her young ward in thoroughly Christian paths is to be found in a most interesting relic in the possession of Mr. W. H. Patterson; M.R.I.A., Belfast. On the inside of the cover of a volume of Miss Edgeworth's popular tales is the autograph inscription, written by Lady Hamilton when she made her judicious gift to Horatia. It is in these words :—

A present to my much Loved Dear, Horatia Nelson, whom God will, I Hope, Bless, protect, succour, and comfort, and I Hope she will be an ornament to Her Sex, and That she will be Religious, virtuous, amiable, and good, and that her education will be solid, free from any affectation, and that she will have the fear of God before her eyes, and that she will be all that her Glorious Father, the Great Nelson, wished her to be. My Life shall be devoted to her improvement. May God Almighty bless her. Amen.

(   ) HAMILTON.

Holding the sacred charge in no light regard, it must be admitted there is no evidence that Lady Hamilton neglected the trust confided to her.

* The spot where the Christian name has been is damaged.

Gratitude to the woman who clung to her at the cost of her reputation should have been boundless. Horatia herself did not consider she was the daughter of Lady Hamilton; the epithet "mother," which her ladyship applied to herself, was merely one of her poetic effusions, for does she not write that a *governess* must act as a mother? Therefore she uses the word "mother" in reference to her ward's prospective teacher. The clever and rebellious young lady would not seem to have been much moved by the kindly meant advice, for a few months later her transgressions assumed a mightier character, and, incapable of appreciating the hand that used necessary firmness in restraining growing tempers, she made the complaint that Lady Hamilton had ill-used her. What wonder that the sorely tried woman who had suffered so much for her adherence to this child, should feel deeply hurt at the circulation of such a statement? That the punishment requisite to curb strong passions should be magnified into ill-usage, must have been greatly aggravating to her whose every wish was to form her charge into a respected and good-living being. Lady Hamilton never lost sight of the great trust that had been reposed in her, and proudly reported the girl's advancement in her various accomplishments. In her sincere endeavour to curb the high spirit of the growing girl, she fell under the lash of her unbridled tongue, with the result that, in self defence, Lady Hamilton threatened to call a council of inquiry from among her friends. In all probability, the letter was but a ruse to cure the girl of tattling. The important document announcing the impending proceedings (!) runs thus*:—

October 31st, 1813.

HORATIA,
Your conduct is so bad, your falsehoods so dreadfull, your cruel treatment to me such that I cannot live under these afflicting circumstances. My heart is broken. If my poor mother was living to take my part, broken as I am with grief and ill health, I should be happy to breathe my last in her arms. I thank you for what you have done to-day. You have helped me on nearer to God, and may God forgive you! In two days all will be arranged for your establishment; and on Tuesday, at 12, Colonel and Mrs. Smith, Trickey, Mr. and Mrs. Denis (and) Dr. Norton will be here to hear all. Every servant shall be put on there oath, as I shall send for Nancy at Richmond, Mr. Slop, Mrs. Size, Mr. Deare, and get letters from the Boltons and Matchams, to confront you and tell the

* The Morrison MSS.

truth, if I have used you ill; but the all seeing eye of God knows my innocence. It is therefore my command that you do not speak to me till Tuesday; and if you do speak to me, I will that moment let Colonel and Mrs. Clive into all your barbarous scenes (schemes) on my person, life, and honner.

EMMA HAMILTON.

Poor Emma! her duties of chaperonage were far from pleasant. Those who knew the young lady when more fully developed assert their belief that this awe-inspiring correspondence (!) was perfectly justifiable.

Fearing re-arrest under the claims of her former coachmaker (which demand afterwards proved to be fictitious), Lady Hamilton, accompanied by Horatia, contrived to escape from Temple Place with the assistance of Alderman Smith. They managed to obtain a passage in a small sailing vessel bound for Calais, which was moored alongside the Tower. With what humid eyes must not the hunted fugitive have gazed on the shores of the land that should have held her in honour. The passage was an unusually bad one, and was prolonged to three days. Owing to the roughness of the sea, the ladies suffered severely from indisposition. On arriving at the French coast, Lady Hamilton fixed herself at the Hotel Dessin, Calais; the flight occurred in the early part of the year 1814.

Conscientiously performing her duty to her young ward, her first act was to place her at a sound day school. Limited though finances were, the child suffered no stint of education or of accomplishments; this, Horatia herself acknowledged in after life to Sir H. Nicolas, in these words:—"With all Lady Hamilton's faults, and she had *many*, she had many fine qualities which, had she been placed early in better hands and in different circumstances, would have made her a very superior woman. It is but justice on my part to say that, through *all her* difficulties, she invariably, till the last few months, expended on my education, &c., the whole of the interest of the sum left me by Lord Nelson, and which was left entirely at her control."

After a brief period of rest and quietude, combined with the enjoyment of absolute freedom, the unfortunate woman regained somewhat of her broken health and spirits. From a letter to Mr. Rose, information is gathered as to her movements from the time of her arrival in France:—

LADY HAMILTON.

HOTEL DESSIN, CALAIS, *July* 4.

We arrived here safe, dear Sir, after three days' sickness at sea, as for precaution we embarked at the Tower. Mr. Smith got me the discharge from Lord Ellenborough. I then begged Mr. Smith to withdraw his bail, for I would have died in prison sooner than that good man should have suffered for me, and I managed so well with Horatia alone that I was at Calais before any new writs could be issued out against me. I feel so much better, from change of climate, food, air, large rooms, and *liberty*, that there is a chance I may live to see Horatia brought up. I am looking out for a lodging. I have an excellent Frenchwoman who is good at everything; for Horatia and myself, and my old dame who is coming, will be my establishment. Near me is an English lady, who has resided here for twenty-five years, who has a day school, but not for eating and sleeping. At eight in the morning, I take Horatia; fetch her at one; at three we dine, and then in the evening we walk. She learns everything—piano, harp, languages grammatically. She knows French and Italian well, but she will still improve. Not any girls but those of the first families go there. Last evening we walked two miles to a *fête champêtre pour les bourgeois*. Everybody is pleased with Horatia. The General and his good old wife are very good to us, but our little world of happiness is in ourselves. If, my dear Sir, Lord Sidmouth would do something for dear Horatia, so that I can be enabled to give her an education, and also for her dress, it would ease me, and make me very happy. Surely he owes this to Nelson. For God's sake, do try for me, for you do not know how limited. I have left everything to be sold for the creditors, who do not deserve anything, for I have been the victim of artful mercenary wretches, and my too great liberality and open heart has been the dupe of villians. To you, Sir, I trust, for my dearest Horatia, to exert yourself for me, &c.*

Really upright in money matters, her life was wrecked solely because her props were suddenly withdrawn, leaving her in a vortex of debt from which she was unable to extricate herself. Nelson well knew that *she* would be faithful to the legacy that he left in her keeping, and she rigidly executed her trust in spite of difficulties that should never have existed. Poverty-stricken and destitute, as far as her own means went, her exemplary fulfilment of her duty, and the expenditure of the child's own income on a first-class educa-

* *The Diaries of the Hon. G. Rose*, by L. V. Harcourt.

HER CREDITORS.

tion, at least merit admiration. Again and again she sought Ministerial aid on behalf of Nelson's adopted child, finding it useless to make application in her own interest. Each appeal was rejected. Taking the young girl to school, calling for her when lessons were over, accompanying her in her walks, and superintending her education—these were the daily occupations of the disheartened lady. She had never been wanting in religious sentiment, and very shortly after she arrived at Calais, as she found her life embittered, she sought consolation in the fold of the Roman Catholic Church, to whose tenets she had had a strong leaning ever since her residence in Naples.

After the demise of her old admirer, Charles Greville, the Welsh estates which had been willed to him by Sir William Hamilton passed to his brother the Hon. R. F. Greville, who had been warned by certain lawyers that he must not pay any money to Lady Hamilton, as she had made over her annuity for the benefit of creditors whom they represented. Uncertain how to act, he withheld her allowance, which for some time accumulated in his keeping. Running very short of funds, she sent a letter of which the annexed is a copy, to beg him to forward her one hundred pounds:—

COMMON OF ST. PIERRE, 2 miles from Calais.
Direct for me CHEZ DESIN. *Sept. 21st*, 1814.

SIR,

You know that my jointure of eight hundred pounds a year has been now for a long time accumulating; if I was to die I should and have left that money away, for the Annuitants have no right to have it, nor can they claim it, for I was most dreadfully imposed upon for my good nature in being bail for a person whom I thought honorable. When I came away I came with honor, as Mr. Alderman Smith can inform you; but mine own innocence keeps me up, and I despise all false publications and aspersions. I have given up everything to pay just debts, but annuitants I never will. Now, Sir, let me entreat you to send me a hundred pounds, for I understand you have the money. I live very quiet in a Farm House, and my health is now quite established. Let me, Sir, beg this favour to

Your humble servant,

E. HAMILTON.

To this application the Hon. R. F. Greville made reply expressive of his willingness to remit the funds if he could only be assured of the propriety of his doing so; for he knew not how to act, and, as a man of business, it was necessary to protect himself against the chance of a second demand being made for the money paid out. His answer was as follows :—

Gt. Cumberland St.,
Oxford St., *Sept.* 27*th*, 1814.

Madam,

Your letter of Sept. 21 I received only by yesterday's post. It is now some time since the regular payments from me of your annuity of eight hundred pounds a-year were very unexpectedly interrupted by a notice addressed to me by professional persons, and on the ground that you had made over the greater part of the same for *pecuniary considerations received by you*, and in consequence warning me not to continue the payment of your annuity otherwise than to them to the extent of their claims.

Not hearing from you in the long intermediate time which followed respecting your not receiving your payments as usual, I could scarce doubt the unpleasant statements I had received. Still I have demurred making any payments when called on, and under existing circumstances I must not venture to make payments in *any direction*, until this mysterious business is made known to me, and whereby my acts by legal authority may be rendered perfectly secure to me. This done, of course I shall pay arrears, and continue all Future payments *whenever they shall be due* with the same precision and *punctuality* as has hitherto *always* been maintained by me, and which were attended to *to the Day*, until thus interrupted. But now, *my own Security* requires that I should clearly *know how this mysterious business actually stands*, e'er I shall deem it prudent or safe for me to take a step in a case where I am resolved not to act on doubtful reports.

I remain, Madam,
Your obedient humble servant,
ROBERT F. GREVILLE.

To Lady Hamilton.[*]

It was from no spirit of malevolence that Mr. Robert Greville detained the annuity, but when his explanatory letter reached the applicant she was rapidly nearing her end, and incapable of sending any reply that would clear up the unpleasant business to Mr. Greville's satisfaction. Hence her financial straits were dire indeed, and for the last few weeks of her fleeting life she

---

* The Morrison MSS.

LADY HAMILTON
THE LAST PORTRAIT OF HER PAINTED BY
R.

HORATIA'S APPEAL TO EARL NELSON.

knew absolute privation. The disease from which she suffered, and which ultimately caused her death, was water on the chest.

As her indisposition increased, Horatia became painfully aware of their very straitened circumstances, and young as she was, she wrote to the Earl Nelson to solicit an advance of her annuity. That she had occasion to do so, demonstrates forcibly that this most undeserving man was perfectly regardless how they were living. Acknowledged, or merely adopted, child of his brother—no matter which—it was the child whom it would have been his pride to rear and care for had he lived. Be it noted to the eternal shame of that wealthy relative who was in the enjoyment of the awards that Nelson morally intended to be shared by the child, the brother who was wearing the coronet earned in death, left these two helpless creatures to struggle with poverty, while he revelled in luxuries purchased at the cost of a life!

Is ever a hand extended to raise the fallen idol? No, as it falls so it lies. With the knowledge of her painful end how preposterous do her aspirations seem. Thus ran the lines which she lived to realise were vainly written, and the hand that penned them rent them in twain, "If I can be buried in St. Paul's I should be very happy to be near the glorious Nelson whom I loved and admired, and as once Sir William, Nelson, and myself had agreed we should all be buried near each other. If the King had not permitted him a public funeral this would have been, that three persons who were so much attached to each other from virtue and friendship should have been laid in one grave when they quitted this ill-natured, slanderous world." As she lay on her wretched bed with life fading painfully, must not the brilliant scenes in which she had been queen regnant have passed in slow succession before her dim eyes. Who is there that would not pity the poor outcast who so little merited her wretched fate? What must her mental sufferings have been as the courts she had held, returned and passed in silent review from shadowland. The fate of Emma Hamilton is one more instance of the fleeting reign of a popular favorite, and the thankless return meted out to so many patriots who have used their bright intellects and firm wills to advance their country's cause. Our Emma, emulating Joan of Arc, gave heart and energy to assist a country's leaders to glorious victories. Did not Lord St. Vincent call her the "Patroness of the Navy?" Her battles ended, and her life's work done, the well-earned pension would have procured comfort in her days of sickness, and relieved the keen want which sorely oppressed her as she lay on her bed in wretchedness and distress.

The blissful sleep of death, bringing rest for evermore, came to the sufferer on January 15, 1815. The ground in which her remains repose had formerly been the pleasure gardens of Elizabeth Duchess of Kingston. Its use as a cemetery was brief; unmargined by hedge or fence, it was desecrated and converted into a storage place for timber, and gradually all traces of the graves disappeared.

As an instance of the recklessly audacious assertions which were made concerning the poor woman even in death, an extract is quoted which appeared in the *Gentleman's Magazine* for February, 1815: " In the village of Calais where she (Lady Hamilton) died there was no Protestant clergyman, and no Catholic clergyman would officiate because she was a heretic; she was even refused Christian burial; no coffin was allowed, but the body was put into a sack, and cast into a hole. An English gentleman hearing of this barbarity, had the body dug up and interred, though not in the churchyard." This mendacious statement appeared one month after her decease in one of the leading magazines of the day. Not one line of sympathy, pity, or horror that the remains of a once idolized woman should have been treated in so inhuman and unnatural a manner—the paragraph seems rather to gloat over the wretched end. In it is evidence of the daring untruths which were uttered against her, and which tarnished her name for future ages; the venom of the men of the period, from amongst whom Sheridan culled the characters for his "School for Scandal," when sarcasm was the accomplishment of the wits, and men excelled the women in slander.

The contradiction which the aforesaid serial inserted in its next issue is a serious reflection on the eagerness with which the most unfounded fables were sent out, without a pause to inquire whether so unnatural a tale had groundwork for circulation. No thought was given that their malicious publication would cling to the memory of the already down-trodden woman. Truly, the evil men do lives after them. The statement in which they endeavoured to unsay the fabrication appeared as follows:—

> The article in page 183 relative to the interment of Lady Hamilton, we have since been assured is inaccurate. Her body was not refused Christian burial on account of her religion, such an objection could not have been

HER FUNERAL.

made, as a Catholic priest performed the last offices of prayer, and administered her the sacrament a short time before her dissolution, no Protestant minister being at hand. The fact is that that lady having incurred many very considerable debts at Calais and its neighbourhood, no person would undertake to furnish her funeral, and she was on the point of being buried in a spot of ground appropriated to the poor, when an English merchant resident in Calais, considering the services she had formerly rendered her country, and the wretched situation of the daughter of Lord Nelson (who in compliance with her father's wishes had never left Lady Hamilton), offered to become responsible for the charges of her funeral, which was respectably performed at the *cimetière* (churchyard) at Calais; all the English gentlemen in Calais and its vicinity to the number of fifty attending as mourners. The merchant above alluded to, finding that a process was commenced to detain the person of Miss Horatia Nelson for Lady Hamilton's debts, conveyed that young lady on board a vessel for England, and on her arrival placed her in the hands of Mr. Matcham, the late Lord Nelson's brother-in-law, with whom she is now residing.

A Mr. Henry Cadogan conducted the funeral ceremonies, receiving his instructions from her genuine friend through all adversity, Mr. Alderman Smith. Mr. Morrison holds the bill of expenses in connection with Lady Hamilton's interment. Mr. Smith himself fell into difficulties a few years later, and made over a portion of the effects he had bought from Lady Hamilton to his man-servant, one Kinsey. This man eventually sold a quantity of autograph letters and other valuables to an old curiosity dealer, named Evans, of Maddox Street, Regent Street, and so the documents found their way into circulation. Among them was the funeral bill, and Mr. Cadogan's receipt to Mr. Smith for the money wherewith to defray it. As Lady Hamilton was an admitted member of the Church of Rome, she had received the administrations of the clergy of that body, and the funeral rites were in accordance with their ceremonies, and many sea captains whose vessels were in port attended to mark their respect for the deceased lady. The bill and receipt are as follows: —

  Funeral expences of the late Lady Emma Hamilton, as paid by me, Henry Cadogan, at Calais, in France, Jan^r, 1815.
  An oak coffin, corked (caulked). Church expenses, Priests, Candells, Burial Ground, men sitting up, dressing the Body, spirits, &c., &c. £28 10s.

LADY HAMILTON.

Copy of receipt for money to defray above :—

Received Feb^r 4, 1815, of J. J. Smith, Esq^{r,} the Sum of Twenty-eight pounds ten shillings, being the Amount of Funeral expences for the late Lady Emma Hamilton, at Calais, in France, as paid by me,

HENRY CADOGAN.

This document is written on an eightpenny stamp, and places it beyond doubt that religious services were performed over the remains by the Roman Catholic clergy, though it was owing solely to the intervention of Mr. Smith that they escaped interment in a spot of ground set apart for the lowest description of poor, from want of means to defray expenses. In time, a stone was placed over the grave of Lady Hamilton, with a Latin inscription, which remained until 1833, when grave and stone were lost in the altered character of the place. When Dr. William Beattie visited Calais, in 1831, he found the stone partially erased, very little of the Latin inscription being traceable. His soul was exercised as he stood in the midst of the desecrated ground and meditated on the ignominious end of that once idolized woman. He penned the following lines on the scene of neglect and decay :—

> And here is one, a nameless grave ; the grass
> Waves dank and dismal o'er its crumbling mass
> Of mortal elements. The wintry sedge
> Weeps, drooping o'er the rampart's watery edge.
> The rustling reed, the darkly rippling wave,
> Announce the tenant of that lowly grave.
>
> Crushed in a pauper's shell, the earth scarce heaves
> Above the trodden breast. The turf scarce leaves
> One lingering token that the stranger found
> "Ashes for hope" in that unhallowed ground,
> And "dust for mourning." Levelled with the soil,
> The wasting worm hath revelled in its spoil—
> The spoil of beauty. This the poor remains
> Of one, who living, could command the strains
> Of flattery's harp and pen ! where incense, flung
> From venal breath, upon her altar hung
> A halo ; while in loveliness supreme
> She moved in brightness like the embodied dream

LINES ON LADY HAMILTON'S GRAVE.

Of some rapt minstrel's warm imaginings,
The more than form and face of earthly things.
Ah! when has heart so warm, have hopes so fair,
Been crushed amidst the darkness of despair?
With broken heart, and head in sorrow bowed,
Hers was the midnight bier and borrowed shroud.

Few bend them at thy bier, unhappy one!
All knew thy shame, thy mental sufferings none.
All knew thy frailties, all thou wast and art;
But thine were faults of circumstance, not heart.
Thy soul was formed to bless and to be blessed
With that immortal boon, a guiltless breast,
And be what others seem. Had bounteous Heaven
Less beauty lent, or stronger virtue given,
The frugal matron of some lowlier hearth
Thou hadst not known the splendid woes of earth;
Dispensing happiness, and happy there,
Thou hadst not known the curse of being fair;
But like yon lonely vesper star, thy light,
Thy love—had been as pure as it was bright.

I've met thy pictured bust in many lands;
I've seen the stranger pause—with lifted hands—
In deep, mute admiration, while his eye
Dwelt sparkling on thy peerless symmetry.
I've seen the poet, painter, sculptor's gaze
Speak with rapt glance their eloquence of praise.
I've seen thee as a gem in Royal Halls
Stoop like presiding angel from the walls,
And only less than worshipped; yet 'tis come
To this, when all but Slander's voice is dumb,
And they who gazed upon thy living face
Can hardly find thy mortal resting place.

The perusal of these touching lines must impress the reader that the dead woman had been deeply loved and respected by her associates. Her own bright and winning nature surrounded her with a halo of love which held both sexes captive as with enchanted chains.

The records of the municipality of Calais contain the following entry:—
"A.D. 1815, Janvier 15, Dame Emma Lyons, agée de 51 ans, née à Lancashire, à Angleterre, domiciliée à Calais, fille de Henri Lyons, et de Marie Kidd, Veuve de William Hamilton, est decédé le 15 Janvier, 1815, à une heure après midi au domicile du Sieur Damy, Rue Française." In the timber-yard just without the fortifications, on the left hand of the stroller to St. Pierre, lie the remains of the unfortunate woman whose death is thus recorded in the language of the foreigner.

The Maison Damy, now Graudin, in a room of which poor Lady Hamilton breathed her last, is situated in the Rue Française, the street running parallel with the southern rampart and the *fosse*, and is at present numbered 111. From its aspect being due north, the house is as cheerless and dreary as can well be imagined; not a ray of sunshine ever gladdens the side of the street in which it is located, or plays for an instant even in summer on the ever-shaded, cold-looking casements. From the portals of this dismal abode, or rather refuge, in the bleak month of January, were the remains of this unhappy woman removed to their final resting-place under the escort of a Sergent de Ville!

Is it not a matter of deep regret that we can hear from every French gossip that the loved friend of the Saviour of our Country died almost deprived of the common necessaries of life, and was buried in a foreign town, every native of which had just cause to deem Nelson a mortal enemy? This scandalous taunt, in spite of the dying hero's last words, uttered in plaintive anguish to his executor: "Take care of poor Lady Hamilton." Upon the ear of no Government save our own could such words, spoken at such a moment, by such a man, have fallen ignored—leaving it in the power of a foreign country to hold a record in its keeping of British heartlessness. Our national humanity and respectability are compromised through this never to be forgotten episode in the annals of Calais.

The darling of a luxurious Court found her last long resting-place in an obscure grave; the exiled patriot, driven by poverty from the shores of the country she had so faithfully served, had to seek refuge and sleep for evermore among strangers – to die in the land of the enemy whom she had helped to defeat.

Emma Hamilton only paid the price which all must pay for celebrity in some shape or other—the sword or the faggot, the scaffold or the field, public hatred or private heartbreak—what matter? Poor woman! her failings were the result of her brilliant surroundings, and men's lavish flattery, which would have undermined a more sound and thoroughly good heart than that of the lovely and luckless Emma.

The sleep of death is given in mercy, and the future concealed in loving kindness. Had the struggling career that was in store for his two dear ones been suggested to Lord Nelson, would not his death agonies have been increased a hundredfold? Better that he should die as he did in trusting reliance on his fellow men that they would care for those whom he bequeathed to them in the terrible pangs of death.

MRS. HORATIA NELSON WARD.

CHAPTER XXVII.

HORATIA'S TROUBLES. THE PRINCE CONSORT ENDEAVOURS TO BEFRIEND HER. SHE APPEALS FOR A PENSION. PLEASING RECOLLECTIONS OF LADY HAMILTON'S ASSOCIATES. INTERESTING RELICS AND FINALE.

WHO can regret that Earl William lived to see the destruction of his hopes, for his promising son died before him, aged only nineteen years. His body lies in St. Paul's, in the same tomb as that of his revered uncle; the lad whom Nelson had fondly wished to marry his adopted child, and thereby put her in possession of the position that he had earned. He sank under an attack of typhus fever on January 17, 1808, an amiable youth, who died regretted. By his demise the national honours and estate of Nelson passed to the eldest son of the hero's favourite sister, whose worthy descendant now holds them.

Upon hearing of the death of Lady Hamilton, the contemptible coroneted cleric, Earl William, put in an appearance, not to take any part in the burden of decent interment for the poor creature who had too surely used her witcheries for his aggrandisement, and her own destruction. No, far from it! Not to do honour to her poor remains was he present, but to see if there were anything of worth or value which he could lay claim to and carry away. Lady Hamilton's little belongings were valued at nine pounds English money, besides a few of her treasures which necessity had caused her to pawn at the Mont de Piété—they had been parted with to avert utter want. He was mean enough to evade payment of the natural expenses in connection with their redemption, and sooner than pay the interest he left them in bondage. Poor little Horatia's legacy—the " all that I die possessed of"—was not worth carrying away!

Punch, dated January 19, 1850, severely enlarges on the omission of common courtesy to the dead woman on the part of Earl William, and in an outburst of righteous indignation (which we surmise to have emanated from

the caustic pen of Douglas Jerrold) he denounces the cruel neglect thus :—
"The Parson Earl did not erect a handsbreadth of stone, yet to him stone must have been cheap enough. The man must have carried a quarry inside of him." And who would defend him against this well-merited outspoken denunciation of his heartlessness?

For two years after Lady Hamilton's death, Horatia resided with Mr. and Mrs. Matcham, and at the expiration of that time she joined the family of Mrs. Bolton, whose son eventually became second Earl Nelson. The sisters at least recognised their obligation of gratitude to the dead brother, and cared for the friendless girl. These ladies, who may be supposed to have been as keen as others of their sex, never considered Horatia to be Lady Hamilton's daughter, and though constantly in her company at the period of the child's supposed birth, they saw no reason to conclude that she deserved the slanders which were rife. It was most praiseworthy that these two good women countenanced and supported Lady Hamilton in the days of her tribulation, when they certainly had nothing to gain by continuing the intimacy; they naturally were chary of their own reputation, but, knowing her thoroughly well, they honestly remained true when she was attacked and accused by scandalmongers. When Horatia reached her seventeenth year, she became engaged to the Rev. Mr. Blake. As she was beginning to relinquish all hopes of obtaining a pension for herself, she wrote to the Hon. G. Rose to ask him to render her the essential service of procuring a preferment for her suitor. Upon receipt of her application, Mr. Rose transmitted the following letter to the Prime Minister:—

MUDIFORD, *Oct.* 29, 1817.

MY DEAR LORD,

I am most deeply concerned at the situation of the writer of the enclosure, recommended to my best attention by the Hero in parting from him when he last sailed from Spithead (at which time I had never seen her), and strongly recommended to his Country in his very last moments. She will not have wherewithal to buy Cloathes on the death of Mr. Matcham. She is, it seems, engaged to be married to the gentleman she mentions, but his friends refuse their consent unless some modest preferment can be procured for him; he is now a Curate. Do you think the Chancellor could be moved for him? supposing a Pension of £200 a year be quite impossible. I hope to hear that your health is perfectly restored. I have not profited by a month's residence here as I expected. I return to Cufnels on Saturday.

I am, my dear Lord, most truly yours,

G. ROSE.

In this letter we find Mr. Rose acknowledging Nelson's final injunctions to him at Spithead, at which farewell he was accompanied by Mr. Canning. If Horatia were mentioned, we may be sure that Lady Hamilton's necessities were broached, as Nelson always named the two in the same breath, although Canning repudiated it.

It is to be presumed that the Chancellor was not to be moved on behalf of Mr. Blake, and that the application was unsuccessful, for in 1822 Horatia married the Rev. Philip Ward, by whom she had eight children. In the *Gentleman's Magazine* for March, 1822, appears the announcement of their wedding thus :—" Feb. 19, at Burnham, Norfolk, by the Rev. W. Bolton, the Rev. Philip Ward to Horatia Nelson Nelson,* the adopted daughter of the late Admiral Lord Viscount Nelson." Troubled about the mystery which attached itself to her birth, Horatia questioned the acknowledged holder of the secret, Mr. Haslewood, but no persuasion could induce him to break the trust which had been reposed in him. The only satisfaction which he felt at liberty to give was an intimation that her mother and Lady Hamilton were totally distinct persons. Dr. Scott asserted the same. The letter from Mr. Haslewood was copied by Mrs. Ward, and sent to Mr. Paget, the writer of more than one interesting article on Lady Hamilton. It appears in the number of *Blackwood's Magazine* for May, 1888, among other correspondence with which she favoured him, and is worded thus :—

BRIGHTON, 26th *September*, 1846.

MY DEAR MADAM,

I dare not write so fully as I could wish on the topics referred to in your kind letter of the 23rd, lest the secret which I am bound to keep should be rendered too transparent. Thus much only may be said without incurring such risk. Your mother was well acquainted with Lady Hamilton, and saw you often during your infancy ; but soon after her marriage she went to reside at a considerable distance from London, which

---

* On Sept. 30, 1806, George III granted a license to Horatia Nelson Thompson, an infant, to use the surname of " Nelson " only.

or (*sic*) never visited afterwards. Lamenting that I cannot be more communicative, I remain always, my dear Madam, faithfully yours,

W^{M.} HASLEWOOD.

To this day there are unreasonably prejudiced people who would fain believe and insist that the courteous and upright old gentleman invented the fable of the mother marrying in order to divert the onus from Lady Hamilton, but common sense prohibits such an interpretation of his letter. His silence was not out of regard for her ladyship, for there was no great friendship between the two, inasmuch as he acted as solicitor for Earl Nelson ; there was, if anything, a tendency to mutual dislike, often verging on open rupture. When Mrs. Cadogan is found writing to her daughter in this strain, in January, 1806 : " Let me know wether you have a copy of the will or not, as I understand the executors are to pay every expence for six months after the death. Pray write me word wether you have employ'd a lawer against Haslewood. Let me know in particular, for if you have not, I will ; " again, in the February of 1806, when the same correspondent says : " I had a very canting letter from Haslewood yesterday, saying the Earl and him was coming down to-day ; " it requires no great stretch of imagination to see that no consideration for Lady Hamilton prompted him to retain the secret, for he was well aware that by his doing so, she would be sacrificed to uphold the reputation of one whom he deemed more worthy. Great reliance may be placed on Mr. Haslewood's intimation that Horatia might claim another for her mother, for there is nothing to show that the old lawyer was actuated by any motive in screening one who had considered herself his opponent in legal matters.

During the lifetime of the late Prince Consort, the case of Mrs. Ward aroused the sympathy of many of her countrymen, and an effort was made to raise a fund for her benefit under the heading of " the Nelson Memorial Fund." Application was made to His Royal Highness, soliciting his support to the movement. Although commiserating the lady's position as a clergyman's wife of contracted means, surrounded by a large family, yet his public capacity would not allow him to head the undertaking by his patronage. In accordance with His Royal Highness' wishes, C. B. Phipps, Esq. replied to the gentleman who had sought to secure his kind participation in the scheme to fulfil Nelson's legacy. The letter of good intent runs as follows :—

LADY HAMILTON.

BUCKINGHAM PALACE, *March* 16, 1850.

DEAR SIR,

I have received the commands of his Royal Highness the Prince Albert to inform you, that although his Royal Highness does not feel that he could with propriety head the public subscription for Mrs. Ward, not being able to separate himself from the Gov^t, yet in his private capacity his Royal Highness was anxious as far as lay in his power to assist Mrs. Ward in the education of her children. The Prince has at present a presentation to Christ's Hospital, and has directed me to request that you will have the goodness to offer this presentation to that lady in case any one of her sons should be of an age (between 7 and 10) at which he would be admissible.

Believe me, sincerely yours,

C. B. PHIPPS.

The presentation was unfortunately not of any service, as the lady's youngest son had reached the age of sixteen years at the time of the offer. The friend who had received the intimation from C. B. Phipps, Esq., communicated the contents of his letter to Mrs. Ward. Her reply thereon is interesting, as it contains a record of the names and ages of her children who were then living. The annexed lines are a copy:—

MY DEAR AND OLD FRIEND,

Many, very many thanks for your kind letter; it was only put into my hands as I was starting for London, and I was too much knocked up to answer it till this evening. I thank Prince Albert much for his kind intentions, but my children are all too old to avail themselves of his offer, the youngest boy being sixteen in the early part of May. You ask the ages and occupations of my children. Horace, 27 the 8th of Dec. last, is now his father's curate, and has been so for two years. Ellen, 26 in April. Marmaduke, 25 in May, now an assistant-surgeon at Melville Hospital, Chatham. Nelson, 22 in the early part of May, I GREATLY FEAR will have an appointment to India; he has served his time to a solicitor. William, 20 next April, has a cadetship to India. Horatia, 17 last Novr Philip, 16 in May. Caroline, 14 last January. I have written the above with some trouble, as, alas! I am neither in mind or body as in days of yore. Thank you much for all your exertions, and believe me that whatever the result may be, the kind feelings which have dictated them have

HORATIA'S PARENTAGE.

sunk deep into my heart. Your advice agrees with my own feelings. I am sure that further publicity in the daily prints w^d be injurious, and only under the idea that such an extract as that introduced into *The Times* and the country papers was calculated to do me much harm, was I induced at all to appear in them, and afterwards by the book itself and Mr. Neale's reply to my denial, did I find that a misquotation had found its way into the *Liverpool Albion*, and from thence been copied into *The Times*, &c., &c. When I return, and have quiet and rest, I will again write. Give my affec^{ate} love to Mrs. B. and Emma.

Sincerely and truly,

H. N. WARD.

The letter of Mr. Neale to which Mrs. Ward refers, appeared in *The Times* of February 23, 1850, and its insertion will tend to strengthen the evidence in Lady Hamilton's favour. It was the testimony of a living witness, who had held converse with Dr. Scott, and was issued in the following form :—

To the Editor of "THE TIMES."

SIR,

Mrs. Ward's letter in *The Times* of to-day* demands an immediate answer at my hands. The information relative to "Horatia," Nelson's, but not Lady Hamilton's, daughter, was derived from a clergyman (intimately acquainted with Mrs. Ward and her family), on whose testimony I felt I could rely.

That my information was gathered from the lips of Horatia herself is an erroneous inference from the contents of *The Life-book of a Labourer*. No such statement is there made.

I adhere, however, to the averment which has caused so much controversy, and respectfully repeat it. Horatia is not Lady Hamilton's daughter. One who knows most of Lord Nelson's secrets told me many years ago, " Horatia is as much Lady Hamilton's child as I am! She is the daughter of a woman of high rank, a woman infinitely superior to Lady Hamilton in morals and station. Nelson told me the whole secret—a secret it must remain. But that Lady Hamilton was the mother of Horatia is all fudge."

* February 21, 1850.

The speaker was Nelson's intimate friend, chaplain and secretary, Dr. Scott.

Trusting that you will oblige me with an early insertion of my reply,

Believe me to be, Sir,

Your very humble servant,

ERSKINE NEALE.

RECTORY, KIRTON, NEAR WOODBRIDGE,
Feb. 21, 1850.

Another item of evidence is supplied by Mrs. Horatia Sophia Elder (daughter and part biographer of Dr. Scott), in the shape of a letter which was placed in *The Times* of February 21, 1850, and reads thus:—

To the Editor of "THE TIMES."

SIR,

It was with much surprise that I read in some of the newspapers the statement so confidently expressed that "Horatia," the acknowledged daughter of Lord Nelson, was also the child of Lady Hamilton, yet notwithstanding the reason I had for believing the contrary, I did not at first consider it worth while to contradict this statement, thinking that the indirect testimony of so humble an individual would have little effect in upsetting a received opinion; since, however, another has come forward in denial of this fact, I now beg to state, in corroboration of such denial, that I have frequently heard the subject mentioned in presence of my late father, Dr. Scott (Vicar of Catterick, Yorkshire, and formerly private secretary and chaplain to Lord Nelson), and that to all queries respecting the parentage of "Horatia," his answer invariably was that "she was not the daughter of Lady Hamilton." This reply he has often made in presence of his family, even to more direct questions as to Nelson being the father, evading the latter query by asserting, in the most positive manner, that "He knew all about the matter, but that 'Horatia' was not Lady Hamilton's daughter." There was evidently a secret with which he was as evidently acquainted, but which was, of course, never divulged. From all we could gather at different times, however, there was an impression in our family that the mother of "Horatia" was a foreigner (if not a Neapolitan), and a lady of very high rank. At this distance of time, I can give no especial reason for such an impression, but can only state the fact that it existed.

My father was much beloved by Nelson, who employed him in many intricate and delicate negociations, and we have several precious relics of the hero in our family: a few letters in his (left) handwriting, some of his hair, and the old black leather chairs (still untouched) which so often served him for a couch on board the "Victory."

I am, Sir, your very obedient servant,

HORATIA SOPHIA ELDER (*née* SCOTT).

9 VERNEY PLACE, ST. SIDWELLS,
EXETER, *Feb.* 18, 1850.

Atoms in a generation, but links in a great chain of important evidence. How often has insignificant correspondence been conducive to right asserting itself?

Punch, December, 1849, sympathising with the struggles of Horatia, refers to the better fate of a sheep of Lord Nelson's that was given with other live stock by Captain Hardy to Captain Griffiths, then commanding a frigate. The sailors would have foregone fresh meat rather than kill the animal. It was sent ashore to the farm of a Mr. Henty, and visitors to Worthing used to visit the pampered little animal on account of its having belonged to Nelson. "Our wonder is," says friend *Punch*, "that Nelson's reverend brother did not pounce upon the animal, butcher it, and flay it for its meat and wool. Nelson left his one ewe lamb to the care of his country, but how—with shame as Englishmen we ask it—how has his country responded to the noble confidence of its tutelary hero? Horatia, for any care she has received of Nelson's countrymen, had better been a sheep." About the same time an appeal appeared in *The Times* on behalf of an old cook of Nelson's, whereon *Punch* sarcastically remarked that "the kitchen bars had a better claim on the sympathies of some folk—far better than any sort of bar sinister." He proposed that a slot be made in the plank of the "Victory" upon which Nelson died in his country's cause, and a money box be placed beneath it, in which the faithful could drop their contributions on behalf of Horatia.

By the efforts of many staunch friends who personally contributed, a fund was raised for the benefit of Mrs. Ward. Attention was called to Nelson's unfulfilled legacy in a prospectus, which took the following form:—"The Nelson Memorial Fund.—'I also leave to the beneficence of my country my adopted daughter, Horatia Nelson Thompson, and I desire she will in future use the name of Nelson only. These are the only favours I ask of my King and country at this moment when I am going to fight their battle. May God bless my King and country, and all those I hold dear.' Such were Nelson's words, written in the codicil to his will on the morning of the *memorable twenty-first of October*, 1805, when in sight of the combined fleets of France and Spain, off Cape Trafalgar. Again, after receiving his fatal wound, and almost with his expiring breath, he said, '*Remember, I leave my daughter Horatia to my country; never forget Horatia.*' Nearly five and forty years have elapsed, and this request *has never been complied with*. Although large sums have been bestowed on Nelson's family, and although we have raised, and are still raising, monuments and statues to his memory in various parts of the kingdom, yet this, the nearest and dearest desire of his heart, uttered in the agonies of death by the greatest of naval heroes, remains to this day unfulfilled by the Government or the country. *Nelson's Horatia still survives*, the exemplary wife of an excellent clergyman with a small income and a large family. Will the British nation now at length perform the long neglected duty, or will they still refuse to entertain this last claim on their gratitude till reparation be no longer possible, and regret unavailing?"

We have the pleasure to insert a portrait of Mrs. Ward, taken in later life, and copied with fidelity, as prepared for the family album! To those who will become familiar (through the medium of this work) with her struggles to rear and place her large family, the acquaintance with the features of the widowed lady must prove of great interest. There is still in possession of Mrs. Ward's relatives a full-length portrait of her as a child of seven years, with fair hair and blue eyes, in a high-waisted white frock with short sleeves, coral necklace round the bare neck, and the costume finished with blue shoes.

Mrs. Ward died on the 6th of March, 1881, at Beaufort Villa, Woodridings, Pinner, in her eighty-second year, after a widowhood of twenty years.

The wars in which Lady Hamilton had played so prominent a part ended in the peace of Europe in 1815, the identical year in which peace came to that faithful and troubled heart.

In the *Recollections of the Table Talk of Samuel Rogers* is to be found his mention of personal memories of Lord Nelson and Lady Hamilton, and similarly to each remembrance left by men of letters and note who had

actually associated with the two celebrities, the lines he has written are in affectionate memory. He says: "At a splendid party given by Lady Hampden to the Prince of Wales, &c., I saw Lady Hamilton go through all those 'Attitudes' which have been engraved, and her performance was very beautiful indeed. Her husband, Sir William, was present. Lord Nelson was a remarkably kind-hearted man. I have seen him spin a teetotum with his *one* hand for a whole evening for the amusement of some children. I heard him once during dinner utter some bitter complaints (which Lady Hamilton vainly attempted to check) of the way he had been treated at Court that forenoon—the Queen had not condescended to take the slightest notice of him. In truth Nelson was hated at Court, they were jealous of his fame. There was something very charming in Lady Hamilton's openness of manner; she showed me the neckcloth which Nelson had on when he died. Of course I could not help looking at it with extreme interest, and she threw her arms round my neck and kissed me. She was latterly in great want." This wonderful woman was a pleasing memory to her old associates, one and all of whom cherished her name in tenderness. Not to them can her defamation be traced.

Some within our own time have loved to speak of their acquaintance with her. Mr. W. P. Frith tells us in his *Reminiscences*, how Lord Northwick had shown him his collection of engravings executed from the great numbers of pictures of Lady Hamilton, many lovely heads by Romney among them. To use Mr. Frith's own words, "many a sigh heaved the old gentleman as he produced them." The late Sir Moses Montefiore had dined with Lord Nelson on board the "Victory." To a young friend who enquired what the great admiral was like, Sir Moses replied, "Ah, my dear boy, I had no eyes for anyone but Lady Hamilton." The Duke of Sussex derived great pleasure from his memories of Lady Hamilton's exquisite singing with Mrs. Billington.

The old ship "Victory" has become a national relic. Once, in the year 1841, it was actually proposed to break up the vessel, but this was mainly averted by Mr. John Poole, the author of "Paul Pry," who wrote a very forcible article in the *Brighton Gazette* against the national sacrilege, which was copied into many leading journals, and the protest that was raised prolonged its existence. The dry-rot got into the vessel about the year 1886, and again, after much argument, the day of destruction was postponed, and the good old ship repaired; and as long as the planks will hold together an effort should be made to preserve her in memory of the great sea-fights in which she took so prominent a place.

On the anniversary of the battle of Trafalgar, 1844, Queen Victoria was on a visit to Portsmouth. While sailing in the harbour she noticed the "Victory" bedecked with flags, and her mastheads adorned with laurels. She naturally enquired the cause of the unusual display of the emblem of conquest, the laurel; and on being informed that it was the *fête* day of the old ship in memory of Trafalgar's fight, she immediately said she would like to go on board. Accompanied by Prince Albert, she was shown over the ship. On reaching the spot where Lord Nelson received his death wound, she read aloud the inscription which is inserted on a brass tablet sunk into the deck: "Here Nelson fell." She stooped and picked two of the laurel leaves from the wreath in which the tablet was enshrined. Her Majesty went to the poop-rail, where, above the steering-wheel, was inscribed in letters of gold, the words of the memorable signal: "England expects every man will do his duty." This inscription was likewise encircled in flowers and laurels. She then desired to be shown the place where Nelson died. The royal party were conveyed to the cabin, where the actual spot is still marked by a painted funeral urn, surmounted by Nelson's flag, and on the top, in a wreath, the record: "Here Nelson died." Thus did Her Majesty do honour to the great and brave sea conqueror. Who is there who could stand unmoved in such a situation while mentally rehearsing the scenes of carnage which surrounded the dying man? Who is there so heartless as to turn from that hallowed spot reflecting that his legacy was unfulfilled, without murmuring the words: "It should have been accomplished"?

A capital effigy of Lord Nelson is to be found among the waxen models in Westminster Abbey, which is considered so correct that it is constantly delineated by artists who have occasion to introduce his figure into their works. It is clothed in the garments worn in life, with the exception of the coat, which is a copy only of his attire as admiral. He stands with his foot on a veritable piece of the "Victory."

When Maclise was painting his "Death of Nelson," he wished to portray the Admiral's hat on or near him, and he waited on Dean Stanley to solicit an inspection of the one on the effigy. The Dean caused the case to be opened, and the hat was found to be stained with grease and sweat marks

MINIATURES OF LADY HAMILTON.

on the part that had touched the wearer's head, except where the edge of the eye-patch had protected the lining. The maker's name (somewhere in St. James Street) was inside, together with the stamp acknowledging payment of the tax on the article. Maclise borrowed the hat, copied it, and returned it to the effigy.

The effigy of Lord Nelson was made merely for exhibition, and was not used or carried in his funeral obsequies.

Nelson's hatchment still hangs upon the wall on one side of Merton Church.

There is a great resemblance between all the miniatures of Lady Hamilton, no matter by what artist they have been executed, and more reliance can be placed upon them for accurate portraiture than on the larger paintings, which were mostly taken in character.

At the Army and Navy Club, Pall Mall, there is a most interesting miniature of Lady Hamilton,* a half-length, showing full face, with a lace scarf thrown over her head. It was presented to the Club by a member, Mr. Percy Williams, of the Royals, and bears the following inscription:—

> The accompanying miniature of Lady Hamilton hung up in Nelson's cabin at the time of his death. It then became the property of Lord Howe, who presented it to his private secretary, Mr. Aubin, from whom it descended to his son. It then became the property of a mutual friend of Mr. Aubin and myself, from whom I had it.
>
> (*Signed*) J. PERCY WILLIAMS.
> ARMY AND NAVY CLUB,
> *Nov.* 22, 1853.

After Lord Nelson was wounded at Trafalgar, a miniature of Lady Hamilton was removed from his neck. Of this relic Mr. A. Davison became possessed, and at the sale of his effects it was purchased by Lord North. The last mention we find of it is in *Notes and Queries*, May 17, 1862, at which time it was the property of a gentleman signing himself "F. J. O." In the back was a lock of Lady Hamilton's hair, and her initials, the latter being inserted in small pearls.

In the Mayer Collection in the Liverpool Museum is a pretty girlish portrait, signed (almost illegibly) "Steveley." The head is surmounted by a

* We have used this beautiful miniature as the frontispiece to this book.

turban, from beneath which flows the hair in superabundance. The neat flowered dress is the essence of modesty.

An interesting tale is told regarding Lady Hamilton's watch, which passed to her cousin, Richard Reynolds, who intended it for his daughter when she should be old enough to value it. Miss Thomas, a descendant of the Hawarden doctor, was desirous of acquiring it, and offered sixteen guineas to its owner, who said he was reserving it for his little girl, but that she should decide for herself. The watch and pile of gold were placed upon the table; the child was sent for and asked to make her choice; she laid her hand upon the watch, which decision was final. She grew up and married, and on an occasion when her husband was suffering from monetary embarrassment, he, laying no historic store upon the watch, took it to Chester, and sold it to Mr. Low, one of the most respectable jewellers in the city. The young woman's father was greatly distressed when informed of the transaction, and at once despatched one of his sons to endeavour to repurchase it. In spite of all the expedition he could use, he arrived too late, for Mr. Low told him that he only bought that kind of watch for the sake of the case, and it was already absorbed in the contents of the melting pot.

The old man set great store on the relics which had once belonged to his illustrious relative, and in bequeathing to his son the china breakfast service (which had come to him through Sarah Reynolds), the remnant of Merton household treasures, it was with these words, "Never part with these, not even if you want bread."

Frances, Dowager Viscountess Nelson, Duchess of Bronté, outlived her illustrious husband many years; she lived to be sixty-eight years of age, and died on May 4, 1831, at her residence in Harley Street, her son, Josiah, having predeceased her in the previous year.

The Rev. Earl William Nelson lost his wife, Sarah (daughter of the Rev. Henry Yonge), on April 15, 1828, aged seventy-eight years, their married life having covered a period of forty-two years. Little did the young bride (daughter of a country clergyman) dream on her wedding day that her brows would ever wear a coronet. The widower displayed little feeling at the loss of his really estimable wife, and in spite of his advanced years and recent bereavement, he took to himself a second spouse in less than twelve months from the day of the death of his first Countess. The lady of his selection was Hilare, widow of George Ulric Barlow, Esq. The Earl himself expired on February 28, 1835, aged seventy-seven years.

The old mistress outlived most of the players in this romance. Good Mrs. Thomas died on October 5, 1821, and rests beside her husband in the quiet country churchyard at Hawarden.

Before closing these memoirs it will be as well to draw up a brief summary of the chief grounds on which a complete exoneration of Lady Hamilton has been based. Would it be possible that a graceful exhibition of the "Attitudes" could have been given four weeks prior to the child's advent? Supposing the lady capable, what about the audience, who in this case were moved to tears by the pathetic exposition, the leading figure being admired by every distinguished spectator? On the 29th December, 1800, she returned from Bath to London, where her time was next occupied in settling into her new house in Piccadilly; could such a circumstance have taken place unnoticed in the upset and bustle necessarily caused by workmen and upholsterers following their various avocations? Where was the infant for the few days before it was delivered to the nurse, and how could it escape all notice from the inmates of the house? If Mrs. Cadogan acted as *accoucheuse*, as has been asserted without a tittle of evidence, why did not *she* at once convey the child to the nurse, which would have been the only course adopted immediately on its birth if the affair were to be surreptitious? Who could calculate or provide against mishaps which would lead to exposure by keeping the infant one full week before removing it? Would the ever-considerate Mrs. Cadogan have allowed her daughter to incur so serious a risk as to drive out on a winter's night when she herself was at hand? No! there was no need for her services. A lady approaching her fortieth year is incapable of emulating the feats of a girl in her teens, and the impossibilities of nature must be placed against the improbabilities invented to found a slander. Lady Hamilton was no working woman, bound to arise and do for her family; there was no reason why a lady in her position should not indulge and nurse herself during an ailment, which could so easily have been effected without arousing suspicion, and which she most assuredly would have done, had she passed through the ordeal with which she has been charged. Such risks as she incurred would have had a fatal result; nature would never have allowed such pranks to be played by a luxuriously living woman without exacting a serious penalty. Is it credible that a good-living, religious man, such as Lord Nelson invariably proved himself to be, could have been so fiendishly treacherous as to hold the hand of his dying friend, to keep the night-watch by his bedside, and receive his last breath on his breast as he heard his parting words of faith and trust, if he had led the wife into infidelity? The very thought of this iniquity is preposterous, and the act totally impossible to God-fearing Nelson. The man must be judged by his life, which is in every way at variance with deception—honest and foolishly simple he may have been, but never wicked.

Attention has already been drawn to the absence of remark prior to the event. Considering the importance of a prospective heir to Sir William, no ingenuous friend seems to have uttered the congratulatory whisper; in fact, the old gentleman died in the positive consciousness that no such charge could be laid on Lady Hamilton, his trusted wife, whom he assured with his dying breath that she had been exemplary in her conduct towards him. The clear-headed old man was no foolish dupe, he retained his full senses up to the last, his brain-power only ceasing in death.

On the 28th of January, 1801, Nelson wrote to Mr. Davison, and his letter contained these remarkable lines: " Either as a public or private (man) I wish nothing undone which I have done." These are indeed words to be pondered over, written as they were upon the eve of an occurrence which has been arranged to bear so much import to himself. This work has been produced to show the impossibility of Lady Hamilton being Horatia's mother. There is absolutely nothing to *prove* that Nelson was her actual father. Lady Nelson never thought so. To call her " his child " might, in one of his true nature, be only regarded as testimony of his thorough and earnest completion of the adoption. In point of fact, Nelson never uttered one word of self-upbraiding or reproach. He assured his revered father that he was blameless ; and, in dying, whispered into his chaplain's ear that he had " not been a very great sinner." As a clergyman's son, eminently religious, he could not have quibbled with his moral sense of right and wrong.

Seeing that Lady Hamilton's daughter, Emily, had at no time been a permanent inmate of her household, it is most improbable that any child bearing similar relationship to herself would have been brought to the front. Conscience would have filled herself and Lord Nelson with apprehension that the introduction would lead to the unveiling of the truth, and they would have

PLATE XII. ATTITUDE OF LADY HAMILTON, FROM A DRAWING BY REHBERG.

zealously guarded against anything that would lead to suspicion or disclosure.

Both the lord and the lady were fond of exaggerating their sentimental passion. Lady Hamilton saw in Nelson the popular hero whom it was her pride to lead enchained: his glory reflected itself upon her, enabling her to shine as *la grande dame*; it was, therefore, her policy to hold his simple nature enthralled by the effusive adulation which was so acceptable to him, and by this means she kept herself to the front, and shared in his notoriety; apart from this, there is no evidence of sincere affection. It was the "glorious" Nelson whom she worshipped, and whom she incited to great achievements; her heart was broken for the loss of her hero, not for the death of her lover. Extravagant in the display of her feelings, she showed to all the world her adoration of the man she idealized. Real love and a secret attachment would not have blazoned itself forth so prominently. It was his renown of which she would partake, and, sailor like, he wore his fetters with complacency, while Sir William smiled, and exulted in the laudation of wife and friend.

The letters of Lady Hamilton and Greville, at present in the possession of Alfred Morrison, Esq., of Fonthill House, Wiltshire (from whose collection many in this work have been copied), were formerly owned by Edward H. Finch Hatton, Esq., who lent them to the late Lord Lytton for perusal. His summary in returning them is noteworthy, his valuable criticism being in itself a brief eulogy. He wrote:—

> My dear Sir,
>
> I return you with many thanks the papers you have so kindly lent me. They are deeply interesting. I know not when I have been equally attracted by any biographical study. For the letters of Lady Hamilton are the epitomized history of a very remarkable woman, and a very marvellous career. Emerging from a position so poor and lowly, occupying for so many years a position so brilliant and eminent, and dying down once more into poverty and contempt. I quite agree with you, that Lady Hamilton was not as black as she has been painted. Her letters to Greville are in part extremely touching, evince great warmth of affection, great goodness of heart, and flashes of native talent as well as generosity, contrasting all defects of education and rearing.
>
> There is something very curious in the condition of morals and manners

in that day. . . . One can see that she must have had wonderful attractions besides beauty, and that she seems to have taken great pains to accomplish herself. Poor woman, one cannot but pity her. The study of so singular a life is a new insight into character. I wish it could be completed by a better or clearer knowledge of her connection with Nelson from the beginning to end.

To judge by the house bills at Merton, she must have been accustomed to a very uneconomical mode of life, and one may guess how the £800 a year came to grief. With repeated thanks for the great treat you have afforded me, believe me truly, yours obliged,

LYTTON.

SATURDAY NIGHT,
ARGYLE HALL, TORQUAY.

The perusal of her artless letters, and sympathy with the details of her troubled later life, will in time produce a reaction in favour of the recklessly calumniated woman. The intelligent reading public only require facts to be placed before them as they existed, and not, as has so often been the case, fictitiously represented; their own discernment, freed from dictation, will lead them to pity the down-trodden woman, and pity is akin to love. Every effort has been made to lay before the reader a true statement. Prejudice with some runs high against Lady Hamilton, the outcome of the old garbled tales for which there can be discovered no absolute foundation; and it must be borne in mind that every person of note who was acquainted with her liked her. The preservation of her letters is a powerful aid to her justification; she wrote too much to merit the application of artfulness. In so much correspondence craftiness must have arisen to the surface had it existed. She rather erred on the side of outspoken honesty, and for that reason perhaps was unappreciated by the men of the time, who with hand on heart, and head abjectly bent, bandied the most hollow and insincere compliments with their fellows. Her faults were the fashion of the age under the demoralized rule of the Georges, and should be regarded with leniency on taking into consideration the laxity of the morals in high life at the period when she lived.

Beauty rules the world, and in no case has the maxim been more faithfully exemplified than in the person of the most marvellous woman of her day—Emma, Lady Hamilton, so lovely, so highly gifted, so well endowed with virtuous tendencies, cruelly led astray while but a child, leaving the stigma of those early days clinging to a memory that should have held high place among England's finest women. Of what avail were her own regrets for the sins of her young life? They rose like a haunting ghost and defeated a righteous acknowledgment of national obligation, and in death encircled her name with dishonour. Those who tempted her received promotion, and ended their career with honourable burial; while their victim became a marked woman, branded as infamous in life; dying in poverty, an object of compassion—for in all the varied phases of adversity it is difficult to find a more heartrending subject than the destitute female outcast, whose name is only uttered with bated breath.

In Lady Hamilton's character were many shining lights, and her transcendant abilities were never questioned. In every age beauty and wit have proved a misfortune to a woman in a friendless situation. All readers who have perused her interesting letters must see in them her earnest desire to do right, and each will form the same conclusion as that expressed by Lord Lytton, a man of acknowledged ability and discernment—"She is not as black as she has been painted," than which there seems no more suitable phrase to use in writing these closing lines in the memoir of Emma, Lady Hamilton.

LETTER OF HORATIA TO LADY HAMILTON,

WRITTEN ACROSS ONE FROM HER GOVERNESS, MISS CONNOR, DATED OCT. 4 (1805), ADDRESSED TO MISS CHARLOTTE NELSON, AT THAT TIME ON A VISIT, IN COMPANY WITH LADY HAMILTON, TO THE REV. W. NELSON. THE CLOISTERS, CANTERBURY.

My dear my Lady I thank you for the Docks. I drink out of my loving cup every day give my love to him every day when you write & a kiss. Miss Connor gave me some kisses, when I read my book well. I have three kisses my love to Miss Nelson my dear my lady I love you very much

Horatia

INDEX.

Abercorn, Marquess of, page 66.
Accounts, housekeeping, 42, 177.
Ackermann, 214.
Acton, Sir John, 98, 99, 118, 190, 249, 250.
Addington, Mr., 187, 188, 189, 220.
Albert of Naples, Prince, his sad death, 106.
Allan, David, his portrait of Sir William Hamilton, 27.
Allot, the Rev. Brian, 103.
Allot, Dr., 191.
Andrews, Miss, young Nelson's love, 92.
Argyle, Duchess of (Elizabeth Gunning), 56.
Art:—Mme. le Brun's portrait of the Prince Regent, 6; Romney's paintings of Lady Hamilton, their prices and purchasers, 15; the origin of "Sensibility," 16; "The Spinstress," 17; Mr. Christian Curwen purchases it, 17; Sir Joshua Reynolds' and Hoppner's portraits of Lady Hamilton, 18; Hayley describes the "Circe," 19; David Allan's portrait of Sir William Hamilton, 27; Sir William wishes to buy some of Romney's pictures, 48; Emma's portraits in demand, 55; Mme. Le Brun's painting of her as the "Bacchante," 59; the price paid to Sir Joshua Reynolds for his "Bacchante," 59; Mme. Le Brun's "Sybil," 60; Lawrence's portraits of Lady Hamilton, 61; she again favours Romney with sittings, 62; Rehburg depicts "the Attitudes," 70; the Queen of Naples gives a miniature of herself to Lady Hamilton, 115; Sir W. Beechey's portrait of the Rev. Edmund Nelson, 117; his portraits of the Duke and Duchess of York, 117; Romney's painting of Mrs. Trench, 122; Abbott's portrait of Nelson, 129; Gillray's caricatures, 168; Mr. Burt engraves two plates of Nelson, 176; Sir William bequeathes to Lord Nelson an enamel, by Bone, of Lady Hamilton, 181; her portrait on a cup, 192; Lady Hamilton performs the "Attitudes" for the French princes, 238; Lady Hamilton's miniature by Dun, 245; Mrs. Ward's (Horatia) portrait as a child, 282; miniatures of Lady Hamilton found in the cabin and on the neck of Nelson after death, 285; another in the Mayer collection, Liverpool, 285.
Augustus, Prince (Duke of Sussex), 97, 126, 212, 253, 283.

Ball, Captain, 116, 163, 246, 251, 252.
Banti, Mme., praises Emma's singing, 55; her own accomplishments, 55; she sings at Fonthill, 131; at Sir William's, 153.
Barlow, Miss (Sir William's first wife), 25; her musical talent, 26, 27.
Bartolozzi engraves "The Spinstress," 18; engaged on work for Sir William, 36.
Bath, Lady, her nervousness, 84.
Beattie, Dr., 270.
Beckford, Mr., 126; the Fonthill revels, 131, 132, 133, 134; his eccentricity, 135, 136.
Beechey, Sir William, 117.
Berry, the Misses, 67, 212.
Berry, Captain, 100.
Betty's noted fruit shop, 6.
Bianchi, Mme., 228.
Billington, Mrs., 175, 257, 283.
Bish, Mr., persecutes Emma with attention, 6.
Blackburn, Mr. and Mrs., take charge of Emma's child, 25; their discretion, 73.
Blackwood, Captain, 197, 208, 255.
Blake, the Rev. Mr., 275.
Bolton, Mr. (Nelson's brother-in-law), 113.
Bolton, Mrs. (Nelson's sister), 127, 146, 180, 187, 216, 217, 225, 237, 275.
Bolton, Eliza and Anne, 158.
Bolton, Lady, 197.
Booth, Mr., 185, 188.
Boydell, Alderman John, 3.
Boydell, Josiah, 3.
Brenton, Captain, his literary errors, 108, 112.
Bristol, Lord, at Naples, 82; an anecdote of, 83.
Brueys, Admiral, 100.
Budd, Dr. (Emma's master), 5.
Bulkeley, R., Esq., 218.
Burnham Thorpe Rectory, 89.
Burt, Mr., 162, 176.
Burt, Mrs., 4, 75, 162.

Cadogan, Mrs. (Emma's mother), resides with her daughter in Edgeware Road, 13; her illness, 34; accompanies Emma to Italy, 41; her efficient housekeeping, 42; Sir William's gratitude for her services, 81; takes charge of Miss Knight, 102; *en route* for England, 120; Mrs. Trench's estimate, 122; resides at Merton, 158; visits Chester, 161, 162; in charge of the house in Clarges Street, 185; her letter to Mr. George Rose, 217; birthday letter to Lady Hamilton, 229; invited to stay with Mrs. Matcham, 238; her death, 239; extract from letters, 277.

P P

Cadogan, Mr. Henry, 269.
Caetano, 177.
Calonne. Monsieur de, 169.
Cambridge, Duke of, 212.
Canning, Mr., 243, 244, 245, 254, 256.
Capel, Captain, 156.
Caracciolo, 107, 108, 109, 110, 111.
Caroline, Princess of Wales, 212.
Casabianca, Louis, 100.
Casabianca, son of Louis, his filial devotion, 100.
Castelcicala, the Countess, 169.
Cawdor, Lady Caroline, 121.
Charlotte, Queen, refuses to receive Lady Hamilton, 67.
Chatham, Lord, 96.
Cheeseman engraves "The Spinstress," 18.
Chester Courant, The, 3.
Clarence, Duke of, 95, 96, 179, 215.
Collier, Commodore, 108.
Connor, Charles, 182.
Connor Miss Cecilia, 193, 240.
Connor, Sarah, 230.
Connor, Ann, 236.
Consort, the Prince, presents Nelson's coat to Greenwich Hospital, 216; he desires to help Horatia, 277; he visits the "Victory," 284.
Conway, General, 67.
Cornwallis, Admiral, his care of Nelson, 92.
Cosacelli, the tenor, 57.
Coutts, Mr., 159, 161, 185.
Cribb, the gardener, 199.
Curtis, Mrs. (Mrs. Siddon's sister), 11.
Curwen, Mr. Christian, buys "The Spinstress," 17.

Damer, Mrs., the sculpiress, 46, 215.
Darnwood, Mrs., 25.
Davison, Mr. Alexander, 115, 138, 144, 164, 171, 174, 181, 196, 202, 215, 285, 288.
De Luc, Mr., too learned for Mrs. Hannah More, 28.
Denis, Mrs. 241.
Deutens, the Rev. Mr., Lady Hamilton's gift to him, 64; he witnesses her marriage, 66.
Devonshire, Duchess of, 159.
Doran, Dr., his summary of Lady Nelson, 139.
Duckworth, Admiral, 118, 137.
Duff, Captain, 203.
Duke de Berri, 238.
Duke de Bourbon, 238.

East India Company, their gift, 130.
Edinburgh Review, the, 124.
Elliot, Mr., 124, 176.
Elliot, Mrs., 122.
Elliott, Lady, her account of Lady Hamilton's favourable reception at Naples, 71
Elliot, Sir Gilbert, 158.
Elliston, Mr., 173.
Emma (little), 7; her personal appearance, 22; her childish quarrel with her mother, 24; she is placed with the Blackburns, 25;

Greville transfers the cost of her keep, 72; her letter to Lady Hamilton, 241.
Esterhazy, Prince, 120.
Evans, of Maddox Street, 269.

Featherstonehaugh, Sir Harry, his connection with Emma, 7; his desertion of her, 8.
Ferdinand IV, King of Naples, 70, 76, 79, 98, 99, 105, 107, 110, 114, 115, 247.
Fish (Nelson's playfellow), 89.
Fonthill Revels, the, 131, 132, 133, 134.
Fox, Mr., 245.
Foxhall, Mr., 138.
Froeling, Sir F., 257.
Frith, Mr. W. P., 135, 283.
Fuller, Mr., M.P., 228.

Gallini offers Emma an operatic engagement, 54.
Gentleman's Magazine, The, 11, 131, 136, 180, 268.
Gibbs, Mr. Abraham, 190
Gibson, Mrs. (Horatia's Nurse), 140, 143, 145, 148, 149, 192, 193, 222.
Gillray, James, his caricatures, 102, 168.
Goldsmid, Mr., 231.
Goodall, Admiral, 118.
Gore, Mr., 174.
Gordon, the Duke of, 169.
Gordon, Sir William, 169.
Graefer, Mr., Nelson's agent at Bronté, 190.
Graefer, Mrs., 76, 230.
Graham, Dr., his gorgeous show, the "mud bath," 10; his well-merited sentence, 11; his death, 12.
Grenville, Lord, 85, 243, 248.
Greville, the Hon. Charles, reproves Emma for extravagance, and relieves her necessities, 8; he empowers Romney to sell "The Spinstress," 17; he sends Emma to Parkgate, 21; he visits the Welsh property, 25; his financial dilemma, 29; he consults Sir William, 30; letter to Sir William about his matrimonial wishes, 31; his good opinion of Emma, 32; designs to improve the Welsh estate, 33; his real object in wishing to place Emma with Sir William, 34; Emma's journey postponed, and further plans for the Welsh property, 35; audacious remark to his uncle relating to his heirship, 38; allusion to Emma's age, 39; Emma departs for Italy, 41; reminds Sir William of the King's commission, 47; letter to Sir William about little Emma, 72; he is appointed Vice-Chamberlain, 80; his unwillingness to oblige his uncle, 121; unconscious of any cause that would disturb his heirship, 154; sole heir, 180; he takes possession, 184; his meanness to Lady Hamilton, 230; death, 232; improvements at Milford Harbour, 232, 233; Sir William entrusts him on his death-bed with a message to the King to solicit a pension for Lady Hamilton, 254.

INDEX. 295

Greville, the Hon. R. Fulke, 232, 265, 266.
Griffiths, Captain, 281.
Gwynne, Nell, 210.

Hackwood, Mrs., her unpaid account, 81, 82, 85, 86.
Hallowell, Captain, 101, 211.
Hamilton, Sir William, K.B., parentage, marriage, and appointment at the Court of Naples, 25; his antiquarian tastes, 26, 27; Sir Nathaniel Wraxall's reminiscences of, 26; Mrs. Trench astonished at his agility, 27; his collection of vases purchased by the nation, 27; his portrait, by D. Allan, 27; his introduction to Mrs. Hart (Emma), 28; he returns to Naples, 29; his intention to make his nephew his heir, 30; he suggests that Emma shall be sent to Naples to do the honours of his house, 37; he tries to ingratiate himself, and loads her with favours, 45; his courtesy to Mme. Le Brun, 59; his marriage to Emma, 66; his illness, 73; he attends an important council, 98; his desire that his wife shall receive due credit for service to the fleet, 99; he soothes the alarm of the King of Naples on seeing the dead body of Caracciolo, 110; his recall, 119; his regret at leaving Naples, 119; he declines the pension offered to his wife by the Queen of Naples, 121; he invites Nelson to reside with him, 138; his letter announcing their occupation of Merton Place, 166; caricatured by Gillray, 168; he dances the Tarantelle, 169; his death, 179; obituary notices, 180; his legacy to Lord Nelson, 181; Lady Hamilton's mention in her petition of the reason her husband left her so ill provided for, 247.
Hamilton, Lady, née Amy Lyon, known as Emma Hart, birth and parentage, 1; in service with Mrs. Thomas, 3; her mother obtains a situation for her in London, 4; keeps late hours at Wepre Fair, 4; servant to Mrs. Linley, 5; romantic attachment to young Sam. Linley, 5; escapade of herself and fellow servant, 5; she derides Mr. Perry on London Bridge, 6; coincidence in after life, 6; resides with Mrs. Kelly, 6; her unfortunate visit on an errand of mercy, 7; want of education responsible for her faults, 7; in distress she applies to Greville, 8; her baptismal certificate, 9; Dr. Graham's show, 10; protected by Greville, 13; she attracts attention at Ranelagh Gardens, and her trouble at Greville's reproof, 14; Sits to Romney, list of the portraits he painted of her, 16; "Cassandra," "Emma," and "Sensibility," 16; the Rev. John Romney defends his father's memory, 19; Emma visits the seaside and writes to Greville, 21; her good resolutions,

23; proceeds to Naples, 42; her household accounts, 42; the arrival in Italy, and the sensation she creates, 44; Sir William falls in love, 45; Greville's silence, 48; her description of the eruption of Vesuvius, 52; offers of operatic engagements, 54; entertained by the Dutch Commodore, 55; projects returning to England, 57; sits to Lawrence, 61; her marriage, 66; Queen Charlotte declines to receive her, 67; kindness of Marie Antoinette, 69; anxious about little Emma, 73; she sends her grandmother her annual allowance, 74; she writes to Mrs Burt about her grandmother's circumstances, 75; help for her Uncle Thomas, 77; admitted to friendship by the Queen of Naples, 79; her happy married life, 79; congratulates Greville on his appointment at Court, 80; simplicity in dress, 81; Lady Bath's nervousness, 84; advises England of the defalcation of the King of Spain, 87; introduction to Lord Nelson, she obtains the order to supply necessaries to the British Fleet, 98, 99; her excitement on hearing of the victory of the Nile, 100; hospitality to Nelson, 102; she aids the Royal Fugitives, 105, 106; slanders concerning Caracciolo's execution, 107; the Queen of Naples gives her minature to Lady Hamilton, 115; to the rescue of the Princess of Naples, 118; she subdues the excited Leghornese, 120; she sings to the accompaniment of Haydn, 120; Mrs. Trench sits in judgment, 122, 123; the gift of the citizens of Norwich, 126; important portrayal of "The Attitudes," 134; Mary Johnstone's statement, 140; Harrison's ingratitude, 141; Lady Hamilton places Horatia with the nurse, 148; error concerning Lady Hamilton's birthplace, 162; assistance for the starving Maltese, 162; caricatured by Gillray, 168; the Tarantelle, 169; Merton Place, 171; she resents an insult, 173; Sir William dies, 179; Nelson asks her to take charge of Horatia, 193; troubled by slander, 195; she urges Nelson to apply for active service, 197; distress at his departure, 198; her last letter to Nelson, 205; Nelson confides her to his country, 209; grief at his death, 216; condolence, 218; letter to Hayley. 218; her services ill-requited, 225; her kindness to humble relatives, 234; her will, 235; she performs "The Attitudes" to oblige the French Princes, 238; death of Mrs. Cadogan, 239; letter from Lady Hamilton's daughter, 241; efforts for a pension, 243, 244, 245; her petition to the Prince Regent, 246; her death and burial, 268, 269; Dr. Beattie's verses on her neglected grave, 270; official entry of death, 272; summary, 287.

LADY HAMILTON.

Hamilton, Emma, the foundling, 157.
Hamilton, Lord Archibald, 25.
Hamilton, Lady Jane, 25, 27.
Hamilton Miss, 28.
Hamilton, Gavin, his admiration of Emma, 35; he escorts her to Italy, 41.
Hamilton, Mrs Gavin, chaperones Emma, 42.
Hamond, the Rev. Dr., 89
Hampden, Lady, 282
Hardy, Captain, 112, 136, 142, 155, 201, 205, 207, 209, 216, 219, 232, 281.
Harrison, Nelson's biographer, 141.
Hart, Emma (Lady Hamilton) 1; her account book, 42; her marriage, 66.
Hart, Mrs. (Lady Hamilton), 61, 68.
Haslewood, Mr. W. (Nelson's legal adviser), 127, 129, 146, 154, 155, 170, 192, 193, 276.
Hastings, Mrs., 68.
Hatton, Edward H. Finch, Esq., 289
Haydn, his elation at the victory of the Nile, 102; he accompanies Lady Hamilton, 120; "The Farewell Symphony," 120; his death, 121.
Haydon, the artist, 213.
Hayley, the poet, suggests the attitude for "Sensibility," 16; his tribute to Lady Hamilton's talents, 19; the good influence of his poems, 65; letter from Lady Hamilton, 218.
Hazlitt, W., 214.
Heard, Sir Isaac, 172.
Henty, Mr. 281.
Herz, Mrs. Philipp, 126.
Hillyar, Captain, 182.
Holden, the Rev. Mr. 151.
Hood, Lord, 96, 247.
Hood, the Hon. A. N., 191.
Hoppner, John, R.A., his portraits of Lady Hamilton, 18.
Hoppner Lascelles, 214.
Horatia Nelson Thompson (afterwards Mrs. Ward), Nelson's adopted daughter, 112, 140, 143, 148, 150, 156, 159, 160, 161, 165, 187, 193, 209, 229, 232, 238, 240, 241, 260, 261, 262, 263, 264, 269, 275, 276, 277, 278, 279, 280, 281, 282.
Hudson, Nelson's errand boy, 198.
Hughes, Lady, 93; her limited gratitude, 94.

Jennings "*la belle*," an anecdote of, 5.
Jerdan, W., 257.
Jerrold, Douglas, 275.
Jervis, Sir John, 87, 171, 206, 247.
Johnson, the Rev. Jacob, 126
Johnstone, Mrs. (Nurse Gibson's daughter), 140, 141.
Jones, Mr., Master of Paston Grammar School, 91.

Kauffman, Angelica, 49, 184.
Keith, Lord, 118, 119, 196, 251.
Kelly, Mrs. (the Abbess), 6.
Kelly, Michael, his anecdotes of Sir William, 26; reminiscence of Lady Hamilton, 240.
Kemble, Mr., 169.

Kent, Duke of, 200, 212.
Kerouelle, Louise de, 224.
Kidd, Mrs. (Emma's grandmother), her occupation, 2; attacked by thieves, 2; her cottage, 3; she is entrusted with Emma's infant, 7; her kindness to her granddaughter, 21; her poverty, 75; her receipt for the annuity allowed by her granddaughter, 75.
Kidd, Mr. (Emma's grandfather), his occupation, 2.
Kidd, Thomas (old), Emma's idle uncle, 77.
Kidd, Thomas (young), 234.
Kilem Effendi, 251.
King Charles II, 210, 224.
King of Spain, 87, 246, 247.
Kingston, Duchess of, 68, 268.
Knight, Lady, 151.
Knight, Mr. Richard Payne, 71.
Knight, Miss Cornelia, 102, 120.

Lamb, Charles, 214.
La Michelle, le Comte, 248.
Lawrence, Sir Thomas, paints Emma's portrait, 61.
Le Brun, Mme., the Prince Regent's conversation with, 6; Emma sits to her, 59; her account of the Madonna de l'Arca, 60; she paints the portraits of the Queen of Naples and her daughters, 60; her remarks on Lady Hamilton's return to Naples, 71; Lady Hamilton portrays "The Attitudes" at her request, 238.
Lewis, Mr. T., 258.
Leyland, Mr. Thomas, Mayor of Liverpool, 107.
Linley, Mr., part-owner of Drury Lane Theatre, 4.
Linley, Mrs. (Emma's mistress), 5.
Linley, Samuel, Emma's romantic attachment for, and grief at his death, 5.
Locker, Captain, 95, 196.
Lord Nelson's Letters and Dispatches, 143, 194.
Low, Mr. (of Chester), 286.
Lyon, Emy (Lady Hamilton), 1; marriage, 66.
Lyon, Henry (Lady Hamilton's father), 1; his trade, 2; his burial certificate, 2.
Lyon, Mary (Emma's mother), afterwards Mrs. Cadogan, 1; she obtains employment as needlewoman, 3; she sends for Emma to go to London, 4.
Lyon, Emma, the neighbours' good opinion of, 4.
Lytton, Lord, 289, 291.
Letters of Lady Hamilton, 8, 21, 23, 45, 48, 52, 57, 63, 74, 75, 78, 80, 82, 83, 85, 86, 148, 188, 189, 195, 198, 205, 218, 219, 225, 230, 243, 244, 255, 258, 259, 260, 262, 264, 265.
Letters of Lord Nelson, 92, 103, 106, 107, 113, 114, 115, 129, 130, 137, 138, 145, 155, 156, 159, 160, 161, 164, 165, 167, 170, 171, 172, 180, 181, 182, 183, 186, 187, 188, 190, 191, 193, 194, 196, 199, 202, 203, 204, 206.
Letters of Lady Nelson, 117, 129.
Letters of the Rev. Edmund Nelson, 103, 167, 174.

INDEX.

Letters of Greville, 8, 17, 30, 31, 32, 35, 36, 37, 38, 39, 41, 47, 50, 51, 72, 185.
Letter of Sir Thomas Lawrence, 61.
Letter of George Romney, 65.
Letters of Horace Walpole, 67, 68.
Letter of Captain Hallowell, 101.
Letter of Rear-Admiral Duckworth, 118.
Letters of Lord Nelson to Lady Hamilton (the anonymous work of 1814), 141, 142.
Letters, the "Thomson," 142, 143, 144, 145, 148, 149, 150.
Letter of the Rev. William Nelson, 153.
Letter of Sir Gilbert Elliot, 158.
Letters of Sir William Hamilton, 164, 166.
Letter from Mr. Gore to Mr. Elliston, 174.
Letter from Mrs. Powell, 175.
Letter of Mr. Oliver, 184.
Letter of Mrs. Ullock, 194.
Letter from H.R.H. the Duke of Kent, 200.
Letters of Mrs. Cadogan, 217, 229.
Letter of the Rev. Dr. Scott, 226.
Letter of Thomas Kidd (young), 234.
Letter of Emily, Lady Hamilton's daughter, 241.
Letter of the Hon. R. F. Greville, 266.
Letter of the Hon G. Rose, 275.
Letter of Mr. W. Haslewood, 127. 276
Letter of C. B. Phipps, Esq., on behalf of the Prince Consort, 278.
Letter of Mrs Ward (Horatio), 278.
Letter of Mr. Erskine Neale, 279.
Letter of Mrs. Elder (Dr. Scott's daughter), 280.
Letter of Lord Lytton, 289.

Mack, General, 250.
Maclise, 284.
Macpherson, Sir John, 169.
Malmesbury, Lady, 71, 124.
Mann, Sir Horace, his account of the fatalities attending the marriage of Ferdinand of Naples, 70.
Margaret, Lady, a humble eccentric at Hawarden, 2.
Marie Antoinette, Queen, her kindness to Lady Hamilton, 69; her personal appearance, 69; Lady Hamilton's petition, 247.
Marlborough, Duke of, 173.
Matcham, Mrs. (Nelson's sister), 113, 127, 146, 159, 175, 216, 238.
Matcham, Mr., 238, 269.
McPherson, Mr., 57.
Melville, Commodore, 55.
Merton Place, 165, 166, 169, 170, 171, 198, 230, 231, 237.
Middleton, Lord (of Nottingham), Greville wishes to marry his daughter, 31.
Mills, Dr., of Norwich, 126.
Minto, Lord, 171, 196, 198.
Minto, Lady, 124.
Mitford, John, 108.
Moira, Lord, 71.
Montague, Mrs., 5.
Montefiore, Sir Moses, 283.
Moore, Amy and John, aunt and uncle to Lady Hamilton, 2.

More, Mrs. Hannah, wearies of Sir William Hamilton's Geology, 28.
Morrison, Mr. Alfred. 43, 176, 269, 289.
Mortimer's *History of the Hundred of Wirral*, 2.
Murray, Captain, 181.
Murray, Lady Augusta. 126.

Nelson. Admiral Sir Horatio, birth, 89; schooldays, 89, 90; freak for a wager, 90; theft for bravado. 91; his uncle, Maurice Suckling, takes him to sea, 91; he begs his uncle, William Suckling, to assist him in his love affairs, 92, 95; Lady Hughes records his exemplary discipline, 93; his marriage, 94; he returns to England and ruralizes, 96; his injuries during engagements, 96; his introduction to the Hamiltons, 97; sends envoy to Naples, 98; letter to Sir William, 99; wounded with shot, 100; nursed at the Embassy, 102; his fealty to his wife, 102; his letter to her, 103; his account of the death of Prince Albert of Naples, 106; receives the Freedom of the Town of Liverpool. 107; divides between his relatives a portion of the gift of the East India Company, 113; his letter to his wife, describing fêtes in his honour, 114; to his father, 115; the fête champêtre at Palermo, 116; he remembers the poor, 117; he gives a ball on his vessel, 118; aggrieved at being superseded, 118; sails to Malta with the Hamiltons, 119; he departs for England, 119; the homeward progress. 122; his Court attire, 123; he arrives in England, 125; he describes a Neapolitan fête in his honour, 129; the gift of the East India Company, 130; his farewell to his wife, 136; he joins the Channel Fleet, 136; the "Thomson" letters, 142, 143, 144, 145; a spurious will, 146; genuine and spurious writing, 147; actual relationship to Horatia questioned, 155; letter to Horatia, 155; he writes her important missives, 159, 160, 161; he deputes Lady Hamilton to purchase Merton, 164; he resents an imposition, 172; his triumphal tour, 173; his regret at the death of Sir William Hamilton, 179; his discipline, 182, 183; he comments on Greville's meanness, 186; his short stay in England, 187; he allows Lady Hamilton an annuity, 189; unprofitable Bronté. 190; his allowance to Nurse Gibson. 192; Lady Hamilton takes charge of Horatia, 193; his goodness to the widow of his brother, 194; affectionately mobbed, 196; he resumes command of the Fleet. 197; farewell to Merton, 199; the embarkation at Portsmouth, 200; sad forebodings. 202; troubles with the Admiralty, 203; his last letter to Lady Hamilton, 204; the battle of Trafalgar and death of Nelson, 208; his funeral, 211, 212, 213; Nelson's

coats, 215; disregard to his legacy, 216; his brother claims his private letters, 222; Lady Hamilton's petition, 246, 247, 248, 249, 250, 251, 252, 253, 254, 255.
Nelson, Lady, her marriage, 94; letter from her husband, 103; her discontent at his generosity, 113; letter from Nelson, describing fêtes in his honour, 114; the portrait of old Mr. Nelson, 117; her son undermines her confidence in her husband, 117; her cool reception, 126; her jealousy, 127; her affectionate letter to Nelson, 129; her inaccurate inventory, 130; Nelson's parting words, 136; she widens the breach, 137; Nelson's declaration that the day of his marriage was the happiest in his life, 151; her annual allowance from her husband, 189; she is responsible for the course of events, 226; her faith in Nelson, 232; her death, 286.
Nelson, the Rev. Edmund (Lord Nelson's father), his marriage, 88; rector of Burnham Thorpe, 89; he writes to an old friend, 103; his high spirit, 113; letter from Nelson, advising him of his creation as Duke of Bronté, 115; letter to Nelson, 167; his death, 174; letter to Nelson, 174.
Nelson, the Rev. William (afterwards Earl Nelson), 90, 113, 136, 146, 152, 153, 172, 185, 196, 216, 219, 220, 221, 222, 227, 228, 229, 230, 231, 255, 259, 267, 274, 286.
Nelson, Mrs. (Nelson's mother) her connection with the house of Walpole, 88; her death, 90.
Nelson the Rev. Suckling, his death, 113.
Nelson, Mrs. William, 153, 164, 187, 222, 286.
Nelson, Lady (second wife of Earl William), 286.
Nelson, Maurice, 193.
Nelson, Mrs. Maurice, 194.
Nelson, Horatio (Lord Nelson's nephew), 160, 274.
Nelson, Charlotte, Miss. 158, 159, 255.
Nelson Memorial Fund, the, 281.
Newcomb, Mr., 235.
Nicolas, Sir N. H., 127, 143, 145, 171, 194, 263.
Nile, Battle of the, 100 101.
Nisbet, Dr. (Lady Nelson's first husband), 95.
Nisbet, Josiah (Nelson's stepson), 95; he saves his stepfather's life, 96; his misconduct, 98; injudicious reports to his mother, 117; unfit to command his vessel, 118; disrespect for his stepfather, 137; death, 286.
Noakes, Mr. (Nelson's schoolmaster), 89.
Noia the Duke of, 169.
Northwick, Lord, 112, 283.

Ogilvy, Mr., the banker, 36, 72, 86.
Oliver, 150, 151, 184.
Orleans, Henrietta, Duchess of, 224.

Paget, Mr., 276.
Paget, Sir Arthur, 119
Parker, Sir Hyde, 128, 150, 164.

Parsons, Lieutenant, G. S., 258.
Payne, Captain, makes overtures to Emma, his desertion of her, 7; he is appointed Comptroller to the household of George IV, 7.
Peddicson, Mr., 198.
Perrin, Sir John and Lady, 231.
Perry, Mr., follows Emma and her fellow-servant, 6.
Pettigrew, Dr., 142, 143, 144, 145, 156.
Pitt, Mr., 217, 221, 244, 254.
Poole, Mr John, 283.
Powell, Mrs. Jane, escapade at Cocksheath camp, 5; coincidence in later days, 6; her letter to Lady Hamilton, 175
Prince Regent, the, remembers Emma in her days of poverty, 6; sits to Mme. Le Brun, 6; invites himself to the Hamiltons, 153; buys Emma's portrait, 182; letters concerning Nelson's legacy, 222, 223; he urges Earl Nelson to forego the deanery, 228; Lady Hamilton beseeches him to assist Horatia, 236; her petition, 246.
Prince Royal of Naples, Leopold, 54, 116.
Prince of Wales (Frederick), his partiality for Sir William Hamilton's mother, 25, 27.
Punch, 221, 274, 281.
Pyle, Mrs. Joyce (Nelson's godmother), 89.

Queensberry, Duke of, 68, 169, 189, 236, 237, 238
Queen of Naples, Maria Caroline, her personal appearance, 69; her distress at a court ceremony, 67; fatalities anterior to her marriage, 70; her friendship for Lady Hamilton, 79, 82, 84; she signs the mandate to the governors of Sicily, 98, 99; troubles at Naples, 105; flight to Palermo, 105, 106; her gift to Lady Hamilton, 115; her alarm at the populace of Leghorn, 119; her parting present to her English friends, 121; she offers Lady Hamilton a pension, 121; Nelson solicits her assistance, 188; the charge she placed with Lady Hamilton, 230, 231; Lady Hamilton recounts affairs at Naples in her petition for a pension, 246.
Queen Victoria. Her Majesty, visits the "Victory," 284.

Rehburg draws "The Attitudes," 70.
Reynolds. Sir Joshua his portrait of Lady Hamilton, 18; his jealousy of Romney, 18.
Reynolds, Richard (Lady Hamilton's cousin), she refunds him for her uncle's keep, 77; he treasures her property, 286.
Reynolds, Sarah, 229, 235.
Rigby, the Misses, 245.
Rogers, Samuel, 136, 282.
Romney, George, is introduced to Emma by Greville, 13; her portraits, 15; his rapid execution of pictures, 20; refutation of the scandals in connection with him and

INDEX.

Mrs. Hart (Emma), 39; proposed as her trustee. 51; she sits to him on her return to England, he is troubled at her coolness, 62; his letter to her, 65; his true friendship, 218.
Romney, the Rev. John, details the portraits of Lady Hamilton painted by his father, 15; he vindicates his father's memory, 18.
Rose, the Right Hon. George, 188, 217, 219, 236, 243, 254, 256, 259, 263, 275.
Rovedino, Signor, 228.
Rumbold, Sir Thomas, his attention to Emma on her first arrival at Naples, 46.
Rumbold, Lady, her heartless conduct to her stepson, 46.
Russia, the Empress of, commissions an artist for a portrait of Emma, 55.
Russia, the Emperor Paul of, 163, 223, 252.

Scott, Dr. (Nelson's chaplain) 94, 208, 214, 219, 225, 226, 227, 228, 256.
Scott, Mr. (Nelson's secretary), 208, 213.
Scott, Sir William, 189, 255.
Sewell, Dr., 203.
Sheridan, R. B., 268.
Sidmouth, Lord, 214.
Signior, the Grand, 123, 129, 251.
Smith, Alderman J. J., 257, 263, 264, 265, 269.
Snelling, Mrs. Sarah, 158.
Southey, 105, 197, 200, 210.
Spencer, Earl, 112, 173.
St. George, Mrs. (*See* Mrs. Trench).
St. Vincent, Earl, 98, 116, 118, 128, 136, 172, 267.
Stanley, Dean, 284.
Stewardson, the artist, buys one of Emma's portraits by Romney (Joan of Arc), 16.
Stormont, Lord, 28.
Suckling, Maurice (Nelson's uncle), 91, 93.
Suckling, William (Nelson's uncle), 92, 95.
Sutton, Mr., surgeon, 3.
Symonds, the Rev. Mr., 90.

Thomas, Mr., of Hawarden, his marriage and benevolence, he practises inoculation, 3.
Thomas, Mrs., of Hawarden, her marriage, she becomes Emma's mistress, 3; her attachment to her nursemaid, 4; her death, 286.
Thomas, Miss, of Hawarden, 286.
"Thomson" Letters, the, 141, 142, 143, 144.
Thorpe, Phillis, 177.
Trench, Mrs. (Mrs. St. George), astonished by Sir William's agility, 27; her diary, 122, 123, 124.
Tresham, Henry, the artist, 13.
Troubridge, Captain, 98, 116, 248, 249.
Tuscany, Louisa, Grand Duchess of, 60.

Wallace, Sir Richard, 182.
Walpole, Horace, chronicles Sir William's arrival in England, 28; and his departure, 29; his sarcasm on Queen Charlotte, 68; in writing to the Misses Berry he applauds Lady Hamilton's singing, 58, 124.
Walpole, of Wolferton (Lord), 89.
Walton, Isaac, 171.
Ward, Captain, 140.
Ward, the Rev. Philip (Horatia's husband), 140, 276.
Watson, Captain, erected the first monument to Nelson's memory, 214.
West, Benjamin, P.R.A., 65.
Westminster Abbey, a tradition of, 211.
Wheatley, Miss, 241.
White, Mr. (Nelson's butler), 177, 184.
Whitworth, Lord, 163, 252.
Wilkie, David, repudiates Lady Hamilton's posing at the Life School, 12.
Williams, Mr. Percy, 285.
Willoughby, Miss, 245.
Wolcot, Dr., 176.
Wolsey, Cardinal, 212.
Woodward, Frances Herbert (Lady Nelson), 94.
Wraxall, Sir Nathaniel, his reminiscences of Sir William Hamilton, 27; and of the French and Neapolitan Queens, 69; he visits the Hamilton's, in London, 169.
Wyatt, Mr., architect, 133.

York, Duke of, 212.